THE LOUSY RACKET

THE LOUSY RACKET

Hemingway, Scribners, and the
Business of Literature

ROBERT W. TROGDON

The Kent State University Press · Kent, Ohio

For Bob and Virgie Trogdon

© 2007 by The Kent State University Press, Kent, Ohio 44242
ALL RIGHTS RESERVED
Library of Congress Catalog Card Number 2006028371
ISBN: 978-0-87338-904-4
Manufactured in the United States of America

11 10 09 08 07   5 4 3 2 1

LIBRARY OF CONGRESS CATALOGING-IN-PUBLICATION DATA
Trogdon, Robert W.
    The lousy racket : Hemingway, Scribners, and the business of literature / Robert W. Trogdon.
        p. cm.
    Includes bibliographical references (p.   ) and index.
    ISBN-13: 978-0-87338-904-4 (alk. paper) ∞
    ISBN-10: 0-87338-904-2 (alk. paper) ∞
    1. Hemingway, Ernest, 1899–1961—Relations with publishers. 2. Charles Scribner's Sons. 3. Authors and publishers—United States—History—20th century. 4. Literature publishing—United States—History—20th century. I. Title.
    PS3515.E37Z8925 2007
    813.'52—dc22   2006028371

British Library Cataloging-in-Publication data are available.

CONTENTS

ACKNOWLEDGMENTS

This work would not have been possible without the support, encouragement, and insight of Matthew J. Bruccoli of the University of South Carolina. He is and will remain my greatest teacher. This work was also improved by the insights and suggestions of my other USC professors, Joel Myerson and Patrick Scott. None of my Hemingway work would have been possible without the early guidance and support of Michael S. Reynolds. The long revision process this work has undergone was facilitated by S. W. Reid, director of the Institute for Bibliography and Editing at Kent State University, and by Susanna Fein and Ronald Corthell, former chair and chair of the Department of English at KSU. Fine-tuning was supplied by Fred Svoboda and Al DeFazio.

This work was facilitated by these protectors of the papers of Ernest Hemingway and Charles Scribner's Sons: John Delaney and Alice V. Clark at the Princeton University Library; Megan Desnoyers and Stephen Plotkin, curators of the Ernest Hemingway Collection of the John F. Kennedy Library; Timothy Murray and L. Rebecca Johnson-Melvin at the University of Delaware Library; Beth Alvarez and Deborah Volk at the University of Maryland Library; George Riser of the Alderman Library at the University of Virginia; and Jean Ashton at the Butler Library, Columbia University.

I would also like to thank the many friends and associates who have read drafts or heard (perhaps too much) about this project: Angela Cisco, Keith Perry, Robert Moss, Steve Luyendyck, Martha Cutter, Cathy Tisch, Carl Eby, and David Earle. And I would like to thank my family—my father, Bob; mother, Virgie; brother, Michael; sister, Dawn; brother-in-law, Larry; nephew, Walker; and niece, Liza—for their love and support.

The author wishes to thank Kirk Curnutt and the Hemingway Foundation and Society and Lydia Zelya of Simon & Schuster for assistance in securing permissions. This work was improved greatly by the work of the staff at the Kent State University Press, especially Will Underwood, Mary Young, and Joanna Craig (the Maxwell Perkins of her time).

AUTHOR'S NOTE

This is the first study of the relationship between Ernest Hemingway and his primary American publisher, Charles Scribner's Sons. As such, the author has drawn heavily from unpublished materials from the Archives of Charles Scribner's Sons at Princeton University and from the Ernest Hemingway Collection at the John F. Kennedy Library.

All quotations from the letters of Ernest Hemingway, Maxwell Perkins, and others have been transcribed as accurately as possible. The correspondents' errors in spelling and punctuation have been retained; no emendations have been made.

If they feel disappointed and still want my "literary Credo" in a book on bull fighting they can run an insert saying "F—ck the whole goddamned lousy racket."
   —Hemingway to Perkins, 28 June 1932

Never trust a publisher,
Or you'll sleep on straw.
   —Hemingway, "Advice to a Son"

But Charles Scribners Sons are my publishers and I intend to publish with them the rest of my life.
   —Hemingway to Charles Scribner III, 28 June 1947

I believe the writer anyway, should always be the final judge, and I meant you to be so. I have always held to that position and have sometimes seen books hurt thereby, but at least as often helped. "The book belongs to the author."
   —Perkins to Thomas Wolfe, 16 January 1937

HEMINGWAY AS PROFESSIONAL AUTHOR AND THE HOUSE OF SCRIBNER

Ernest Hemingway dominated American literature in the twentieth century. For most of his professional career, he was both a literary
artist and a popular writer. Like Mark Twain in the previous century,
Hemingway cultivated both sides of his career. This, he understood
from the beginning, was his strength. As he explained to Horace Liveright in 1925 upon accepting Boni and Liveright's offer to publish *In
Our Time,* "My book will be praised by highbrows and can be read
by lowbrows. There is no writing in it that anybody with a high-
school education cannot read."[1] It was by publishing with Charles
Scribner's Sons that Hemingway was able to develop both aspects
of his career, and an understanding of the nature of his relationship
with the firm—the way he and the publisher's employees edited his
works and how his books were published and promoted by Scribners—broadens our understanding of Hemingway the writer.

While Hemingway saw himself foremost as an artist, he would not
have been content to keep his works in his desk drawer. He wanted
his works to be read by as many people as he could reach and thus

had to balance the demands of art with those of a popular audience for most of his career. Writing was his job, and Hemingway strove both for critical acclaim and for a large readership. William Charvet defined the profession of authorship in terms that apply well to Hemingway: "The terms of professional writing are these: that it provides a living for the author, like any other job; that it is a main and prolonged, rather than intermittent or sporadic, resource for the writer; that it is produced with the hope of extended sale in the open market, like any other article of commerce; and that is written with reference to buyers' tastes and reading habits. The problem of the professional writer is not identical with that of the literary artist; but when a literary artist is also a professional writer, he cannot solve the problems of the one function without reference to the other."[2]

For most of his adult life, Hemingway did not need to write to make a living. His first wife, Hadley Richardson Hemingway, had several small trust funds that provided the couple with between two and five thousand dollars a year;[3] because of the low cost of living and the favorable exchange rate for American money, this was a more than adequate income for a family living in France during the 1920s. Hemingway's second wife, Pauline Pfeiffer Hemingway, was substantially wealthier, and Hemingway reaped the benefits. Her uncle, Gustavus Adolphus Pfeiffer (a major shareholder in Richard Hudnut's cosmetics empire), was generous to the author and his niece. He gave Hemingway money after his separation from Hadley, paid the rent on Ernest and Pauline's first Paris apartment, bought the couple a Model A Ford in 1928, financed their 1933–1934 African safari, and purchased a house for them in Key West.[4] During their marriage, Pauline "shared her money . . . generously and discreetly" with her husband.[5] He led an active life and needed large infusions of cash to support his travels and other leisure pursuits. But his income from writing, along with the contributions made by his first two wives, was usually sufficient to meet his expenses. He was never the starving artist in a garret (despite his portrayal of himself as such in *A Moveable Feast*), producing masterpieces that would be appreciated only after his death.

To understand how little Hemingway made from his writing during his early years as a professional writer, it is helpful to compare his magazine income with that of his friend and fellow professional F. Scott Fitzgerald. In 1926, Hemingway published four stories in mainstream American magazines: "The Killers," "In Another Country," and "A Canary for One" in *Scribner's Magazine,* and "Fifty Grand" in the *Atlantic Monthly.* For the serial rights, he received $850, which would equal $8,981.30 in 2005 dollars.[6] That same year, Fitzgerald sold five stories to the *Saturday Evening Post:* "Jacob's Ladder," "The Love Boat," "A Short Trip Home," "The Bowl," and "Magnetism." Fitzgerald, after paying his agent 10 percent of these sales, netted $15,300, or $161,663.43 in 2005.[7] Even in 1929, when Hemingway received $16,000 for the serial rights to *A Farewell to Arms,* Fitzgerald still made more money, selling eight stories for a net of $27,000.[8] In 2005 terms, Hemingway would have received $172,875.25 to Fitzgerald's $291,726.98. Hemingway might have made more money if he had wanted to do so. Early in his career he was averse to big money deals that might influence the way he wrote. But with the Pfeiffers supplementing his income, Hemingway could afford not to sell to the large-circulation magazines.

Hemingway made money from the sale of his books during the 1920s and 1930s, but it was only after the publication of *For Whom the Bell Tolls* in 1940 that he made enough to support himself from writing alone. Sales of the Scribners and Book-of-the-Month Club editions over five years brought in over $200,000. In addition, Paramount paid $100,000 for the film rights. By the late 1940s, he could name his price to magazines and usually get it. In 1950, *Cosmopolitan* paid $85,000 for the serial rights to *Across the River and Into the Trees.* Two years later, *Life* bought the serial rights for *The Old Man and the Sea* for $40,000. During the latter part of the 1940s and 1950s, his income, in addition to the royalties Scribners was paying for book sales, was further increased by the sales of movie, television, and paperback rights.

Hemingway's sense of himself as a writer was shaped to a certain degree by his financial independence. Because of this freedom, he could more readily write about what he wanted. He did not necessarily have to write the type of works that most readers wanted. Thus, after the highly successful novel *A Farewell to Arms,* his next project was *Death in the Afternoon,* his exhaustive treatise on bullfighting, a subject of limited appeal to American readers. In 1935, despite advice from Maxwell Perkins, his editor at Scribners, that what his readers wanted was another novel, Hemingway published a nonfiction account of his safari, *Green Hills of Africa.*

Hemingway developed his aesthetic values early in his career in the first half of the 1920s, while he was under the tutelage of Gertrude Stein and Ezra Pound in Paris. He was essentially a realist, but his sense of realism was different from the conception of it in the nineteenth century. Hemingway's aim was not merely to produce an objective mirror of reality. There is always a subjective aspect to his writing—an attempt to depict and re-create in the reader the emotion of the situation. In the first chapter of *Death in the Afternoon,* Hemingway described what he was attempting in his writing:

> I was trying to write then and I found the greatest difficulty, aside from knowing truly what you really felt, rather than what you were supposed to feel, and had been taught to feel, was to put down what really happened in action; what the actual things were which produced the emotion that you experienced. In writing for a newspaper you told what happened and, with one trick and another, you communicated the emotion aided by the element of timeliness which gives a certain emotion to any account of something that has happened on that day; but the real thing, the sequence of motion and fact which made the emotion and which would be as valid in a year or in ten years or, with luck and if you stated it purely enough, always, was beyond me and I was working very hard to try and get it.[9]

Hemingway's prose, when successful, makes the reader think that he has experienced what is depicted. The best writers transport the readers, as Hemingway said in *Green Hills of Africa:* "For we have been there in the books and out of the books—and where we go, if we are any good, there you can go as we have been."[10]

Hemingway's supposedly simple style belies a complex representation of reality. His most famous explanation of his method is his comparison of writing to an iceberg: "If a writer of prose knows enough about what he is writing about he may omit things that he knows and the reader, if the writer is writing truly enough, will have a feeling of those things as strongly as though the writer had stated them. The dignity of movement of an ice-berg [*sic*] is due to only one-eighth of it being about water."[11] Hemingway seldom used stream of consciousness to reflect his characters' psychological states, as James Joyce and William Faulkner did, nor did he use lyrical descriptions to capture the mood of a scene, as F. Scott Fitzgerald was able to do. Rather, reading Hemingway forces the reader to piece together what a character's actions and other clues in the text show about the situation. An emotion may be evoked, but the reasons why are not always evident. A perfect example of this type of writing is in the story "The Doctor and the Doctor's Wife." The focus is apparently on Dr. Adams's argument with Dick Bolton, but the real story is about the relationship between the doctor and his wife and is revealed indirectly to the reader. Mrs. Adams is a Christian Scientist, ironic for the spouse of a doctor. The Adamses maintain separate bedrooms. Mrs. Adams questions her husband about what happened between him and Bolton, which apparently shows that she does not know. But when Dr. Adams leaves the cottage, he speaks to his wife through an open window; this indicates that she has probably heard or witnessed the argument between the two men. If so, her inquiries afterward are merely a means to attack and belittle her husband.[12] Thus, through indirection and subtle clues, Hemingway presents a story of an unhappy and destructive marriage, never once telling the reader how to feel or interpret the situation.

Because he always wanted to present things as they were, Hemingway fought against the confining conventions of his day. He always sought to reproduce in writing language as it was spoken. To do this, he often needed to use obscene language. When writing of soldiers in battle, Hemingway felt that it was important to use the words that soldiers would have used, words such as *shit, fuck,* and *cocksucker.* He made his opinion clear to Perkins: "I hate to add any worry to you with my attitude on the publishable or unpublishable word business—But that is only official worry remember—You know what I want—All we can possibly get. It's a fight with me for the return of the full use of the language and what we accomplish in that direction may be of more value in the end than anything I write. I never use a word if I can avoid it—but if I must have it I know it—Then if you decide it is unpublishable really unpublishable I suppose I must leave it blank. But I want the blank to indicate what the word is."[13] Hemingway's sense of artistic integrity demanded that he use all the tools at his disposal to mirror experience. For him, being a writer was defined (as he explained to Perkins) as follows: "But I am a careerist, as you can read in the papers, and my idea of a career is never to write a phony line, never fake, never cheat, never be sucked in by the y.m.c.a. movements of the moment, and to give them as much literature in a book as any son of a bitch has ever gotten in the same number of words. . . . The story is there but I dont tell it to them in so many words."

The curious thing about Hemingway was that, even with the adequate financial support he had, he still desired acceptance by a large readership and strove to get it. He knew that his experimentation was lost on most readers and that the so-called common reader wanted something different. In the same paragraph to Perkins quoted above, Hemingway went on to define what he tried to give this type of reader: "But that isn't enough. If you want to make a living out of it you have to, in addition every so often, without faking, cheating or deviating from the above to give them something they understand and that has a story—not a plot—just a story that they can follow instead of simply feel, the way most of the stories are."[14] Hemingway knew that his popular, as opposed to his critical, reputation rested on stories of action, as he explained to Perkins when they were establishing the contents of *Winner Take Nothing:* "At present I know that the book needs one more simple story of action to balance some of the difficult stories it contains. I thought I had it with the last story I wrote, one I just finished about the war, but that turned out to be a hell of a difficult one ['A Way You'll Never Be"]. Stories like Fifty Grand, My Old Man and that sort are no where near as good stories, in the end, as a story like Hills Like White Elephants, or Sea Change. But a book needs them because people understand them easily and it gives them the necessary confidence in the stories that are hard for them."[15] The challenge was to find a way to reconcile the demands of art with the desire to satisfy the perceived needs of the majority of his readers.

Hemingway seems to have eventually achieved a balance between the two. By the mid-1950s, he had received the Nobel Prize for Literature, and his work was the subject of four scholarly books.[16] At the same time, he was the most recognized writer in America and perhaps the world. As John Raeburn writes,

Hemingway's face was a familiar sight on magazine covers in the years after *The Old Man and the Sea.* Although occasionally appearing on the covers of periodicals with a continuing interest in literature—the *Atlantic, Saturday Review, Wisdom*—he was more frequently featured by magazines with only a minimal interest in high culture. These included *True, Look,* the Luce magazines *Time* and *Life, Fisherman, Popular Boating,* the Sunday supplements *Parade* and *This Week,* and the gossip magazine *See.* What this signified, beyond the obvious fact that he was the best-known writer of his time, was that he had transcended his literary calling and become a figure of importance to his entire culture.[17]

Hemingway, in the last two decades of his life, had been embraced by both highbrows and lowbrows.

Hemingway's capture of the American public owed much to his publisher, Charles Scribner's Sons. He would have produced great literature for whatever publisher he worked with, but without Scribners, the course of his career would have been vastly different. Scribners was a respectable mainstream publisher who gave Hemingway the freedom to write what he wanted and at the same time offered him wide, usually tasteful, exposure. For Hemingway, Maxwell Perkins was Scribners. The legendary editor was the best collaborator the legendary writer would ever have. During his thirty-seven years with the firm, Perkins helped launch and shape the careers of some of the twentieth century's most famous and important writers, among them F. Scott Fitzgerald, Thomas Wolfe, and Marjorie Kinnan Rawlings. Perkins had started in the firm's advertising department in 1910 before his move to the editorial department in 1914. At that time, Charles Scribner's Sons (which had been founded in 1846) was still grounded in the nineteenth century, as described by Perkins's biographer, A. Scott Berg: "The Scribner list was a backwater of literary tastes and values. Its books never transgressed the bounds of 'decency.' Indeed, they seldom went beyond merely diverting the reader."[18] This situation changed when Perkins successfully fought for the acceptance of F. Scott Fitzgerald's first novel, *This Side of Paradise* (1920). The novel was a best seller and launched both the author and the editor into prominence. Scribners granted Perkins more control in the selection of writers and books to be published, and he began to bring in younger, more experimental authors: "In what seemed a personal crusade, he gradually replaced the hackneyed works in the Scribners catalog with new books he hoped might be more enduring. Beginning with Fitzgerald and continuing with each new writer he took on, he slowly altered the traditional notion of the editor's role. He sought out authors who were not just 'safe,' conventional in style and bland in content, but who spoke in a new voice about the new values of the postwar world. In this way, as an editor he did more than reflect the standards of his age; he consciously influenced and changed them by the new talents he published."[19] Perkins himself was a rather reserved New Englander who never said anything stronger than "my God"—and that only when very upset. One story has it that when Perkins reported to Charles Scribner II that there were three words in Hemingway's *A Farewell to Arms* that could not be printed, Perkins could not bring himself to say them, so Scribner told him to write them down. Perkins wrote the first two down as requested but had to be forced by Scribner to write the third. When Scribner saw the word, he supposedly said, "Max . . . what would Hemingway think of you if he heard that you couldn't even write that word?"[20]

Perkins has the erroneous reputation of having been a hands-on editor, of having actively worked with his authors to create their books. He did so when it was necessary, as it was in the case of Thomas Wolfe's second novel, *Of Time and the River* (1935). In 1934, Perkins helped Wolfe cut and reshape the manuscript into publishable form. But he did not think such a collaboration should be standard for an editor. In 1946, he defined the role of an editor as he saw it for the members of a publishing seminar conducted by Kenneth McCormick, editor in chief at Doubleday: "An editor does not add to a book. At best he serves as a handmaiden to an author. Don't ever get to feeling important about yourself, because an editor at most releases energy. He creates nothing. . . . The process is so simple. . . . If you have a Mark Twain, don't try to make him a Shakespeare or make a Shakespeare into a Mark Twain. Because in the end an editor can get only as much out of an author as the author has in him."[21] When Fitzgerald, who was revising *The Beautiful and Damned* (1922) at the time, disagreed with one of Perkins's suggestions, Perkins responded, "Don't ever *defer* to my judgment. You won't on any vital point, I know, and I should be ashamed, if it were possible to have made you; for a writer on any account must speak solely for himself."[22] When he sent Hemingway his first suggestions for revisions to *A Farewell to Arms,* Perkins prefaced his ideas by writing, "I have thought and talked about it for some three months now, and beyond the few slight comments on the margin of the proof I have one or two more serious ideas on it which I dare give you because I know you will know easily whether to reject them, and won't mind doing it;—and if you do it I'll believe you're right: I see plainly that you go down to the very bottom at any cost to test the truth of everything. Only you can do that—not many writers, even, have the strength to—and that brings the right decision."[23] Even with Wolfe, Perkins saw that his role was that of an assistant rather than a partner. In 1937, after Wolfe had claimed that Perkins had forced him to cut *Of Time and the River*, the editor wrote Wolfe:

> If it were not true that you, for instance, should write as you see, feel, and think, then a writer would be of no importance, and books merely things for amusement. And since I have always thought that there could be nothing so important as a book can be, and some are, I could not help but think as you do. . . . But my impression was that you asked my help, that you wanted it. And it is my impression too that changes were not forced on you (you're not very forceable, Tom, nor I very forceful), but were argued over, often for hours. But I agree with you about this too, fully, and unless you want help it will certainly not be thrust upon you. . . . I believe the writer, anyway, should always be the final judge, and I meant you to be so. I have always held to that position and have sometimes seen books hurt thereby, but at least as often helped. "The book belongs to the author."[24]

Perkins did not attempt to force his writers to write in the same ways. Rather, he encouraged the natural growth of their talents, helping them to write as they had to write. Perkins did make suggestions, most of which concerned matters of structure and characterization. But he made it clear to his authors that the final decisions on such matters would be left to them.

Perkins left the routine editorial tasks to others. He did not himself line edit or check his authors' works for errors in grammar, spelling, and punctuation. His handwritten letters show that he was as poor a speller as Fitzgerald and Hemingway, and that his punctuation was idiosyncratic. He relied on his secretary, Irma Wyckoff, to catch his errors in his correspondence.[25] Others at the firm also edited Hemingway's books. For *For Whom the Bell Tolls*, the copyediting was handled by Wallace Meyer. Charles Scribner III (who had become president of the firm in 1932) also made suggestions for revision. Meyer, like Perkins, had moved from the advertising department to editorial. (Meyer had planned the advertising campaign for *The Sun Also Rises*.) After Perkins's death in 1947, Meyer and Scribner became Hemingway's main editorial contacts at the firm and were active in the editing and launching of *Across the River and Into the Trees* (1950).

Perkins's taste in reading was grounded in the nineteenth century; his favorite book was Tolstoy's *War and Peace,* and he often sent a copy to new authors.[26] Like Hemingway, Perkins most admired realistic fiction. Before publication of *Green Hills of Africa,* he wrote Hemingway, "Even at worst I still believe—+ its written in all the past—that the utterly real thing in writing is the only thing that counts, + and the whole racket melts down before it."[27] Perkins understood what Hemingway was trying to accomplish in his prose. He did not make many suggestions about the structure of Hemingway's work. He understood that Hemingway was in many ways his own best editor and did not readily accept advice. Hemingway rejected Perkins's suggestions about including a preface to *The Sun Also Rises* and revising the ending of *A Farewell to Arms.* He did, however, sometimes solicit Perkins's advice, as he did when he was troubled about the ending of *For Whom the Bell Tolls.*

This is not to say that Perkins was merely a conduit from Hemingway to the reading public. Perkins did serve an important role in Hemingway's career by protecting his author from suppression and libel. The correspondence from Perkins to Hemingway is filled with requests to emend obscene words and to change characters to make them less recognizable to the people on whom they were based. The only editorial change Perkins requested for *Green Hills of Africa* was for Hemingway to delete the reference to Gertrude Stein as a "bitch." Perkins had to fight to get Hemingway to remove the three obscene words from *A Farewell to Arms,* but in the end these actions protected the author from many potential libel suits and large-scale suppressions.

For Hemingway, Perkins was his liaison with other members of the firm. When Hemingway had a story to submit to *Scribner's Magazine,* he sent it directly to Perkins, preferring not to correspond directly with editors Robert Bridges and Alfred Dashiell except when forced to do so by circumstances (as when the magazine was serial-

Ernest Hemingway, Charles Scribner III, and Maxwell Perkins, November 1935 (Scribners Archives)

izing *A Farewell to Arms* and *Green Hills of Africa*). He liked Meyer and Charles Scribner III and wrote frequently to them,[28] but there is no evidence of any correspondence with Charles Scribner II (who was president when Hemingway signed with the firm in 1926) or with his brother Arthur Hawley Scribner (president from 1929 to 1932); it is doubtful whether Hemingway even met these two men. Hemingway viewed most of the publisher's staff with contempt; he loathed the head of the sales department, Whitney Darrow, because he thought Darrow did not work hard enough to sell his books and was too quick to place them with cheap reprint houses. He never liked the way the advertising department promoted his works, with the single exception of the campaign for *The Sun Also Rises*.[29] Perkins had to mediate between the demands of Hemingway and those of the firm. It was he who handled Hemingway's complaints about advertising budgets and justified the reprint arrangements Darrow made. Perkins had the corrections charges for *Death in the Afternoon* cancelled after Hemingway complained that they were excessive, and he got his author a $6,000 advance on *Winner Take Nothing*—an advance that the book's initial sales did not cover. Perkins even acted as agent for Hemingway. After *Scribner's Magazine* rejected "Fifty Grand," Perkins attempted to place it with another magazine, and until Hemingway hired lawyer Maurice Speiser in 1933 to handle sales of foreign and film rights, Perkins handled inquiries about sales of these rights for Hemingway.

The Lousy Racket is an explication of the working relationship between Ernest Hemingway and Charles Scribner's Sons. The most important aspect of this relationship is the way in which Hemingway and Perkins (and, later, Hemingway, Meyer, and Scribner) edited the author's works for publication. The members of the House of Scribner served as collaborators with Hemingway and significantly influenced the final form of his works. The following chapters also examine the way the publisher promoted Hemingway and his books, since how Scribners advertised the works affected Hemingway's reputation and sales. Hemingway's business relationship with the firm is also examined. Hemingway did not write primarily for money, but he was a shrewd businessman who insisted on the maximum reward for his works; money earned was a tangible gauge of his success as an author, proof that he was being read and that the firm valued him. This description of how Hemingway and Charles Scribner's Sons published thirteen books between 1926 and 1952 details the evolution of Hemingway both as a literary artist and as a professional writer and helps to show how his reputation was shaped for the public. Hemingway's longest and most enduring relationship, lasting from 1926 to 1961, was with Charles Scribner's Sons. The following chapters document the nature of that relationship.

CHAPTER 1

LEARNING THE TRADE

Boni and Liveright, In Our Time, *and the Move to Scribners*

Ernest Hemingway's name and promise as a fiction writer were brought to the attention of Maxwell Perkins, editor at Charles Scribner's Sons, by F. Scott Fitzgerald. In October of 1924, Fitzgerald wrote from the Riviera to his editor in New York: "This is to tell you about a young man named Ernest Hemmingway, who lives in Paris (an American) writes for the transatlantic Review + has a brilliant future. Ezra Pount published a collection of his short pieces in Paris, at some place like the Egotist Press, I havn't it hear now but its remarkable + I'd look him up right away. He's the real thing."[1] Fitzgerald had yet to meet Hemingway. His opinion of Hemingway's literary talent must have been based only on the vignettes in *in our time* (Paris: Three Mountains, 1924)—the sixth volume of Ezra Pound's "Inquest into the State of Contemporary English Prose"—and on Hemingway's contributions to the *Transatlantic Review,* which at the time consisted of some gossipy news items; an appreciation of Joseph Conrad; and one story, "Indian Camp." Whether Fitzgerald had seen Hemingway's *Three Stories and Ten Poems* (Paris: Contact,

1923)—which included "Up in Michigan," "Out of Season," and "My Old Man"—is uncertain. In any event, Fitzgerald's judgment, while based on scant evidence, in this case proved dependable.

Ernest Hemingway, a veteran of the Red Cross Ambulance Service and a freelance reporter, had been learning his trade as a fiction writer in Paris for three years. Since his arrival in 1921 with his first wife, Hadley Richardson Hemingway, he had forged the types of relationships important for a young writer, relationships with important older writers, editors, publishers, and opinion makers: Gertrude Stein, Ezra Pound, Ford Maddox Ford, Robert McAlmon, Harold Loeb, Edward O'Brien, and Sylvia Beach. Hemingway's first works appeared in the little magazines with expatriate connections—*This Quarter, Transatlantic Review, Little Review*—and as the small editions published by McAlmon and William Bird—*Three Stories and Ten Poems* and *in our time,* respectively. In the space of three years, Hemingway had integrated himself into the Paris literary scene and was fast becoming an important force in it.

However, importance in Europe meant little in America. Hemingway could not get his work published in American magazines. And without exposure in a magazine like the *Saturday Evening Post* or the recommendation of someone connected to a New York publisher (a power lacked by most of his Paris friends), Hemingway would have had difficulty getting signed by a mainstream American publisher. Hemingway may have been important on the Left Bank, but his standing in the world of letters was nothing compared to the one held by his soon-to-be friend Fitzgerald. A gauge of their relative positions is provided by a comparison of the printings of Hemingway's first two books with those of Fitzgerald's first two novels, *This Side of Paradise* (1920) and *The Beautiful and Damned* (1922). The edition of *Three Stories and Ten Poems* consisted of 300 copies; that of *in our time* was 170 copies.[2] By the end of 1921, Fitzgerald's first novel had gone through twelve printings totaling 49,075 copies; his second novel had three printings in 1922 for a total of 50,000 copies.[3]

Fitzgerald's recommendation to Perkins gave Hemingway exactly what his career needed: the attention of a major American publisher. Perkins, who had joined Charles Scribner's Sons as advertising manager in 1910 and had become an editor in 1914, had made his mark as the discoverer and champion of young innovative writers. His first notable success was *This Side of Paradise,* which not only launched

Fitzgerald's career but also transformed the firm from a "backwater of literary tastes" to a company committed to publishing the best new fiction and nonfiction.[4] During the reign of Perkins, the reputation of the firm would be one of respectability combined with innovation.

Perkins immediately sought out evidence to substantiate Fitzgerald's claim. On 18 October 1924 he wrote to Fitzgerald, "I think I shall soon have got something by Ernest Hemmingway though probably from abroad."[5] By 19 December, Perkins informed his author that "something by that Hemingway" had arrived.[6] Perkins waited until 21 February to write to Hemingway. In this letter, he praised *in our time* but admitted that he thought the work was too short to interest a commercial publisher. He concluded this letter by asking Hemingway to consider submitting a longer book to Scribners.[7] Two days later, Perkins related his opinion of Hemingway's work to Fitzgerald: "As for Hemingway: I finally got his 'In our time' which accumulates a fearful effect through a series of brief episodes, presented with economy, strength and vitality. A remarkable, tight, complete expression of the *scene*, in our time, as it looks to Hemingway. I have written him that we wish he would write us about his plans and if possible send a ms.; but I must say I have little hope that he will get the letter,—so hard was it for me to get his book. Do you know his address?"[8] When John Peale Bishop gave Perkins Sylvia Beach's bookshop as Hemingway's Paris address, the editor sent another letter, along with a copy of that of 21 February, to Hemingway on 26 February.[9]

Hemingway was vacationing in Austria at the time, and Beach held his mail, which included Perkins's letter, until he returned in April.[10] It would have made no difference even if Beach had forwarded Perkins's letter. While Perkins had been waiting for *in our time,* friends of Hemingway (most notably the humorist Donald Ogden Stewart and the novelist Harold Loeb) had been working to find him a New York publisher. In September of 1924 Hemingway had sent Stewart, who was in New York, the typescript of what would eventually become *In Our Time.* Loeb had introduced him to Leon Fleischman, literary scout for Boni and Liveright, Loeb's publisher.[11] Stewart had submitted the typescript to his own publisher, George Doran (who rejected it), and had taken it to H. L. Mencken with the idea that if the critic liked the stories he might pass them on with a recommendation to his publisher, Alfred Knopf.[12] No recommendation came from Mencken, and Knopf made no move at that time to sign Hemingway.

By the end of January 1925, the search for a publisher for Hemingway had ended. Loeb and Stewart both cabled him that *In Our Time* had been accepted by Boni and Liveright. On 5 March, Horace Liveright cabled Hemingway in Austria, offering to publish the short-story collection for a $200 advance ($2166.08 in 2005). Hemingway accepted by return cable.[13] Liveright sent Hemingway a contract for the book in the form of a letter on 17 March. According to the terms, Hemingway would receive a royalty of 10 percent of the retail price on the first 2,500 copies sold, 12.5 percent on the next 2,500, and 15 percent on any copies sold thereafter. Liveright added in his letter to Hemingway, "It is understood and agreed by you that we shall be permitted to make such excisions as we deem necessary and we shall eliminate the story which we now believe to be censorable." The contract also contained the following clause:

> In consideration of our publishing this book at our own expense, it is agreed that we are to have the option to publish your next three books, one of which shall be a full length novel, on the same terms as outlined in this agreement with the following exceptions: On your second book you are to receive from us on our acceptance an amount equal to the sum earned in royalties by your first book up to date of publication, and on the third book you are to receive as an advance against royalties on our acceptance of the manuscript an amount equal to the sum earned in royalties by your second book up to the date of publication. It is agreed on our part that unless we exercise our option to publish your books within 60 days of our receipt of the manuscripts, our option shall lapse, and that unless we publish your second book, we relinquish our option on the third book.[14]

On 31 March, Hemingway returned the signed contract to Liveright. He also sent the typescript of "The Battler" to replace "Up in Michigan," which Liveright thought suppressible. He also asked that no part of his work be altered by anyone at the firm without his consent and closed with the hope that he would "become a property" for the firm.[15]

The surviving evidence suggests that at this point Hemingway was perfectly happy to be published by Boni and Liveright. Only one piece of his had been published in America (the fable "A Divine Gesture," which had appeared in the New Orleans little magazine *Double Dealer* in 1922), and thus his American market was almost nonexistent; in short, he was not in the position to make demands of the one publisher who had offered him a contract. The letter he had received from Perkins was tentative at best about whether Scribners would publish what he wrote. In addition, at that time he did not personally know any Scribners author and had no knowledge of how Perkins and the firm handled their authors and their books.

Hemingway nevertheless on 15 April 1925 responded to Perkins's letter. He outlined the option clause in his Liveright contract. He also mentioned that he did not care about writing a novel and hoped to one day write a study of bullfighting. He was not surprised that Perkins had trouble getting a copy of *in our time,* since he himself did not have one. Hemingway added that if he were "ever in a position to send" anything to Perkins he would do so.[16] Hemingway was keeping the lines of communication open in case things went sour with Boni and Liveright.

Perkins must have responded immediately upon receiving Hemingway's letter. On 28 April, he wrote the author that it was "rotten luck" for Scribners to have missed the chance to publish him and asked that Hemingway remember that Scribners was one of the first to show interest in his work. He also sent along his copy of *in our time,* stating, "Certainly you ought to have it before me."[17] The gesture pleased Hemingway, who sent another copy of the work to Perkins on 9 June, writing that Perkins's gift "was one of those very pleasant things that sometimes happen to one and which give a good feeling whenever they are remembered."[18] By this time Hemingway had met and become friends with Fitzgerald, who no doubt informed Hemingway of the pleasures of working with Scribners.

Based on the surviving evidence, it appears that Hemingway was satisfied with his relationship with Liveright until after the publication of *In Our Time* (5 October 1925). Although Liveright refused to include "Up in Michigan" and asked for major revisions in "Mr. and Mrs. Elliot," Hemingway met the publisher's demands almost cheerfully.[19] Fitzgerald and Perkins do not appear to have actively attempted to lure Hemingway to Scribners until after he had become dissatisfied with Boni and Liveright in the fall and winter of 1925.

Hemingway's desire to break with Liveright was the result of many factors, the most important having to do with the handling (or mishandling, in Hemingway's mind) of *In Our Time*. For one thing, Liveright was having financial difficulties. During the summer of 1925, Liveright sold the Modern Library to Bennett Cerf for $200,000 and sold Donald Friede a half interest in Boni and Liveright for $110,000.[20] On 14 July 1925, Fitzgerald wrote Perkins that Liveright had sold the Modern Library.[21] In a 31 December 1925 letter to Fitzgerald, in which he informed his friend that he was free of his contract, Hemingway indicated that Liveright's financial problems were a cause for concern, and one of the reasons he had wanted to change publishers: "God it feels good to be out from Liveright with the disturbing reports I have had from Fleischman etc. Liveright supposed to have dropped $50,000 in last venture. Has sold ½ business sold Modern Library etc."[22] To Hemingway, the instability of the firm would have meant that his works would not be given the attention they needed; he had to have a publisher with the assets and position necessary to capture an audience for him.

Another possible concern for Hemingway was the types of books Liveright published. While the firm's fall 1925 list included some of the best new American literature and reprints of several world classics (including Theodore Dreiser's *An American Tragedy; The Plays of Eugene O'Neill;* Robinson Jeffer's *Roan Stallion, Tamar and Other Poems;* Laurence Sterne's *The Life and Opinions of Tristram Shandy, Gent.;* and *The Decameron of Giovanni Boccaccio*), Hemingway found his story collection on the same list with such titles as Thomas Dixon's *The Love Complex* (in which, according to the firm's sales department, "love at first sight is revealed as a tremendous sex impulse—fierce, savage, and blind"), Dr. William Stekel's *Frigidity in Woman in Relation to Her Love Life,* and Gertrude Atherton's *The Crystal Cup* (the story of the thawing of a frigid woman).[23] Liveright had a history of fights with John Sumner and the New York Society for the Suppression of Vice in the twenties because he published allegedly prurient works. Whether Hemingway knew of Liveright's reputation before he signed the contract is not known, but he could not have remained unaware for long. He may have felt that he was the victim of a double standard when Liveright asked for changes in *In Our Time* in order to avoid suppression, since Liveright had willingly fought such cases for his other authors. His requests for revisions may have indicated to Hemingway that Liveright lacked faith in both him and his book.

By the fall and winter of 1925, Hemingway may have had a more personal reasons for changing publishers. His acquaintance with Harold Loeb, whose novel *Doodab* was also being published by Liveright that fall, had soured after their trip to Pamplona in the summer of 1925, which Hemingway incorporated into *The Sun Also Rises* during the summer and fall, transfiguring Loeb into the weak-willed Robert Cohn. No doubt Hemingway also wanted to cut ties with one of his former mentors, Sherwood Anderson, who had recently signed with Liveright as well and whose work many critics saw as the major influence on Hemingway. He was obviously not concerned about hurting either man's feelings but probably wanted to cut professional ties with Loeb and Anderson as he cut personal ones.

The last and most compelling reason for Hemingway's dissatisfaction with Boni and Liveright was the marketing of *In Our Time.* Liveright was more interested in what Hemingway would do in the future than in his initial American publication. Short-story collections typically sold badly, especially when they were the first books of unknown authors.[24] Liveright appears to have treated the book as a lost cause right from the beginning, publishing it only to secure the talented author for the firm. Liveright ordered a first printing of 1,335 copies, indicating that a large sale was not expected.[25] In contrast, the firm published 2,000 copies of the first separate book publication of Eugene O'Neill's *Desire Under the Elms* in April of 1925 and ordered a first printing of 2,500 copies of William Faulkner's *Soldier's Pay* in 1926,[26] which perhaps indicates how Boni and Liveright would have treated Hemingway if he had been an established author, like O'Neill, or had written a novel, like Faulkner. The firm's advertisements for its fall 1925 list include only one mention of *In Our Time,* and this on the second page of a five-page spread in the 26 September 1925 issue of *Publishers Weekly;* Hemingway's work is mentioned at the bottom of the third column of the page, the last of eighteen books listed.[27] From 31 August to 30 November 1925, Liveright spent only $653.10 to advertise the collection.[28] In its catalog of books for the fall of 1925, Boni and Liveright did not mark *In Our Time* for distinction, describing it thus on page 25:

In Our Time

Stories by Ernest Hemingway

We are privileged to offer the first collection in book form of the stories of Ernest Hemingway, a man who has become an authentic and important figure on the literary horizon.

Hemingway has taken his time. He has walked carefully and slowly. The catholicity of appreciation of Hemingway may be evidenced by such names as Sherwood Anderson, Ford Madox Ford, James Joyce, Donald Ogden Stewart, Ezra Pound, Edmund Wilson and Edward O'Brien. "His tales are full of the feel of life," writes Anderson. "The pen feels good in his hand and his people flash suddenly up into odd elusive moments of glaring reality." "I regard this volume," says O'Brien, "as a permanent contribution to the American literature of our time. He has seen life stripped to its fundamentals, and written a brave book not only for us but for posterity."[29]

The description is vague, relying on the reputation of the writer and critic quoted, rather than the content, to sell the book. This was the same strategy employed by the jacket designer, who surrounded the title with six quotes from O'Brien, Anderson, Gilbert Seldes, Stewart, Waldo Frank, and Ford. How Liveright's sales force presented Hemingway's work to booksellers is not known, but it was probably not singled out for special attention by them, if the firm's advertising is any indication. This and the other factors soured Hemingway's opinion of his publisher.

In Our Time was not widely reviewed, although Boni and Liveright did send out 189 copies to reviewers.[30] In his scrapbook, Hemingway had only nineteen clippings of reviews for the collection.[31] While this might only be a result of the fact that Hemingway was unknown in America, it might also indicate that Boni and Liveright did not send out the review copies in a timely manner. Only two reviews of the book came out in the month of October, and these, Herschel Brickell's in the *New York Evening Post Literary Review* (17 October 1925: 3) and an unsigned review in the *New York Times Book Review* (18 October 1925: 8), ran two weeks after the book's publication date. Of the ten reviews that appeared in major magazines and newspapers, five were published in 1927, after the publication of *The Sun Also Rises*. All signs indicate that the firm did very little to garner notice by the critics. This lack of attention was reflected in the sales; by the end of 1925, Boni and Liveright reported only 642 sales.[32]

Fitzgerald and Perkins, the evidence suggests, did not actively try to lure Hemingway away from Liveright. They did, however, closely follow the development of Hemingway's talent, sought to assist him in other ways, and watched with interest and dismay Liveright's handling of *In Our Time*. Following publication of the collection, Fitzgerald wrote his editor, "Isn't Ernest Hemmingway's book fine? Did you read the last story ["Big Two-Hearted River"]?"[33] Perkins responded on 27 October, "I have just been away for ten days. I did not know that Hemingway's book was out. I certainly shall get it."[34] On the first of December, Fitzgerald asked Perkins if Robert Bridges, the *Scribner's Magazine* editor, would "be interested in Hemmingways new short pieces."[35] Perkins responded on 15 December: "I have been reading Hemingway's book most of which I had read before, and I wish we would have something of his in the magazine. If you or he will ever send me anything that seems to suit—and I think the idea of short pieces is right—I will certainly do my best for Hemingway."[36] One of the advantages Charles Scribner's Sons had was its ownership of *Scribner's Magazine*. Although it did not publish Scribners authors exclusively, it did provide the firm's authors with a periodical that gave them financial rewards and exposure, which in turn built up the readership for their books. Between 1926 and 1933, the magazine published seven of the ten Hemingway short stories that appeared in American magazines at that time, as well as the serializations of *A Farewell to Arms* (1929) and *Green Hills of Africa* (1935).

Throughout 1925, situations that would drive Hemingway away from Boni and Liveright and to Charles Scribner's Sons arose. In May of that year, Fitzgerald had told Perkins, "If Liveright doesn't please him he'll come to you."[37] During the summer of that year, Hemingway produced the first draft of what every fiction publisher wanted: a novel.[38] He went from being an unknown author in America to one who had one book published there (no matter that it had poor sales); this exposure would draw the attention of other publishers, publishers who, unlike Liveright, would work hard to sell his books. Hemingway's criteria for success was no doubt enlarged by his friendship with Fitzgerald, a man who made money as a writer, unlike Hemingway's former Montparnasse associates, some of whom had to pay to have their books published. By November of

1925, Hemingway was clearly not pleased with Liveright and set out to move to another publisher.

That month, Hemingway had decided that *In Our Time* had been neglected by Liveright, when it should have been strongly pushed, and that things would have to change. Sometime in November 1925, Hemingway wrote Harold Loeb, voicing his opinion of Liveright's handling of *In Our Time*. He told Loeb that Liveright had not sent copies to Sylvia Beach or Brentano's and that he was "annoyed" that the firm had done nothing to push the book in Chicago. He added that he had received "three swell offers" for the novel.[39] This letter was not signed and thus was probably not sent. It does make clear that Hemingway was ready and willing to leave Liveright.

For him to do so, the contract with Liveright had to be broken. Hemingway believed that the firm would gladly accept *The Sun Also Rises* as the second book asked for in the contract. Therefore, he had to give the firm something they would never think of publishing. In ten days in late November Hemingway wrote a parody of Sherwood Anderson's *Dark Laughter,* Liveright's then-current list leader. Published along with *In Our Time,* 22,297 copies of the novel had been sold by the end of the year.[40] Hemingway had to know that Liveright could not take the chance of offending Anderson by publishing the parody, which he titled after a novel by Ivan Turgenev, *The Torrents of Spring.* In a letter to Liveright dated 7 December 1925, which accompanied the typescript, Hemingway pointed out that the work was not the novel he had written, but a parody in the vein of Donald Ogden Stewart. He asserted that he had "made no kick" about the handling of *In Our Time,* but that this book could sell if it were pushed. To ensure that Liveright would do this, Hemingway asked for a $500 advance ($5415.20 in 2005). In case Liveright had missed the point of the parody, Hemingway pointed it out to him: "The only reason I can conceive that you might not want to publish it would be for fear of offending Sherwood. I do not think that anybody with any stuff can be hurt by satire. In any event it should be in your interest to differentiate between Sherwood and myself in the eyes of the public and you might as well have us both under the same roof and get it coming and going."[41] Hemingway made no attempt to deny the true nature of the work, making sure that Liveright knew exactly why he should reject *The Torrents of Spring.*

Around the same time, Fitzgerald also wrote Liveright about Hemingway's parody. Fitzgerald claimed that he was writing to Liveright and editor T. R. Smith because Hemingway was worried about how they would receive the work. Fitzgerald stated that in his opinion

> It seems the best comic book ever written by an American. It is simply devastating to about seven-eighths of the work of imitation Andersons, to facile and "correct" culture and to this eternal looking beyond appearances for the "real," on the part of people who have never even been conscious of appearances. . . . Frankly I hope you won't like it—because I am something of a ballyhoo man for Scribners and I'd some day like to see all my generation . . . that I admire rounded up in the same coop—but knowing my entheusiasm and his own trepidation Ernest agreed with me that such a statement of the former might break the ice for what is an extraordinary and unusual production.[42]

Like Hemingway's letter, Fitzgerald's gives Liveright a reason to reject the satire. However, his honest statement that he wanted Hemingway to join him at Scribners suggests that Fitzgerald was not part of Hemingway's scheme to break his contract. If he was part of Hemingway's plan, Fitzgerald was, as Bruccoli states, "a master of the disingenuous letter."[43]

On 30 December, Liveright cabled Hemingway (who was again vacationing in Austria), "REJECTING TORRENTS OF SPRING PATIENTLY AWAITING MANUSCRIPT SUN ALSO RISES WRITING FULLY."[44] In a letter of the same date, Liveright argued that aside from being a "vicious caricature" of Anderson, the parody was too cerebral for the general reader. He also defended the firm's handling of *In Our Time*.[45] Liveright's letter indicates that he had some hope of keeping Hemingway, a hope he repeated in a letter to Fitzgerald also written on 30 December: "You know we have a contract with Hemingway for three more books and you know too that we all, and I, especially, believe in Hemingway.[46] I think he has a big future. And I'd hate you to get so hilariously enthusiastic about our rejection of Torrents of Spring that you would make yourself believe that we were in any way giving up Hemingway. We're not, and we expect to absolutely go through on our contract with him."[47] Liveright soon came to see that there was little point to fighting to keep an author who did not want to remain with his firm.

Hemingway wrote Fitzgerald on 31 December, probably the same day he received Liveright's cable. In the letter, Hemingway quoted Liveright's cable and outlined his contract, making it clear to Fitzgerald that he was free to change publishers. He also added that both Knopf and Alfred Harcourt were interested in signing him. In most of the letter, however, Hemingway made it clear that he wanted to go to Scribners and that he wanted Fitzgerald's help to clear the way. He asked Fitzgerald to send Perkins his opinion of *The Torrents of Spring* and told him that he would instruct Donald Ogden Stewart to forward the typescript of it to Scribners. He also told his friend that *The Sun Also Rises* would be ready for publication in three to four months and gave him instructions on how to get his letter to New York via the fastest mail boat.[48]

Fitzgerald did what Hemingway wanted, writing Perkins from Paris in early January 1926. This letter indicates that Fitzgerald held no illusions about the hastily written satire, which he estimated would sell no more than 1,000 copies. He informed Perkins of Harcourt's and Knopf's interest in Hemingway. But Fitzgerald thought he could get the satire to Perkins, who could then get Hemingway to sign a contract for both it and the novel at the same time. He also reminded Perkins that Hemingway wanted to get "a foothold" in *Scribner's Magazine* (to which Fitzgerald had already sent Hemingway's "Fifty Grand" in December). Fitzgerald suggested that Perkins send a strong wire to Hemingway "to show you were as interested, and more, than Harcourt." He closed this section of the letter by telling Perkins, "I think the novel may be something extraordinary—Tom Boyd and E. E. Cummings + Biggs combined."[49]

It is doubtful, even though he wanted Hemingway with Scribners, that Fitzgerald would have written Perkins in such detail had it not been for Hemingway's all-but-stated request of 31 December that he do so. In essence, Hemingway was using Fitzgerald as his agent, knowing that his friend could write to Perkins in a more open manner than he could. Hemingway did not have the clout necessary to make demands of Scribners, and it would have been bad form for him to tell Perkins himself that other publishers wanted to sign him. Hemingway does not seem to have actively pursued these other offers before he went to New York in February, using them mainly as leverage with Scribners. The only publisher Hemingway wanted after leaving Liveright was Charles Scribner's Sons.

Fitzgerald, perhaps worried by the time it would take for his letter to reach Perkins, cabled the editor on 8 January: "YOU CAN GET HEMINGWAYS FINISHED NOVEL PROVIDED YOU PUBLISH UN-PROMISING SATIRE HARCOURT HAS MADE DEFINITE OFFER WIRE IMMEDIATELY WITHOUT QUALIFICATIONS." The same day Perkins replied, "PUBLISH NOVEL AT FIFTEEN PERCENT AND ADVANCE IF DESIRED ALSO SATIRE UNLESS OBJECTIONABLE OTHER THAN FI-NANCIALLY."[50] On the eleventh, Fitzgerald cabled Perkins, "HEM-MINGWAY MATTER TENTATIVE AND CONFIDENTIAL," to which Perkins replied the same day, "Confidence absolute Keen to publish him."[51] Perkins had seen neither *The Torrents of Spring* nor *The Sun Also Rises;* Fitzgerald had seen only the parody. The terms Perkins proposed were generous. In contrast, the royalty Fitzgerald had received for *This Side of Paradise* was 10 percent of list price on the first 5,000 copies sold, and 15 percent for every copy sold thereafter.[52] Perkins's judgment was based on Fitzgerald's reports and on the evidence provided by the small Paris publications and *In Our Time,* perhaps Hemingway's strongest short-story collection.

On 13 January, Perkins sent Fitzgerald a fuller account of his views about the satire and Hemingway. Perkins feared that if the satire proved to be suppressible (in which case Scribners would not publish it), the firm would lose its chance with Hemingway. He then went on to present an argument for why Hemingway should sign with the firm:

> But in any case, I think it was bully of you to have acted in our behalf in that way. I was much pleased that you did it. As for Harcourt, I think him an admirable publisher and haven't any criticism of him. But I believe that as compared with most others, Hemingway would be better off in our hands because we are absolutely true to our authors and support them loyally in the face of losses for a long time, when we believe in their qualities and in them. It is that kind of publisher that Hemingway probably needs, because I hardly think he could come into a large public immediately. He ought to be published by one who

believes in him and is prepared to lose money for a period in enlarging his market.—Although he would certainly, even without much support, get recognition through his own powers.

I have not tried to communicate with him because I did not know how far I ought to go, particularly after getting your second telegram. The fact is that we would publish the satire however certain it might be of financial failure because of our faith in him,—and perhaps also because of the qualities of the work itself, of which I cannot speak.[53]

Like Hemingway, Perkins was using Fitzgerald as a mediator, knowing that Fitzgerald could handle Hemingway better than he could since he was closer. No doubt he expected Fitzgerald to pass on to Hemingway his reasons why Scribners was the right publisher.

Around the same time, Fitzgerald wrote to Perkins offering more information on the parody and advice on how to handle Hemingway:

Now, confidentially, as to Hemminway. He wrote a satire 28,000 words long on Sherwood Anderson, very funny but very cerebral, called *The Torrents of Spring*. It is *biting* on Anderson—so Liveright turns it down. Hemminways contract *lapses when Liveright turns down a book, so Hemminway says*. But I think Horace will claim this isn't a book and fight it like the devil, according to a letter I saw which he wrote Ernest—because he's crazy to get Ernests almost completed novel *The Sun Also Rises*. It is such a mess that Ernest goes to N.Y. next month.

Meanwhile Harcourt & Knopf are after him but he's favorably disposed toward you because of your letters and of the magazine. He's very excitable, though and I can't promise he'll know his own mind next month. I'll tip you off the moment he arrives. Of course if Bridges likes his work + if you'll take Torrents he's yours absolutely—contingent, of course, on the fact that he isn't bitched by some terrible contract with Liveright. To hear him talk you'd think Liveright had broken up his home and robbed him of millions—but thats because he knows nothing of publishing, except in the cucoo magazines, is very young and feels helpless so far away. You won't be able to help liking him—he's one of the nicest fellows I ever knew.[54]

In answer to Perkins's letter of 13 January, Fitzgerald allayed Perkins's fears but stressed the importance of getting a signed contract for *The Sun Also Rises:*

> Ernest will reach N.Y. as soon as this. Apparently he's free so its between you and Harcourt. He'll get in touch with you.
>
> There are several rather but not very Rabelaisian touches in Torrents of Spring (the satire) *No worse than Don Stuart* or Benchley's Anderson parody. Also Harcourt *is said* to have offered $500. advance *Torrents* and $1000. on almost completed novel. (Strictly confidential.) If Bridges takes *50 Grand* I don't think Ernest would ask you to meet those advances but here I'm getting involved in a diplomacy you can handle better. I don't say hold *50 Grand* over him but in a way he's holding it over you—one of the reasons he verges toward you is the magazine.
>
> In any case he is tempermental in business. Made so by these bogus publishers over here. If you take the other two things *get a signed contract* for *The Sun Also Rises* (novel) Anyhow this is my last word on the subject—confidential between you & me. Please destroy this letter.[55]

Around the eighth of February, Fitzgerald informed Perkins that Hemingway could be reached care of Henry Strater in New York.[56]

While Fitzgerald was handling matters with Perkins, Hemingway was completing his break with Liveright. On 19 January, he wrote his soon-to-be ex-publisher:

> As The Torrents of Spring is my second completed book and as I submitted it to you and as you did not exercise your option to publish it; according to my contract with you your option on my third book then lapses. This is quite clear. The contract is quite clear that if you do not exercise your option to publish the second book within sixty days of the receipt of the manuscript your option lapses and the contract further states that if your option lapses on the second book it lapses on the third book. There can be no doubt on this point.
>
> There was nothing in the contract about what order books should be submitted in, whether the second book was to be a

collection of short stories, a humorous book, or a novel. The contract said one of my next three books must be a full length novel. There was nothing in the contract which said that a full length novel must be the second book which I should submit to you. On the other hand the contract is quite explicit that your option on further books lapses if you reject my second book. . . .

I therefore regard myself as free to give The Torrents of Spring and my future books to the publisher who offers me the best terms.

As you know I expect to go on writing for some time. I know that publishers are not in business for their health but I also know that I will pay my keep to, and eventually make a great deal of money for, any publisher. You surely do not expect me to have given a right to Boni and Liveright to reject my books as they appear while sitting back and waiting to cash in on the appearance of a best seller: surely not all this for $200.[57]

With that, Hemingway prepared to go to New York and finalize the break.

No concrete evidence survives explaining what Hemingway did in regard to finding a new publisher between 31 December 1925 and 3 February 1926, the day he sailed for New York aboard the *Mauretania*. According to remarks made in Fitzgerald's letters to Perkins, he and Hemingway must have discussed the matter at some length during this time. Perkins seems to have made no attempt to contact Hemingway personally, and Hemingway does not appear to have written Perkins. There was no need, since Fitzgerald was in contact with Hemingway. When Hemingway landed in New York on 9 February, nearly all was ready for him to become a Scribners author.

On 10 February, Hemingway went to the Boni and Liveright offices. Liveright let Hemingway go—satisfied that the refusal of *The Torrents of Spring* had voided their contract, and unwilling to make the necessary fight to keep him with a publisher he did not want.[58] Liveright reported the meeting to an unknown member of the firm this way: "Hemingway was in and absolutely proved that our contract specified if we rejected his second book we relinquished our option on the third book. He also proved that Torrents of Spring was a good and honest delivery on his second book. The various people here in the office had nice chats with Hemingway who would be willing to take away from the publishers who have Torrents of Spring if we would reconsider our decision. In spite of some things that we said to him in Paris he would like to stay with us but our decision on Torrents of Spring is irrevocable."[59] Liveright may have been lying to save face, but the possibility that Hemingway would have stayed with Liveright if better terms could have been arranged cannot be ignored. Even at this early point in his career, Hemingway was proving to be a savvy businessman.

The next day Hemingway met Perkins for the first time. The editor had read the satire by this point and did not believe it to be suppressible. The publication of "Fifty Grand" in *Scribner's Magazine* was a different matter; the story was thought to be too long for the magazine, but Perkins would later attempt to place it with other magazines.[60] Hemingway had not brought the manuscript of *The Sun Also Rises* to New York, but he and Perkins may have discussed it in detail. In any event, Perkins agreed to publish both books. A contract for both works, dated 15 February 1926, was drawn up. Hemingway would receive 15 percent of the list price for every copy sold. (*Torrents* had a list price of $1.50, and *The Sun* sold for $2.00; Hemingway would thus receive twenty-three cents per copy of *Torrents,* and thirty cents per copy for *The Sun.*) In addition, he got a $1,500 advance ($15,849.36 in 2005). There was no option clause.[61] After missing him a year before, Perkins had signed Hemingway; he would remain with the firm for the rest of his life.

Hemingway, however, made sure that if things with Scribners did not meet his expectations he would have another publisher to go to. After meeting with Perkins, Hemingway went to see Alfred Harcourt. After he had explained that he had given Perkins the right of first refusal and that they had come to an agreement, Harcourt told Hemingway that he "would always be welcome at Harcourt, Brace if the occasion ever arose."[62] Perkins probably did not know about this meeting. In any event, Hemingway now had laid the groundwork for a move to Harcourt, Brace if he ever wanted to do so.

On 4 March, Perkins wrote Fitzgerald to inform him that he had signed Hemingway. Perkins wrote that Hemingway had been willing to give Scribners options on his other works, but Perkins had not wanted to do so. He then thanked Fitzgerald for his assistance and interest in the matter.[63] In his letter of reply, written around the middle of the month, Fitzgerald wrote Perkins, "I'm glad you got Hemmingway—I saw him for a day in Paris on his return & he thought you were great. I've brought you two successes (Ring & Tom Boyd) and two failures (Biggs & Woodward Boyd)—Ernest will decide whether my opinions are more of a hindrance or a help."[64] Fitzgerald's latest find for Charles Scribner's Sons would prove to be his biggest.

CHAPTER 2

STRENGTHENING THE BOND

The Publication of The Torrents of Spring, The Sun Also Rises, *and* Men Without Women

The first two years of Hemingway's association with Charles Scribner's Sons proved extremely satisfactory to both the author and the firm. In this period, Scribners published three books by Hemingway: the satire, *The Torrents of Spring;* Hemingway's first novel, *The Sun Also Rises;* and his second story collection, *Men Without Women.* In addition, despite the trouble placing "Fifty Grand" and "An Alpine Idyll" caused, with Perkins's help Hemingway finally broke into the American magazine market, publishing five stories (three in *Scribner's Magazine*) in 1927. Most importantly, Hemingway and the firm were able to effectively introduce the author and his works to the public, which thereby permitted Hemingway to gain a substantial readership and an established market for his later publications. In short, Scribners did what Boni and Liveright did not: help Hemingway successfully launch his career as a professional author in America.

Perkins began establishing promotion and publishing strategies for Hemingway's works during their first New York meetings. On 15 February 1926, in a note asking Hemingway to come to the office the next day to sign the contract, Perkins promised to show him a preliminary design for *The Torrents of Spring*.[1] Two days later, Perkins wrote asking for Hemingway to come to the office on the nineteenth to see a dummy for the book and, possibly, a sketch for the jacket.[2] Hemingway's reaction to these initial plans is not known.

In addition to preparing a salesman's dummy for *Torrents*, Perkins pursued other means of promoting his new author, the main way being the placement of Hemingway's work in an American magazine. On 19 February Perkins wrote that "Fifty Grand" had been rejected by *Collier's*, but that he would send it on to *Liberty* and the *Saturday Evening Post*.[3] At some point after Hemingway had signed with the firm, Perkins also sent out copies of *In Our Time* to reviewers and other literary opinion makers, no doubt as a means to enhance their receptivity to the works Hemingway would publish with Scribners.[4]

Hemingway left New York for Paris on 20 February. While waiting for *Torrents* to be set in galleys and for Hemingway to send the typescript setting copy of *The Sun Also Rises* to New York, Perkins continued to try to place "Fifty Grand" in a large-circulation American magazine. Hemingway seems to have lacked confidence in his editor's skill as an agent; he wrote Perkins on 10 March that he expected the *Saturday Evening Post* and *Liberty* to reject the story as well, since it was unlike most of the fiction published by those magazines. "It is quite hard in texture and there is no reason for them to take something that is not absolutely what they want and are used to until the name means something to them." Hemingway's letter was not totally pessimistic, as he also told Perkins that he had only five chapters of *The Sun* to revise and would send it to New York in May.[5] By 24 March, Perkins declared himself defeated as an agent and engaged the services of Paul Reynolds to aid in placing "Fifty Grand."[6]

Work on *Torrents* proceeded rapidly. On 15 March Perkins sent Hemingway galley proofs for the book. In a separate letter, Perkins suggested only two revisions. The first was obvious: change the name of the publisher from Horace Liveright to Scribners in the "P.S.—To The Reader" in chapter 8. The other suggestion was to remove the mention of Maude Adams, an American actress famous for her starring role in J. M. Barrie's *Peter Pan*, from the book due to her "extreme sensitiveness." Perkins also forwarded the dust jacket, pointing out that it contained no blurb about the satire: "All that ought to be said should be about you."[7] Perkins's statement about the dust jacket indicates that Scribners was more interested in selling Hemingway, rather than his satire, at this point. Hemingway replied to Perkins on 1 April that he expected the proof that day or the next and would return it via the *Aquitania* on 3 April. He also agreed to change Maude Adams to Lenore Ulrich or Ann Pennington, "which should," he wrote, "be funnier and will make the same joke."[8] Hemingway also informed his editor that he had finished rewriting *The Sun Also Rises* and was having it retyped.[9]

Hemingway did not send the proof back until 8 April. In a letter that accompanied the galleys, he included a list of twenty-three people who should receive either advance proofs—reviewers such as Burton Rascoe, Edmund Wilson, Isobel Patterson, and Alan Tate—or copies of the book—friends and other authors, including Donald Ogden Stewart, James Joyce, Elinor Wylie, and Sinclair Lewis.[10] Hemingway added that there was no reason for him to see page proofs for *Torrents* and told Perkins that *The Sun* would be back from the typist that day and, after reading it over once more, he would send it to New York on Wednesday (14 April).[11] On 19 April, Perkins acknowledged receipt of the *Torrents* galleys, promised that page proof would be read "carefully, but very quickly," and estimated that the book should be out by 21 May.[12] Perkins's estimate was off by seven days; priced at $1.50, *The Torrents of Spring* was published 28 May 1926.

Neither Perkins nor Hemingway seemed to hold any illusions about the literary value of the satire or the reasons for publishing it. Only three months had elapsed between the signing of the contract for the book and its publication. Changes by both editor and author had to be kept to a minimum in order to get the book out quickly. Furthermore, the Scribners sales department did not have the time necessary to prepare a large-scale campaign for the book. *Torrents* was not listed in Scribners' regular spring 1926 catalog, but the following announcement ran on the first page of the firm's *Supplement to List of Spring Publications:*

> It is necessary to preface an announcement of this book by one of the most promising young writers of the period—his volume of stories, "In Our Time," could hardly have received more favorable comment—with the statement that Hemingway as a writer is in revolt against the soft, vague thought and expression that characterizes the work of the extremists in American fiction today.

Hemingway's writing is utterly direct and completely fearless. He follows through to the very end without wincing. When he writes of a bull-fight or a prize-fight, the reader knows exactly what it is like. His stories, "In Our Time," are so clear and complete in their expression of actuality that they give one a shock like cold water.

"The Torrents of Spring" is in reality a broad satire on that "great race" of writers who are responsible for the vogue which Hemingway refuses to follow. Specifically, in style and substance, it is a burlesque of Sherwood Anderson's "Dark Laughter," but in the course of the narrative other literary tendencies associated with American and British writers akin to Anderson, such as D. H. Lawrence, James Joyce, John DosPassos [sic], etc., come in for satirical comment. Aside from its satirical intent, this is a highly entertaining story to read, due to the extraordinary talent of the writer, a talent which will be even more clearly revealed when his first novel, "The Sun Also Rises," is published next fall.[13]

This announcement placed emphasis on Hemingway's talent as writer, not on the book itself.

There was only one announcement of the book in all the issues of *Publishers Weekly* for 1926, no doubt because the firm had already purchased most of its advertising space for spring books in that periodical before *Torrents* had even been accepted. The firm ran thirty-five ads for the book between mid-March and October 1926 at a cost of $796.54. While some space was purchased in magazines (*Atlantic Monthly, Forum, Harpers,* the *New Republic,* and *Scribner's Magazine*), most were placed in trade magazines such as *Book Review* and in newspapers. No advertisements were placed in newspapers outside New York and Boston.[14] The *New York Times* advertisements were typical of the firm's strategy. The first, in the 30 May 1926 issue, listed Hemingway's work with eleven other books and described the work as that of "a brilliant young writer" and as "a sharp satire of present day tendencies in fiction."[15] The second ad of 13 June featured only *Torrents* and repeated the first half of the second paragraph of the catalog's description.[16] Two weeks later the third and final ad for the book appeared in the *New York Times Book Review; Torrents* headed the list of six Scribners titles (among them Fitzgerald's *All the Sad Young Men* and Ring Lardner's *The Love Nest and Other Stories*), accompanied by quotes from four reviews, including the Franklin P. Adams mention and one from Ernest Boyd's review in the *Independent*.[17]

During its first month of publication, *Torrents* was reviewed by only four major newspapers and magazines: *New York World* (30 May), the *Independent* (12 June), the *New York Times Book Review* (13 June), and *Time* (28 June). For all of 1926, only nine major organs reviewed the satire; however, Hemingway's scrapbook for the book contains clippings of over two hundred notices, reviews, and mentions for *Torrents* from newspapers and magazines across the country, many syndicated versions of reviews first appearing in major publications.[18] Most of the critics thought the satire was competent, but, as the unsigned reviewer for the *New York Times Book Review* put it, "not precisely what might have been expected of the author of *In Our Time*."[19]

Evidence indicates that the firm did not think that *Torrents* sales would be great. The modest advertising campaign points to this conclusion, as does the small first printing Scribners ordered. Owning its printing facilities allowed the publisher to control its inventory and meet unexpected demands. On 6 May 1926, the Scribners Press printed 1,250 copies of *The Torrents of Spring*. On 8 July, 510 additional copies were produced. These 1,760 copies would satisfy the demand for the book for two years. There were only two additional printings of this edition: one of 515 copies on 20 March 1928 and one of 510 copies on 13 September 1930.[20] In all, the edition consisted of only 2,785 copies. Except for its inclusion in *The Hemingway Reader* in 1953, the satire was not reprinted in America until 1972. Assuming that all the copies sold, Hemingway would have made only $626.63 ($6,621.12 in 2005 dollars).

Hemingway never made any attempt to have Scribners reissue *Torrents* after it had gone out of print, nor did he force Jonathan Cape, Ltd., his British publisher, to accept it. Cape did eventually bring the work out in England, but not until 1933, when Hemingway was better known as the author of *A Farewell to Arms*. Perkins also understood that Charles Scribner's Sons had published *Torrents* only to abet Hemingway's break with Boni and Liveright. On 18 June 1926, Perkins wrote Fitzgerald that he "did not rate so very high" Hemingway's satire.[21]

Regardless of *The Torrents of Spring*'s less than overwhelming reception amongst literary opinion makers and readers, Hemingway now had two books published in America. The stage was set for his first novel.

During the editorial work on *Torrents,* Perkins's main desire was to see the typescript of *The Sun Also Rises.* The editor went so far as to prepare a salesman's dummy for it in mid-April, six weeks before he had received any of the typescript.[22] On 27 April, Perkins wrote Fitzgerald that he thought *Torrents* would be fine once published but added, "It's the novel I am most eager to see, 'The Sun Also Rises'!"[23] Perkins soon got his wish.

On 24 April 1926, Hemingway sent Perkins the typescript of the novel. In a letter of the same day, Hemingway wrote, "It will probably be much better for you to have it so that you can go ahead on it and I can do additional working over in the proofs. There are plenty of small mistakes for the person who reads it in Mss. to catch before it goes to the printer—Mis spelled words, punctuation etc. I want the Mss. back with the proofs."[24] After discussing his British and French publication plans, the latest news of Fitzgerald, and the current crop of World War I books, Hemingway closed the letter with "This is a long drooling letter but if it arrives at the same time as the Sun A.R. (the pig that you bought in a poke) you'll probably be so busy reading the pig that whatever this letter says will not be very important—nor is it."[25] Despite the heretofore good relations between the author and editor, Hemingway's flippant tone may have been his way of masking his fear that the novel would be rejected, a fear that could only be dispelled after Perkins had read the typescript.

Allowing for the time necessary for the typescript to reach New York from Paris and be read, Perkins responded with almost unqualified praise as soon as he could. If he had any serious misgivings about the novel, Perkins kept them concealed from Hemingway in his 18 May letter. He began by praising the humor of the novel and Hemingway's ability to make the reader feel that he had had the experiences described. He brought up a "hard point" about Bill Gorton's speech on Henry James and wrote that he had two or three other concerns he would mention when the proof was ready. He concluded: "The book as a work of art seems to me astonishing, and the more so because it involves such an extraordinary range of experience and emotion, all brought together in the most skillful manner—the subtle ways of which are beautifully concealed—to form a complete design. I could not express my admiration too strongly."[26] The "hard point" dealt with the fishing episode in chapter 12, in which Gorton refers to the apocryphal story that James had been rendered impotent by a horseback- or bicycle-riding accident. But for the time being Perkins appears to have thought it best not to really force the issue with Hemingway, preferring instead to use most of his letter to assure Hemingway of his commitment. This would become Perkins's usual way of handling submission of a new Hemingway work.

But Perkins was not as confident as he attempted to appear to Hemingway. Although he had a great amount of power in the office, Perkins did not have the final say over what books Charles Scribner's Sons would or would not publish. At the monthly board of editors meeting, Perkins faced strong opposition from Charles Scribner II, who, as John Hall Wheelock, a poet and associate editor at the house, stated, "would no sooner allow profanity in one of his books than he would invite friends to use his parlor as a toilet room. Rumor even circulated around the office that Scribner had rejected the book and that Perkins was going to resign."[27]

The situation does not seem to have reached such a serious level, but Perkins did have to garner considerable support to carry his point with the conservative Scribner. His strategy included getting a favorable report on the novel from the firm's editor in chief, William Cary Brownell. Brownell had been with Scribners for nearly forty years, and his tastes and sense of propriety were similar to those of Charles Scribner. In short, Scribner would be inclined to trust his opinion. In the Charles Scribner's Sons Archive, there is a typed copy of Brownell's statement, upon which Perkins wrote, "Report by Brownell on Hemingway's 1st Book":

We were speaking of the only other fastidious houses the other day. But our range is wider our business larger in scope and our sympathies broader. Of an occasional slip in holding our equally strict standards we might excusably therefore be more tolerant ourselves and expect friends to be—especially as we have no material or moral interest in incurring the reproach of pedantry by excercising a censorship over what the Time Spirit not only accepts but calls for. Practically, doing so would involve the greater evil of impairing one of our greatest assests of energy and enterprise and vitality—a step in the direction of what you once called the danger of "drying up." I should think, accordingly, we might go ahead and see what happens. A single mistake would not be fatal and would be a guide for the future. Besides, are there not better *judges* of what is publishable than we who object to so much that is published? What I read seemed somehow by its triviality to counteract somewhat the objectionability of the scheme and idea. Also the tragedy is real and *impressive* as an incident of war that must often happen and that few have ever thought of as one of war's inevitable horrors, and not, probably, as exceptional as some others. Perhaps here it is all the more impressive for not being better done. And doubtless, for that matter, it is well enough *done*—quite "in the vein" now.[28]

Whether the report was made for Perkins, Scribner, or some other member of the firm is not known, but Perkins clearly had Brownell on his side.

Brownell's qualified approval of *The Sun Also Rises* no doubt helped Perkins's cause but did not make approval automatic. During the monthly meeting, Scribner supposedly shook his head from side to side as Perkins pleaded his case.[29] The best account of the meeting was provided by Perkins himself in the first section of a 27 May letter to the publisher's son and future head of the house, Charles Scribner III:

You wanted to know the decision on Hemingway: We took it,— with misgiving. In the course of the debate I argued that the question was a crucial one in respect to younger writers;—that we suffered by being called "ultra-conservative" (even if unjustly + with malice) + that this would become our reputation for the present when our declination of this book should, as it would, get about. That view of the matter influenced our decision largely. Wheelock was called in, with a curious result: I thought he had been so much out of the world on that balcony of his, + in his generally hermit like life, as to be out of touch with modern tendencies in writing + therefore over sensitive; but to my amazement he thought there was no question whatever but that we should publish. There was of course a great one. I simply thought in the end that the balance was slightly in favor of acceptance, for all the worry + general misery involved.—But you wont see Hemingway: he's in Spain, Bull fighting I suspect.[30]

With the matter of whether or not to publish *The Sun Also Rises* decided, Perkins turned to the task of editing the novel.

Hemingway had already set about this task. On 5 May, two weeks after sending the typescript, Hemingway sent Perkins "An Alpine Idyll" for the editor to pass on to *Scribner's Magazine.* He also informed Perkins that the title of the novel was *The Sun Also Rises,* noting that nothing would be gained from the use of the archaic word *ariseth.*[31] He also availed himself of Fitzgerald's editorial advice while the two men were vacationing at Juan-les-Pins. Fitzgerald read a carbon of the typescript and sometime before 5 June wrote for Hemingway a ten-page memo with suggestions for revisions. Fitzgerald's criticisms centered on the first thirty pages of the typescript, noting, "Ernest I can't tell you the sense of disappointment the beginning with its elephantine facetiousness gave me." He suggested that Hemingway totally rewrite the novel's opening, reducing it from seventy-five hundred to five hundred words by taking out the "worst of the *scenes.*"[32]

Hemingway accepted Fitzgerald's advice, but not wholly in the way that the other writer intended. On 5 June he wrote Perkins, "I was glad to get your letter and hear that you liked The Sun a.r. Scott claims to too." He then went on to explain what he intended to do with the novel's opening and to defend his anecdote about Henry James. He told his editor that he was deleting the first fifteen pages of the typescript, claiming that Fitzgerald agreed with this decision—rather than saying that it was Fitzgerald's suggestion. As for the James reference, Hemingway stated that since James was dead, he did not see any harm in it. He added that "Scott said he saw nothing off-color about it."[33] While he reduced Fitzgerald's editorial contribution, Hemingway used the other author's opinions to justify himself to Perkins. Hemingway was in, for him, uncharted waters and was using Fitzgerald as a means to convince Perkins that such a drastic cut from the novel and the retention of Henry James's name were good ideas.

Perkins responded on 16 June. The magazine had rejected "An Alpine Idyll" because the subject matter was too strong, but he added that it "belongs in a book, and would there be appreciated." Perkins did not discuss editorial matters relating to the novel in depth in this letter, probably preferring to wait until galley proofs were ready to make his suggestions, but he did assure Hemingway that he did not consider the James reference to be a sneer.[34]

Before the proofs were finished, Perkins wrote Hemingway on 29 June to give him a progress report. *Torrents* was getting good reviews, and thirty-eight galleys of *The Sun* were on his desk. But Perkins's main purpose was to prime Hemingway for the excision from the novel of certain words that might be considered obscene: "There are several places I must then bring up for your consideration. You know, I guess, that the majority of people are more affected by *words* than things. I'd even say that those most obtuse toward *things* are most sensitive to a sort of *words*. I think some words should be avoided so that we shall not divert people from the qualities of this book to the discussion of an utterly impertinent and extrinsic matter.—Then there might conceivably be some question about Hilliare Belloc;—I don't know about it and will look at the passage again. Probably it's O.K."[35] As this letter indicates, Perkins was going to great lengths to prepare Hemingway for the necessary editing.

Hemingway's response of 24 July was relatively reasonable. He accepted the fact that certain words could not, because of the standards of decency of the time, be published, but he did give a defense of his use of them:

> I imagine we are in accord about the use of certain *words* and I never use a word without first considering if it is replaceable. But in proof I will go over it all very carefully. I have thought of one place where Mike when drunk and wanting to insult the bull fighter keeps saying—tell him bulls have no balls. That can be changed—and I believe with no appreciable loss to—bulls have no horns. But in the matter of the use of the *Bitch* by Brett—I have never once used this word ornamentally nor except when it was absolutely necessary and I believe the few places where it is used must stand. The whole problem is, it seems, that one should never use words which shock altogether out of their own value or connotation—such a word as for instance *fart* would stand out on a page, unless the whole matter were entirely rabelaisian, in such a manner that it would be entirely exaggerated and false and overdone in emphasis. . . .

I think that words—and I will cut anything I can—that are used in conversation in The Sun etc. are justified by the tragedy of the story. But of course I haven't seen it for some time and not at all in type.

The reason I haven't sent any more stories to the magazine is because Scott was so sure that it would buy anything that was publishable that my hopes got very high and after I'd tried both a long and a short story—and I suppose the stories aren't pleasant—and both were not publishable and it made me feel very discouraged; as I had counted on that as a certain source of income, and I suppose I have been foolish not to copy out more stories and send them. But I will when we get back to Paris the 10th of August. As yet no proofs have arrived.[36]

While Mike's statement was changed to "Tell him the bulls have no horns," reference to Brett as a "bitch" remained in the printed version.[37] The matter of the use of obscene language would continue to be one of disagreement and compromise between Hemingway and members of the firm for the rest of their professional relationship.

As for the matter of the short stories, Hemingway's statement shows that one of his reasons for coming to Scribners was its connection with *Scribner's Magazine.* By adopting the pose of the discouraged author, he was probably hoping to shame Perkins into forcing the magazine's editor, Robert Bridges, to take his next submission. In any event, Hemingway's statement on the magazine to Perkins illustrates what would become his way of dealing with *Scribner's Magazine;* he almost never dealt directly with its editors—Bridges and, from 1929 to 1937, Alfred Dashiell—preferring instead to use Perkins as a liaison.

Four days earlier, on 20 July, Perkins had sent the entire proof of the novel off to Hemingway. In a letter of the same date, Perkins for the first time addressed all the possible problems with the work: the scene with Roger Prescott, the references to Hilaire Belloc and Joseph Hergesheimer, the James anecdote, and the use of the words *balls* and *bitch* and the implied *shitty* in Gorton's "Irony and Pity" song. Perkins suggestions are tactful; as he wrote, "You write like yourself only, and I shall not attempt criticism." He believed that the original opening was needed to properly introduce the reader to the world of the novel but did not attempt to force the issue with his author.[38] The points he did want Hemingway to change show that as an editor Perkins was not concerned with matters of the style, characterization, or plot in *The Sun Also Rises;* what he feared were libel suits from the use of real names and the possibility of suppression due to obscene language, even if the language was only suggested. "Roger Prescott" was a thinly veiled portrait of the American novelist Glenway Westcott. The Belloc reference occurs in the first fifteen pages of typescript; it is part of an anecdote about Braddocks (Ford Maddox Ford), who mistakes the diabolist Aleistair Crowley for Belloc.[39] In chapter 6, Joseph Hergesheimer, an American author, is called a garter snapper by Harvey Stone (Harold Stearns), who says the story came from H. L. Menken. The galley proofs for *The Sun Also Rises* have not been located (with the exception of the first three with the deleted opening), so what corrections Perkins or Hemingway may have made upon them cannot be determined. On 27 July, Perkins sent a one-page follow-up letter to Hemingway in which he wrote, "Take your time over [the galleys] and change them all you wish,—only do take seriously the points that I brought up."[40]

According to his 21 August letter to Perkins, Hemingway got the proofs on 11 August. In the letter Hemingway addressed all Perkins's editorial points. The Belloc incident had been eliminated when the first fifteen pages were cut. "Prescott" and "Hergesheimer" became "Prentiss" and "Hoffenheimer." Henry James lost his last name. Mike now claimed that "The bulls have no horns." In two areas, Hemingway did not defer to Perkins. The "Irony and Pity" was unchanged, as was Brett's use of the word *bitch*. In the same letter, he also enclosed the typescript for "The Killers" for Perkins to forward to Bridges. He closed with a promise to send the proof and another story by the end of the week. Hemingway's editing satisfied Perkins's concerns. The most interesting part of this letter, however, is Hemingway's reasoning for why he "commenced with Cohn." The anecdote about Belloc is only a small part of the original beginning, and Hemingway had already mentioned the possibility of starting with Cohn, per Fitzgerald's instructions, in his 5 June letter to the editor. Therefore, his statement that the opening "would have been pointless to include with the Belloc eliminated" must be viewed as an attempt on Hemingway's part to make Perkins feel guilty and thus easier to manipulate.[41] Hemingway seems to have genuinely liked Perkins, but while his readiness to accept editorial advice from

Perkins and Fitzgerald at this stage of his career indicates that he felt more than a little insecure in his new role as novelist, his statement to Perkins about the cut shows that he was not above lying to gain an advantage over his editor.

Perkins must have begun to worry over the rapidly approaching publication date. On 31 August, he cabled Hemingway, "Better return proof in sections as read and to hasten publication."[42] Perkins did not have to wait long, cabling his author on 8 September, "Fighters ["The Killers"] grand Bridges writing offer Sun proof received."[43] The same day, the editor gave his assessment of Hemingway's revisions and informed him of changes he had made after rereading the proof: "The proof of 'The Sun' came back, and so lightly corrected as to put us in an excellent position to put it through. Certainly you have done all that we could have asked,—and I hated to ask as much as I did. I think *Henry* will do. I ventured one further correction myself by changing Roger Prescott to Robert Prescott, because of your telling me of a man named Roger Prescott. I thought that was slightly dangerous, and that the change would do no harm. If you think it does, tell me and I will change it back." Perkins also added that he had fixed the bad type of the front matter and placed the two quotes (Gertrude Stein's "You are all a lost generation" and Ecclesiastes 1:2, 4–7) on the page opposite the dedication since they were long.[44] But Perkins stressed to Hemingway, "Remember that the book is your book, and should be as you want it." Aside from his aesthetic judgment, Perkins optimistically predicted good sales: "I was delighted to find that, when they got around to reading it, our advertising men felt as I did about the book. This means a great deal, for though they are supposed not to take their predilections into consideration, of course, they of course do, for they cannot help it. The quality of their work is inevitably affected;—and in this case it would be affected in the most favorable way."[45] The next day, Perkins wrote Hemingway that "a little short of 1400 copies" of *The Torrents of Spring* had been sold, adding, "If we can do what we hope with 'The Sun' it will stimulate 'The Torrents' considerably."[46]

Things were going just as well on Hemingway's end. On 7 September, he wrote Perkins that he was not discouraged about not making any money, as it "has always been much more exciting to write than to be paid for it." He also had good news about possible publicity help for *The Sun:* "O'Brien has written today for permission to publish The Undefeated, a story I do not know if you ever saw, in his 1926 volume. I suppose that all becomes publicity. It might help The Sun Also Rises as the Undefeated has something to do with bulls and neither of the two mention any of the embarrassing appendages."[47] Along with the good news about *The Sun, Scribner's Magazine* accepted "The Killers," paying Hemingway $200 for it.[48] Hemingway did not see page proofs for the novel; instead, he approved the changes Perkins had made in a letter of 28 September. In the same letter, he noted that "Fifty Grand" was being edited by Manuel Komroff, Reynolds having had no luck placing it.[49]

While Perkins and Hemingway were editing the novel, the advertising department and book designers at Scribners were preparing the campaign and jacket design that would successfully introduce the novel to book sellers and readers. The first advertisement for *The Sun Also Rises* was in the firm's fall 1926 catalog, where the following description appears on page 32:

BY ERNEST HEMINGWAY
Author of "In Our Times" [*sic*]
The Sun Also Rises

This, the first novel by Mr. Hemingway, quivers with life. The characters, who belong to that group of English and American expatriates who frequent the Quarter in Paris to-day, are so palpable that one, after reading, would recognize them upon the street. They belong to that war generation too strongly dosed with raw reality of which Gertrude Stein is quoted as saying, "You are all a lost generation." Through the Cafés of Paris, the Fiesta of Pamplona, the bull-fights, one accompanies them with amusement sometimes tinged with horror, and a deep sense of underlying tragedy for their sense of life—all illusions shattered, all reticences dissipated—is that of the futile repetitions of the Book of Ecclesiastes from which the title comes.

In the narrative one seems to observe life directly, not through a literary medium—and with a curious consciousness of its beauty and its cruelty. Yet the book is full of humor, sometimes pure fun, but often of a satirical sort. In fact, one can see that it was written in a spirit of literary revolt; and in disgust with hazy, subjective, sentimentalized presentations which result in certain popular novels. Life is hard and bright, and in the eyes of persons of vitality, objective. Let us face it at any cost—so Hemingway seems to say.[50]

This copy was reprinted in a condensed form on the inside front flap of the dust jacket of the first edition. The cover featured an illustration by CLEON of a lounging woman in classical dress under the title, with "ERNEST HEMINGWAY|Author of|'IN OUR TIMES' [*sic*] and 'THE TORRENTS OF SPRING'" running at the bottom. The back flap had a notice for *Torrents* consisting of quotes from three reviews. A drawing of Hemingway by John Blomshield and a facsimile of Hemingway's signature occupied the entire back cover.[51] The decision to use a drawing of the author rather than a photograph was a publicity decision, as Perkins explained to Hemingway in a 26 November 1926 letter: "The thing in its favor is the fact that a drawing is much more easily used on all sorts of paper and is therefore more widely published than a half tone."[52] Perkins, hoping that Hemingway's good looks would help sell the book, wanted the drawing to be widely copied by newspapers and magazines.

The advertising campaign, which was handled by Wallace Meyer (who would become a copy editor in later years and, after Perkins's death in 1947, Hemingway's editor), was extremely thorough and would become for Hemingway the model by which all other advertising efforts for his books were measured, as it was for *A Farewell to Arms* ("If it can come after Christmas it will be grand—The Sun did"), for *Death in the Afternoon* ("You will have to stick with it hard, *as though it were selling big*, through Christmas no matter *how* it goes. Like Sun also"), and for *To Have and Have Not* ("Will you tell me, quite frankly, whether you plan to try to sell anymore copies of the book? I remember how you pushed the Sun Also after it got away to such a slow start and sold it for a long time after the first of the year").[53] For 1926, Scribners ran three advertisements that mentioned or featured *The Sun Also Rises* in *Publishers Weekly*. In the first, on 25 September, it is the second of twenty-seven Scribners books listed in a one-page spread.[54] The other *Publishers Weekly* advertisements featured Hemingway's novel alone. The first of these, on 30 October, features the illustration by Blomshield with the statement that the novel will "command the sharpest attention."[55] The

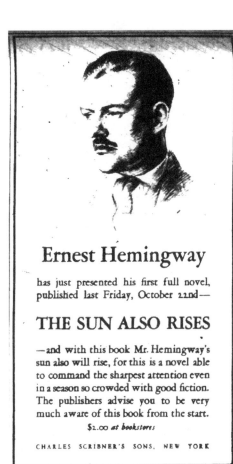

Ernest Hemingway

has just presented his first full novel, published last Friday, October 22nd—

THE SUN ALSO RISES

—and with this book Mr. Hemingway's sun also will rise, for this is a novel able to command the sharpest attention even in a season so crowded with good fiction. The publishers advise you to be very much aware of this book from the start.

$1.00 *at bookstores*

CHARLES SCRIBNER'S SONS, NEW YORK

New York Times (24 October 1926) advertisement for Hemingway's first novel, featuring the John Blomshield drawing (Scribners Archives)

latter ran in the 25 December issue; along with reproductions of the Blomshield and CLEON drawings, the advertisement ran quotes from reviews by Conrad Aiken and the *New York Times Book Review* and a quote from Gordon Lewis, owner of the New Dominion Bookshop in Charlottesville, Virginia. The headline of the advertisement reads, "Watch for January Advertising of 'The Sun Also Rises.'"[56]

Between September and December of 1926, Scribners ran seventy-five advertisements for the novel in book-trade journals and in mainstream magazines and newspapers, spending $3,433.56.[57] In the *New York Times Book Review,* for example, Scribners ran nine advertisements between 24 October and 12 December that mentioned or featured Hemingway's novel.[58] Of these, only the ones of 24 October and 5 December (p. 40) featured *The Sun Also Rises* by itself.

The first was a variation of the *Publishers Weekly* advertisement for 30 October, while the second made use of quotes from four reviews. This was typical of Scribners' advertisement schemes, in that they relied on statements from reviews for later advertisement copy.

The Sun Also Rises was published on 22 October 1926 and sold for $2.00 a copy. The novel received only sixteen reviews or notices in major newspapers and magazines. However, Hemingway's scrapbooks indicate that there were well over one hundred notices, mentions, or reviews of the novel in American newspapers and magazines in 1926 and 1927.[59] The reviews were for the most part good, with a few exceptions. The poet Conrad Aiken, writing in the *New York Herald Books,* singled out Hemingway's use of dialogue, by which, he claimed, Hemingway "almost entirely . . . tells his story and makes the people live and act."[60] The unsigned reviewer for the *New York Times Book Review* called the novel "unquestionably one of the events of an unusually rich year in literature."[61] The critic Ernest Boyd, in his *Independent* review, noted, "The technique of this book is fascinating" in reference to Hemingway's use of dialogue and accretion of details.[62] And Allen Tate, writing in the *Nation,* stated, "His perception of the physical object is direct and accurate; his vision of character, singularly oblique."[63] Most of the negative reviews dismissed the novel because of its subject matter, not its style. The reviewer for *Time* wrote that since *In Our Time,* while Hemingway's "writing has acquired only a few affectations, his interests appear to have grown soggy with much sitting around sloppy café tables."[64] The notice in the *Dial* remarked that Hemingway seemed "content merely to make a carbon copy of a not particularly significant surface of life in Paris."[65]

After publication, Hemingway and Perkins began planning future advertising for the novel and their next publishing move. In a 30 October letter to Hemingway, Perkins, who had never seemed entirely convinced of the advisability of cutting the novel's original beginning, advanced the idea of including in future printings of the novel a preface that would explain what had been deleted.[66] In his response of 16 November, Hemingway told Perkins that he was against the preface idea since it would "break up the unity of the book." In the same letter, Hemingway also outlined how he hoped his career and his relationship with Scribners would develop: "You see I would like, if you wanted, to write books for Scribner's to publish, for many years and would like them to be good books—better all the time—sometimes they might not be so good—but as well as I could write and perhaps with luck learning to write better all the time—and learning how things work and what the whole thing is about—and not getting bitter—So if this one doesn't sell maybe sometime one will—I'm very sure one will if they really are good— and if I learn to make them a lot better—but I'll never be able to do that and will just get caught in the machine if I start to worrying about that—or considering it the selling."[67] Hemingway at this point was looking beyond *The Sun Also Rises* and was making it clear that he was depending on Perkins and Scribners to handle the business of selling his books so he could concentrate on writing them. In his answer of 26 November, Perkins agreed that despite the fact that a preface would end the confusion some readers felt about Brett, he now agreed that including it would be a bad idea.[68]

By this point *Scribner's Magazine* had accepted three stories by Hemingway: "The Killers," "A Canary for One" (which Bridges had accepted by 23 November), and "In Another Country" (sent by Hemingway on 22 November).[69] "Fifty Grand" was still being circulated, and Hemingway advanced the idea of placing it with *College Humor* in his 23 November letter before Komroff sent it to the *Atlantic Monthly* in late December.[70] In late November Perkins advanced the idea of following the novel with a story collection to be published in March: "The question is whether it would be wise to publish another book as early as this spring, with the prospects of 'The Sun Also' running strongly through that season."[71] By 3 December, he had pretty much decided against publishing the collection in the fall because he did not want to overshadow the magazine's publication of the three stories it had: "I told [Bridges] that our attitude would be against publishing a book of short stories if it would interfere with his publishing the stories he had, in any way. I want them to have a full chance to announce these stories beforehand, and to make the most of them."[72] Hemingway was in agreement with the plan. On 6 December the author wrote his editor, saying that he had ten stories written, but asking, "Do you think it would be wise to have another book out so soon as Spring—rather than wait until early fall? . . . Don't you think we might give them a rest? Or isn't that how it's done?"[73] Both men had arrived at the same conclusion: wait on the story collection until after sales of *The Sun* had significantly dropped off.

Scribners handled *The Sun Also Rises* very well, especially in 1927. The novel went through three printings in 1926—5,090 on 9 October; 1,970 on 24 November; and 2,290 on 29 November—for a total of 9,350 copies, a respectable number for a first novel.[74] But Perkins thought that the novel's sale could continue through 1927. On 10 December he wrote Hemingway that the magazine was planning on running all his stories in one issue; he also outlined the advertising strategy for 1927: Scribners was easing up until after the glut of advertisements for Christmas "gift books" was over, "saving our fire and opening up after New Years."[75] The advertising records indicate that this was what the firm did; in 1927 Scribners bought 104 advertisements for the novel, 70 alone in the first three months of the year, spending $3,124.37 above the $3,433.56 they spent promoting the book in 1926.[76] In addition, notices for the novel ran in the Scribners trade catalogs for spring and fall of 1927 and 1928. This steady attention added to the influence provided by word-of-mouth exposure and had a palpable effect on sales. The novel was reprinted five times in 1927 for a total of 18,530 copies. From 1928 to 1945, there were six additional printings. In all, between 1926 and 1945, Scribners printed 36,140 copies of this edition of *The Sun Also Rises*.[77] At a 15 percent royalty rate, the novel would have provided Hemingway with only $10,842.[78] (This sum would equal $113,424.90 in 2005.) The sale of dramatic and movie rights brought in more, but this did not occur until 1932, when RKO bought the rights for $15,200.[79] Hemingway saw very little of this money, since he gave Hadley Hemingway all income from the novel to facilitate their divorce proceedings. Hemingway asked Perkins, however, that in regard to the $1,500 advance for *Torrents* and *The Sun,* $1,000 should be for the novel, with payments to Hadley to begin after the advance had been met.[80] But while Hemingway did not grow rich from *The Sun Also Rises,* it did sell well for a first novel and prepared the way for future volumes.

After the first of the year, Perkins returned to the idea of publishing a short-story collection by Hemingway. On 20 January 1927, he wrote his author, "Remember that it won't be so very long before we shall be planning for the book of short stories. So you ought to have it in mind, and think about it, and what you will put into it, and the order and that sort of thing."[81] Hemingway's only thought about stories at this time seemed to be centered on publishing the ones he had in periodicals. On 20 January, he asked Perkins to send "Fifty Grand" to the *Atlantic Monthly* and "An Alpine Idyll" to the *American Caravan,* a literary yearbook to which he had promised a "long bull fight story called A Lack of Passion."[82] The story had seemed good to Hemingway when he wrote it, but he "decided it was no bloody good at all and that re-writing wouldn't save it."[83] Perkins in his 4 February letter to Hemingway reiterated that he had to have setting copy and the title of the collection soon in order to prepare a campaign for the book.[84]

The prodding by Perkins produced the desired results, for on Valentine's Day, Hemingway sent from Switzerland his proposed title, a tentative table of contents, and information on the new stories:

> As for the book of stories for the fall—I have been working very hard and concentrating on a title etc. Want to call it
>
> Men Without Women
>
> | and it will have | The Undefeated | 15,000 |
> |---|---|---|
> | | Fifty Grand | 10,000 |
> | | The Killers | 3,000 |
> | | Today Is Friday | 2,000 |
> | | An Alpine Idyll | 1,500 |
> | | A Pursuit Race | 1,800 |
> | | Banal Story | 1,000 |
> | | A Simple Enquiry | 1,200 |
> | | Up In Michigan | 1,600 |
> | | | 40,000 words |
>
> etc.
>
> In all of these, almost, the softening feminine influence through training, discipline, death or other causes, being absent.
>
> The number of words is approximate but fairly accurate I think. Will have some other stories probably. . . . My head is going well again and I am writing some stories that seem pretty good. . . .
>
> The way the stories are listed is not the order they will be in the book. I just wanted to give you an idea of what you would have so they could go ahead with it. You have seen most of the stories so you will know about what it is like. . . . Up In Michigan I'm anxious to print—it is a good story and Liveright cut it out of In Our Time. That was the reason I did not want to stay there. I

think it is publisheable and it might set Mr. [Allen] Tate's mind at rest as to my always avoiding any direct relations between men and women because of being afraid to face it and not knowing about it. Anyway when I get to Paris in March I will get them all in shape—you have the Fifty Grand—and send them over. Is that about right for length?[85]

All but two of the stories Hemingway listed for inclusion had been or would be published before *Men Without Women* came out in the fall: "The Undefeated" in *This Quarter* (Autumn–Winter 1925–1926: 203–32) and *The Best Short Stories of 1926* (New York: Dodd, Mead, 1926), "Fifty Grand" (*Atlantic Monthly,* July 1927: 1–15), "The Killers" and "In Another Country" (*Scribner's Magazine,* March 1927: 227–33; and April 1927: 355–57), *Today Is Friday* (Englewood, NJ: As Stable, 1926), "An Alpine Idyll" (*American Caravan* [New York: Macaulay, 1927], 46–51), "Banal Story" (*Little Review,* Spring–Summer 1926: 22–23), and "Up in Michigan" (*Three Stories and Ten Poems* [Paris: Contact Press, 1923]). But none of these previous publications would have exposed any of the stories to a large American audience. While both *Scribner's Magazine* and *Atlantic Monthly* were important periodicals, they did not have the circulation of the *Saturday Evening Post* or *Collier's.* What is more unusual is the fact that Hemingway did not include "In Another Country" or "Now I Lay Me" in the contents, even though the first story had been published in *Scribner's Magazine* and the other was completed in December. In any event, Perkins had probably seen all the works that had been published, except perhaps for "Up in Michigan," which had the potential to cause new problems, as Hemingway's statement that it was the reason he left Liveright indicated. For the time being, however, Perkins was pleased with the state of affairs, as expressed in his reply to Hemingway of 28 February: "I think 'Men Without Women' is a splendid title. Forty thousand words is rather short, but it will do and it will be better that it should do, than that you should feel forced into writing more against your inclination. Maybe you will write more, and that will be an advantage, but one we can forego."[86]

The publication of *The Sun Also Rises* marked a change in Hemingway's dealings with American magazines, as he explained to Perkins in a letter of 19 February:

I wrote about a week ago giving an outline of the stories for the book and a title. Men Without Women may have struck you as a punk title and if it did please cable me and I'll try and work for another one. I don't know anything about titles here in Gstaad. You wrote once you wanted one by March—that was why I hurried it.

Have now had requests for articles stories or serials from New Yorker, Vanity Fair, Harper's Bazaar, Hearst's etc. This all looks so much like the fast smooth flowing shutes that I've watched so many of my ancestors and contemporaries disappear over that I've decided not to sell or send out anything for a year—unless I have to sell a story to eat. In that event I'll send them to you and the magazine can have the first crack. Really I should have an agent, if for no other reason to take this story selling business off your hands. Do you know of one who would try and sell the stuff and yet would not write me letters trying to get me to do serials etc.?[87]

The tables had turned for Hemingway; now instead of trying to sell his pieces to magazines, they were attempting to buy stories from him. Hemingway never got an agent to handle his stories, but he did not really need one.[88] He did not have to sell stories to make a living as Fitzgerald did, since his future wife's family provided him with a comfortable living. Therefore, more unpublished stories could make it into his collections, which in the end may have improved their sales. In the letter, Hemingway also complained about rumors that had arisen about his early life and asked that Scribners "lay off the Biography."[89] Hemingway was learning that one of the costs of being a famous writer was the loss, to a certain extent, of control of his life, and he was fighting this loss as well as he could.

By 1 April, Perkins had a dummy of the book ready, using "The Killers" as text. He also added that the book, according to Hemingway's estimate, would be short. Hemingway, Perkins thought, must have had more stories, and he set about persuading him to beef up the volume: "But Scott thinks that you must have much more material than forty-five or fifty thousand words. He spoke of various things that I had never heard of. If you have other stories that would go into this book without any regret on your part, send them too.—But if you are not satisfied that they are good ones, let the book remain short, and we shall do very well that way. Anyhow I suspect there are many more words according to our figuring than you think."[90] From Paris, where he was preparing to marry Pauline Pfeiffer, Hemingway responded that he would send the stories off after he had looked them over again. He added that there "should be two or three more to add to the ones I scheduled." Hemingway also said that he had had to go to Italy "after some stuff, which I couldn't get." The trip, in March with Guy Hickok, provided Hemingway with the material for "Italy 1927," which the *New Republic* would publish in May, but Hemingway's statement might also indicate that he was checking facts for "Now I Lay Me," a story about World War I in Italy. He also asked Perkins for a "$650 or $700 advance."[91] On 9 May, Perkins responded by sending a check for $750, adding that Hemingway should send any stories he wrote after sending the setting copy for the book: "If we have time we will put them in; otherwise I shall—if you approve of it—put them in the hands of Paul Reynolds."[92]

As he waited for the copy, Perkins sought Fitzgerald's advice about "Up in Michigan." On 10 May, he wrote Fitzgerald:

> I had a letter from Hemingway saying that he was about to send off his stories for the book, "Men Without Women" but there is one story there, called "Up in Michigan" I think, which he says Liveright refused to publish in "In Our Time" and that it was on this account that he left Liveright. I think you spoke to Charlie Scribner about this story and said that it was ridiculous that he should think it could be published. Could you tell me about it some time? Certainly we cannot go as far as Liveright is willing to. At least, I look upon him as an extremist in that respect. On the other hand, Mrs. [Hadley] Hemingway told me that the story could be made acceptable even for conservatives, by striking out a few physiological details.[93]

From Edgemoor, Delaware, Fitzgerald wrote approximately two days later with the facts about the story and to explain how to handle Hemingway:

> It seems a shame to put business into a letter thanking you for such a gift but just a line about Ernest. It is all bull that he left Liveright about that story. One line *at least* is pornographic, though *please* don't bring my name into the discussion. The thing is—what is a seduction story with the seduction left out.

Yet if that is softened it is quite printable. However I trust your judgement, as he should. . . .

(Explain to Hemmingway, why don't you, that while such an incident might be lost in a book, a story centering around it *points* it. In other words the material raison d'être as opposed to the artistic raison d'être of the story is, in part, to show the physiological details of a seduction. If that were possible in America 20 publishers would be scrambling for James Joyce tomorrow.)[94]

Again, Fitzgerald served as Hemingway's editor, although Hemingway never knew of it.

Perkins did not have to reject "Up in Michigan," for when Hemingway submitted most of the setting copy the story was not included. On 4 May, Hemingway sent most of the stories along with instructions and opinions to Perkins:

This copy of Fifty Grand is the one Komroff cut. I marked all the cuts *stet* so will you mark it for them to pay no attention to the pencilled cuts and set them up as it was originally typed.
Dear Mr. Perkins:
    Enclosed is the copy on hand for Men Without Women.
    The stories go in this order
        The Undefeated
        Today Is Friday
        In Another Country
        The Killers   You have these
        A Canary For One
        Pursuit Race
        An Alpine Idyll
        A Simple Enquiry
        Banal Story }will send this week
        Fifty Grand
[*In right margin*] You better this any way you wish. I've just drawn it up tentatively.
    Within three weeks at the latest I plan to send you two more stories—Italy 1927 and After The Fourth [retitled "Ten Indians"]—these I am re-writing now. I hope by the middle of June or so to have three more—(Not *absolutely* sure on this) A Lack of Passion—a long bull fight story which I am re-writing—and a

couple more. These should make a full sized book I imagine. Will you let me know until what date I can get stories in for the book? I have been unable to decide about the Up In Michigan. Want a little more time to look at the revised version. . . .

I think there is nothing in the stories to bother any one except a couple of words in Pursuit Race and if I find any way of re-placing those in proofs I will. You know I never want to shock with a word if another will do—especially if the word will shock beyond it's context—but if there is nothing to be done sometimes that is all there is to be done.

Any suggestions you would make about the order of the stories I would greatly appreciate. It is not at all finally fixed if you think it can be bettered.

I have not sent copies of The Killers, Canary, or In Another Country as you can get them from the March and April Scribner's.

There will probably be quite a good deal more material if there is time to get it in. I want the book to be full $2.00 size but there is no use sending stories that would just be filler. Though I need some quiet ones to come in between the others. Hope to have something good next month.[95]

Hemingway seems to have decided on his own not to include "Up in Michigan," perhaps judging that the material he had in hand, along with the stories he was writing and revising, would be enough.

However, the skimpiness of the volume was still a worry for Perkins. His 16 May letter to Hemingway, which also contained a request to find a replacement for the word *shit* in "A Pursuit Race," was designed to encourage the author to send what new stories he had: "As for the length, we have now forty-eight thousand words, and ten stories. This amounts to about fifty thousand words in the case of a novel, because the space taken up between stories. If you can send us the long bull fight story—'A Lack of Passion'—and if two or three others turn up, we will have a very impressive collection, even in a physical sense. . . . I shall wait until the first of July for other stories, but then we shall have to get under way, particularly as we shall lose a great deal of time in sending the proof to and fro between here and wherever you will be. I think the book will make a stir."[96] Perkins's prodding had the desired effect. On 27 May, Hemingway sent "After the Fourth" and "Now I Lay Me." In a further effort to increase the volume's size, he asked that the article "Italy 1927" be inserted.[97] In his reply of 8 June, Perkins expressed his satisfaction with the variety of the volume and his hope that "A Lack of Passion" could be revised in time to be included in the volume.[98]

Hemingway was sent the contract for *Men Without Women* on 27 May.[99] The contract had the same terms as the one for *Torrents* and *The Sun:* Hemingway's royalty was a straight 15 percent of the retail price of the book ($2.00), or thirty cents a copy.[100]

Perkins had to leave New York for London in June due to his father-in-law's illness. On 10 June, while he was gone, Hemingway sent the last story for the book, "Hills Like White Elephants."[101] He also apologized for being unable to get "A Lack of Passion" in order but stated that he thought they had enough stories anyway. He told Perkins that he felt lukewarm about "A Banal Story." By this point, Perkins had sent a trial jacket, for which Hemingway in this letter expressed his dislike; he thought the bull on the cover looked too much like a cow and sent Perkins photos and drawings of Spanish fighting bulls to give the Scribners artist a better idea of what he wanted. He promised that he would try to change the words in "A Pursuit Race," and he retitled two stories: "Italy 1927" became "Che Ti Dice La Patria?" and "After the Fourth" became "Ten Indians."[102] This letter marked the end of most of Hemingway's work on the book. He received proofs on 16 August and had finished going over them the next day, his only addition being to dedicate the book to his wife's sister, Virginia (Jinny) Pfeiffer.[103] However, he changed his mind about the dedication, cabling Perkins on 6 September to change it to read "TO EVAN SHIPMAN," a minor poet and horse-racing fancier.[104]

After his return from London, Perkins brought up in his 14 July letter the possibility of adding "A Lack of Passion," even though he would be sending galley proofs soon.[105] A week and a half later, Perkins sent the proofs of *Men Without Women* to Hemingway, who was still vacationing in Spain. The editor, in answer to Hemingway's 10 June letter, said that he too would not mind dropping "A Banal Story," but that it was needed to bulk up the book. This letter contains Perkins's main editorial contribution for this volume; he suggested beginning with "The Undefeated," placing "Fifty Grand" in the middle, and concluding with "Now I Lay Me." He considered these to be the best of the fourteen stories.[106] Hemingway evidently agreed, for this was the eventual placement of these stories in the book.

Further evidence of the importance Perkins placed on "The Undefeated" and "Fifty Grand" exists in his 9 September letter to Hemingway. Perkins wrote that there had been a "tussle" over the bull on the cover, but that he did not want to lose it, as "he is a valuable little mark for the book, useful in advertising." The bull's penis is clearly visible, and this was probably what was worrying the officials at Scribners. Perkins's desire to keep the bull, to include "A Lack of Passion," and to place "The Undefeated" as the book's first story indicate that he was attempting to associate the story volume in the critics' and readers' minds with bullfighting, no doubt hoping to link it with *The Sun Also Rises*. In the same letter, Perkins told Hemingway that the firm was not letting Edward O'Brien have "Fifty Grand" for his *Best Short Stories of 1927* because it was too important to *Men Without Women*.[107]

Prospects for a large sale must have seemed very good, for the firm advertised the book extensively. The first advertising efforts, aimed at booksellers, appeared in the firm's fall 1927 catalog: "In all these stories by that writer who awoke the literary world to astonished admiration with his first novel, "The Sun Also Rises," the softening feminine influence is absent—either through training, discipline, death or situation." The firm drew directly from Hemingway's 14 February 1927 letter to Perkins for this description of the collection. After a paragraph giving brief descriptions of "The Undefeated," "A Pursuit Race," "A Simple Enquiry," "In Another Country," "The Killers," "An Alpine Idyll," and "Fifty Grand," the catalog copy concludes thus: "Like all literature of the first order, they make a book seem a miraculous thing—miraculous in that it can encompass such emotion and yet look so insignificant."[108] The first advertisement mentioning the book in *Publishers Weekly* appeared in the 24 September 1927 issue; it headed the list of twelve fiction titles in the firm's two-page spread announcing its fall list.[109] The prepublication announcement for *Men Without Women* in the *New York Times Book Review*'s "Books to Come Before Christmas" included a photo of Hemingway.[110] The firm's faith was also indicated by the relatively large first printing it ordered on 3 October: 7,650 copies. Sales were rapid, as the printing records indicate; in the last three months of 1927 there were four printings, for a total of 16,835 copies.[111]

Men Without Women was published on 14 October 1927. The volume received reviews or notices in ten major American periodicals between September 1927 and May 1928. Hemingway's scrapbooks contain clippings of forty-eight notices of the collection in American publications—fewer than the number for *The Sun Also Rises*, yet still fairly large for a story volume.[112] A better indication of Hemingway's growing importance in the literary world is the people who reviewed the new work: Virginia Woolf in the *New York Herald Tribune Books* (9 October 1927: 1, 8), Dorothy Parker in the *New Yorker* (29 October 1927: 92–94), and H. L. Mencken in the *American Mercury* (May 1928: 127). The reviews for the most part were mixed (Woolf in particular disliked it), but the significance of the number and the prominence of the reviews should not be underestimated in an assessment of their positive effect on sales.

The book also received wide exposure through the firm's advertisements of it. Between October 1927 and December 1928, the firm purchased 153 advertisements for the collection (129 in 1927 alone), spending $4,599.70 on them.[113] In the *New York Times Book Review* between 16 October 1927 and 20 May 1928, twelve of the firm's advertisements listed or featured *Men Without Women*.[114] From 16 October to 18 December, the firm advertised the book every week. Six of these advertisements included either Hemingway's picture or one of the dust jacket, which featured a silhouette of a fighting bull. Beginning with the advertisement of 30 October, the firm, per its usual practice, began quoting from reviews. This procedure was also followed by the jacket designers as well; beginning with the third printing, the front cover of the dust jacket included quotes from reviewers.[115]

The collection, as the printing records indicate, sold fairly well for many years. Following the 16,835 copies produced in 1927, the firm ordered two additional runs for a total of 5,990 copies in 1928. No additional printings were ordered until 1932 (990 copies).[116] In all, this edition consisted of seven printings for a total of 23,815.[117] Assuming a consistent list price of $2.00, Hemingway's royalty (15 percent of list price) for the 1927 edition of *Men Without Women* would have been $7,144.50, a sum payable over a period of eleven years. Adjusting for inflation from 1928 to 2005, this sum would be equivalent to $44,197.95.

Hemingway never complained directly to Perkins about the sale of *Men Without Women*. As was typical of him, he complained over what he saw as lack of advertising for it.[118] Hemingway, though, may not have felt that the volume was as good as he could have made it, attributing this to his belief that Perkins's desire to enlarge it made him include material he should not have. In a letter circa late October 1927 to Fitzgerald (which Hemingway never completed or sent), Hemingway answered Fitzgerald's assessment of the volume, which Fitzgerald had made in a letter of October 1927. Hemingway wrote, "What do you think about quitting either writing or publishing? The only reason I publish the damn stuff is because that is the only way to get rid of it and not think it is any good. There is certainly no other way to show up that shit to yourself. I didn't care anything about that 10 Indians story either and wouldn't have published it except they wanted enough for a book aid like White Elephants and In Another Country—I suppose that last is a swashbuckling affectation too."[119] Hemingway was of course reacting to the reviewers, but he was also reacting to his new status as professional author, which meant having to make compromises with his publisher and with the public. This was the cost of fame. While on the whole Hemingway's first three publications with Scribners had gone smoothly and he was now on the verge of becoming the most famous writer in America, he was still wary. Soon this wariness and his limited ability to compromise with his publisher and the public would be thoroughly tested, when in 1928 he and Perkins began preparing for the publication of *A Farewell to Arms*.

CHAPTER 3

"IT'S NO FUN FOR ME ON ACCT. OF THE BLANKS"

The Serialization and Publication of A Farewell to Arms

The publication of *The Sun Also Rises* and *Men Without Women* established Hemingway's presence in the American literary market; he had proven himself as a money-making author for Scribners. However, even with the publication of four books in America, Hemingway had yet to become a blockbuster author or achieve the level of fame a writer like Sinclair Lewis enjoyed. The stage was set for Hemingway to achieve this level of success, and with the serialization and publication of *A Farewell to Arms* in 1929, he would do so.

Hemingway began writing his next novel, which he described as a "Modern Tom Jones," sometime in the early fall of 1927.[1] But Hemingway abandoned this novel, the story of a revolutionist and his son, by March of 1928 and never resumed work on it.[2] Instead, Hemingway began work on what would be called *A Farewell to Arms*, telling Perkins in a 17 March 1928 letter that he would "go on with the other one I am writing since two weeks that I thought was only a story but that goes on and goes *wonderfully*."[3]

Even before Hemingway had started writing his World War I novel, the way in which it would be published was being decided. On 24 June 1927, Hemingway wrote his editor that Ray Long of Hearst's magazines had offered to buy the serial and movie rights of his next novel for $10,000 and $15,000, respectively. Although Hemingway wrote that he was tempted to take the offer, he declined and returned the advance check for 25,483.40 francs Long had sent him. In his reply of the same day to Hearst's European representative, Mildred Temple (a copy of which Hemingway sent to Perkins), Hemingway wrote, "I will send you some stories for Mr. Long when I have them, and I give you my word that I will not enter into negociations with any one else for serializing the novel. When it is done if I decide to serialize it Mr. Long can have it if he wishes at the price stated in the offer, $12,000 with the $30,000 movie option." Apparently, Hemingway had revised the agreement (which has not been located) to reflect his asking price for the serial and movie rights; he wanted $2,000 more for the serial rights and $15,000 more for the movie rights than Long had originally offered. Hemingway added, "I do not want to take an advance which might even unconscously affect the writing of a novel because of the necessity of submitting it for serialization."[4] The $12,000 would have been the most money he had received for any of his works. More and more the man of business's affairs began intruding on those of the man of letters.

However, events that would make is harder for Hemingway to keep his promise to Long were developing in the Scribner offices in New York. In mid-1927, Robert Bridges and Alfred Dashiell (then associate editor of *Scribner's Magazine*) began developing a plan to revamp the magazine, beginning with the January 1928 issue. Part of the plan, as outlined in an undated memo from Dashiell to Bridges, called for more serializations and, under the heading "*Follow up previous successes*," noted, "Ernest Hemingway—ask him for more stories. All the other magazines are after him, but fortunately Hemingway is not anxious to appear in Cosmopolitan, Collier's, etc."[5] Dashiell saw the value Hemingway's name and work was acquiring and knew they would be assets to the magazine.

After publication of *Men Without Women*, Perkins wrote Hemingway on 14 October to inform him of the periodical's new format and to ask that he consider submitting his new novel to Bridges and

Dashiell. He also added that Dashiell had written about his "urgent desire" to get a new story by Hemingway. Perkins closed his letter by writing, "I will say no more about it, but since all the other magazines have said something, I thought if we did not, you might possibly not realize the strength of our interest."[6] The novel in question was "A New Slain Knight," not *A Farewell to Arms*. Even though Hemingway had garnered success for the firm, Perkins's near promise of acceptance of a novel he had not seen is unusual and indicates his great desire to keep Hemingway happy and with Scribners.

As Hemingway worked on *A Farewell to Arms,* he kept Perkins informed of his progress and how it affected publication plans. On 21 April 1928, he wrote the editor, "I wish I could have it for Fall because that seems like the only decent time to bring out a book but suppose, with the time necessary to leave it alone before re-writing, that is impossible." He raised the possibility of not publishing the novel until the fall of 1929, while writing and publishing stories to keep his name before the public, thereby also having the material for a story collection to publish in 1930 as a follow-up to the novel.[7] In his reply of 27 April, Perkins stated, "We can certainly expect to publish at the very beginning of the year anyhow, unless serialization intervenes;—and even then we could publish a year from the present time. I wish it might be sooner, but I think you are dead right in proceeding the way you do."[8] Again, Perkins was combining praise and prodding, wanting to keep his author happy while getting the novel delivered as soon as possible.

Negotiations, in a limited fashion, continued through the summer. From Kansas City, where he had gone to be with Pauline as she delivered their first son, Patrick, Hemingway wrote Perkins wanting to know how much *Scribner's Magazine* would pay for serialization rights.[9] In his response of 8 August, Perkins hedged the question a bit; he also hinted at possible problems. While he did not doubt the quality of the novel, Perkins was worried that the "character" of it might make it "unavailable" for serialization (i.e., that it might contain obscene language and scenes of sexual intercourse that a respectable magazine would not print). He was also concerned about the price. *Scribner's Magazine*'s top price had been around $10,000 for long serials by John Galsworthy and Edith Wharton; Hemingway had asked Long for at least $12,000 to serialize the novel in one of Hearst's magazines. Perkins did not know if Bridges could meet such a price. Having seen none of the new novel, Perkins was hesitant about committing the magazine to accepting it.[10]

Hemingway noticed this ambiguity on Perkins's part and reacted to it. In a letter of 20 August from Wyoming, he informed his editor that the first draft was finished and that he would be coming to New York either in mid-October or the first of November. But he did not seem optimistic about the prospects of serialization:

> I havent thought about serialization much—need the money but am afraid the magazine wont take a chance under Dr. Bridges—I am sure he would not have run The Sun—He wanted me to cut 50 Grand—Owen Wister—who seems a fine man—told me he was once going over some letters of Roosevelt's for his sister and all the good ones were one's B. had refused for the magazine.
>
> So I dont know how much hope to give myself—But now my earnings are down to $90 a month again must look forward to something as life is expensive.
>
> The fate of my stuff has been to always be turned down as too something or other and then after publication everybody say that of course they could have published it and it would have been fine—I think you'll like the book—The Mss. is in the safe in the bank of Piggott.[11]

Hemingway appears to have been making yet another play on Perkins's sympathy. These statements also show Hemingway's distrust of everyone at the house—with the exception of Perkins.

In an unusual move, Perkins wrote Hemingway to assuage his fears on 17 September. The move was strange because Perkins's letter was handwritten. This way there was no carbon copy for the files, thus the nature and contents of the letter would be known only to Perkins and Hemingway:

> I'm writing by pen partly because of my stenographer's vacation, but more that I may speak personally, rather than officially, on the Serial question.—This is the truth: there is nothing that Scribner's wants as much as a Serial by you + they will do everything they can to get it, + if they do, will make more of it than they ever made of anything. That's absolutely straight, + from me to you. Against this, stands only the one danger that

the story may have in it some element that would unfit it for magazine use,—as there was in The Sun Also. Other wise there is absolutely no ghost of a question. If there is any such element it would presumably unfit the Story for any magazine, but what of it! The book sale should be large, to Speak moderately. The Size of the advance would be what would Suit You, + it would be paid as you pleased, beginning any time from now on. I could not over-state the degree to which this house is interested in this book, or in You;—+ if they were not it would be time to re-organize as a Dry Good House.[12]

Perkins's optimism is a contrast to Hemingway's pessimism. Against this, Perkins admits that certain elements of the novel could adversely affect the magazine's decision. At the time, the U.S. Post Office had the power to strip a magazine of its second-class postage rate if it judged that the magazine was publishing obscene material; such a move would increase the cost of a periodical to such an extent that very few readers could afford to buy it. This would not, as Perkins points out, prevent the novel's publication in book form. Four days later, to further secure Hemingway's faith, Perkins wrote again about the serialization, offering to send a $5,000 advance on the serial rights. He added that for Hemingway to accept this offer would not bind him to accept the final offer, but that the gesture was made "to give you palpable evidence of the Magazine's interest."[13]

Perkins's offer of $5,000 is proof of the firm's desire to keep Hemingway happy, and the author saw it this way as well. In his reply of 28 September, he appeared to be ready to accept the magazine's offer and thanked Perkins for the promise of the $5,000 advance. However, he did bring up a point both he and Perkins seemed to have forgotten—he had promised Ray Long of Hearst's *Cosmopolitan* the right of first refusal of the serial:

The only draw back to accepting the 5000 advance is that I quite gratuitously promised Ray Long would let him have the first look at my next book if I decided to serialize it. I did this to shut them up when they were worrying me with propositions while I was working. To be completely frank I would greatly prefer to serialize in The Magazine—I do not care for serializing in Cosmopolitan and the difference of a few thousand—2 or 3—would not make me switch from Scribners to the International Magazine Co. I think it would be a good thing for me to serialize because it is not a good plan to wait *too* long between appearances and as will not have a book out this fall—nor until next fall—due to work so long on this one—it is good to keep something going.

As I said the money would be very welcome. I would write Ray Long and tell him but am afraid he would think I was trying to bid him up which is the last thing I want. If you can see anyway out of this would be very happy. In the meantime I feel like a damned fool not to take the check—I worry about the whole business and am prevented from writing the stories I wanted to do now in between by worrying about these bloody money matters.[14]

In none of their previous letters had Hemingway or Perkins mentioned Long or Hemingway's promise to him. Now, with a virtual promise from Perkins that *Scribner's Magazine* would take the novel, Hemingway was worried about offending Long and thus losing an outlet for his future work. *Cosmopolitan* was one of the better-paying magazines of the day—with deeper pockets than *Scribner's Magazine*—and Hemingway foresaw that one day he might need some of Hearst International's money. Yet he could not afford at this time to accept Long's offer and thus annoy his publisher, who was his biggest backer and promoter.

Perkins once again provided the answer, this time in his 2 October letter, in which he also reassured Hemingway of every member of the firm's faith in him:

Anyway, I send you the cheque, and feel easier for doing it, because, as we regard you, and as things have worked out, it seems as though we had sent you very little money. If in some way Ray Long does get this serial, the sum can stand as an advance against the book;—and in view of our expectations, or of your position now as a writer, we are certainly justified in making it, even on a very conservative business estimate.—I hope it will work out the way I proposed though, we to take whatever risk there may be of availability for serialization. When the manuscript is ready you could rightly, to the minds of publishers, including the Mind of Ray Long (sounds like a book title) say: that as Scribner's was the first general magazine to publish your stories, and as that house was publishing your books, it seemed only fair that they should have a chance at this serial.—This argument, easily enlarged on, would and should appeal to a publisher or editor, though it might not and need not appeal to an author. (There would be no reason, of course, why you should recognize this claim to priority unless you wanted to). I know Ray Long would recognize it since as editor he has urged it, and he might freely acknowledge it and clear the whole question. But I'd favor forgetting the question now, wholly, until the manuscript it finished. I didn't like to raise it, I knew it would be disturbing, but I saw there was some doubt in your mind over the Magazine and I had to try to make the thing plain. I suspected you thought the Magazine rather luke-warm because they didn't take the "Fifty Grand," and only urgent because of the enthusiasm of the house in general, and pressure therefrom. The truth is, Bridges and Dashiel have asked me a thousand times when that serial by Hemingway would be finished. I was mad enough that they didn't break their blooming rule and give the whole issue to "Fifty Grand" if necessary,—as they would have done had Mr. Scribner been here then.—But how many people know when to break a rule! They are fully awake now to your significance and would put forward a serial by you with a vigor and emphasis that no one could excel.—And I believe, personally, that you would do better to appear in Scribner's than the Cosmopolitan,—which is the last word I'll volunteer on a perplexing subject, best forgotten until the time comes to act.[15]

In essence, Perkins told Hemingway to invoke the concept of courtesy of trade, which, simply stated, meant that a publisher would not steal or attempt to lure away an author who had a commitment to another publisher. In his reply of 11 October, Hemingway thanked Perkins for the check and his advice, stating that he would present the case to Long as Perkins had suggested.[16]

During the second week of November, Hemingway was in New York—going to prize fights, seeing friends, and meeting frequently with Perkins to discuss the novel.[17] During the first week of December he was back in New York to pick up his eldest son, Bumby, from Hadley. On this trip, Hemingway met Ring Lardner, to whom he was no doubt introduced by Perkins.[18] It is not clear whether he and Perkins discussed the publication of the novel during this second trip. However, there is no evidence that Hemingway brought the manuscript, or any part of it, to New York for these meetings. The conclusion that suggests itself is that Perkins's advice about publication was based solely on what Hemingway told him. Once again, Perkins had essentially accepted a Hemingway book without reading any of it.

On his and Bumby's return train-trip to Key West, somewhere between New York and Philadelphia, Hemingway was informed by wire of his father's suicide.[19] This somber postscript to his New York trip marked a change in his relationship with Perkins. Whereas before both men had been reserved with each other, heading their letters "Dear Hemingway" and "Dear Mr. Perkins," at Perkins's request this changed, as the opening of Hemingway's mid-January 1929 letter shows:

> Dear Max—
> I'm sorry to have mistered you so long—Early got the habit of mistering anyone from whom I received money—on the theory of never make a friend of either a servant or an employer—But we have been friends for a long time and it is cockeyed splendid that you are coming down.[20]

By this point thirty-four chapters of the novel had been typed, and Perkins was coming to Key West to fish and, more importantly, to finally read the work.

Perkins arrived the first of February and stayed a little over a week. Here, Perkins was wholly in Hemingway's world, and the two spent most of their days fishing. Unfortunately, their discussions about the novel during this time were not documented. When he left, Perkins took the typescript with him. On his way home, the editor, aboard the Havana Special, wrote his author on 9 February to praise the work and to assure Hemingway that he was on his side: "Dear Ernest:—I've just finished re-reading the book. It's a most beautiful book I think,—perhaps. Especially the last part, after they get into Switzerland. . . . As for the proprieties, I'm in complete agreement with You personally, + have argued that way all my life. I said all that before + this letter is superfluous as well as realy illegible.—But after You put down such a book You've got to say something."[21] Perkins may have been preparing for the possibility of rejection by the editors of *Scribner's Magazine.* In any event, the letter introduces a new phase in Hemingway and Perkins's discussions about the novel.

Perkins's fears of possible rejection by *Scribner's Magazine* never materialized. Both Bridges and Dashiell were enthusiastic about the novel, and on 13 February they offered Hemingway $16,000 for serial rights.[22] Perkins informed the company's chairman of the board, Charles Scribner II, of this in a letter of 14 February; the letter includes a synopsis of the work, the reactions of the staff, and an outline of possible problems with the publication:

> Its quality is that of "The Sun," though its range is much larger and its implications consequently more numerous and widely scattered. Its story in outline is not objectionable but many words and some passages in it are: we can blank the words and the worst passages can be revised.—The reading of the book will still be a violent experience because of the force, directness, and poignance of the writing. . . .
>
> Mr. Bridges thinks the book a very strong one and its motif—a revelation of the tragic degradation of war, of which this love affair is a part—a fine one. Dashiel is very enthusiastic and regrets that even one word must be changed. I do not think that given the theme and the author, the book is any more difficult than was inevitable. It is Hemingway's principle both in life and literature never to flinch from facts, and it is in that sense only, that the book is difficult. It is not at all erotic, although love is represented as having a very large physical element.

Perkins could not, since his secretary was typing this letter, directly address what the obscene words were, as he noted in a handwritten postscript: "P.S. I was somewhat constrained in bringing out the difficult points in 'A Farewell' by dictating this to Miss Wykoff, but I thought your familiarity with Hemingway's way would sufficiently suppliment what I have said."[23] This would not be the last time during the publication of *A Farewell to Arms* that the problem of obscene words and passages would vex Perkins.

On the same day Hemingway had wired, "AWFULLY PLEASED PRICE OK."[24] Two days later he followed this with a letter to Perkins in which he gave his opinions on omissions and how he wanted them to be handled:

I'm awfully glad they are going to serialize and the Price is fine.

About omissions—They can only be discussed in the concrete examples—I told you I would not be unreasonable—dont mind the leaving out of a word if a blank is left if the omission is unavoidable and as for passages—almost every part of the book depends on almost every other part—You know that—So if a passage is dropped—there should be something to show it—That will not hurt the serial and will help the book. People might be curious to see the book and see what that passage contained. It's not a regular serial anyway.

My point is that the operation of emasculation is a tiny one— It is very simple and easy to perform on men—animals and books—It is not a Major operation but its effects are great—It is *never* performed *intentionally* on books—What we must both watch is that it should not be performed unintentionally—

I know, on the other hand, that you will not want to print in a magazine certain words and, you say, certain passages. In that event what I ask is that when omissions are made a blank or some sign of omission be made that isnt to be confused with the dots that writers employ when they wish to avoid biting on the nail and writing a hard part of a book to do.

Still the dots may be that sign—I'm not Unreasonable—I know we both have to be careful because we have the same interest *ie* (literature or whatever you call it) and I know that you yourself are shooting for the same thing that I am. And I tell you that emasculation is a small operation and we dont want to perform it without realizing it.

Anyway enough of talking—I am not satisfied with the last page and will change it—but the change will in no way affect the serializability—(what a word.)

I think you are very fine about the price—If I havent said more about it it is because while we are friends I am no blanket friend of the entire organization and have the feeling from experience, that the bull fighter is worth whatever he gets paid. However I think you are fine about the price. You are generous and I appreciate it.[25]

Hemingway was casting Perkins in the role of his advocate with the firm, the person who was to protect Hemingway's artistic integrity against the demands of business and social conventions. This letter also makes clear how the editing would be handled: Hemingway was to have the final say.

The first test of Hemingway's ability to handle the demands of serialization came on 19 February, when Bridges sent the galleys for the first installment of the serial. In his cover letter, Bridges explained the magazine's editing rationale:

> You will note that in accordance with your talk with Perkins, we have in several places put in dashes instead of the realistic phrases the soldiers of course use. This is not done from any particular squeamishness, but we have long been accepted in many schools as what is known, I believe, as "collateral reading," and have quite a clientage among those who teach mixed classes. Things which are perfectly natural and realistic in a book are not viewed with the same mind in a serial reading. You are, however, familiar with all this, and I need not argue our point of view. I know that you will help us in every way.
>
> On galley 12, I would suggest that you omit the paragraph circled with lead pencil, inserting several dashes to fill out the line after "please," resuming with:
>
> That is how it ought to be, etc.
>
> In these things we have to consider a constituency that has followed the Magazine for a great many years.[26]

The paragraph in question occurs in chapter 6 of the novel; it is Frederic Henry's fantasy about being in bed with Catherine Barkley in a hotel in Milan.

In order to deflect the brunt of Bridges' letter, Perkins wrote Hemingway the same day, repeating some of Bridges' arguments, responding to Hemingway's letter of 16 February, and emphasizing the possible good of the serial:

> Bridges is sending you today the proofs of the first installment, and there is one passage where he thinks a cut should be made, where cutting will go hard. I believe he is telling you why he thinks it necessary,—circulation as collateral reading in schools, and consideration of subscribers, etc. You as an ex-newspaperman know

about such things, and that there is a practical side to running periodicals,—On the other hand, there is this other side which I cannot wholly overlook:—there was a great deal of hostility to "The Sun." It was routed and driven off the field by the book's qualities, and the adherence which they won. The hostility was very largely that which any new thing in art must meet, simply because it is disturbing. It shows life in a different aspect, and people are more comfortable when they have got it all conventionalized and smoothed down, and everything unpleasant hidden. Hostility also partly came from those who actually did not understand the book because its method of expression was a new one. Sisley Huddleston expressed their view.[27] It was the same failure to be understood that a wholly new painter meets. People simply do not understand because they can only understand what they are accustomed to.

Now this serialization is not the real thing, as the book *is*. If we considered "A Farewell to Arms" only in respect to its intrinsic quality, and refused to regard the question from any practical point of view, we would all be dead against serialization. It is an incidental and outside thing, and the best reason for it, to my mind, was on account of the practical aspects of it in widening your public, and in making you understandable to a great many more people, and generally in helping you to gain complete recognition. It is in view of all this that I think—as I judge you do by your letter of today[28]—that cuts can be philosophically made, for if we can keep people from being diverted from the qualities of the material itself, by words and passages which have on account of *conventions*, an astonishingly exaggerated importance to them, a great thing will have been done. Your mind is so completely free of these conventions—and it is fortunate it is—that you do not realize the strength with which they are held. If you know a few of the genteel!

I am afraid this discourse is not very well put, but what I am trying to argue is that if we can bring out this serial without arousing too serious objection, you will have enormously consolidated your position, and will henceforth be further beyond objectionable criticism of a kind which is very bad because it prevents so many people from looking at the thing itself on its merits.[29]

Here, Perkins plays the role he would be forced to play time and again—not only during the publishing of *A Farewell to Arms,* but for the rest of his life—the mediator between the needs of his author and his firm.

In comparison to what Hemingway's reaction to future editorial advice and changes would be, his reaction to the proof of the first installment was calm. In his reply of 23 February, he told Perkins that the "blanks are all right *so far*" and agreed to omit the paragraph in galley 12; he did note, however, that he would never agree to such an excision in the book version.[30] Hemingway may not have been happy with the cut, but Bridges and Perkins's explanation must have satisfied him. Perkins responded on 27 February and attempted to assure the author that the book would be handled differently from the serial. In it, Perkins gave his opinion of the cut and outlined how he would handle the editing of the book version: "The passage you spoke of will do very well for the book and it is necessary really.—But anyhow, I never would ask you to take out anything, not even a word unless it seemed to me that it simply had to be done; and I should not be just playing safe. I should play the other way, in fact."[31] Against the conservatism of the magazine and its editors, Perkins contrasted his commitment to the artist and his art.

The biggest confrontation between Hemingway and the firm over the editing of the serial occurred with the second installment. Bridges had made three cuts, two in galley 2 and one in galley 10, that Hemingway, as he told Perkins in an 11 March letter, saw as evidence that the magazine editor was overstepping his bounds; Bridges had apparently cut the passages in the setting copy, not in proof, as Hemingway wanted. Galley 2 corresponds to chapter 10 of the novel; the cuts Bridges made were in Frederic and Rinaldi's conversation in the hospital, the first being Rinaldi's insinuations that Frederic and the priest are homosexuals, while the second is a cut of five lines of dialogue in which Rinaldi explains the difference between having intercourse with a girl and with a woman. In galley 10 (chapter 14), the scene of Frederic and Catherine's reunion in the hospital in Milan, the lines "Yes, I am. Come on" and "I'm crazy about you. Come on" were changed to "Yes, I am" and "I'm crazy about you." In addition, the following passage was deleted:

"You really do love me?"
"Don't keep saying that. Come on. Please. Please Catherine."

"All right but only for a minute."

"All right," I said. "Shut the door."

"You can't. You shouldn't."

"Come on. Don't talk. Please come on."[32]

In his letter to Perkins, Hemingway reacted violently then calmed down enough to be reasonable:

> If any passages are to be eliminated they must be eliminated from the proof so I can see how it looks and clean it up on the proof—I'd rather return the money and call it all off than have arbitrary eliminations made without any mention of the fact they are being made. If that's to be done let some one else sign it—By E.H. and A.B.—That's just anger! Half the writing I do is elimination. If someone else is doing it let them sign it. . . .
>
> *Later*—
>
> Wrote a calm letter to Mr. Bridges[33]—There was a cut in galley 10 too that I concede if you think it's necessary—but it doesnt seem so. Would you read the installment and my letter to Mr. Bridges and see if it's all right? You know I'm not just trying to be difficult. Am not sore now—But it was snooty to cut passages on Mss. rather than on proof. I think it's fixed up all right.[34]

Although Hemingway had calmed down, it was only a matter of time before new editorial demands would raise his ire again, when the novel was being set in proof for book publication.

Again, Perkins moved to reassure Hemingway that the magazine would do things the way he wanted them done. On 15 March, Perkins wrote: "Truly, Ernest, the change made in the galleys (I have just consulted Mr. Bridges most tactfully, and I have seen your letter to him which was fine) was made for only the one reason of simplifying things and speeding them up;—although I will admit that the simplification could only have been effective at this end. There is, and was, and never will be any idea of making any change without your approval;—and I doubt it there will be any change except a few blanks hereafter, anyhow. I am just writing now to assure you on that point."[35] Perkins's assurance was prophetic; no other indication of problems over Bridges' editing of the remaining installments is present in the correspondence between Hemingway and Scribners.

In his last located letter to Bridges, dated 18 May 1929, Hemingway wrote that he was returning proof of the last installment, with the exception of galley 19, the last of the set: "I have been rewriting the last 3 paragraphs for ten days and hope I now have it almost right—will mail it on the fast boat leaving May 23 due New York May 29."[36] The conclusion of the novel would continue to plague Hemingway for over a month; it was not until he revised the book galleys that he got it the way he wanted it to be.[37]

On 3 April, Hemingway wrote Perkins that he and Pauline would soon be sailing for Paris. He had just finished correcting proofs for the fourth installment. He instructed Perkins not to give Fitzgerald his Paris address, fearing that Fitzgerald's erratic behavior would get them evicted from the apartment, where they were "quiet and comfortable."[38] Hemingway's attempts to avoid Fitzgerald that summer proved unsuccessful, a fact that added to the stress Hemingway felt while editing A Farewell to Arms. In a letter to Lord Chesterfield, Samuel Johnson once wrote, "Is not a patron, my lord, one who looks with unconcern on a man struggling for life in the water, and when he has reached ground encumbers him with help?"[39] That summer in Paris Hemingway felt extremely encumbered by the well-meaning but ill-received advice his friends were giving him. As Hemingway saw it, the writing of the work was his job, the editing was his and Perkins's, and the selling was Scribners'; other parties attempting to help in any of these areas could expect a less than enthusiastic reception.

The first offer of assistance came from Owen Wister, best known as the author of The Virginian (1902). Hemingway had met the older author in Wyoming in August of 1928; by all accounts they got along wonderfully.[40] Wister had encouraged Charles Scribner to serialize A Farewell to Arms.[41] At Wister's request, Perkins sent him a complete set of the serial galleys in April. After reading them, Wister sent a letter praising the novel to Hemingway in late April. But Wister also told Perkins of his reservations about the book, and the two exchanged letters about the novel. No problem would have resulted, but Perkins on 7 May forwarded to Hemingway a copy of a letter Wister had written him (dated 29 April 1929) in which Wister had written about the ending, "I wonder whether those details are absolutely necessary to the emotional effects which he desires to produce. They are so terrible and so painful that I personally shrank from them as I read."[42] In his letter, Perkins commented:

There is one point that he raises some question of about which he is writing you.—Whether the extreme painfulness of the last scenes in the hospital are not too much in that they so completely absorb the reader, so torture him almost, as to obscure other things. This had occurred to me at the beginning, and I thought I would re-examine the passages in the book proof and possibly raise the question.—Although you have always turned out to be so extraordinarily right as to make me hesitate on such points. After all, you are the one who has gone to the bottom of the matter. Still, it is worth considering, especially when one so enthusiastic as Wister thinks it worth considering.[43]

As Alan Price has ascertained, Perkins, "who had his own doubts about the book's structure, used Wister's private comments to buttress his own position."[44]

Hemingway was in the midst of rewriting the ending of the novel for the serial when Perkins and Wister's letters arrived. Reacting to "what he saw as collusion between Wister and Perkins," Hemingway fired off an angry letter to Perkins.[45] Perkins wrote on 31 May to apologize; he accepted responsibility for soliciting Wister's comments, explaining that he thought a positive statement by the older author could be used to defend the serial from attacks. Perkins claimed he saw no possible harm in doing so: "My idea was that you would probably disregard his or any other person's suggestions, but that one might have some validity which you would accept, and that no harm would be done anyhow. There are people who write, and even some quite good ones, to whom you do not dare make suggestions because of an uncertainty in themselves.—I never saw any sign of this in you. Anyway the only way I knew what suggestions Wister made—and I never even thought much about them—was by his briefly mentioning them in order to ask if I thought you would object to his stating them."[46] On 7 June, Hemingway wrote Perkins and told him not to worry. He claimed to understand and appreciate both Perkins's and Wister's suggestions.[47] Hemingway was once again appeased, but his overreaction to Wister's comments indicates his increasing sensitivity to outside criticism.

To a lesser degree, Hemingway reacted in a similar way to Fitzgerald's comments on *A Farewell to Arms.* As he had done for *The Sun Also Rises,* Fitzgerald wrote a long (ten pages) memo to Hemingway with his suggestions for editing the novel. The memo is undated, but Fitzgerald probably wrote it sometime in June. Among other things, Fitzgerald disliked the ending and the way Catherine was characterized at times. Hemingway did act on some of Fitzgerald's ideas, most notably his advice on the ending, but his annotation at the end of the memo—"Kiss my ass EH"—indicates that his reaction to Fitzgerald's comments was similar to his reaction to Wister's.[48] No matter how well meaning the advice, Hemingway was in no state to take it calmly. The only person who seemed even partially safe from his anger was Perkins.

Around this time Perkins briefly considered submitting the novel to either the Book-of-the-Month Club or the Literary Guild.[49] But by June he had rejected this plan. In his letter of 12 June, he explained to Hemingway that he thought that in the case of an established author like Hemingway, the publicity generated by such an arrangement would not outweigh the number of sales taken away from the trade edition.[50] Hemingway agreed, telling Perkins so in his letter of 24 June.[51]

Toward the end of May, with Hemingway's work on the serial galleys complete, work on shaping up the book version of the novel began. On 24 May, before Hemingway's angry letter about Wister had reached him, Perkins mailed the galley proofs of the book to his author in Paris. He reminded Hemingway not to delay reading the proofs, while urging him to take the time to make any revisions he wanted. He also informed Hemingway of the great interest his novel had raised in "those who will be most active in 'pushing' it," the firm's salesmen. The bulk of the letter was taken up, however, by Perkins's suggestions for revisions. Like Wister and Fitzgerald, he was concerned about the ending and the more unpleasant aspects of life depicted in the novel. But Perkins was careful in his comments to make clear to Hemingway that the final decision lay with him: "I have thought and talked about it for some three months now, and beyond the few slight comments on the margin of the proof I have one or two more serious ideas on it which I dare give you because I know you will know easily whether to reject them, and won't mind doing it;—and if you do it I'll believe you're right: I see plainly that you go down to the very bottom at any cost to test the truth of everything. Only you can do that—not many writers, even, have the strength to—and that brings the right decision." Perkins thought that through most of the novel the elements of love and war had been balanced perfectly, but in the last section the war was almost wholly forgotten. He suggested introducing the war in some way at the end in order to leave the reader with both elements. Perkins also advised modifying the depiction of Catherine's labor and death, since the description Hemingway had might shock and distract the reader from the story. Perkins closed by writing, "Otherwise, there's nothing much to say, except that if you could reduce somewhat the implications of physical aspects in the relationship I doubt that harm would be done. But here I may be influenced by the dangers of censorship. My whole intention is to put these things in mind.—I have most absolute confidence in your judgment and wouldn't want to influence it if I could."[52]

The galley proofs contain very few revisions by Hemingway or members of the firm. Most of the revisions are corrections to punctuation and appear to have been made by an unknown copy editor at the house. One instance where Perkins made a suggestion was on galley 23—the section in chapter 13 where Nurse Gage asks Frederic Henry if he would like to use the bedpan. In the margin, Perkins wrote, "I should think this unpleasant implement might be omitted;—for the physiological function it re-lates to has no significance,—here any how." Hemingway replied, "On the other hand this instrument dominates hospital life—I have only mentioned it once I believe I mentioned it to give the natural and unembarrassed attitude of nurse toward all the natural functions. The first and biggest impression one who has never been in a hospital receives E.H."[53] The passage remained unaltered.

The major concern that Perkins did not mention was Hemingway's use of obscene words. Apparently, he had marked the places in the novel where Hemingway had used the words *balls, fucking,* and *cocksucker*. This is clear from Hemingway's response of 7 June, two days after he had received the galley proofs.[54] Hemingway thanked Perkins for having corrections from the serial galleys copied onto the book galleys; noted some of the suggested changes were good, others bad; and accepted those that seemed to make no difference: "I am glad always to make it conventional as to punctuation." The bulk of the letter was dedicated to the matter of the three obscene words. Hemingway presented a two-pronged argument. The first was based on literary precedent. He claimed that two of the words could be found in Shakespeare and would soon be found in the German novel *All Quiet on the Western Front* by Erich Maria Remarque, which would be published in America by Little, Brown in 1929. Next, Hemingway appealed to Perkins's business sense, arguing how sales would be harmed by such cutting, as would his future with the firm:

> I hate to kill the value of mine by emasculating it when I looked up in The Quiet on W.F. book to find the words to show you I had a very hard time finding them. They dont stand out. But you should not go backwards. If a word can be used and is needed in the text it is a *weakening* to omit it. If it *cannot* be printed without the book being suppressed all right.
>
> There has always been first rate writing and then American writing—(genteel writing)
>
> No one that has read the Mss. has been shocked by *words* The words do not stand out unless you put a ring around them
>
> There is no good my pleading the case in a letter. You know my view point on it. What would have happened if they had cut the Sun Also? It would have flopped as a book and I would have written no more for you.

Next, Hemingway addressed the specific cases. He agreed that in some cases blanks could be used. His compromise was to use dashes for part of the word, such as *b——ls* for *balls* and *c——s——r* or *c——ks——r* for *cocksucker,* closing the letter with the weak claim, "Certainly those letters cannot corrupt anyone who has not heard or does not know the words. There's no proof it isnt cocksure."[55]

Before Perkins could respond to Hemingway's claims, a situation beyond their control arose that would govern the remaining discussion of the editing of *A Farewell to Arms*. On 20 June, Boston police chief Michael H. Crowley banned the June issue of *Scribner's Magazine* because the serial's second installment had been judged "salacious." As Scott Donaldson has concluded, the action was rather quixotic: the June issue had been on newsstands for weeks already, and although the action barred distribution of the periodical for the remaining four months of the serial's run, there was little effect on the circulation of the magazine and probably served to increase the eventual sale of the book.[56] The ban was not unexpected; in 1927 *The Sun Also Rises* had been banned in Boston. The firm publicly defended the serial, and on 21 July 1929, a statement by Dashiell appeared in an article on the second page of the *New York Times:*

> The very fact that Scribner's Magazine is publishing "A Farewell to Arms" by Ernest Hemingway is evidence of our belief in its validity and its integrity. Mr. Hemingway is one of the finest and most highly regarded of the modern writers.
>
> The ban on the sale of the magazine in Boston is an evidence of the improper use of censorship which bases its objections upon certain passages without taking into account the effect and purpose of the story as a whole. "A Farewell to Arms" is in its effect distinctly moral. It is the story of a fine and faithful love, born, it is true, of physical desire.
>
> If good can come from evil, if the fine can grow from the gross, how is the writer effectually to depict the progress of this evolution if he cannot describe the conditions from which the good evolved? If white is to be contrasted with black, thereby emphasizing its whiteness, the picture cannot be all white.
>
> A dispatch from Boston emphasized the fact that the story is "anti-war argument." Mr. Hemingway set out neither to write a moral tract nor a thesis of any sort. His book is no more anti-war propoganda [*sic*] than are the Kellogg treaties.
>
> The story will continue to run in Scribner's Magazine. Only one-third of it has yet been published.[57]

Privately, however, Perkins had a more complex view of the Boston ban. The firm had no legal recourse, but it is doubtful if they would have taken any action if they could have. Scott Donaldson has argued that the ban was more troubling to Hemingway than to Perkins since it provided the novel with free publicity and gave the editor another "bargaining chip in his ongoing discussion with the author about his use of objectionable words."[58] On 27 June, Perkins wrote Hemingway about the ban, informing him of Dashiell's statement and the firm's continued support. But he was very clear on what could and could not be printed, using the example of the American publication of *All Quiet on the Western Front* to undercut one of Hemingway's arguments:

> The incident affects the possibility of book suppression. There are things in the book that never were in another,—since the

18th Century anyway. There are points that enemies could make a good deal of. All right then! But I don't think we can print those three words, Ernest. I can't find *anyone* who thinks so. That supreme insult alone might turn a judge right around against us, and to the post office, it and the others, I think, would warrant (technically) action. It would be a dirty shame to have you associated in a way with that Jessica boy and his sort,— people who write with an eye to tickle a cheap public. It would be disgusting. There would follow such an utterance of intelligent indignation against it as in the end would change it.—But harm would have been done,—at least from my point of view. . . .

Will this business disturb you? I had to tell you about it, and you would have heard it anyway. We had previously lost eight or ten subscribers or so, and had a few stupid and violent kicks;— and many people who truly admired the story said they were astonished to see such things in print,—but I heard, or heard of, no cheap comment. Molly Colum wrote a fine indignant letter to the Times about the Boston act. Apparently "The Western Front" was very badly cut here, and the publishers were as much to blame as anyone. Not only many words, but passages, incidents, went.—So there's a book designed only to show how nasty and damaging is war, and its point must be blunted for the very people who ought to want those very things shown and would say they do.[59]

The "Jessica boy" Perkins mentions was Maxwell Bodenheim. His novel about a promiscuous woman, *Replenishing Jessica,* had been published by Boni and Liveright in 1925. The novel was judged obscene by a New York grand jury soon after publication, but although indictments had been issued, no motions for a trial were issued, presumably because Liveright had withdrawn the novel. In 1928, however, motions were issued, mainly due to of Liveright's involvement with Edouard Bourdet's play *The Captive.* The trial was a brief sensation in New York, mainly because members of the jury fell asleep while the novel was being read to them, and in the end Liveright was found not guilty.[60] Perkins's remarks, then, show his desire to avoid such a public spectacle. He did not want Hemingway and Scribners to be embarrassed as Bodenheim and Liveright had been. He did not want *A Farewell to Arms* to be seen merely as sensational trash.

On 12 July, Perkins wired Hemingway that the galleys had arrived in New York and that page proofs would not be sent to him unless Hemingway sent word. But the matter of the obscene words was not finished. Perkins pointed out that there was little that could be done about the Boston ban then went on to outline his fears.

There was, and there is still, considerable anxiety for fear of the federal authorities being stirred up. They seem to take curious activity of late, and if the post office should object, we would be in Dutch.—The thing could be fought out, but it would take so much time as to be very serious.— But we do not have to cross any such bridge as that until we come to it. The question does, however, affect the book in this way:—it has been immensely admired, but also it has aroused fierce objection. This means that when the book appears it will be scrutinized from a prejudiced standpoint, and this taken with everything else, did make us conclude, what we had always felt anyhow, that the three words we have talked so much about, could not be printed, or plainly indicated. This is bad in connection with Miss Van Campen except that I do not see how anybody could fail to get the sense. Anyhow, we went over this thing with the strongest inclination to play the game to the limit with you, and we felt that if we got in trouble in just a matter of words like this, you would be in the least defensible position, because they could easily be defined as indecent and impure, etc., etc. They would from a technical point, and they would arouse prejudice. This point of prejudice I think is hard for you to understand, but there is no question about the fact of it. Anyhow, that is the way the thing worked out after I had talked with Mr. Scribner at great length about it. Everything else in the book goes, of course, as you have put it, exactly.[61]

Perkins's argument rests on the assertion that the firm was acting only to protect its author, whether the author desired or thought he needed this protection or not. In essence, Perkins said that there could be no other way: the three words would have to go.

Hemingway read Perkins's letters as indication that the firm and his editor were frightened. In a letter to Fitzgerald in late July, Hemingway wrote of Perkins's reaction, "Max sounded scared. If they get scared now and instead of using that publicity try and lay off the book I'll be out of luck. Haven't asked for an advance so far. I know I should because in the end it is more difficult to lay off a book if they have money tied up in it already. Max is such a damned fine fellow that I hate to act as I know I should act. Not that I think that they would lay off but there is always a [*rest of letter missing*]."[62]

Hemingway had not received Perkins's 27 June letter when he wrote on 26 July in answer to his editor's letters of 24 June and 12 July. In this letter, Hemingway conceded the point on the three words: "I understand your viewpoint about the words you cannot print—If you cannot print them—and I never expected you could print the one word (C—S—) then you cannot and that lets me out." But he was still angry over having to give up the point, blaming the Catholics in Boston and the book clubs for the rash of censorship, which in turn forced him to censor his own work: [63]

> But do not you get in opposition to me now; ie—you = "me" and me = the author who does not understand the risks of using words. Because we both run risks it is only that where the writer risks hundreds the publisher risks thousands—But it all comes from the writer who doesn't write until he has at least risked that. We all lose in the end. That is the one thing we can be sure of. You'll be dead and I will be dead and that is all we can be completely sure of. This, of course, all seems nonsense but it is really true—And when you write your guts out (and your life out) and you do not write easily it is bad to see a few organized ignorant Irish co-religionists try to sabotage it aided by a few extra dollar seeking book organizations that have given a great blow to all good writing or anyway attempts at good writing. There is damned little good writing and the way things are going there will be less.
>
> I'm sick of all of it. Of course I have nothing to complain of. You have been swell (what a lousy word to mean so much) consistently. But I am sick of writing; of the disaster of a family debacle; of the shit-i-ness of critics—(Harry Hansen IE *Naughty Ernest* in the World which Wister just sent me)[64] of damned near everything but Pauline and to get back to Key West and Wyoming—Paris has been—nasty enough.

After he finished this letter, however, he did think of an adequate replacement for one of the words that would have otherwise remained a blank. At the top of page one, he wrote, "What about saying—kicked in the *scrotum* in connection with Miss Van Campen. Remember the last time balls was changed to Horns—isnt that O.K.?"[65] In his reply of 14 August, Perkins noted that the "synonym or near-synonym you suggested for the blank word" was unusual, but since it was said to a nurse, it would serve.[66]

With the editing of the novel complete, Hemingway turned his attention to his next project. From Santiago de Compostela, Spain, he wrote Perkins sometime in August that he wanted to do a book of nonfiction next, a volume of pieces "about fishing—hunting—about Bull fights and bull fighters—About eating and drinking—About different places—Mostly things and places."[67] Hemingway may have been having trouble writing fiction and was working on these pieces as a way to keep in practice. Perkins's reaction to this proposal is not known. But the letter indicates that Hemingway was already considering his next project after *A Farewell to Arms* was published and had accurately predicted the type of writing he would be doing in the thirties.

While editing and censorship occupied most of Hemingway and Perkins's time, other members of the firm were gearing up the advertising and publicity campaign for *A Farewell to Arms*. The novel received the most exposure of any Hemingway work to date. It first benefited from its serialization in *Scribner's Magazine*. Between April and August of 1929, the magazine ran five advertisements for the serial in *Publishers Weekly*.[68] The campaign focused on the love and war elements of the story, as demonstrated by the copy for the full-page advertisement of 20 April: "A vivid love story woven into the texture of the debacle of Italian retreat." As Perkins had hoped to do, Wister was used to help sell the book; the entire copy for the 10 August advertisement was a quote by Wister, presumably taken from a letter to Perkins. In addition, other newspapers and magazines ran notices, articles, columns, and editorials on the serial and the Boston ban. Hemingway's scrapbook contains fourteen clippings pertaining to the serialization or the ban.[69] This number is low, but it must be understood that the real number of such articles was no doubt much higher, since some of the clippings came from syndicated columns

Publishers Weekly (20 April 1929) advertisement for the serialization of Hemingway's second novel (Scribners Archives)

(such as Harry Hansen's "First Reader"), of which Hemingway would have kept only one copy.

The tone of the firm's advertising efforts for the book publication of *A Farewell to Arms* was established by its description in Scribners' fall 1929 catalog. The full-page announcement features a photograph of Hemingway (who is listed only as the author of *The Sun Also Rises* and *Men Without Women*) with the following description:

> This novel throws a far greater shadow than did the first. Its range is much wider, its implications more numerous, its significance more profound. The title is a bitter phrase: war taints and damages the beautiful and the gallant and degrades every one;—and this book which is a *farewell* to it as useless and hateful, might be grim reading if it were not illuminated with the beauty of the world, of the characters, and by love; and if it were not also lively with incident and often extremely amusing.
>
> It is in Italy during the war and a magnificent episode is the Caporetto retreat in which Lieutenant Henry, the American hero, participates;—it differs from conventional accounts of retreats as widely as does Stendhal's familiar account of Waterloo from the conventional accounts of battle.
>
> The whole book is full of horror, beauty, and sadness, and so is the love story that is the heart of it;—that of Lieutenant Henry and Catharine Barclay, the English nurse, a tall "tawny" beauty. The whole story is tremendously moving. Reading it is a violent experience because of its force, directness and poignance. One could hardly think of a parallel in literature, for beauty, to the final episode of the life of Catherine and Henry in Switzerland throughout a fall and winter. It has the pathos of a happy time that is tinged with sorrow because those having it know that it must end soon, and tragically.
>
> A sense of the beauty of nature and of its permanence, in contrast to the brevity and fluidity of man's affairs, pervades the whole book.[70]

Many of the phrases used to describe the novel are identical to those Perkins used in his 14 February 1929 letter to Charles Scribner. Whether Perkins wrote the catalog copy or the person who did based it on Perkins's letter is not known; what is clear, however, is that Perkins's ideas about the novel were shaping the way it was presented to the public.

The firm made only one other prepublication announcement for the novel in *Publishers Weekly*. The novel is listed first in a list of twenty Scribners titles in a two-page spread in the 21 September 1929 issue.[71] Scribners no doubt assumed that since the serialization had been so widely publicized to booksellers, little else needed to be done. In addition to the *Publishers Weekly* advertisements, the publisher ran three prepublication ads in the *New York Times Book Review*—the first on 23 June, and the last two on 22 September.[72]

The book was published with a list price of $2.50 on 27 September 1929, just as the last installment of the serial appeared in *Scribner's Magazine*. Sixteen reviews for the book appeared in major American newspapers and magazines in 1929 and 1930. Hemingway's scrapbooks contain 215 clippings of reviews for the novel.[73] The majority of the critics reviewed the book favorably, and most considered it Hemingway's best work to date. Fanny Butcher, reviewer for the *Chicago Daily Tribune,* called the novel, "Technically and stylistically the most interesting novel of the year."[74] *Nation* reviewer Clifton Fadiman stated, "There seems no reason why it should not secure the Pulitzer Prize."[75] There were a few holdouts, most notably Robert Herrick, who in his essay for the *Bookman* titled "What Is Dirt?" bemoaned the deletions made in the American edition of *All Quiet on the Western Front* but felt "no great loss to anybody would result if *A Farewell to Arms* had been suppressed."[76] This essay sparked two replies in the *Bookman,* the first in Henry Seidel Canby's "Chronicle and Comment" column in the February 1930 issue, and the second in the Scribners advertisement in the March 1930 issue.[77] Thus even negative comments served the purpose of publicizing the novel.

The firm ran eighteen advertisements for the book in the *New York Times Book Review* after publication.[78] From 29 September through 8 December Scribners ran an ad for the book every week. In addition to advertisements that used comments from American reviewers, the 17 January ad used quotes from English reviewers.[79] These ads, in combination with the stories about the serialization and the Boston ban, and the reviews, made *A Farewell to Arms* the most widely publicized book by Hemingway until the publication of *For Whom the Bell Tolls* in 1940. The firm's advertising records show that the publisher promoted the book well. Between September 1929 and December

1930, Scribners bought 325 advertisements—the bulk appearing in the first six months—spending a total of $20,578.17. As was usual, most of the ads were in New York newspapers and in magazines such as *Harper's,* the *New Republic,* and the *Nation.* But the firm also advertised extensively in newspapers in Boston, Philadelphia, Chicago, St. Louis, Los Angeles, and San Francisco, as well as in the alumni magazines of Ivy League universities. The final analysis shows that Scribners mounted a true nationwide campaign.[80]

According to the firm's printing records, the exposure paid off. The Scribners Press printed seven impressions of the novel, all between 18 September and 7 December 1929. This does not seem large compared to the number of printings for *The Sun Also Rises,* but it must be understood that larger print runs were ordered for the war novel: 31,050 copies on 18 September; 10,000 on 1 October; 10,000 on 9 October; 10,050 on 15 October; 20,350 on 11 November; 10,100 on 30 November; and 10,125 on 7 December. In all, 101,675 copies for this edition.[81] In short, Scribners expected a large sale from the beginning but still had to order larger than usual printings to meet demand.

Hemingway was almost as active after publication as he had been during the writing and editing of it. On 3 October, he wrote that he had trouble finding the book in the stores, a problem he thought caused by the poor jacket design. (The jacket, by CLEON, featured male and female seminude figures in a neoclassical pose.) He also told Perkins that the firm needed to keep pushing the book because it was his only source of income. Again, Hemingway played up the conflict between the commercial writer and the literary artist:

> What I'm afraid of now that I've actually seen it is that in a little while it will all be over and when a respectable number are sold then it will be laid off being pushed and not sell any more and the book will be just the same only no one will ever buy it—I wont have another one for two years anyway
>
> I always figured that if I could write good books they would always sell a certain amount if they were good and some day I could live on what they all would bring in honestly—But Scott tells me that is all bunk—That a book only sells for a short time and that afterwards it never sells and that it doesnt pay the publishers even to bother with it. So I guess it's all just a damned racket like all the rest of it and the way I feel tonight is to hell with all of

it—All I got out of this book is disappointment—I couldn't pay any attention when my father died—Couldnt let myself feel *anything* because I would get out of the book and lose it—Of course the thing as a serial supports them all and the book is going to have to too—But I would rather write and then go over it and when I know it's right stick to it and publish it that way the way it was if it never sells a damned one—That's what I should have done—Instead of starting in on the polite Owen Wister Compromise—The fact I do it on acct. of my family is no excuse and I know it—I'm a Professional Writer now—Than which there isn't anything lower. I never thought I'd be it (and I'm damned if I'm going to do it any more)—But if I can get one copy of it and I can see I got it set up the way it was (rather you set it up and deserve all credit) in type it will take some of the curse off it.

Dont think I'm sore at you—I'm not. You've *always* been grand to me. I just hate the whole damned thing.[82]

This letter's location in the Ernest Hemingway Collection at the John F. Kennedy Library suggests that it may not have been sent to Perkins (no copy of it has been located in the Scribners Archive at Princeton); Hemingway may have thought better of letting his editor see such bitter comments. But it does show that Hemingway, despite the prospect of a big sale, had had enough—he was tired of making his works conform to his publisher's and society's conventions.

Hemingway on 22 October showed exactly what he meant when he said he was a professional writer. Again using Fitzgerald to support his position, Hemingway wrote Perkins: "Scott says he has a contract whereby above certain large amounts of sales the royalty percentage rises. He told me what it was but I forgot it. What about this? Do you want to make some increase over 50,000? over 75,000? and over 100,000? Will you let me know about this. The principal thing I want is for it to keep on going of course and am not avaricious. But have heard this is done so write to ask you."[83] The contract for *A Farewell to Arms* had been sent in March of 1929.[84] This contract has not been located, but its terms, as indicated by the correspondence, were the same as for Hemingway's other Scribners books: a flat royalty of 15 percent of the list price per copy.

Hemingway's disgust over the compromises he had made became a recurring theme in his late-1929 letters to Perkins. For example, he closed his 10 November letter with the following assertions: "Remember O.W. and et al wanting me to tone down or cut out some of the last chapter? That's why they're reading the damned book. It's no fun for me on acct. of the blanks—Now I can never say shit in a book—Precedent—When you make your own precedent once you make the wrong precedent you're just as badly stuck by it—It takes away the interest in writing fiction."[85] This complaining and despair may have been part of a calculated move on Hemingway's part to guilt Scribners into changing the terms of his contract.

Perkins appeared ready to play hardball over this matter, however. On 12 November, he wrote his author and argued that a higher royalty rate would be impossible for the firm:

> In connection with this there is the question about the royalty. When we first published for Scott costs were not what they are now, nor were discounts. 20% after a certain figure left a reasonable margin to the publisher, on account of the big sale he had previously made. The situation is different now, and most publishers feel that 20% is too much,—that 15% is about all that a book will bear if it is to be heavily advertised. Before the advent of the clubs and other influences, it was possible to get a book going strongly and then let it go on its own impetus.—But now along comes the new Club book and Guild book, and a great deal must be done to counteract the tendency of public attention to turn to these new books. The truth is if you demanded 20% royalty, even from the start, we would probably give it to you and face a loss, if necessary, but it is better that the publisher should have an adequate margin so that he may strongly support a book. I will tell you what,—we have this contract now, and the royalty report based upon it will not be rendered until six months after publication;—but of course if you want payments in the meantime, you can have them in advance. But when that report is rendered we shall know what the result of the whole publication is, and I could then give you in a very simple form, the exact figures about the profits, and the advertising, and everything else, and if you thought we ought, we could then revise the terms of the contract retroactively. If you should come through New York, or if I should have the chance to go to Key West, I could easily show you the whole thing, and we could talk it out.[86]

With the stock market crash of 29 October 1929, more concern was being paid to the bottom line. Perkins's position was that Scribners would pay a greater rate if Hemingway wanted it, but he made it clear to his author that such a demand would hurt the firm.

Hemingway received Perkins's letter on 20 November. In his reply of the same date he made very clear that such a wait-and-see attitude was not acceptable to him. He hinted that the firm knew the novel was going to be a big seller because it ordered a first printing of 30,000 copies, as opposed to the 5,000-copy first printing of *The Sun Also Rises*. He noted that he had had offers from other publishers but maintained that he was not trying "to bid up." Finally, he asserted that the cutting of the novel had made him intractable in his demand for a larger royalty:

> You know we have no fights about money. The only fundamental disagreement was about the words—I *knew* certain ones could be published because I saw them in proof and they were all right— They shocked no one—I *had* to have them—It meant everything to the integrity of the book. I was prepared with the book written and published intact as I wrote it to accept no advance—I didnt ask for one. Every one to whom I had obligations could take their chances along with me—If the book was suppressed I knew the suppression would not last and that it would be as well and better for all concerned in the end. I wrote about how I felt and how serious the matter was to me—That is our business—yours and mine—and I have talked to no one outside about it. But when I was over-ruled and knew that it was finally a commercial proposition (as of course it is and rightly so to you because you have the responsibility of Scribner's interests) and it was cut so it would be able to sell—I've had no interest in it as a *book* since. It's something to sell—Some man in Town and Country has written that I am the one who made Joyce's integrity saleable and palatable[87]— All right—with the words in they would see whether I was writing to sell or not—But now that I've lost my integrity on it let it sell By God and fix up my mother and the rest of them.[88]

To what extent Hemingway was truly upset about the firm's censoring of *A Farewell to Arms* at this time is a matter of debate; what is clear is that he played this anger as a trump to increase his earnings.

Scribners obviously felt that Hemingway was too important to its list to make angry and that his demands should be met. Perkins wrote on 10 December outlining his discussion with Scribner and informing Hemingway of the new arrangement:

> Now as to the revision of the contract: I took it up finally today and everything went well about it. Your position and point of view were fully understood and accepted. In fact, I suggested a royalty of 17½% after 25,000 copies, and of 20% after 45,000, and Mr. Scribner said, "No, 20% after 25,000. I think I told you once that if you asked for 20% from the first copy, we would give it, whatever the effect of our own profit on the book might be;—because we think the value of publishing for you is a great one in itself.—So if these new terms do not seem to you satisfactory, you have only to tell us what terms will. That is a fact. I am sure that if you wanted anything else, I could take it up, and they would give it. But from this moment on, you can figure anyhow on 20% after a sale of 25,000,—and the sale must actually have reached 60,000. It is bearly short of that on the royalty card.[89]

The new contract for the novel, dated 25 September 1929, was revised to include the new terms. Hereafter, all new works by Hemingway would contain the same royalty rate: 15 percent of the list price for the first 25,000 copies sold and 20 percent for every copy thereafter.[90] The contract also specified that the first $20,000 in royalties would be paid into a trust fund that Hemingway had established for his mother and siblings.[91]

The difference in the terms would produce a big difference in Hemingway's earnings. Under the old arrangement, Hemingway would have earned only 37.5 cents a copy (15 percent of $2.50), or $38,128.13 for the 101,675 copies of this edition. Under the new terms, Hemingway earned 50 cents per copy (20 percent of $2.50) after the first 25,000 copies. In short, he made $9,375 on the first 25,000 copies and $38,337.50 on the remaining 76,675 copies—a total of $47,712.50. He made $9,584.37 more with the new contract

Overleaf: Contract for Hemingway's fourth Scribner title, the first with his increased royalty rate (Scribners Archives)

Memorandum of Agreement, *made this* — twenty-fifth — *day of* September *19*29

between ERNEST HEMINGWAY

of Paris, France, — — — — — *hereinafter called "the* AUTHOR,*"* *and* CHARLES SCRIBNER'S SONS, *of New York City, N. Y., hereinafter called "the* PUBLISHERS." *Said* — — Ernest Hemingway — — *being the* AUTHOR *and* PROPRIETOR *of a work entitled:*

A FAREWELL TO ARMS

in consideration of the covenants and stipulations hereinafter contained, and agreed to be performed by the PUBLISHERS, *grants and guarantees to said* PUBLISHERS *and their successors the exclusive right to publish the said work in all forms during the terms of copyright and renewals thereof, hereby covenanting with said* PUBLISHERS *that he is the sole* AUTHOR *and* PROPRIETOR *of said work.*

Said AUTHOR *hereby authorizes said* PUBLISHERS *to take out the copyright on said work, and further guarantees to said* PUBLISHERS *that the said work is in no way whatever a violation of any copyright belonging to any other party, and that it contains nothing of a scandalous or libelous character; and that* he *and* his *legal representatives shall and will hold harmless the said* PUBLISHERS *from all suits, and all manner of claims and proceedings which may be taken on the ground that said work is such violation or contains anything scandalous or libelous; and* he *further hereby authorizes said* PUBLISHERS *to defend at law any and all suits and proceedings which may be taken or had against them for infringement of any other copyright or for libel, scandal, or any other injurious or hurtful matter or thing contained in or alleged or claimed to be contained in or caused by said work, and pay to said* PUBLISHERS *such reasonable costs, disbursements, expenses, and counsel fees as they may incur in such defense.*

Said PUBLISHERS, *in consideration of the right herein granted and of the guarantees aforesaid, agree to publish said work at their own expense, in such style and manner as they shall deem most expedient, and to pay said* AUTHOR, *or* – his – *legal representatives,* FIFTEEN (15) ——————————— *per cent. on their Trade-List (retail) price, cloth style, for* the first Twenty-five Thousand (25,000) copies *of said work sold by them in the United* States and TWENTY (20) per cent. for all copies sold thereafter. ——————— *Provided, nevertheless, that one-half the above named royalty shall be paid on all copies sold outside the United States; and provided that no percentage whatever shall be paid on any copies destroyed by fire or water, or sold at or below cost, or given away for the purpose of aiding the sale of said work.*

It is further agreed that the profits arising from any publication of said work, during the period covered by this agreement, in other than book form shall be divided equally between said PUBLISHERS *and said* AUTHOR.

Expenses incurred for alterations in type or plates, exceeding twenty per cent. of the cost of composition and electrotyping said work, are to be charged to the AUTHOR's account.

The first statement shall not be rendered until six months after date of publication; and thereafter statements shall be rendered semi-annually, on the AUTHOR's application therefor, in the months of February and August; settlements to be made in cash, four months after date of statement.

If, on the expiration of   five   years from date of publication, or at any time thereafter, the demand for said work should not, in the opinion of said PUBLISHERS, be sufficient to render its publication profitable, then, upon written notice by said PUBLISHERS to said AUTHOR, this contract shall cease and determine; and thereupon said AUTHOR   shall have the right, at his   option, to take from said PUBLISHERS, at cost, whatever copies of said work they may then have on hand; or, failing to take said copies at cost, then said PUBLISHERS shall have the right to dispose of the copies on hand as they may see fit, free from any percentage or royalty, and to cancel this contract.

Provided, also, that if, at any time during the continuance of this agreement, said work shall become unsalable in the ordinary channels of trade, said PUBLISHERS shall have the right to dispose of any copies on hand paying to said AUTHOR – fifteen (15) – per cent. of the net amount received therefor, in lieu of the percentage hereinbefore prescribed.

It is further understood and agreed that the first Twenty Thousand Dollars ($20,000) of said royalties shall be paid to The City Bank Farmers Trust Company as Trustee.

In consideration of the mutuality of this contract, the aforesaid parties agree to all its provisions, and in testimony thereof affix their signatures and seals.

Witness to signature of
Ernest Hemingway

Henry H. Strater

Ernest Hemingway [L.S.]

Witness to signature of
Charles Scribner's Sons

R. J. Watson

*Charles Scribner's Sons
By Arthur H. Scribner
President* [L. S.]

than he would have under the original contract, assuming that every copy was sold. In terms of 2005 dollars, under the old contract Hemingway would have made $411,963.12 but would have gotten $515,519.39 under the terms of the new agreement, a difference of $103,556.27. At a time when 70 percent of the families in America had annual incomes of less than $3,000, the additional money Hemingway would make was substantial.[92]

Scribners kept the book in print until 1931. That year the firm negotiated contracts with the Modern Library and with Grosset and Dunlap for reprint rights to *A Farewell to Arms*. Hemingway was angry when he received the news of the reprinting since "the putting of a book in reprints amounts, as much as I can gather from looking at the royalty figures, to saying good bye to all further income from its sale for an outright cash payment."[93] The royalty rate from reprinters like Grosset and Dunlap was small, usually about ten cents a copy, which was divided between Hemingway and Scribners per the standard contract of the firm. Perkins explained to Hemingway why the firm made such agreements with reprinters in a letter of 11 June 1931:

In a letter you pointed out the disappointing fact that books do not hold up as you had thought from year to year. We know that well enough. It is increasingly true. And the chief reason for it is the short-sightedness and avariciousness of publishers. They were such fools years ago as to let Grosset & Dunlap, and such reprint houses, get going, and the result was that many people got in the habit of not buying books until they came down to a dollar, or seventy-five cents as it then was. This led to Doubleday, for the sake of their printing which is the big end of their business, starting a dollar library, and this led to other cheap libraries.

At the start, all the publishers refrained from putting in books into these libraries until two years after they had appeared,— which was too long a time for people to just wait until the price came down. But as new, and sometimes low-grade, publishers came into the business—people who were thinking of nothing but quick profit—the time limit was cut down more and more, until now people actually sell editions to printing houses and libraries as shortly after publication as six months, and generally, even, after a year. It was the most short-sighted and selfish policy. It takes a year or eighteen months for a book to get known outside of the centres, and often its biggest sale in the old days came after a year or eighteen months.—But now people generally find what books they want to read in dollar series by that time. That is the great reason why books do not hold up as they did in the old days, and as they ought to do.

Another reason, of course, is the greatly increased number of publishers, and of books, whose pressure on the trade is such as to compel the bookseller practically to give all his emphasis to new books. He is so hard pressed by salesman that he finds all his capital for a season has gone into current orders, and that he has little left with which to order old books for stock.—His inclination is to order them only when people ask for them,—and then of course, he tries to sell them some new book instead. It is an unhealthy situation for literature and an unsound one for publishers. Maybe the present discouraging state of business will end by improving things,—for those who come through.[94]

Perkins essentially said that Scribners had no choice; the buyers who would buy the book at $2.50 already had, and to sell any more copies, the novel would have to be priced near $1.00. The situation was not one of Scribners' devising, nor was it to the firm's liking.

A Farewell to Arms would remain Hemingway's best seller until *For Whom the Bell Tolls*. But its success did not come without a price. The serialization, the Boston ban, and the editing of the book version were very stressful to Hemingway. This, combined with the pressure of dealing with his father's suicide, made him increasingly bitter and harder to handle. Scribners found themselves with a writer who produced best sellers, but one who had to be treated very gently to ensure that he would stay with the firm.

CHAPTER 4

"A WRITER SHOULD NEVER REPEAT"

In Our Time *and* Death in the Afternoon

Hemingway's next project, as he had intimated to Perkins in August of 1929, was a work of nonfiction, a long treatise on bullfighting that would eventually be titled *Death in the Afternoon.* This should not suggest that Hemingway totally turned his back on fiction from 1930 to 1932. During this time he published three new stories in magazines: "Wine of Wyoming" (*Scribner's Magazine,* August 1930: 195–204), "The Sea Change" (*This Quarter,* December 1931: 247–51), and "After the Storm" (*Cosmopolitan,* May 1932: 38–41, 155). In addition, he spent much of 1930 working with Perkins on a new edition of *In Our Time,* which included another new story eventually titled "On the Quai at Smyrna." But his attention and interest were focused almost entirely on his study of bullfighting. By the time *Death in the Afternoon* was published, however, Hemingway had written more than just a description of bulls and bullfighters; the book was his first and most complete treatise on art and his first public articulation of his opinion of writers and writing. From 1930 to 1932, Hemingway worked harder on *Death in the Afternoon* than he had worked or would work on any book published in his lifetime. *Death in the Afternoon,* therefore, deserves special attention for what it shows of Hemingway's views on art as well as what it shows of the way Scribners handled what was then an atypical book for one of its star fiction writers to produce.

Writing a guide to bullfighting had been a dream of Hemingway's at least since 1925. In his first letter to Perkins, dated 15 April 1925, Hemingway had written, "I hope some day to have a sort of Doughty's Arabia Deserta of the Bull Ring, a very big book with some wonderful pictures."[1] His interest was revived in November 1929 when his friend, the poet Archibald MacLeish, asked him to contribute an article on bullfighting as an industry to *Fortune,* a new magazine owned by Henry Luce. MacLeish had taken an editorial job with the business magazine, which agreed to pay Hemingway $1,000 for the 2,500-word article.[2] The article, titled "Bullfighting, Sport and Industry," appeared in the March 1930 issue; it bore little resemblance to *Death in the Afternoon,* focusing almost exclusively on bullfighting as a business, and addressing the economic plights and rewards for the promoters, bull breeders, and bullfighters.[3]

It is not clear exactly when Hemingway began writing *Death in the Afternoon.* In 1953, he gave his clearest statement about the composition to Charles Poore, reviewer for the *New York Times* and editor of *The Hemingway Reader* (Scribners, 1953): "I wrote Death In The Afternoon in Key West, the ranch near Cooke City, Montana all one summer, Havana, Madrid, Hendaye and Key West. It took about two years. The glossary I remember I wrote at Hendaye. It was a bastard to do."[4] If Hemingway can be trusted with the facts, late February 1930, after his return to Key West from Paris, was probably when he began writing the book.

While Hemingway was writing, Perkins was advancing plans to publish, or rather republish, another book. On 25 November 1929, he had written asking if Hemingway would approve of Scribners "making a strenuous effort" to get *In Our Time* from Horace Liveright.[5] But the firm's initial effort failed. On 31 December 1929, Liveright wrote, "We consider Mr. Hemingway's name of value on our list, and in that we published his first book, we have a sentimental feeling about the matter as well."[6] No doubt Liveright thought the big sale of *A Farewell to Arms* might help sales of the collection. Another explanation may be that Liveright was still smarting over the loss of Hemingway to Scribners and viewed this as a perfect opportunity to frustrate Perkins's plans and gain a measure of revenge.

Hemingway and Perkins may have discussed the matter in detail during the editor's second trip to Key West in February of 1930. The subject was next broached in their correspondence by Hemingway in mid-April. He asked if Perkins had approached Liveright again, adding that if Scribners got the book it should be republished with "Up in Michigan" and with "Mr. and Mrs. Elliot" as it had appeared in the *Little Review*.[7] Perkins responded on 30 April that he thought they would have a better chance to get the book if Hemingway approached Liveright when he came to New York in June, adding, "We should lose nothing by not announcing the book until August,—when business ought to be better if it is to continue to go on at all."[8]

Hemingway came to New York in early June for a quick visit before an extended stay in Montana and Wyoming.[9] On 16 June, he met with Liveright, who wrote Scribners the same day to ask what they would pay for the stock on hand and the plates.[10] The exact details of the arrangement worked out by Hemingway, Scribners, and Liveright are not known. Hemingway's bibliographer, Audre Hanneman, reported that Scribners bought the plates, bound stock, and reprint rights from Liveright on 19 June 1930, but she has no information on the price.[11] Liveright often needed ready cash to keep his business afloat, which is probably why he was willing to sell six months after his initial refusal. The matter was closed by 21 November, when Liveright sent the assignment of copyright and the copyright card to Scribners.[12]

On 1 July, Perkins sent Hemingway a copy of *In Our Time* to revise, noting that Hemingway was to add "'Up in Michigan' and the short piece." He also raised the idea of separately publishing the subchapters as they had appeared in *in our time*.[13] The "short piece" was probably "On the Quai at Smyrna," the composition of which Paul Smith dates to the winter of 1926–1927.[14] Perkins may have seen it during his 1930 trip to Key West or during Hemingway's trip through New York in June.

Hemingway received the book on 24 July. The same day he wrote Perkins asking for a copy of *Three Stories and Ten Poems* and an issue of the *Little Review* containing "Mr. and Mrs. Elliot." He wanted to include "Up in Michigan" but leave the vignettes as they had appeared in the Boni and Liveright edition. He also told his editor that he did not want the revision and republication of the short-story volume to take time away from his new work.[15] Despite the chance to publish *In Our Time* as he had originally wanted, to Hemingway it was clearly not worth delaying the progress he was making on the bullfight book. In his response of 1 August, Perkins notified Hemingway that he had sent a copy of *Three Stories and Ten Poems* and "Mr. and Mrs. Elliot" from the New York bookseller (and Hemingway's first bibliographer) Captain Henry Louis Cohn; he also repeated his assurance that *In Our Time* was Hemingway's book and that he should continue to write while he was going well, but that *In Our Time* should be published no later than October.[16]

Hemingway attempted to revise "Up in Michigan" for publication in the book. His revisions indicate that he feared libel suits from the people upon whom the characters in the story were based, as well as suppression of the book due to the frank sexual content of the story. In the copy of *Three Stories and Ten Poems* (which Cohn eventually reacquired), he changed some of the characters names: "Liv Coates" to "Mary Coates," "D. J. Smith" to "F. E. Smith," and "Jim Gilmore" to "Jim Dutton." In addition, he deleted the sentence "Her breasts felt plump and firm and the nipples were erect under his hands." He also emended the sentence "She felt Jim right through the back of the chair and she couldn't stand it and then something clicked inside of her and the feeling was warm and softer" to "She couldn't stand it. She knew she couldn't stand it."[17] But Hemingway abandoned this revision soon after undertaking it; in his 12 August letter to Perkins he explained that he could not revise the story to remove the obscene material without ruining it. He then suggested that an introduction to the volume, written by Edmund Wilson, would help to differentiate it from the Boni and Liveright edition, adding that he was "too busy, too disinterested, too proud or too stupid or whatever you want to call it to write one for it." Above all he did not want to become involved in a libel suit over the old book and suggested that a disclaimer should be inserted. Hemingway also gave his editor a progress report on the new book: "Am going well on the new book—Have something over 40,000 words done—Have worked well 6 days of every week since got here. Have 6 more cases of beer good for 6 more chapters—If I put in an expense account on this bull fight book it would be something for the Accounting Dept to study."[18] Again, Hemingway's first priority was to the book in progress, not to the one he had published five years earlier. Again, Perkins was understanding and deferred to Hemingway's opinion, as shown by his 18 August reply:

> I believe Bunny will do the introduction—I think it is a good idea he should—and I'll write him immediately.
>
> You get us wrong about the book though: we know its value,— at least we think its value very great as it stands. I don't want you to do anything new to put in but merely to put in such things that belong, like that additional "In Our Time" sketch you read me in Key West.—I may be confused about that, for although I remember it vividly, I am more susceptible to stimulation than I look as if I were, and those farewell cups had more effect on me than you probably thought. . . . As for the book, it's to be the way you want it exactly and no complaints on our part either uttered or thought. We don't want artificialities to make a new book of it or do any cheap thing. So just do it—if possible before September 1st—and we'll publish it properly. We regard it as an extremely important piece of literature which broke open a new channel.[19]

The editor's letter demonstrates again his attempt to balance the needs of the firm with the needs of his author. As he had done before and would do again, Perkins let Hemingway know that he called most of the shots and that Scribners would do all they could for him.

Hemingway's progress on the revision of the book seems to have been fairly slow. Aside from restoring the original "Mr. and Mrs. Elliot" and removing the book's epigraph,[20] the only other changes he made were in "A Very Short Story." Hemingway changed the location of the hospital from Milan to Padua and changed the nurse's name from "Ag" to "Luz," no doubt in order to avoid a suit from Agnes von Kurowsky, the nurse he had wanted to marry in 1918.[21] By 3 September, he had done all to the book that he was going to do and shipped it back to Perkins. He included typed setting copy for "Mr. and Mrs. Elliot," indicated that the new piece was to be called "An Introduction by the Author," and told his editor that Scribners published the book at their own risk. He then noted, "I'm on page 174 of this book I'm writing and have had it knocked out of my head for two days working on this In Our Time again and I've no interest in publishing it now, will take no risks and give no guarantees against libels nor slanders." Hemingway then reiterated that the important thing for him was to finish writing the bullfight book. He told Perkins that the firm could advertise *In Our Time* as having "new material" and added that "A certain number of people are bound to buy whatever book I bring out after the sale of A Farewell." In closing, he wrote that he thought that "*any* attempt to bring this out as a new book or as anything new from me in anyway will be altogether harmful."[22] Hemingway's fears are evident in this letter. He did not want to become involved in any legal action, but of equal importance was his desire not to have his old work presented to the critics as something new. He foresaw that such a move would only open him up to attack, a prospect he did not relish.

Perkins responded on 9 September that the publication of the short-story collection might have be delayed until the next year and that he was worried that this might conflict with the publication of *Death in the Afternoon*.[23] Another concern for the editor was how Edmund Wilson would react to the Smyrna piece being titled "Introduction by the Author"; on 24 September he wired Hemingway to ask if "Introduction" could be changed to "Prelude" or "Foreword." Perkins added that the proofs could be read there, indicating that Hemingway did not see them.[24] In a letter of 27 September to Hemingway, Perkins explained his views on the matter:

> I telegraphed you to ask if we could call the piece you entitled "Introduction by the Author" either "Prelude" or "Foreword." It is not in any sense an introduction, and I had a sort of a queer idea that following an introduction by Edmund Wilson which would be a regulation introduction, it might seem as if in entitling this an introduction, when it is not conventionally so, might seem in a way to be saying, "To Hell with introductions" and so reflect a little on Bunny's. It has now occurred to me that if I do not hear from you we shall simply call it "By the Author" then people can take it any way they want to, but certainly on its merits. I think that is the thing to do if you do not get my wire in time to answer it, and if you insist on "Introduction" we can change it in unbound copies and later printings.[25]

Wilson, as well as being a Scribners author, was too influential a critic to risk offending. Perkins's sense of decorum would not allow him to knowingly insult anyone.

Hemingway wrote Perkins on 28 September to report on his progress on the new book (he had nearly reached page 200) and to ask for an explanation of the objection to calling his piece an introduction ("You can call it Preface if you like but it is not nearly as good"). He added that he saw no problem with waiting to publish *In Our Time* in 1931, since he needed to go to Spain the next summer to get the photographs and illustrations for *Death in the Afternoon,* noting that these were "damned important."[26] For some unknown reason he changed his mind about the introduction, for on 3 October he wired Perkins:

ANSWERING YOUR LETTER SEPTEMBER TWENTY SEVENTH BELIEVE MUST INSIST ON INTRODUCTION BY AUTHOR STOP WILSON HAS GOOD SENSE IS ARTIST AND WOULD NOT BE OFFENDED WHERE NO OFFENSE INTENDED OR POSSIBLE STOP CALLED ANYTHING ELSE IT LOSES ALL FORCE AND SIGNIFICANCE STOP I WANTED CONTRAST OF TWO INTRODUCTIONS HAVE NOT READ WILSONS HAVE GREAT RESPECT FOR HIM SO WHY WOULD I INSULT HIM STOP CHANGING IT RUINS IT STOP AFTER ALL IN WRITING YOU GET YOUR EFFECT ONE WORD AT A TIME AND IF SOMEBODY CHANGES THE WORDS FOR YOU THE EFFECT IS GONE[27]

Perkins responded via telegram the same day to say, "INTRODUCTION ALL RIGHT," and that Wilson's would be coming in Monday (6 October).[28] On 14 October, Perkins wrote his author that he had been worried that Wilson would take offense, but that this fear had evaporated after Wilson read Hemingway's piece. He also asked Hemingway if he would be agreeable to running some pieces of *Death in the Afternoon* in *Scribner's Magazine* since the book could not be published until the fall of 1931, at the earliest.[29]

The advertising for and printings of the Scribners edition of *In Our Time* indicate that the firm did not expect a large sale. As feared by Hemingway, the Scribners advertising department initially emphasized the fact that the book would contain new material, as the book's description in the publisher's catalog of fall 1930 books shows:

In Our Time
BY ERNEST HEMINGWAY, author of "A Farewell to Arms," "Men Without Women"
Probably $2.00

The publication of this volume of short stories in 1925 proclaimed the arrival of a new and brilliant talent in American literature. Critical praise was immediate and unanimous. Since then Mr. Hemingway's audience has increased tremendously, but nothing he has written surpasses in vigor, reality and brilliance the fifteen stories—each with its own introductory bit of startling "atmosphere"—of "In Our Time." In the new edition, which Mr. Hemingway has completely revised, there will be one new story never before published in book form, and a new "interlude." The thousands of readers who appreciated "A Farewell to Arms" will find equal enjoyment in these tales that "are full of the smells, the taste, the feel of life." With the reissue of "In Our Time" Charles Scribner's Sons becomes the American publisher of all Mr. Hemingway's books.[30]

The catalog's cover notes that it had been "Revised to August 1," so the description for *In Our Time* was written before Hemingway's decision not to include "Up in Michigan" and before his letter of 3 September to Perkins warning him not to claim that the book had a lot of new material. The only other prepublication advertisement for the book was in the Scribners announcement of its fall list in the 20 September 1930 issue of *Publishers Weekly*. In the two-page spread, which lists twenty-seven titles, *In Our Time* was not singled out in any way; the only description it is given is that it was "with new material" and would cost "probably $2.00."[31]

After the book's publication, Scribners ran only six ads mentioning *In Our Time* in the *New York Times Book Review*.[32] In all but two of these advertisements no measures were taken to make the mention of *In Our Time* stand out amongst the other Scribners titles. The advertisement in the 23 November issue is the first to mention any of the stories included, and the first to use any illustration (a reproduction of the drawing by CLEON for the dust jacket). Still, in this advertisement *In Our Time* is only one of eight books featured. The only advertisement that featured Hemingway's collection alone is the one for 7 December, which along with the CLEON drawing gives two quotes: one from André Maurois and the other from Robert Quotes's review of the collection in the *New Yorker*. The firm spent only $1,564.71 on forty-eight advertisements for the book. Most ran in New York newspapers and in magazines such as *Atlantic Monthly* and *Harper's Monthly* and appeared mainly in the last two months of the year, with only five running in January of 1931.[33]

Perhaps the reason Scribners ran so few ads for *In Our Time* was because this edition received little critical notice. Only three major American periodicals ran reviews for this edition: the *New York Herald Tribune* (16 October 1930: 22), the *New Yorker* (22 November 1930: 116), and the *Saturday Review of Literature* (24 January 1931: 548). Hemingway's scrapbook contains only twenty-six clippings of notice or reviews for this edition of *In Our Time.*[34]

Scribners published its edition of *In Our Time* on 24 October 1930. The initial printing was 3,240 copies, and the book sold for $2.50. Another printing of 1,035 copies was ordered in December, for a total of 4,275 copies.[35] The press used the Boni and Liveright plates, soldering in corrections, revisions, and changes in pagination, for the bulk of the volume, needing only to set type for the front matter and introductions.[36] Hemingway's contract for this edition, dated 10 November 1930, stipulated the same 15/20 percent royalty rate he had received for *A Farewell to Arms.*[37] Therefore, Hemingway would have received, when all these copies had been sold, only $1,603.13, which translates to $17,321.34 in 2005 terms.

In any event, the scant notice and small sales did not seem to bother Hemingway or Perkins. Neither made any complaint about the sales or reviews in their correspondence. All of Hemingway's works were now published by the same firm. The next step was to complete and publish *Death in the Afternoon.*

Hemingway, despite the work he had done on *In Our Time,* had made good progress on the bullfight guide. By 28 October 1930, he was able to report to Perkins, "Am on page *280* on my book. Nearly through. 2 more chapters and the 4 *appendice* to do at Piggot."[38] Hemingway's plans, however, had to be reformulated. On the first of November, Hemingway wrecked his car outside Billings, Montana. The car's passengers, John Dos Passos and Floyd Allington, were unharmed, but Hemingway severely broke his right arm. The injury forced him to curtail most of his writing for nearly six months.[39]

The book was very nearly finished at the time of the accident. In the 303-page manuscript, however, only a small portion of chapter 19 had been completed; chapter 20 had yet to be written, nor had Hemingway completed the endings of chapters 2, 7, 8, 17, and 18. Hemingway had also not incorporated "A Natural History of the

Dead" into the book.⁴⁰ The book at this point dealt almost exclusively with bullfighting. It was in the later additions at the ends of the chapters that Hemingway gave his views on writing and aesthetics.

Hemingway had promised Perkins in December, "I'll let you read some of it when you come down to Key West, if you want to, and are a very good boy in the meantime."⁴¹ During the first week of March 1931, Perkins made his third trip to Key West. Whether the still-recuperating Hemingway let his editor see any of the work in progress is not known. On 27 April, Hemingway wrote Perkins that he had two potential stories for the August issue of *Scribner's Magazine:* "A Sea Change" and "A Natural History of the Dead." The latter story, Hemingway noted, Perkins had read during his visit to Key West.⁴² Neither of these stories would appear in the magazine, and Hemingway did not relate in any of his subsequent correspondence with Perkins why or when he decided to insert "A Natural History of the Dead" as the conclusion to chapter 12 of *Death in the Afternoon.* In May of 1931, Hemingway departed for Spain to get the photographs and additional information for the book. Before he left, he wrote Perkins that he was having the manuscript typed out and was leaving a carbon copy in Key West. He added that it should be finished by the fall, but he did not like the idea of publishing in the spring of 1932.⁴³

Throughout the summer and fall Hemingway kept Perkins apprised of his progress on the book. From Paris on the first of August, he wrote that he would finish the glossary by the end of the week and would then have only two chapters left to write.⁴⁴ After returning to Spain, he cabled on 14 September that he had gotten all the illustrations that he needed.⁴⁵ Back in Kansas City, where Pauline was giving birth to their second son, Gregory, the author reported, "Re-writing going excellently and whipping it into shape and cutting out the crap."⁴⁶ By mid-November, Hemingway wrote more fully about the book and his schedule for completion:

> About the book. Except for the two days interruption of Greg have never been going better—Have been going so swell I hate to end it. Am getting everything in that I knew I had to get in to make it come off completely—all the grand stuff—You'll like it—
>
> As to the estimate of length. I have cut the body of the text in the rewriting to approximately 75,000 words—It may go more— There are, so far 5 appendixes all to be set in same type except

possibly one—the 13,000 word one—(1) of 1,300 words—(1) of 13,000 words—(1) or about 4 pages of the book (a calendar of dates etc.) (1) of about 4 pages (1) of about 6 pages. And a descriptive glossary approximately 20,000 words in length—It takes up 129 pages of long foolscap in my writing. So May take more space since sentences and paragraphs in length as Dialouge.

Does this give you enough of an idea of length?

About the insurance on pictures—The Juan Gris is worth $7500 cash Will be worth an amount impossible to estimate—The others are worth about $300 between them—

How much will the Treasurer have to pay in insurance on 7800 valuation. . . . Everything is completed except this swell last chapter that I am still writing on and the translation of the 13,000 words of reglamento.[47] May get some one to rough out the translation to save me time and work—Then I will correct it and fix it up—. . . . I can have the Mss. ready for delivery before Xmas—the one appendix might not be in shape but can give you the exact length by counting the words. . . .

What about running a few chapters from the Death In The Afternoon [in *Scribner's Magazine*] just before it comes out—Do you think that would be good for it. The book I mean?[48]

Hemingway's estimate was off; it would be nearly two months before he got setting copy to Perkins.

With the conclusion of rewriting seemingly so near, Perkins addressed the idea of running some of the book in *Scribner's Magazine*. On 25 November, he wrote his author, "I have always thought we could run several pieces out of the bull fight book, and if you ever could send a copy of a manuscript, even if it is actually *manuscript*, we could designate which parts we could use. We have fixed up the insurance. Then there is the matter of the royalty.—We can pay at any time you want."[49] Perkins may have hoped to duplicate the success of *A Farewell to Arms* by publishing some parts of the new book in the magazine.

Hemingway wrote his editor on 5 and 6 January 1932 to explain his delay in delivering the book. He gave a litany of problems, from having workmen in the house to nearly every member of the household being sick. He wrote that Archibald MacLeish and John Dos Passos could clean up the manuscript if anything should happen to him.[50] The next week he was able to wire Perkins, "FINISHED

REWRITING BODY OF BOOK LAST NIGHT YOU CANT MISS HAV-
ING IT FIRST OF WEEK.["]51 The same day Perkins wrote that William
Lengle of *Cosmopolitan* was bothering him about the possibility of
serializing *Death in the Afternoon* in that periodical.52 Hemingway
responded on 21 January that he did not want *Cosmopolitan* to have
the book. He added that Scribners was not to use the photo of him
with a sick steer in its publicity.53

The typescript setting copy arrived at Scribners on 20 January.54
Perkins apparently could not give it his immediate attention but did
respond more fully five days later:

> I read the book all yesterday—Sunday—and after it I felt *good*.
> I went to bed happy for it in spite of innumerable troubles (not
> so bad really, I guess). The book piles upon you wonderfully, and
> becomes to one reading it—who at first thinks bull fighting only
> a very small matter—immensely important.
>
> I'll write you about practical matters. It's silly just to write
> you that it's a grand book, but it did do me good to read it. That
> about America, the corn, is utterly right. And I think of corn as
> in New Jersey in the winter,—the most unlikely time and place
> for corn.55

The passage about the corn and America was eventually cut from
the first part of chapter 20.56

Most of the subsequent correspondence between Hemingway
and Perkins about *Death in the Afternoon* dealt with the problems
of the book's format (the page size and the number of illustrations
and way in which they would be reproduced), Hemingway's use
of obscene words, whether or not to excerpt parts for magazine
publication, and whether or not to place it with the Book-of-the-
Month Club. Perkins's main concern was to keep the price of the
book down. With the country in the midst of the Great Depression,
book buyers had less money to spend on books, and publishers were
taking steps to lower prices, as was noted in an editorial in the 12
November 1932 issue of *Publishers Weekly:* "It has been increasingly
clear as the fall publishing developed that the list prices of books in
non-fiction areas have shown a very marked decrease since a year
ago. Publishers, since last spring, have had time to review their pro-
grams and to plan their campaigns on lines that include the closest

possible economies in all publishing costs in order that their books as they reached the bookseller's counters might show an appreciable decline in list prices."[57] Perkins, therefore, was merely reacting the way all publishers were at the time: prices had to be kept down.

The first matter that had to be settled was whether or not parts of the book would be run in *Scribner's Magazine*. On 5 February, both Perkins and Alfred Dashiell (who had become editor of *Scribner's Magazine* after Robert Bridges' retirement in 1929) wrote Hemingway about the possibility. Perkins's desire was not merely to pull out all the best parts of the book, although he acknowledged that running some articles would "from the commercial standpoint . . . help it."[58] Dashiell's plan was to run four articles—one each in the May, June, July, and August issues. The first would be part of chapter 2; the second a section from chapter 11 on fighting bulls; the third would be an article on the bullfighters Maera, Gallo, Gitanello, and Zurito; and the fourth would be an abridgement of chapter 20. Hemingway would receive $2,000 for the articles.[59]

The idea of publishing only parts and abridgements of chapters was unacceptable to Hemingway. On 7 February, he wrote letters to both editors explaining his position. He wrote Dashiell that the price offered was too low and that he did not like the idea of cutting up chapters to make articles, since each chapter was designed to have its own unity.[60] To Perkins, Hemingway repeated the points he had made to Dashiell, adding "Max you know truly that while I'm often wrong in personal matters I've always been right about the handling of my own stuff—literarilly speaking—and I feel awfully strongly about this."[61] Hemingway's attitude killed the plan. On 15 February Dashiell wrote the author that while they could probably come to some agreement about the contents of the articles, the magazine could not pay the $3,600 that Hemingway wanted.[62]

During the months of February and March, Perkins worked on the format problems and the proofs of the book. The problem, as the editor explained to Hemingway on 2 February, was that the book needed to be big enough to "give the pictures a real show, and yet not to put too high a price on it in such days as these are."[63] By 2 April, Perkins had settled on a page size of six and three-eighths by nine inches. In an effort to gain a measure of free publicity for the book, as well as a guaranteed amount of money, Perkins advanced the idea of placing *Death in the Afternoon* with the Book-of-the-Month Club:

"Then there is a question of whether we should let the Book of the Month Club see this. How do you feel about it? The only reason for doing it is the depression. They have only about half the number of subscribers they did have, and they only pay in all about $14,000 or a little more, so that the author would get something over $7,000. But they do have a great deal of publicity value; and in these times we ought to think about the possibility even if we would not in other times."[64] But Hemingway was opposed to this plan from the beginning for many reasons. First, he believed that if Scribners was guaranteed $7,000 from the Book-of-the-Month Club, they would not "make as much of an effort to sell the book in times like these as the writer had to make to write it in the same times." Secondly, he was convinced that the book club would put undue pressure on him to cut out obscene words and passages. Near the end of his response to Perkins, he summarized his views:

> If the publisher need a sure 7,000 from that source all right—but I have to see that two things are not imperilled; the further sale, which helps you as much as it does me, and the integrity of the book which is the most imprtant thing to me. If anyone so acts as to put themselves out as a book of the month they cannot insist in ramming the good word shit or the sound old word xxxx down the throats of a lot of clubwomen but when a book is offered for sale no one has to buy it that does not want to—and I will not have any pressure brought to bear to make me emasculate a book to make anyone seven thousand dollars, myself or anyone else. Understand this is all business not personal. I'm only trying to be as frank as in talking so you will know how I stand and so we won't get in a jam and if I write too strongly or sound too snooty it is because I'm trying to make it frank and honest and clear as possible. So don't let me insult you Max nor find any insults where none is intended but know I am fond of you and that we could not quarrel if we were together and if I'm rude I apologise sincerely.[65]

Perkins on 7 April responded, "As for the Book Club, we don't like it any more than you do."[66] The plan was dropped.

The most daunting problem for Perkins was the photographs for the book. Originally, Hemingway and Perkins had planned to place each photo and drawing at a place appropriate for it in the text.

Cost would depend on the number used and the method of reproduction. On 2 April, Perkins wrote that to keep the retail cost of the book at $3.50, they could include sixteen full-page illustrations reproduced by offset.[67] But Hemingway was completely against this idea, explaining his views to Perkins in his letter of 4 April. He told Perkins that he had to have 112 photographs included to make the book comprehensive. He was willing to eliminate the colored frontispiece to save money but wanted as many photographs included as he could get.[68] Three days later Perkins responded that it would be possible to reproduce sixty-four photographs if they were printed back-to-back as halftones.[69] The next day he wired Hemingway that the book would be brought out as he wanted, but that the list price would depend on how the pictures were reproduced.[70]

Perkins had decided by 13 April to have the photographs reproduced by offset: "All this will probably not result in increasing the cost per copy after enough copies have been sold to pay for the plates and all the original manufacturing expense.—We shall have to sell around 2,500 copies before that is done, but thereafter we shall be operating on a reasonable margin." He then hit upon the idea of grouping all the photographs in one section so that readers would not be distracted from the text.[71] Two days later Hemingway wired that he thought this idea "SEEMS VERY INTELLIGENT AND EXCELLENT SOLUTION."[72] In the end, Scribners was able to reproduce eighty-one of the photographs in *Death in the Afternoon.*[73]

Perkins played a very small role in the actual editing of *Death in the Afternoon,* even though it was very heavily revised in galley proofs. Hemingway revised them in Havana between mid-April and 2 June.[74] John Dos Passos had read some of the book on a brief visit to Key West in February. After he left, he wrote Hemingway with his praise and suggestions for editing:

> The Bullfight book—is absolutely the best thing can be done on the subject—I mean all the description and the dope—It seems to me an absolute model for how that sort of thing ought to be done—And all the accounts of individual fighters towns etc, are knockout. I'm only doubtful, like I said, about the parts where Old Hem straps on the longwhite whiskers and gives the boys the lowdown. I can stand the old lady—but I'm pretty doubtful

as to whether the stuff about Waldo Frank (except the line about shooting an owl) is as good as it ought to be. God knows he ought to be deflated—or at least Virgin Spain—(why not put it on the book basis instead of the entire lecturer?) and that is certainly the place to do it. And then later when you take off the make up and assure the ladies and gents that its really old Uncle Hem after all and give them the low down about writing and why you like to live in Key West etc. I was pretty doubtful—Dont you think that's all secrets of the profession—like plaster of paris in a glove and oughtn't to be spilt to the vulgar? I may be wrong—but the volume is hellishly good. (I'd say way ahead of anything of yours yet) and the language is so magnificently used—(why right there sitting in Bra's boat reading the typewritten pages I kept having the feeling I was reading a classic in the Bohn library like Rabelais or Harvey's Circulation of the Blood or something and that's a hell of a good way to feel about a book not even published yet) that it would be a shame to leave in any unnecessary tripe—damn it I think there's always enough tripe in anything even after you've cut out—and a book like that can stand losing some of the best passages—After all, a book ought to be judged by the author according to the excellence of the stuff cut out. But I may be packed with prunes with all this so for God's sake dont pay too much attention to it—the Books damn swell in any case.[75]

On 26 March, Hemingway wrote his fellow author, "I will work hard on my proofs and try to cut the shit as you say—you were damned good to take so much trouble telling me."[76] By mid-April, he wrote Dos Passos, "Am working hard. Cut a ton of crap a day out of the proofs."[77]

Dos Passos's contributions to the editing of *Death in the Afternoon* must, however, be judged carefully. Hemingway's response to him came before he had done most of his work on the galleys. In fact, Dos Passos on 7 June asked Hemingway to send him, if he could, a set of the galleys: "I'd like to read them over as I didn't read it all in Key West—due to lack of time and want to read it more slowly."[78] To say, then, that Dos Passos helped Hemingway revise the book is to overstate the case: Dos Passos made some general suggestions, a few of which Hemingway accepted. On 30 May, Hemingway wrote his friend:

Have gone over book 7 times and cut out all you objected to (seemed like the best to me God damn you if it really was) cut 4½ galleys of philosophy and telling the boys—cut all the last chapter except the part about Spain—the part saying how it wasn't enough of a book or it would have had these things. That is OK.

Left Old Lady in and the first crack early in book about Waldo Frank's book—cut all other references to Frank. Believe old Lady stuff O.K.—or at least necessary as seasoning.

The four and a half galleys cut were part of chapter 20. This cut appears to be what Hemingway thought Dos Passos disliked.[79]

The galley proofs of *Death in the Afternoon* would seem to verify that Hemingway did put in as much work as he told Dos Passos he did. He reworked the book more extensively at this stage than he did any of his previous or subsequent books. His marked galleys show that he made 405 substantive emendations and 461 emendations to punctuation and spelling in the text.[80] His revisions were so extensive that the firm charged him $145.25 for the alterations that had to be made to the type, the only time Hemingway was ever charged for proof corrections.[81]

Hemingway received the first nineteen pages of galley proof for *Death in the Afternoon* the first of April and sent most of them, "revised—cut and corrected," to Perkins on 2 June.[82] These first nineteen galleys end with the first three pages of chapter 7 (as printed in the first edition), where the Old Lady makes her first appearance. Most of the revisions in this batch of proof are small: additions and deletions that tighten the prose or add more specific information and detail for the reader. For example, in galley 12 (chapter 4, page 40), Hemingway added the phrase "There will be a special bus leaving from the Calle Victoria opposite the pasaje alvarez," important information for anyone using *Death in the Afternoon* as a guidebook to Spain. In galley 14 (chapter 5, page 48), he adjusted his description of dancing to the Bombilla by adding "there in the leafyness of the long plantings of trees where the mist rises from the small river" to the end of the sentence. The revision is small in the context of the book, but it gives the reader a more specific account of what it is like to be in Spain. Some changes serve to make Hemingway's prose more accurate, as in galley 18 (page 58), where he changed the phrase "crowd empties the ring" to "crowd leaves the ring, leaving it empty." Essentially, there is no difference between the two except for the style.

The most extensive revisions to this first batch of proofs, however, are in the latter part of chapter 5 (galley 16), where Hemingway cut or modified three passages about Waldo Frank, as Dos Passos suggested. On what would become page 52, Hemingway deleted the sentence ridiculing the fact that Frank produced *Virgin Spain* (New York: Boni and Liveright, 1926) less than a year after his first visit to the country. He added to the second passage (page 53) and changed the third from "it was an interesting mechanical experiment if only the vision of those writers had been a little more interesting and developed when say, not so congested" to "It was an interesting mechanical experiment while it lasted, and full of pretty phallic images drawn in the manner of sentimental valentines, but it would have amounted to more if only the vision of these writers had been a little more interesting and developed when, say not so congested" (pages 53–54). Hemingway, contrary to his promise to Dos Passos, did not go easier on Frank.

Hemingway made the most extensive revisions to galleys 20 through 84 (the last part of chapter 7 through chapter 20). Many of the emendations were to make the descriptions more specific, as in galley 23 (chapter 8, page 76), where Hemingway changed the description of Gitanillo from "had only been a servant to a gypsy family" to "had only worked as a horse-trader for a gypsy family." Some emendations served to bring the work up-to-date. On galley 25 (chapter 9, pages 84–85) Hemingway added the following phrase to his description of Valencia II: "and a badly sewn wound at the corner of one eye has distorted his face so that he has lost his cockiness." Later, in this same chapter (galley 26, page 88) Hemingway added the following, probably based on his own observation of the bullfighter at the 1931 fights in Pamplona, to describe Nino de la Palma's cowardice: "its fat rumped, prematurely bald from using hair fixatives, prematurely senile form."[83]

Most of the large modifications occurred in the Author and Old Lady exchanges and at the end of chapters, where Hemingway shifted from descriptions of bullfighting to a discussion of aesthetics and writing. Some of the emendations, like those make in the middle of

"A Natural History of the Dead" (chapter 12), add to the humor of passages. In galley 41, Hemingway added the following exchange after his modification of two lines of Andrew Marvell's "To His Coy Mistress":

> I learned to do that by reading T. S. Eliot.
> *Old Lady:* The Eliots were all old friends of our family. I believe they were in the lumber business.
> *Author:* My uncle married a girl whose father was in the lumber business.
> *Old Lady:* How interesting. (139–40)

The addition adds little to the story (except for increasing the absurdity of it), but it does allow Hemingway a chance to attack T. S. Eliot and enhances the book's humorous side.

By far, the most extensive revisions occur in the last four chapters. The original conclusion of chapter 17 was "Do you want conversation? No. All right, we will let it go to-day." Hemingway replaced this with a three-page typed insert on Goya, Velázquez, and El Greco (pages 203–5). Likewise, the conclusion of chapter 18 (pages 228–31) was inserted at this time, which is logical since it deals with the "four new matadors promoted in 1932." This revision demonstrates Hemingway's desire to create not only a history of bullfighting but also a work that could be used as a guidebook.

No part of the book was altered as radically as the last two chapters. The original chapter 20 was longer than it was in the published book; this version was printed on galleys 78 through 84. Hemingway revised galleys 78 and 79, the section dealing with peninsulas and corn that Perkins had admired, but marked another copy of these galleys "Omit" (both of these sets of galleys are in the Kennedy Library). The published conclusion of chapter 19 was shifted from the galleys of chapter 20 (the last quarter of galley 81 and the first half of galley 82). What was eventually printed as chapter 20 was originally all but the first six lines of galley 80, the first three-quarters of galley 81, and a three-page typed insert. There are two sets of galley proofs 83 and 84—one with Hemingway's corrections, the other set marked "Omit."

Galleys 83 and 84, the original conclusion of *Death in the Afternoon,* move the focus of the book wholly away from bullfighting and

Spain toward the craft of writing and Hemingway's views on the profession of authorship. This section begins with a discussion of the need for writers and painters to leave their native land in order to create their art. Otherwise, the writer becomes merely a local-color writer. Hemingway claims that the artist creates the country—rather than merely describing it—and could do so anywhere. He then moves on to state that once a writer has written of something as well as he can he should not do so again. It does not matter, Hemingway wrote in this passage, what personal flaws a writer has; he is an honest writer if he does not lie to himself about what or why he writes. In the concluding paragraph of this statement of aesthetic principles, Hemingway explains how writers become trapped by the economic aspect of writing. He claims that while a writer has a right to make a living anyway he wants and may be lucky enough to do so through his writing, if he does make a lot of money from one book, there will be pressure to write another for money in order to maintain his standard of living. When a writer changes any part of his work because of economic pressure, he becomes a commercial writer and ceases to be an artist (galley 84). Hemingway had said as much before when the subject of selling serial rights to an unfinished novel had been advanced.[84] He was no doubt reacting to the great success of *A Farewell to Arms.* Conventional wisdom would suggest that Hemingway should have followed the successful novel with a similar novel. Here, however, Hemingway the artist balked at the idea of giving the public what it supposedly wanted, as expressed by the huge sale of *A Farewell to Arms.* Hemingway in this section, with which he had originally intended to conclude *Death in the Afternoon,* shows that he wanted to set the trend in literature—not merely pander to a preexisting demand. Exactly why Hemingway chose to delete this section from the book is not known. Perhaps he knew that keeping such material would give critics ammunition against him. This was the section Dos Passos had read and suggested cutting, as he indicated in a 7 June 1932 letter to Hemingway. Dos Passos wrote:

> It sure makes me feel uneasy to hear you've been taking my advice about plucking some of the long white whiskers out of the end of Death in the Afternoon—I may be wrong as Seldes—A funny thing happened about that stuff I've been trying all week to write a preface to the 97 cent edition of "Three Soldiers"—and

yesterday found it pouring out in fine shape—What do you think it was on rereading? Your remarks and the stuff about what you'd liked to have put in the book—and about the lit. game almost word for word—shows there must be something in it to have it stick in just a natural born preface.[85]

On 2 June, Hemingway sent the corrected proof to Perkins, pointing out to his editor what changes he had made: "Have cut a lot of text—With what is gone the book may be less fashionable (all this stating of creeds and principles which does not belong in literature at all by people who have failed in or lost belief in or abandoned writing the minute it got tough to save their bloody souls). But it will be permanent and solid and about what it is about—I will save what I cut and if it proves to be of permanent value you can publish it in my Notebooks." Hemingway added that he would be sending the estimate of Sidney Franklin and would not include the *Reglamento*, since a new one would be out soon. He also included a projected layout for printing some pictures on the same page. He then addressed the issue of obscene words. He instructed Perkins, "About 4 letter words—See your lawyers—If you are unwilling to print them entire at least leave 1st and last letters—You say that's legal—I'm the guy who has been the worst emasculated of any in publishing It's up to you to keep out of jail and from being suppressed I write the books—You publish them—But dont get spooked."[86] Perkins responded on 11 June. After telling Hemingway that it would be fun to publish his notebooks, he gave his author a report of his meeting with the firm's lawyer and what he believed they could safely do:

I did what you suggested about the *words*. I got our lawyer up here and talked to him. He would have infuriated you, and in fact I ended with quite an argument,—but then broke it off because I saw it was foolish. His advice was against the words, of course, and he suggested that "damn" could be used just as well as one of them, and that was where we got into trouble, for I began to try to show him how it couldn't. But further discussion was confined to the legal aspect of the matter which amounts to this:—the words are literally illegal, but much more latitude is now allowed than formerly, and the courts do not consider the words by themselves, but in their context and in their general intent and bearing on it all. But there is a serious danger, since this is the first time in a book of any consequence in which these words have been printed in full, that Mr. Sumner or some of these Prohibitionistic people would make a fight on the matter in order to stop any further progress that way.[87] Lawyers are mighty careful what they say, but I really think he thought that if they did, we could probably win in court, but not until after sales had been held up and publication suspended, etc. His advice was strongly in favor of the omission of the two middle letters, at least.—Even that, he thought would show that an attempt to meet the law had been made, and would be in our favor. You will understand all about it I guess. I have simply sent back the proof as it was because we can change those few instances in the page proof. So I shall send it to you as it stands, and we can look at it all in final form. There is no doubt that these words do seriously interfere with library sales. But that does not amount to very great numbers. It is a good sale though, and it gives a book a permanence and finality to which this book is entitled. This book is even a reference book.[88]

This idea was acceptable to Hemingway, who on 28 June wrote, "If you decide to cut out a letter or two to keep inside the law that is your business."[89] Hemingway apparently did not make these alterations, as they appear only on the galley proofs in the Cohn Collection and not on the set at the Kennedy Library. In addition to transferring Hemingway's revisions, the unknown copy editor emended *fuck* and *fucking* to *f——k* and *f——king*. However, the word *shit* was not changed.[90] Despite these emendations, Hemingway was allowed more latitude than he had been heretofore. No legal action resulted from the book's publication.

Hemingway must have been feeling very touchy by this point, for after receiving galley proofs for the short sections at the end of the book, he wired Perkins on 27 June, "DID IT SEEM VERY FUNNY TO SLUG EVERY GALLEY HEMINGWAYS DEATH OR WAS THAT WHAT YOU WANTED HAVE BEEN PLENTY SICK."[91] Since all the galley proofs, most of which Hemingway had worked over in April and May, had also been slugged in the same way, it seems strange that Hemingway had just noticed this notation. Perhaps he was just tired of working over the book or was irritated by the firm's marketing of the book and used the heading as an excuse to blow off steam. In any event, Perkins wrote him on 7 July to apologize about the heading and to say that he would have had the galleys slugged a different way if he had noticed. In this same letter Perkins acknowledged that all the page proofs had been received. He added that he had hoped Hemingway would not be so hard on Waldo Frank.[92] Hemingway noted in his response of 15 July that he had cut all but one reference to Frank and would cut no more: "After all the lazy punk needs to be stepped on—You've never asked him to tone down anything he wrote about me. Or did you?"[93] Perkins let the remaining reference about Frank stand without further comment.

Hemingway was intensely concerned with how the book would be marketed. Rather than merely wanting more and bigger advertisements, he worried that Scribners' claims that the book was about more things than bullfighting would open him up to attack. The first promotion efforts Scribners made—the salesman's dummy and the description in the firm's fall 1932 catalog—were aimed at booksellers. On 28 June, Perkins wired, "BOOKSTORES IMMENSELY IMPRESSED BY DUMMY AND IDEA OF BOOK."[94] The dust jacket illustration was Roberto Domingo's "Toros" and was retained for the jacket of the trade edition. The first four pages of chapter 1 and four photographs were reproduced. The actual description of the book's contents was printed on the front and back flaps of the jacket. The back-flap copy mainly quoted from the text, specifically Hemingway's account of how he became interested in bullfighting. On the front flap wider claims for the book were made:

> In bringing into focus all that is important and interesting about bullfighting—the bravery and cowardice, the bull, the costume and theatre and personality and craftsmanship and history (all of it beneath the Spanish sun and in the midst of men *consumed with a passion* for bullfighting)—Mr. Hemingway has also brought into focus a great deal that is significant about human living and dying, and about the trade called literature, which attempts to depict human living and dying.
>
> The author has discovered, and put into this book, the profound and subtle reasons why bullfighting is so wonderful to so many men, for so many centuries, why it is so moving and impor-

tant and exalting. By virtue of an undismayed and undeceived honesty he has been able to see what *actually* happens during moments of overwhelming emotion, when the exact cause of the exaltation is usually unnoticed.

There is much collateral information in this book, about life and letters and what it takes to be an artist—a real one. There are dicta about writing so honest and true they will very likely become common axioms, so vivid and sincere and convincing is their presentation. There are also episodes of gorgeous comedy and satire, deliberately injected into the discussion and description of bullfighting and bullfighters.[95]

A similar presentation of the book appeared in the firm's catalog of its fall 1932 list. Along with a small reproduction of the book's frontispiece (Juan Gris's "The Bullfighter"), the publisher ran the following description:

If this were only the first complete book by an American writer about the bullfight, bullfighters, and bulls—as it is, and that American the one who knows more about the subject than any other—it would be supremely worth reading. But it is very much more than that. Blended into its pages are several short stories, one of them, "The Natural History of Death," among the finest that Hemingway has done: there is a chapter on writing in America that contains the author's literary credo stated fearlessly and with smashing directness: there are gorgeously funny dialogues on divers subjects with a hypothetical old lady whose mind finally becomes so depraved that she is dismissed from the story: and there are resounding pages in which Mr. Hemingway enters the arena of current literature and plunges sharp critical banderillas into the sensitive sides of some of the bulls of American letters. It is lavish with color, wisdom, humor, tragedy, and life.

But primarily "Death in the Afternoon" is about the art of bullfighting—"a decadent art in every way, reaching its fullest flower at its rottenest point, which is the present." Here are described and explained the technic and the emotional appeal of the bullfight, "the emotional and spiritual intensity and pure classic beauty that can be produced by a man, an animal, and a piece of scarlet serge draped on a stick." There are chapters about bullfighters, men who live every day with death—Joselito, "to watch him was like reading about d'Artagnan as a boy"; Maera, who with his wrist dislocated killed a bull "made of cement," and many others are vividly delineated. And there are pages about bulls, whose bravery is the primal root of the bullfight and who when they are really brave are afraid of nothing on earth. There is something interesting and vital on every page of this book—one that every admirer of Hemingway will enjoy to the end.[96]

Perkins's role in developing advertising copy for *Death in the Afternoon* is not known. However, Scribners clearly saw Hemingway as a literary artist—a writer of fiction—and the firm was afraid that American readers would not be interested in a technical book about bullfighting. The book, therefore, had to be presented as having more in it.

Hemingway reacted angrily to this strategy. On 28 June, he wrote his editor to correct the firm's advertising:

What you will do is get everyone disappointed—I put all that stuff in so that anyone buying the book for no matter what reason would get their money worth—All that story, dialogue, etc is thrown in extra—The book is worth anybodys 3.50 who has 3.50 as a straight book on bull fighting—If you go to advertizing that it is so many damned other things all you will do is make people disappointed because it hasnt a cook book and a telephone directory as well.

If you try to sell it as a great classic Goddamned book on bull fighting rather than some fucking miscellany you may be able to sell a few—Let the critics claim it has something additional—But suppose all chance of that is gone now with that lovely Hauser stuff[97]—If you want to try to find someone to speak well of it ask Dos Passos. . . .

If you feel disappointed and still want my "literary Credo" in a book on bull fighting they can run an insert saying "F——ck the whole goddamned lousy racket"—Hemingway[98]

Hemingway had obviously seen the catalog copy by this point, as his reference to his "'literary Credo'" makes clear. By 15 July, he had seen the dust jacket and asked Perkins to discontinue making similar claims on the jacket copy since, he claimed, reviewers reviewed the blurbs and he wanted them to read the book.[99] Nearly a month later, he wrote Perkins that the now-revised jacket was fine ("Seem restrained, to make no false promises, and know what the hell it is about"), but he added that Scribners would have to strongly back the book to ensure a large sale: "If you advertize like hell and realize there is a difference between Marcia Davenports Mozart etc (nice though they must be) you can sell plenty. If you got spooked or yellow out on trying to sell then naturally they will flop in these times—You will have to stick with it hard, *as though it were selling big*, through Christmas no matter *how* it goes. Like Sun also. Then it will go. It is really a swell book."[100] This was Hemingway's familiar call when publication of a book was near, and something Perkins had heard many times before.

Hemingway's instructions must have arrived before copy was ready for Scribners' prepublication advertisements in *Publishers Weekly*. The firm ran two notices in the trade periodical for *Death in the Afternoon*. The first, in the 10 September 1932 issue, was a one-page spread for Hemingway's book and for James Truslow Adams's *The March of Democracy*. The copy mentioned only bullfighting and the many photographs in the book.[101] The second advertisement was in the 17 September issue and was part of the firm's two-page announcement for its fall books. The description emphasized the book's strengths: "Bullfighting, bulls and bullfighters plus much collateral observation on life and letters. Drama, color, action, humor, *and* 80 amazing pictures. Every Hemingway admirer is a sure sale . . . and it will interest a public that his novels hasn't [*sic*] touched."[102] However, the statement was vague about the types of "collateral observations" and exactly who the Hemingway admirers are. Although the publisher had an extensive nonfiction list, it seems that they were having a difficult time deciding how to present a work of nonfiction by a writer who was known almost exclusively for his fiction.

Death in the Afternoon was published on 23 September 1932 and sold for $3.50. The first printing consisted of 10,300 copies. Between the date of publication and June 1933, fourteen reviews of it appeared in major American newspapers and magazines. Hemingway's scrapbook contains clippings from some sixty-five reviews or notices from American publications.[103] Most of the major reviewers admired the breadth and detail of the treatise. The reviewer for *Time* called it a "complete, compendious, and appreciative guide."[104] Laurence Stallings, writing in the *New York Sun*, described it as "a superbly colored and capricious essay on human pride."[105] Nearly all the reviewers liked the style; the *Saturday Review of Literature* reviewer, Ben Ray Redman, wrote that the descriptions in the book were "couched in a prose that must be called perfect."[106] Some reviewers, however, such as R. L. Duffus in the *New York Times Book Review* and Curtis Patterson in *Town and Country*, thought the style was too dense and not as good as it had been in Hemingway's previous work.[107] Many reviewers also disparaged Hemingway for his attacks on other writers, as *New Yorker* reviewer Robert M. Coates did, and for his use of "obscene" language, which was H. L. Mencken's only criticism in his review in the *American Mercury*.[108] The reviews on the whole can be described as good, but not overwhelmingly positive.

The advertising campaign for the book was extensive, but probably not as extensive as Hemingway would have wanted. In addition to the notices in *Publishers Weekly,* Scribners ran prepublication advertisements in *Retail Bookseller* and *Book Dial*—advertisements aimed primarily at booksellers—and in *Scribner's Magazine,* the *Saturday Review of Literature,* the *New York Herald,* and the *New York Times*—advertisements aimed primarily at book buyers. The firm bought notices for *Death in the Afternoon* until February 1933, but most of its advertisements ran from September to December of 1932 (only four ran in 1933). In all, Scribners purchased 178 notices for the book. Most (78) appeared in New York newspapers. Twenty-seven of the advertisements were in book trade publications. Thirty-one appeared in general-circulation magazines like *Harper's Monthly,* the *Forum,* and *Atlantic Monthly.* The rest appeared in newspapers in Boston (13), Philadelphia (8), Chicago (9), and California (2), and in Ivy League alumni magazines like the *Princeton Alumni Weekly* and the *Yale Review* (4). Total expenditure for these advertisements were $8,581.14.[109] This strategy shows that the firm did not have high hopes for a large sale; little effort was made to promote the work outside the northeast of the United States. In contrast, the firm promoted *A Farewell to Arms* from September 1929 until December 1930, spending $20,578.17.

Examination of the advertisements for *Death in the Afternoon* does show that Scribners attempted to push the book but did not have a clear idea of how to do so. From 25 September to 18 December 1932, Scribners advertised *Death in the Afternoon* every week in the *New York Times Book Review.*[110] In all but four of these notices (those appearing between 23 October and 13 November), Hemingway's book had to share the spotlight with other Scribners books. These advertisements also show a shift in Scribners' strategy. Initially, the book was pushed only as a guide to bullfighting, with quotes from reviewers first used in the advertisement for 9 October. By 13 November, however, Scribners began describing the book as a "best seller" in "New York Chicago Philadelphia and points West." These claims gave way in December to advertisements that, against Hemingway's wishes, promised a book with many "digressions into literature and life."

These shifts in focus indicate something the printing records and Perkins's letters bear out: *Death in the Afternoon* was not selling. Scribners had ordered an initial printing of 10,300 copies. Between September and 1 November, three more printings were made for a total of 9,780 copies—20,080 copies total for all four printings. The next, and last, printing for this edition was on 27 August 1934—700 copies.[111] Soon after publication, the sales outlook was good. Perkins reported two weeks after publication that "well over 12,000 copies" had been sold.[112] The first hint of trouble come on 3 November, when Perkins wrote his author that sales had started dropping off two weeks earlier.[113] Nine days later, Perkins explained more fully what problems the book faced:

> It is very hard to say anything definite about the sale. It has been very good indeed in New York, and distinctly good in Chicago, and good in other big cities. The booksellers outside of the several big cities took it well in general, but they are in the worst shape of all booksellers, and it is to them especially that we have sent so many books "on sale." We do not get good reports from them about it, even from those who were most enthusiastic, like one in Los Angeles and one in Frisco. They say that they find it very difficult to sell because their customers say "they are not interested in bull fighting." The first reaction to the book even in the big cities was more or less of that sort on the part of customers, but it was immediately overcome in the big cities where reviews and advertisements have most effect. In these lesser places it was not overcome to any such degree, and we do not really know how they will work out with it. From them we have had a great many returns.[114]

The sales situation seemed so hopeless, as Perkins reported to Hemingway on 21 November, that the firm adopted a direct-mail campaign, sending out two circulars—the first to 161,000 people, the second to 10,000—in hopes of stirring interest in the book.[115] This effort seems to have had little effect.

Death in the Afternoon, then, met with two equally difficult obstacles to overcome: the harsh economic conditions caused by the Great Depression and the indifference of the so-called common reader. American readers did not care to read a book on bullfighting. This view was expressed by an A. E. Howard in a letter to the editor of the *New York Times Book Review,* which appeared in the 9 October 1932 issue:

> If we are to believe Mr. Hemingway, high adventure and a lust for blood fuse in the Castilian bullring. One might question wherein a bullfight differs from a dogfight, or a cocking main, or terriers in a ratpit, or shooting at pigeons from a trap, save, indeed, that a bullfight endangers human life. Certainly there is a mean between baiting the bull and "bedside mysticisms" as there is between bulldogging and the study of sex eugenics.
>
> But it certainly is a non sequitur to infer that the aficionados at an actual bullfight are more redblooded than the spectators of a moving picture featuring gangster warfare. Both assay as bleacher fans simon pure. Neither play the game; neither are in added fear of, or in increased love with, death by violence. And the theories advanced by Mr. Hemingway as to tauromania simply recall the brainstorms born of the Thaw trial at the beginning of this century.[116]
>
> I have never so much as seen the cover of one of the 2,000-odd Spanish books and pamphlets bearing on the subject, nor, after reading the utter maudlin tosh distilled by Mr. Hemingway, do I desire to do so. My strong impression is that a peerless short-story writer wrote "Death in the Afternoon" purely to put across a sensational book which would find a ready market.[117]

The "ready market" Howard and Scribners assumed Hemingway would have was not there. Faced with such resistance, Hemingway could not hope that this work would be as successful as his fiction had been. If all 20,780 copies were eventually sold, Hemingway would have made only $10,909.50 ($132,561.75 in 2005 dollars).[118] This is a respectable amount for 1932, but a far cry from the $47,712.50 the sale of 101,675 copies of *A Farewell to Arms* had netted Hemingway in 1929.

The final insult came in March of 1933, when the first royalty report for *Death in the Afternoon* was sent to Hemingway. Included in the report was a charge of $145.25 for excess corrections of the galley proofs. Hemingway reacted angrily in a letter of 31 March to Perkins. He cited the $600 he spent on photographs and his reasonable requests for advances as proof that he had been reasonable with the firm.[119] As usual, Perkins gave in to Hemingway's demands, writing his author on 3 April, "I thought that you would not feel that the cost of the corrections was fair, and we shall cancel it. Corrections are frightfully expensive things and really unreasonably so, and due to union charges. They seem particularly hard to bear under present conditions."[120]

This essentially marked the end of the story of the publication of Hemingway's first nonfiction book. *Death in the Afternoon,* especially after the great success of *A Farewell to Arms,* must have been a great disappointment to him and Perkins in terms of sales and reception. The public did not want such a book from Hemingway. As the thirties wore on, both Hemingway and Perkins would become convinced that the Hemingway works that sold were fiction—especially novels. But Hemingway would not produce another novel until he had tried his hand at another nonfiction work: *Green Hills of Africa.*

CHAPTER 5

"YOU CAN'T BE POPULAR ALL THE TIME"

Winner Take Nothing *and* Green Hills of Africa

While *Death in the Afternoon* did not sell as well as Hemingway's previous books and could therefore be considered a failure, its sales were respectable. It would be with his next two ventures, *Winner Take Nothing* and *Green Hills of Africa,* that Hemingway and Scribners would meet with real failure. Hemingway's return to fiction in book form, *Winner Take Nothing,* sold very poorly in comparison to *Men Without Women. Green Hills of Africa,* his account of his 1933–1934 African safari, was his second nonfiction book and the last such book he would publish in his lifetime; aside from *In Our Time* and *The Torrents of Spring, Green Hills of Africa* had the weakest sales of any work by Hemingway. A combination of many factors, one of which was the poor economy, lead to these failures (as they were defined by Hemingway). But the main reason was the author's difficult attitude.

Even before *Death in the Afternoon* was published, Perkins began planning for Hemingway's next book; as was typical, Perkins thought that the work to follow should be a short-story collection. On 19 September 1932, he wrote Hemingway, "Won't you have a book of stories for spring publication?"[1] A month later, Hemingway responded from Wyoming, "Will have some swell stories. Need 4 more which I plan to write when leave here."[2] Writing from Key West on 26 October, he informed his editor, "Starting to work on stories now—Any subject you would like a story about?"[3]

Hemingway had ten stories on hand by this time: "Wine of Wyoming," "The Sea Change," "A Natural History of the Dead," "After the Storm," "God Rest You Merry, Gentlemen," "Homage to Switzerland," "The Light of the World," "The Mother of a Queen," "A Way You'll Never Be," and—probably—"A Clean, Well-Lighted Place." Only the first four had previously been published as of October 1932. By May of 1933, all but three of these stories would be published. *Scribner's Magazine* rejected "The Light of the World," and there is no evidence to suggest that Hemingway ever attempted to place "The Mother of a Queen" or "A Way You'll Never Be" with any periodical. Three of these stories—"Wine of Wyoming," "A Clean, Well-Lighted Place," and "Homage to Switzerland"—had or would appear in *Scribner's Magazine*. "A Natural History of the Dead" had been included in *Death in the Afternoon*. "After the Storm" had been published in the May 1932 issue of *Cosmopolitan*. The remaining two stories had had very limited exposure. "The Sea Change" had appeared in the little magazine *This Quarter* in December 1931, and "God Rest You Merry, Gentlemen" would be published (without the comma) in a limited edition (300 copies) by Louis Henry Cohn's House of Books in April 1933.

Hemingway seems to have made minimal progress in October and November. He wrote Perkins on 15 November 1932: "Have been working like hell writing. Have four stories ready to be typed. Will send you two. No obligation to take them but they are very good stories. I now have ten ready for a book. Need two, possibly three more. Next fall might be a good time."[4] The letter indicates that Hemingway had probably spent much of his time revising stories he had written. The stories he sent were "Homage to Switzerland" and "A Clean, Well-Lighted Place." The other two stories ready to be typed were "The Gambler, the Nun, and the Radio" and, probably, "One Reader Writes." In his response of 18 November, Perkins applied gentle pressure to his author: "You know what you have to do, but if the book of stories could be published in the spring, which might easily be as late as May, or even June, it would be better in some ways. A book of stories would not conflict at all with 'Death in the Afternoon' and it would keep the whole matter to the front and be helped by it, and help it. And there really does seem to be strong reason to think that we are coming to the end of this depression. . . . If you had the other three stories done in the next three months, you would be in time enough. You would have almost as many stories than as were in 'Men without' and 'In Our Time.'"5 Perkins's hope was not that the story collection would be a success but that the attention it would receive would revive interest in the bullfight book. In a postscript to his letter of 3 December to Hemingway, Perkins reiterated his call, again leaving the final decision to his author: "Let me know as soon as you can about the book of stories. We ought to announce it in the spring list if it is to be published before August. If it is to be ready in time to be published before August, I believe it ought to be. If it is to be published later than June, or perhaps even in May, it should be a fall book. But I think it would help with 'Death in the Afternoon' and everything if it could come out in the spring. Don't hurry it though,—of course you wouldn't."6 Hemingway does not seem to have tried very hard to meet the deadline for spring publication. In his letters to Perkins he gave no indication that he was trying to do so.

By early February, Hemingway informed his editor that he had nearly finished "The Gambler, the Nun, and the Radio." He also asked about the royalties for *Death in the Afternoon* and made a difficult request of his publisher:

> Also are you or will you be prepared to advance me $6,000 on the book of stories—This is figured as 15% on 20,000 sale at $2.00. The 20,000 is the minimum sale I have to have Mr. Darrow carry in his mind. Also the minimum that will hold poor old Papa's affectionate loyalty. The advance mentioned is less than the sale on day of publication of this last $3.50 masterpiece.
>
> Would it be any more palatable to you to advance 3000 or 4000 and the balance at say $200 a month?
>
> If I take an advance on the new book will not need that Death In Aft royalties until they are due. But anyhow let me know when they are due.7

Perkins's response of 10 February illustrates the poor business climate and how in spite of it the firm was willing to try very hard to keep the author happy:

When a man calls for $3,000 or $4,000 even in boom times he is likely to get only $3,000, and he is likely to get only that in these times.—So we deposited only $3,000,—but we are bent upon doing exactly what you want. And we realize that you are trying to help us in suggesting the $200 a month.—So tell me when that ought to begin. The royalties on "Death in the Afternoon" are strictly due ten months after publication, which is July 23rd. We are altogether willing though to pay them now. I have got to take up with Charlie how we should charge this $3,000, whether as much as possible against the royalties, or whether as an advance on the stories.[8]

Hemingway seems to have been understanding of the firm's plight but was determined to have things his way. On 23 February, he sent the story (now titled "Give Us a Prescription, Doctor") and told his editor that he had four chapters done on a novel.[9] He also restated his opinion about the advance:

Thanks for making the deposit—My point about the advance was that I wanted 6000 *before the book came out.* Explained why. Didnt realize how few months intervened. Only suggested those monthly payments as a convenience for you in order not to draw too much out of your treasury at once. I detest any monthly payment status. Said 3 or 4 grand on same basis. What I ask for unqualifidly as to times is 6000—before book is out—15% on 20,000 @ 2.00—Look over the record and you will find I have always been reasonable about advances and want to protect myself, my financial careeh (career) rather, and through me, you.[10]

Perkins responded on 3 March: "We are quite ready to give you as much of an advance as six thousand in all on the next book."[11] The same day Hemingway had written that he did not need the other $3,000 but did want it before publication.[12] Still, at the end of the discussion, Hemingway got what he wanted.

Of paramount importance to Perkins at this time, as was typical for him when he was working on a story collection by one of his authors, was the promotion and publicity. For the campaign Perkins had to have the book's title and its contents. On 29 March, he wrote Hemingway to get him to send both so that he could have a salesman's dummy ready by 1 May.[13]

But before Perkins could get the title and contents he would have to solve another problem. The first real threat to the publication of the still-untitled collection came at the end of March, when Hemingway received the royalty report for *Death in the Afternoon* and saw the charge for correcting the galley proofs. He said that he would pay the charge but told his editor, "Do not expect me to do anything against my interests in the matter of speeding up in the future." Most serious, however, was his threat to stall publication of the story volume: "I am not going to rush on a title. Perhaps it may not be such a good idea to get out a book of stories now anyway. Will be very pleased, in case you feel you are being badly treated, to send you back your advance three thousand dollars with interest. Or, if you want it, the 667.08 that statement says I owe you. Stories that are any good do not get sour and I am in no particular rush to publish."[14] Again, Perkins defused the situation, writing on 3 April that the firm was canceling the correction charges.[15]

With the flap over the correction charges settled, Hemingway set out to provide Perkins with a title. On 8 April, he wrote that he had thirteen stories ready and was considering calling the collection "After the Storm and Other Stories," but that he thought he could come up with a better title. He also told his editor that he had been working on a novel. In addition, Hemingway provided Perkins with his theory of what a good story collection should be:

At present I know that the book needs one more simple story of action to balance some of the difficult stories it contains. I thought I had it with the last story I wrote, one I just finished about the war, but that turned out to be a hell of a difficult one ['A Way You'll Never Be"]. Stories like Fifty Grand, My Old Man and that sort are no where near as good stories, in the end, as a story like Hills Like White Elephants, or Sea Change. But a book needs them because people understand them easily and it gives them the necessary confidence in the stories that are hard for them. A book of stories, that is a good one, is just as much a unit as a novel. You get the overtones by the juxtaposition of the stories or by what you put between them. You cannot just have one good story and a lot of crap that you published in magazines as Scott's last book of stories was and make a book of it. Nor can you put everything you ever wrote together, as you did with Ring, and not have the hate in them, the righteousness, and the cheating at the end of the bulk of them choke and throttle the fine ones.[16]

Nor can you publish them all. What makes a book of stories sell is *unpublished stories*.[17]

Hemingway's attitude is very revealing. He understood his readership to a certain extent, believing that the "common" reader wanted what could be called "adventure" stories rather than works of psychological realism.

When Perkins received Hemingway's letter of 8 April, he wired on the tenth that the firm needed the setting copy for the book by 7 August.[18] He followed this wire with a letter two days later in which he more fully explained what Scribners needed. Perkins admitted that "After the Storm and Other Stories" was a weak title. He wanted to publish in early October and restated that Hemingway had to get setting copy to Scribners by 7 August. Perkins, though, wanted to announce the upcoming publication as soon as possible: "The only thing is that if it seems to you that the chances are stronger that you will have a book ready in the fall than not, we ought to announce it to the trade through our salesmen and in the Publisher's Weekly. The title is not so important as the mere fact. Your name is very important, then the title."[19] Perkins understood that the firm was by this point selling Hemingway as much as they were his books.

Hemingway wired on 24 April, "OK ANNOUNCE BOOK STORIES FOR FALL WILL SEND TITLE SOON AS HAVE IT."[20] But Hemingway had greater than expected difficulty finding a title. On 20 May, writing from Cuba, he told Perkins, "Havent written because I wanted to send the title and havent gotten it yet—Have 3 good ones—but none of them is right." He also wrote that he was leaving for Europe and then Africa on 7 August, noting that he could cable his approval for any changes to the galley proofs of the book since "Stories arent like a novel."[21]

It would be another month before Hemingway would wire Perkins the title and the epigraph for the collection (along with a promise to break Max Eastman's jaw over his review of *Death in the Afternoon,* titled "Bull in the Afternoon," in the 7 June issue of the *New Republic*).[22] Perkins responded the next day: "Think title excellent stop And you are absolutely invulnerable to Eastman and others."[23] Perkins did not seem to know that the title and epigraph were Hemingway's invention, even though the author claimed to have gotten them from an "old book about gaming."[24]

On 13 June, in a letter mainly dedicated to attacking Eastman and other critics, Hemingway told Perkins, "Sorry I could not send the title sooner but did not have it any sooner. Now you can make up the dummy with that title. Would it be any help to you if I sent the 12 stories that I have ready—for you to set up and follow with the other two I am working on. Finished 24 page story yesterday."[25] The just-completed story was the one that would eventually be titled "Fathers and Sons." Unfortunately, Scribners had already prepared a dummy that used the beginning of "Give Us a Prescription, Doctor" as a sample; the title page read "STORIES | (TITLE TO BE DETERMINED)."[26]

Three days after receiving Hemingway's letter of 13 June, Perkins sent him the contract for *Winner Take Nothing*. The terms were the usual for Hemingway: he would receive 15 percent of the retail price for the first 25,000 copies sold, and 20 percent for sales over 25,000 copies.[27] Perkins also added, "I wish you would send us the stories you are sure are all right because we could set them up, and keep the type standing until the others came. It would be a good thing to do, too,—save time."[28] But it would be nearly another month before Hemingway did so. In his accompanying letter, dated 13 July, he included his order for the stories and other instructions for the handling of the book. He wanted "The Light of the World" to be the first story, followed by "A Clean, Well-Lighted Place" and "After the Storm." He had one new story called "The Tomb of His Grandfather" ["Fathers and Sons"] that would be "either next to last or last in the book." Hemingway added that he wanted to remove the asides of the Author and the Old Lady from "A Natural History of the Dead." He also gave Perkins his opinion on how the book might best be advertised:

> You might stress the fact that 6 of the stories in the book have never been published—One has been in a limited edition of 300 copies (verify number from Cohn) another only published abroad—(although copied freely here and a copy published by your esteemed selves) . . .
> Another thing—
> Either I will mention in a foreword that A Natural History of The Dead was included because it was only available in a book published at 3.50 or you can say that I so requested in the front

matter or the jacket—It was added to the original number of stories—Not put in to fill up.[29]

The contents of the book were set. Perkins acknowledged receipt on 18 July, promising to have galley proofs as soon as possible.[30] Hemingway had only to wait for the proofs and revise that last story. He had left little time to get the book set in type for the 7 August deadline.

Despite Perkins's pleas to be as quick as possible, Hemingway did not rush. On 26 July, he wrote his editor that he was starting the rewrite of "The Tomb of My Grandfather." He gave his itinerary: he would be in Spain for half of August, all of September, and (perhaps) October before leaving for Africa in November. He was also bitter about what Gertrude Stein had written about him in *The Autobiography of Alice B. Toklas,* which he had been reading in the *Atlantic Monthly.* Hemingway, toward the conclusion, brought up the matter of obscene words: "I imagine you are in more or less of a stew about certain words but tell me what you can and can't do and we will work it out. I'm not the little boy writing them on the wall to be smart. If I can make the effect without the word will always do so but sometimes can't. Also it is good for the language to restore its life that they bleed out of it. That is very important."[31] Three days later, he forwarded the completed story with what he believed would be a temporary title, "Fathers and Sons." He also included instructions for sending the proofs to Spain, indicating that he knew that Scribners could not get the galleys to him in Key West before he left.[32]

Perkins does not seem to have had much of a problem with the obscene words. However, in a wire of 31 July, after promising to send the entire proof by airmail to Havana, he asked that Hemingway consider putting another story first instead of "The Light of the World."[33] Hemingway replied the same day, "WRITE DETAIL YOUR VIEWS ORDER STORIES LIGHT WORLD BETTER AND SHORTER STORY THAN MAISON TELLIER."[34] Two days later, Perkins explained his objection:

My point about the order of the stories is simply a practical one. The story you have put first is the one to which people will most object.—Utterly enrage all those who do get enraged in the most hateful way about those things. Its most conspicuous position would give it a tremendous emphasis, and would greatly damage the book in sales, and I think in other ways too, in reviews of such things. So I hoped you could put it elsewhere. I have underlined the words and phrases I think you ought to get around. There is one in "God Rest You" that you did not have in the version I read.[35] I really think that one of the best of all the stories is "A Clean Well-Lighted Place" though it is of that kind, I suppose, which not many people would respond to as much as to others. I think "After the Storm" is probably the most popular sort of story.[36]

"The Light of the World," with its focus on two prostitutes, was no doubt too bawdy to lead off the book. Hemingway apparently accepted Perkins's reasoning, as there is no objection from him in the located correspondence.

The proofs, which lacked sufficient postage, did not get to Hemingway before his departure. From the ship, Hemingway wrote his editor an angry letter, berating Perkins for failing to get the proofs to him in time and for his perceived attitude about the stories:

> I suppose, from the tone in which you write (ie. *cautious defense of one or two stories*) that me having been attacked by your pal Eastman and poor old Stein you are all about ready to ask waivers—
>
> But if you will go over the record you will find that I have cost the house of Scribner very little money—And I am in better shape and going better than I have ever been—It happens to be a time when I could appreciate a little loyalty (having just seen actions of Eastman, Stein and Co.) and if you feel you have been robbed by me taking a 6,000 advance (*Less* than the previous *non*fiction book had earned) (taking it in driblets so as not to embarrass you market comittments) (The state of the stock market being the accepted measure of a publishing enthusiasm for literature) will be very glad to return the
>
> 500
>
> 1000
>
> 750
>
> advance and call it all off—
>
> But I tell you very sincerely that you would be very short sighted to do so—
>
> *After* the stock market crash I turned down offers guarantying 25,000 advance etc. I have turned down plenty since—I paid

for all the things in Death In The Afternoon that you promised to pay for—Your memory may be short or maybe you werent thinking about book but about something else and that's how I got impression I did. But didnt hear anything for 10 days after sent Mss. Then this letter—

And out of what has happened to me this year (details *not furnished on request*) you will make plenty when I write it—It wont be one of those Conrad Aiken stories So when your friends, who ardently hope for it, tell you that I am all washed up—I wouldnt take too much stock in it. Because I have a good ⅓ of a better novel done than any of the poor twirps you publish will ever come within a 100 leagues of doing—and am well and healthy and feeling fine—

And contrary to Gertrude I *last* where the other bastards break—

Thats why she said that—because being untrue she thought it would hurt me—

I will go over the order of the stories—When I asked you to write me in detail I had hoped you would—The book means something to me, you know too.[37]

Perkins again was bearing the brunt of Hemingway's anger. The author felt that he was being attacked on all sides and saw even his closest advisor as a foe.

Again, Perkins uttered mea culpa, writing on 14 August to explain the mistake:

I just got your letter and felt perfectly sick about the proof. I harried the press to get everything on the machines and run it off as quickly as could possibly be done, to be sure that you had it for the boat. And it was done in time. I told them to be sure to get on enough postage, and to take every kind of pains. I should have looked up the postage myself I suppose, and put on the stamps.—For I suppose it must have been insufficient postage that interfered. So now I am simply sending off instantly another set of proof. But it is too late to give you the chance to read it that you should have had on the boat. . . .

I am awfully sorry about the proofs. I didn't think anything could go wrong with them. I know it will turn out that they did not put the right postage on, although Miss Bearn went down to the post office to be sure she had everything right.[38]

The next day Perkins wired that he was sending another set of proofs to Spain, adding, "Not such a blank fool to misjudge present or future."[39] Perkins followed this cable with a handwritten letter meant to assure Hemingway of the high regard Perkins had for him and of his imperviousness to attacks:

> Dear Ernest: I meant *Your* present + future in my cable. Never, since I read the first In Our Time have I had any question about You as a writer on *real* grounds. I have been terribly anxious on other grounds (not financial ones which I dont by nature think so much about) + I am somewhat now. A writer, + any artist, does reach a point after his first great sucess when he must meet opposition,—whether by the law of action + re-action, or from just plain cussedness in man, or what. But the real ones beat the opposition simply by having the reality or authenticity of their art. It can't be beat. You do give the opposition something obvious + easy to go against by ignoring the conventions + arouse a vicious hostility. But I know that while Bromfield etc. might + in the sort of writing they are willing to do, perhaps should, consider these things, the real writer should not. He should not be thinking about such things, of course, when he's writing. I really have been a buffer in this matter + I ought to be.—And I hate to speak to You about these things now because you're not the one to be worried about them. Then too You know everything I can tell You, I guess. I certainly think that I sound mighty silly in saying what I think of You, as a writer. That has to go without saying. Suppose You heard someone tell Tolstoi he thought War + Peace was a great novel! By the way, I do think the last story You sent *is* a great story!

Perkins closed by repeating that he was to blame for the proofs not having gotten to Hemingway on time.[40] He again defused a potentially disastrous situation for the firm. The letter also gives a glimpse of Perkins's understanding of what his authors were trying to do; he understood that Hemingway saw himself first and foremost as a literary artist and not as a strictly commercial writer, and he treated him accordingly.

Hemingway was calmer when he responded to Perkins on 31 August. He apologized for his 10 August letter and told Perkins not to worry about him and the "opposition." He then explained what he had done in the galley proofs:

> I have changed the places you underlined and eliminated the three Anglo-Saxon phrases.
>
> I do not do this happily. But I see your point very clearly and having taken money have no choice. Better to perform operation myself than have anyone else do it! If you want to leave off the K at the end of the word F——K in The Natural History of the Dead you can do so. It has been published once—So I dont care—I mean this seriously—I have never gone in much for fighting the conventions But for fighting the *Genteel* tradition which has been strangler of all English and U.S. literature. . . .
>
> You can put The Light of The World 3rd opening with After The Storm—A Clean Well-Lighted Place 2nd—Then The Light if you think that better—
>
> I do not want it any further down on account of it's chronological position in book—Also I thought it best to open with an unpublished story—However if you feel as strongly as you wrote about it put it in 3rd place—
>
> It may make no difference anyway—
>
> I might as well leave that last story as Fathers and Sons.

Hemingway also asked that a note be made that "A Natural History of the Dead" was reprinted at the author's request because it had previously been in a book that sold for $3.50. Before closing, Hemingway explained that he needed the full support of the firm, noting that in the end he would make more money for Scribners than his imitators would.[41] Hemingway mailed the galley proofs to New York two days later; he pointed out to Perkins that he had changed and inserted a footnote to "up at the end he shits the bed full" in "A Natural History of the Dead." He also noted that he had made many corrections to "Fathers and Sons" so that it needed to be gone over very carefully before final proofs were sent.[42] The book was nearly complete.

Perkins received the galley proofs by 14 September and sent Hemingway the page proof on 21 September.[43] The next day he wrote Hemingway about what he had done about the proofs:

We ought to publish in October, and so we are going straight ahead. It seems to me that everything is all right. It was the first time I had seen the collection all as one, and I think it a most impressive one. All your stories in every book are better the fifth time you read them, which can be said of hardly anybody else, and I do not think you ever wrote a better story than "Fathers and Sons" (We have kept that title. We think it throws back into the past and future the way the story does more than any of the others, though "Tomb of a Grandfather" is a fine title). I did knock off that K. I ought to do the worrying, and I ought not to urge you any further toward concessions to the genteel than I can help.—And I admit too, that in the past I have probably gone too far that way because many things I feared have never happened. . . . But the Genteel have managed to murder several of the best writers there ever were;—though they were more fragile boys than you, and I suppose it was more on account of their conduct than their writings, too. We do want for every reason to stand back of everything you do and I am always afraid of being too timid about it because I come for people who were conventional in those regards, although never genteel. . . . Those "un-named worries" are all on that score,—the fear of unconquerable prejudices. But it is true that you have been righter than I have been so far, and I have always remembered that.[44]

Three days later, Perkins wrote that the few obvious mistakes in the page proof, such as a misplaced asterisk in "A Natural History of the Dead," had been corrected and for Hemingway not to worry about them.[45]

Ten days later, on 5 October, Perkins sent a description of the dust jacket and outlined publication details:

[The jacket] is striking,—black and red, not like any we have had previously, only type matter. It sounds badly as I put it, but I cannot describe it and I think you will like it. We have a note on the flap which includes the statements that you want, like that about "A Natural History of the Dead." . . .

We are going right ahead with the book in the idea of publishing it this month. But we shall print a rather small edition so that if there are any small things you want to change that won't upset the re-paging, we can do it even in the first edition in unbound copies, by cancelling any page that is wrong.—But I do not think anything will be wrong.[46]

Hemingway took his time going over the page proofs, finally cabling Perkins on 20 October, "PROOF OK PAGE THIRTY SHOULD READ YOU CAN INTERFERE WITH THIS ONE."[47] Perkins acknowledged receipt on 25 October, stating that the book would come out Friday (27 October) and that prospects looked good.[48]

Winner Take Nothing was published on 27 October 1933 and sold for $2.00. The firm ordered a printing of 20,300 copies on 6 October.[49] According to the "Fall Book Index, 1933," which appeared in the 16 September 1933 issue of *Publishers Weekly,* 6 October had been the initial publication date; the delay of three weeks was necessitated by the time needed to get corrections from Hemingway in Paris.[50] The delay no doubt adversely affected review schedules and hence the publisher's plans.

Before publication, the Scribners advertising department had begun promoting the book. The prepublication advertisements stressed that this was a work of fiction and the fact that *Men Without Women* had sold well for a story collection. The firm announced the collection in the 20 May 1933 issue of *Publishers Weekly,* calling it "A Book of Stories (Title to Come)" in a two-page spread with five other Scribners titles for the fall. No individual story titles are mentioned, but the fact that almost half of the stories had not been previously published was stressed.[51] The announcement for the book in the firm's fall 1933 catalog is more specific, stressing Hemingway's record:

WINNER TAKE NOTHING
by Ernest Hemingway *Tentative Date, October. $2.00*
author of "Death in the Afternoon," "A Farewell to Arms," etc.

  The Author: *"The Sun Also Rises" and "A Farewell to Arms" placed Mr. Hemingway at the head of American novelists. His short-story collections, "In Our Time" and "Men Without Women," are critically recognized as among the best in their field. "Death in the Afternoon," Mr. Hemingway's "bullfighting book," published last year, revealed a new phase of the author's genius.*

The Book: Ernest Hemingway's first new book of fiction since the publication of "A Farewell to Arms" in 1929 contains fourteen stories of varying length. Some of them have appeared in magazines but the majority have not been published before. The characters and backgrounds are widely varied. "A Clean, Well-Lighted Place" is about an old Spanish beggar. "Homage to Switzerland" concerns various conversations at a Swiss railway-station restaurant. "The Gambler, the Nun, and the Radio" is laid in the accident ward of a hospital in Western United States, and so on.

Ernest Hemingway made his literary start as a short-story writer. He has always excelled in that medium, and this volume reveals him at his best.

The Market: *The Hemingway fiction following will want this book. "Men Without Women" was one of the best-selling volumes of short stories ever published. This one has exactly the same kind of appeal.*[52]

Winner Take Nothing was also listed in the firm's two-page spread announcing its fall list in the 16 September 1933 issue of *Publishers' Weekly,* but nothing was done to distinguish it from the nine other titles listed.[53]

Despite the stress placed on the fact that *Winner Take Nothing* was a return to fiction by Hemingway, the book received scant notice by reviewers compared to his previous books. Only nine reviews appeared in major American newspapers and magazines, only three of which were published within a week of publication, the change in publication date no doubt affecting the reviewers' schedules. Hemingway's scrapbooks contains only about thirty clippings of reviews or notices for the book.[54] As with *Death in the Afternoon,* the reviews were mixed. While Horace Gregory, reviewer for the *New York Herald Tribune Books,* claimed that the collection revealed growth on Hemingway's part, others, like Clifton Fadiman, writing in the *New Yorker,* saw the stories as mere copies of what Hemingway had done before and asked that he write about different subjects.[55]

The firm did not advertise *Winner Take Nothing* as vigorously after publication as it had other Hemingway titles. Between publication and the end of the year, the story collection was featured or listed in only six Scribners advertisements in the *New York Times*

Book Review.[56] What is even more unusual is that in none of these notices is *Winner Take Nothing* featured alone. At best, the book was one of four titles listed (29 October); at worst, it had to share the spotlight with twenty-two other Scribners titles (3 December). Scribners' advertisements for November also included two additional notices in *Publishers Weekly,* one in the 11 November issue and one in the 18 November issue. Again, neither of these is for *Winner Take Nothing* alone. The former, a four-page spread, is an advertisement for twelve titles; the latter lists five Scribners books.[57] In the final analysis, the campaign appears to have been a lackluster one. Scribners bought only ninety ads for the book, three of which appeared before September, while only five ran in 1934. Only ten appeared in newspapers outside New York City. In total, the publisher spent only $2,442.16 on advertisements, less than a tenth of what it had spent on *A Farewell to Arms.*

As usual, Hemingway reacted angrily to the reviews and the sparse advertisements. On 17 November, five days before he left for his African safari, he wrote Perkins about what he thought of the firm's efforts and the critics:

> The advertizing is your business—not mine. But if a publisher seems to give no importance to a book and make no Boom Ha Ha the public takes the cue from the publisher very quickly.
>
> One of the reasons I always stuck by you was (in a commercial way) because you kept on pushing The Sun Also Rises through a terrificly slow start—And one of the things I did not care much about was the way after a wonderful start they dropped Death In The Afternoon absolutely cold. You know yourself.
>
> This happens to be a book *you* have to do a little work to push—But in the end it doesnt do anyone any particular harm to publish literature once in a while—Especially as I have always paid my way.[58]

Hemingway's rage was not destined to be stilled by the sales of the book. A week after publication, the outlook was good; Perkins reported that sales were close to 9,000 copies.[59] On 10 November sales had surpassed 10,000 copies.[60] Sales dropped off sharply in November; by 12 December only a total of 12,500 copies had been sold.[61]

After the first of the year, orders had come to a halt; Perkins reported on 12 January 1934, "The sale at the present moment amounts to thirteen thousand, six or seven hundred copies. We are now at that stage at which you came in last year:—many copies are on consignment of all the leading books, and we do not know what we may have sold out of the consignments. I hope we shall get to fifteen thousand by the time that is cleared up."[62] The printing card indicates that as of October 1937 the firm still had on hand 2,350 of the 20,300 copies printed in October 1933. Another note, made on 24 June 1940, indicates that 2,000 copies were "Jobbed" to "Outlet" (i.e., remaindered to the Outlet Book Company), while 250 copies were kept by the firm.[63] The best estimate, therefore, would be that Scribners sold only 18,300 copies of its 20,300-copy printing. At a 15-percent royalty rate, Hemingway would have made only $5,490 for this edition of *Winner Take Nothing*. The sales did not cover the $6,000 advance.

Hemingway would consider and analyze this failure later. From December 1933 to February 1934 what mattered most to him was Africa. Led by Philip Percival, a white hunter who had been on safari with Theodore Roosevelt, Hemingway discovered a new world. Despite his bout with amoebic dysentery, the safari was one of the high points of Hemingway's life, culminating with the killing of two greater kudu bucks on the last day.[64] Writing from Nairobi (where he had gone for treatment of his dysentery) on 17 January 1934, Hemingway told Perkins, "This is the finest country I've ever been in. Believe we will settle here. Wonderful people and splendid climate. Pauline is mad about it."[65] The last month of the safari would serve as the basis for Hemingway's next book, *Green Hills of Africa*.

The Hemingways returned to America at the beginning of April 1934; no doubt Hemingway met with Perkins soon after landing in New York. Using an advance for future contributions to *Esquire* from editor Arnold Gingrich, Hemingway made a down payment on a fishing cruiser, the *Pilar*.[66] He and Pauline then headed for Key West. Back home, he returned to the publication of *Winner Take Nothing*. He claimed that he had gotten the book out too quickly because he had taken an advance. The collection, he wrote, needed another simple story that would have been easy for the readers to understand, to which he added, "But I am a professional and professionals learn by their mistakes instead of justifying them. So that won't happen again."

After giving his opinion of Fitzgerald's recently published novel, *Tender Is the Night*,[67] he left Perkins with some good news: "Am going well but it is hard going. Have 20 good pages now on a story and 30 bad ones—discarded—Some are certainly easier to write than others. But am writing the kind that is hardest for me to do. Will do one of the easier ones next." He did not tell Perkins exactly what he was writing, but this is clearly the beginning of his book on Africa. Although he called it a story, his statement that it was "the kind that is hardest for me to do" indicates that the piece was nonfiction, since earlier in the letter, when discussing Fitzgerald, he had written, "using actual stuff is the most difficult writing in the world to have good."[68]

Despite his fishing nearly every day on his new boat and the necessity of writing a "Letter" every month for *Esquire,* Hemingway made rapid progress on his safari memoir.[69] Instead of covering the whole trip, the piece recounted only the final month and the quest for the greater kudu, thus giving it a sharp focus. Although he did not give Perkins any details about the work, he did give frequent reports on his progress and state of mind. For example, on 20 June, just two months after beginning, he wrote his editor:

> I have been headover heels, under water, not coming up to breathe or however you wish to characterize it on this thing I am writing. Am on page 141 of the mss. (something over 20,000 words of triply re-written shit-removed mss. so far. Will run another 10,000 it looks.)
>
> Am not troubled by the lack of confidence, what will the critics say, general impotence jeebies that seem to be driving the boys to religion, religious economics, or just not finishing anything. And am getting the old fourth dimension into the ladscape again. So feel pretty good.[70]

Hemingway was only in the middle of what would be chapter 5 of the published book at this point.[71] He still had much writing ahead of him. Perkins, however, did not seem to take much notice of Hemingway's progress; during the summer of 1934 he was too busy helping Thomas Wolfe edit what would become *Of Time and the River.*[72]

By the beginning of October, Hemingway was able to report from Havana that he had "50,000 some words done on this long thing."

He also mentioned a novel that he had been writing and an idea for an omnibus collection of his short stories, tentatively titled "The First Fifty-Seven."[73] Perkins apparently confused the projects, thinking that Hemingway had 50,000 words done on a novel. Answering his author on 6 October, Perkins wrote:

> That about the novel is wonderful news. I won't worry about how it compares with other people's novels. I'd felt morally certain you were doing a novel, but not quite, because when you were here you spoke of having written a great deal on a narrative and of thinking you might reduce it to a story. Sidney Franklin did not know what you were writing, but he did tell me you had written a lot. You do a novel, and we shall strain every muscle for it. Things look better now, too,—if only they don't break them down in some new way. But let me know soon if The First Fifty-Seven could be published in the fall or the spring, or when. If the novel were imminent I would do the novel first.[74]

Hemingway did not correct Perkins's misconception at this time.

In mid-November, seven months after beginning the composition of the safari memoir, Hemingway wrote Perkins, "I finished the long bitch this morning, 492 mssspages, average, I suppose, something over a hundred and twenty words to the page."[75] On 20 November he wrote Perkins more fully about the work and his ideas for publishing it:

> I've been over a little more than half of it 3 times re-writing and cutting so I dont imagine will cut more than 3 or 4 thousand words out of the last.
>
> I started it as a short story about while we were hunting in Africa, wanting it to be a damned fine story to go at the end of the First Fifty Four and kept going on and on—Until now it is as long as I tell you—But it has a beginning and an end—it the action covers almost a month—and after you have read it I think you will have been there—
>
> It is more like the story at the end of In Our Time—Big Two Hearted river than anything else—in quality—It is as much landscape painting, making the country come alive, but a hell of a lot happens in this one and there is plenty of dialogue and action.

There is plenty of excitement, I think—But you will know when you read it—I had never read anything that could make me see and feel Africa—It was not at all as I had imagined it or like any thing I'd ever read—When I started the story that was what I wanted to make—But just the straight story, the actual things that happened on that wonderful Goddamned kudu hunt—the relation between the people and the way it all worked up to a climax—seemed to me a very fine story. Anyway I have it done now—

Been starving me to do it for 8 months.

One thing I have learned this last year is how to make a story move—So that it seems short when it is really very long. I think this has that—Anyway we will see—

I've written it absolutely truly. *absolutely* with no faking or cheating of any kind but I think I have learned to make it smoother without sacrificing any honesty—This is as honest as the Big Two Hearted River and much more exciting—I make the excitement with the country—But there is so much more going on too.

Hemingway then suggested that, despite the safari narrative's length, he wanted to publish it either in a collection of his *Esquire* "Letters," calling it "The Highlands of Africa and Other Pieces," or in his collected stories, which he wanted to title "The First Fifty-Four": "It is a hell of a good book by its-self—but I want to get out a book of *super value* for the money—That is the best way to sell a hell of a bloody lot of them—After whichever is published first—either the collected stories or the collected Essays—I want to follow with a novel that will knock them cold. But I am not in a hurry about it—And can always publish both books first—I'd even write another novel and let this one wait. There is no hurry on anything that is any good."[76] Hemingway apparently thought that if he could not get good reviews and large sales with the quality of his work, he could do so by giving critics and readers a book so large they could not ignore it.

Perkins responded on 28 November. After telling how much he liked the *Esquire* pieces, Perkins suggested modifying the title to "In the Highlands of Africa," since this would make the book sound less like a travel book. He used most of the letter to argue against Hemingway's plans to publish the story in a collection:

I do not want to put anything so emphatically that it will embarrass you to overrule me if you must, but it is my strong conviction that this story ought to be published by itself. It detracts from a book to add anything else to the same volume. It does not make it more desirable, but less so. This comes partly from the fact that publishers always are padding books, and everybody is on to it. They get a story of 25 or 30 thousand words and it is too short to interest the trade,—the price would be so low that the margin is too small. The public seems to object to small books, so then they proceed to pad it. Either they pad it by putting in a great many half titles and some illustrations, or much more often by asking the author for short pieces to add to it, or short stories. It is never so good as a complete unit. What is more, I do not think it is so good absolutely. "Spring Freshets" is really a long story, but it ought to be published by itself because it is a masterpiece, and ought not to be thought of with anything else, but only by itself.[77] If this book were only 40,000 words, I would say, publish it alone. Then, to revert to the purely practical: when the reviewers review the book with the short pieces added, their comments would be somewhat vitiated by being scattered to some extent over the other pieces. I hope you will publish it by itself.

The other possibility was to put it in the lead of "The First Fifty-Seven." That would make a very big book for one thing. But the chief objections I have to it are the same ones that apply to the addition of the Esquire pieces. The reviews then would be of all the stories. I see that you regard this as a story, not a novel, but that makes no difference.—It is a complete unit and considerably longer than would be necessary to make a full book. Besides, with this story you are writing you will have plenty to give "The First Fifty-Seven" the element of new material that is needed and fine things too.[78]

Perkins's arguments must have convinced Hemingway, for in his 14 December letter to his editor there is no mention of his plans for either omnibus. Instead, Hemingway now raised the idea of serializing the work; he also urged Perkins to come to Key West so he could read the manuscript and they could then talk face-to-face about Scribners' publication plans.[79] While visiting his in-laws in Piggott, Arkansas, Hemingway wrote Perkins on 28 December to iron out details for the visit to Key West. He said that he would be back in Florida by 5 January but wanted a week to ten days alone to go over the typescript before he met with Perkins.[80]

Perkins and his wife, Louise, arrived on 23 January for an eight-day stay. No complete record of the author and editor's discussion exists, but they did talk about serializing *Green Hills of Africa* in *Scribner's Magazine*. Perkins seems to have been pleased with what he read. On 31 January, he sent Fitzgerald a postcard, on which he wrote, "HEMS BOOK IS ABOUT HIS OWN HUNTING IN AFRICA, BUT DIFFERENT FROM ANY OTHER HUNTING BOOK MAGICAL IN THE LAST THIRD."[81]

Despite his admiration for the work, Perkins did not make an offer to serialize during the trip to Key West, as he needed the approval of Dashiell and Charles Scribner II. After his return to New York, Perkins wired on 4 February that all at the firm wanted to serialize it, but that they needed to see the work first.[82] The next day he wrote to outline the preliminary serialization plans:

> I talked with Charlie and with Dashiell almost the moment I got here, and gave them an account of the book, explaining everything I could about it. They were both greatly taken with the idea of serializing, and so I sent the telegram. The point is that we run the magazine on a monthly budget. The amount paid for a serial has to be apportioned equally to the number of issues it appears in. If we ran it in very large sections it would run way above our budget for the number. We want to run this if we possibly can, in seven numbers, with the idea of publishing the book in October. In order to figure it out that way we have to see how the book would divide up, and I could not remember it at all in the mechanical way that would be required to judge of the number of words between one incident and another. It is rather a hard problem, but we have every kind of will to work it out and if you will send the manuscripts, we shall do it quickly.[83]

Gone were the days when Perkins could essentially accept serials for the magazine himself.

Hemingway had supposedly turned down an offer from *Cosmopolitan* to serialize the book because they had asked him to cut it to 45,000 words.[84] He sent the typescript to Perkins around 7 February. In the accompanying letter, he revealed his frustration over the magazine's delay in making him an offer:

> The reason I waited was because, you may remember, you were to let me know as soon as you got back what was the price you could pay for serialization so I would know how to make my plans. By *not* letting me know and by asking for the mss. you jeopardise my disposing of it otherwise as it will be too late to make other plans for serialization and still publish in the fall. Being a business man you must know that. I have held up all marketing of it while waiting to hear from you and you are losing me plenty of money.
>
> Nevertheless am sending the mss. today with a sheet of paper enclosed suggesting a division of seven installments. You may wish to modify this according to space requirements; but it is one possible division. . . .
>
> If it will help you out to pay the serial price, provided it is satisfactory, each month out of the months budget rather than have to raise it in a lump sum that would be all right with me.[85]

Perkins apparently thought arrangements could be worked out to everyone's satisfaction, for on 8 February, before the typescript had arrived in New York, he wrote Hemingway to express his admiration for the work and to request that he send some photographs of the safari to the magazine's illustrator, Edward Shenton.[86] Shenton had recently drawn the pen-and-ink illustrations used in the serialization of *Tender Is the Night* in *Scribner's Magazine;* these drawings were so effective that they were also included in the book.

Perkins received the typescript on 11 February.[87] Around this date he sent Hemingway a handwritten letter, once again probably to ensure that no file copy could be made. Perkins wrote that when he was in Key West he thought that the serial could run in six or seven installments, for each of which Hemingway would be paid $600: "What was in my mind *then* was $4,200,—600 a number, twice what we pay for anything else. You, when we last talked, mentioned $5,000. Can't we stop here till we get the ms. I'll do rightly + wont let you be put in a jam by any personal considerations. The whip is in *your* hand if we come to that."[88] With the poor business climate and state of the magazine, Perkins seems to have been trying to prepare Hemingway for a lower than expected offer.

Four days after receiving the typescript, Perkins wired that the magazine would pay $4,500 for the serial and that Scribners expected to publish the book in October.[89] He also sent a letter the same day to explain the decision:

> You know how we feel about price, and in reality we stretched it a great deal more than would seem to be warranted on a money basis, to get it to forty-five hundred. It is not a question of what "Green Hills" is worth intrinsically at all, but of what we can rightly pay for it and still run the magazine on as nearly sound an economic basis as the present situation allows, which is not a sound one. Three hundred dollars for a single piece is the highest we ever pay now. A serial should cost more, even looked at by installments, but this is over twice as much. We do not intend that there shall be any hard feelings about the price, but I do want to tell you as plainly as I can what the facts are.
>
> It seems to us that the narrative divides up very well, and 10,000 words an installment is really long enough for a serial, and we exceed that by a little.[90]

Hemingway received Perkins's letter on 18 February, and that night he fired off an angry telegram with a list of Scribners' supposed past crimes against him and a veiled threat to leave the publisher as he had left Boni and Liveright:

> LETTER JUST RECEIVED SORRY UNABLE UNDERSTAND YOUR ATTITUDE PRICE UNLESS YOU MEAN YOU WANT ME TO REFUSE IT TO RELEASE YOU FROM PURCHASING STOP WHAT DOES WE NOT INTEND THERE SHALL BE ANY HARD FEELINGS ABOUT PRICE MEAN STOP AND ON HOW SOUND AN ECONOMIC BASIS DID I OFFER IT TO YOU STOP THE MAGAZINE HAS NEVER BEEN ON A SOUND ECONOMIC BASIS AND NEITHER HAVE I BUT IVE NEVER COST A PUBLISHER ANYWHERE ANY MONEY EITHER EXCEPT LIVERIGHT BY LEAVING HIM STOP WHEN OFFERED YOU FIFTY GRAND YOU WANTED TO CUT IT AS TOO LONG LATER YOU GAVE FIVE THOUSAND DOLLARS FOR A LONG SHORT

STORY CONTEST STOP I TURNED DOWN THREE TIMES WHAT
YOU PAID ME TO PUBLISH FAREWELL IN THE MAGAZINE STOP
CAN YOU WONDER WHY DON'T UNDERSTAND THIS WHEN OUR
CLEAR AGREEMENT WAS YOU WERE TO WIRE ME AS SOON AS
YOU REACHED NEW YORK WHAT YOU COULD PAY[91]

The money itself does not seem to have been the real issue. Rather, it was what the money represented to Hemingway: tangible proof that he was valuable to the publisher and that he held the upper hand in his dealings with the firm. By the next day, however, Hemingway had calmed down and wired his agreement to the terms, saying that he would send some photographs for Shenton.[92]

That same day Perkins wrote a letter (probably right after he read Hemingway's wire of the eighteenth) to clarify the firm's position:

When there is a misunderstanding it never does any good to attempt explanations. It generally makes things worse. But the truth is my attitude has always been perfectly simple and there has never been in it any intention that it should be anything else. What I intended you to think was that we would make you the highest price we possibly could in view of the situation of the magazine, which I tried to explain, and that in order to do this, if the road was clear for the serial, we would have to spread it over as many numbers as we could without detriment to time of book publication, for the sake of spreading the payment. If I misled you, it was not in discussing the price more specifically when I was there at the time you mentioned five thousand. I had begun by saying between four and five thousand, and that was all that was said because I could not tell how many numbers we could run the serial in, and I thought it possible, though unwise, that we might be able to catch an earlier number to start with, and run it in eight, which would have made the five thousand easy. When I got back that was impossible. Anyway, it would have been too many numbers. Seven is a good many to stretch something over that ought, ideally, to be in one number. Surely I could never have given you the idea that we did not want the serial. I had never considered the possibility of serialization before you brought it up because I knew our price would seem low to you, and I simply regarded the thing as beyond our reach. In each of my letters I pretty clearly said that we would meet your price for we always have been completely for you since the first day we had anything here of yours,—unless you accept the matter of "Fifty Grand" and the magazine of that day.[93]

Dashiell (perhaps with urging and assistance from Perkins and Scribner) came up with another $500, for Perkins wired on 19 February that they would pay the extra $500 if he wanted it.[94] Apparently, all concerned thought it best to keep the increasingly difficult Hemingway—who was seeing an erosion of his critical reputation and of the big money he was accustomed to being offered—happy.

Hemingway responded to Perkins's letter on 22 February. After stating that he thought it best not to include any drawings of dead animals in the serial, he explained why he had blown up at his editor. Hemingway wrote that while he trusted Perkins, he thought the editor had mishandled the negotiations with the magazine. He added that he was now tired of discussing the matter.[95] Perkins replied on 27 February, confirming that Hemingway would get $5,000 for the serial and adding, "I guess you got me beaten with that analogy about fishing because that immediately fills me with an inferiority complex which I cannot override. So anyhow everything is all right with me. I only did not want you to think that I would do anything but wholly on the level."[96] Once again there was peace between Hemingway and Scribners.

Perkins did not take an active role in editing the serial of *Green Hills of Africa*. He did, however, serve as a liaison between Hemingway and Dashiell. The complete typescript was sent back to Hemingway for further editing on 20 February.[97] By 5 March, proofs for the first installment had been sent to the author.[98] Hemingway apparently revised this section fairly quickly, for he wrote Perkins around 8 March, "I sent the proof of the first installment off to Dashiell by air-mail from Miami yest. afternoon. I believe I improved it some. Am going over the second installment again. If you can get any reader into the third installment you won't have to worry about them stopping it. Its tempo increases all the time as it goes along. From Droopy's country on its probably best prose I've written."[99]

While Dashiell was getting the serial ready, Perkins was considering how to handle the publication of the book for the fall. The Hemingways had taken many photographs while on safari, and Perkins considered the advisability of including some in the book. He advanced the idea of including some photos at the end of the text, as had been done in *Death in the Afternoon.*[100] But he was not convinced, as he explained to Hemingway in a letter of 4 April:

> I am having a sample page made up for "Green Hills of Africa," the book, which I shall soon send you. The thing that has troubled me is what I spoke of yesterday,—that the book has the quality of an imaginative work,—is something utterly different from a mere narrative of an expedition. (I am not trying to tell you this, of course, but have to say it the way you have to begin in geometry by saying that a straight line is the shortest, etc.) Just the same, it has also the value to hunters and people who care for adventure, of a record. It tells so much about animals and the way things are in Africa, about shooting and hunting.— This value it has as a record is enhanced by photographs, but the other and greater value, is injured by photographs. I therefore wondered if we could not put the photographs at the end of the book, except for a frontispiece. We could use sixteen of them that way, and I hoped that you would write long captions for each one which would be aimed at the people who would value the book as a record, and as telling about animals and hunting. We could then make a book to sell at $3.00 . . . What do you think of this plan? $3.00 is not too high for the book, which according to the Magazine estimate comes to almost 90,000 words, if not quite to that. In fact a good many novels, though they are long ones, are sold for that price without apparently injuring the sale.[101]

Hemingway agreed that the book had more of the qualities of a purely imaginative work than of a hunting memoir. In his letter to Perkins before he left Key West for Bimini, Hemingway vetoed the idea of running photographs:

> About the book. The only pictures that have to do with it are the one looking over the country from the hill for rhino, the picture of the kudu horns and Kamau against the hut, and possibly the lion turning to look back. They are swell. The other fine lion pictures have nothing to do with it.

Why not just run it straight and use, perhaps, one swell picture as a frontispiece? You could use another in the jacket perhaps, or for the back of the jacket. I don't think pictures help the book. I make the pictures in it. If I had wanted pictures would have had other and better ones. I have them, beautifully, on the cinema film but do not believe they would enlarge large enough. Remember I have a certain standard of pictures to beat in Death In The Afternoon and if I were writing a book with pictures would want to beat those.

This is my reaction at present.

That way the book would sell for 2.50 wouldn't it?

Don't advertise the book as a novel. It is neither a novel nor a travel book. It is a book that you can sell as well as Fleming's first book with the additional advantage of haveing a known name to it if you handle it right.[102]

If you cant get anybody to figure out what sort of book to call it will try to help you out.[103]

Hemingway was attempting to achieve with nonfiction the same effects that the best fiction had and therefore did not want *Green Hills of Africa* to be marketed merely as a travel book. Throughout the work he had addressed what good writing should do to the reader, and he used these same criteria and terms when writing about *Green Hills of Africa*. In the memoir, the narrator (Hemingway) tells Kandisky that the best writing has a "fourth and fifth dimension." Later, when the safari stops at midday, Hemingway reads Tolstoy's "The Cossacks" and is "living in that Russia again" before considering how the best writing is able to make him feel as if he had lived those experiences.[104] Time and again in his correspondence with Perkins about *Green Hills of Africa* Hemingway would say this was the effect he had achieved with the book.

Green Hills of Africa began appearing in *Scribner's Magazine* in the May issue and ran through November.[105] Hemingway was mostly pleased with the presentation, writing Perkins on 1 May, "I think Shenton is damned good in the first number."[106] One mistake occurred when a "220-grain bullet" was referred to as a ".220-caliber bullet," but Dashiell promised to catch that in the subsequent installments.[107] Additional editorial help was soon available. In Bimini, Hemingway was reunited with Baron von Blixen, former husband of the Danish author Isak Dineson, and Philip Percival's partner in Kenya. Blixen offered to correct the Swahili and the place-names in the work. On 3 June, when he sent setting copy of the August and September installments, Hemingway requested that a set of proofs be sent to Blixen as well.[108] Perkins, sending the first batch of galley proofs for the book on 5 June, said that he would send Blixen copies of the published installments and proofs of those not yet published to correct.[109]

Few problems arose during the serialization. On 10 June, Dashiell wrote Hemingway asking that the word *condom,* used twice in the fourth installment, be removed or changed.[110] After getting both proofs for this installment and the first batch of book galleys, Hemingway wrote Perkins on 19 June:

> I will go over the installment proofs I have just received from Dashiell at once and send them to him by the next mail—ie next Wed. or before if I have any way of getting them off. He queries the word Condom. I can change this to used rubber in one instance but it spoils the prose. It is a very serious passage. The description of the gulf stream. The word isnt put in to shock anyone but is used seriously. I am always the one who is asked to cut something out and I never use a word unless it is serious or necessary. Look at what other writers are allowed to use. No one would object to that word used as it is, where it is. If you spoil the prose in this book you spoil everything. Still I suppose a magazine has certain restrictions since people subscribe to it. But it was just because old Bridges was such a Dodo that he didnt know what it was about that everything in the first installment of A Farewell wasnt queried and cut out. It didnt seem to harm anyone.[111]

Answering Hemingway on 28 June, Perkins wrote that they should not run photographs in the book; he also explained the need to remove the word *condom:* "I think we shall have to go against that word. I know that everything you say is precisely true.—That passage is one of the finest you ever wrote, or anyone else ever did.—And nobody could have any right objection to it. But it is fanaticism that we have to meet,—it is the only way you can describe it. There is no sense or reason in it. We are always fighting with people about the question of words."[112] *Condom* is used twice in the passage describing the Gulf Stream in chapter 8. In the end, the phrases "occasional condom" and "empty condoms of our great loves" were changed to "occasional fishskins" and "empty rubber [*sic*] of our great loves" in the serial text; the words *condom* and *condoms* were restored in the book text.[113] The change no doubt upset Hemingway because the description of the Gulf Stream as a metaphor for the permanence of true art is the work's centerpiece. Another excision of obscene material in the serial text did not elicit any recorded remark from Hemingway. In Part V, Hemingway, after hearing Karl shoot, relates the following: "I remembered the old saying of the Indian in camp, 'One shot, meat. Two shots, maybe. Three shots, heap shit,' and I got out the dictionary to translate it for M'Cola. However it came out seemed to amuse him and he laughed and shook his head." The passage appeared in the manuscript but was cut in the serial text. It was restored in the book text.[114]

Hemingway was optimistic about the book's chances. On 2 July, he wrote Perkins to go ahead and run Shenton's drawings in the book. He then went on to give his thoughts on why it should sell and how Scribners should handle it:

I hope you can put it over. It may be what people want to read. We have hit that a couple of times ahead of the others and this may be another one. Nobody that I know has read it without getting excited and being held by it. . . .

I will send the proof off on the next boat. You make Blix's corrections from the installment in Droopy's Country that he read (I have that and will do it too) and from the others. Once Dan is referred to as Ben We must catch that. I will let you know about the advance. I think it should be based on a certainty of a sale of at least 15,000 copies if the book is handled rightly and given sufficent backing. I believe it should sell better than 20,000—Winner Take Nothing had not one element of popularity and everything to make it unpopular. This book has many elements that should make people like it—It is a long and good story. It is straight and absolutely true autobiography with no pulling of punches or lack of frankness with plenty of story interest, suspense and lots of conversation and it takes people bodily to a place they have never been and most of them can never go. Also it's the best writing I've ever done and the more often I read it the more I think it gets that extra dimensional quality I was working for—I think that Darrow should realize that he has something that he can sell aside altogether from its permanent value.[115]

The advance, based on 15,000 copies at 15 percent of the retail price ($2.75), would have been $6,187.50. However, the contract, dated 14 October 1935, specifies that the advance was $4,800. It is possible that Hemingway assumed that the price would be at or near $2.00. The royalty rate for *Green Hills of Africa* was Hemingway's by-then standard 15 percent of the retail price for the first 25,000 copies sold, and 20 percent thereafter.[116]

The same day that Hemingway wrote about the advance (2 July), Perkins wired because Blixen had not gotten his copy of the fifth installment proofs to Scribners; the editor suggested that they might get an expert in African languages to verify doubtful words.[117] Hemingway replied on 4 July to ask Perkins not to do so, since it would destroy the special sense of realism he was working toward in the book:

> [Blixen] wrote me it would be a great mistake to put all the Swahili in correct grammatical form as I state I am speaking it in monosyllables and as a sort of pigeon swahili. So *please* do not hire an African authority to buggar up all my intentions by putting in a lot of fancy spellings and erudition. I write it as it was spoken by and with Walsamba, Kibuyu, Masai and M'Bulus—To none of whom it is a native language but rather a foreign language used as a sort of pigeon english. It is only native to the coast tribes where it is a highly developed and very interesting Bauti tongue. But please don't let some African authority try to make everyone talk in a way they do not talk.[118]

Hemingway's intentions required even the language of the natives to be true to his experience, not true to the dictates of a linguist. This had been expressed in the text in chapter 3 (p. 52) where the narrator Hemingway thinks, "I used to make up sentences in Swahili with Arkansas and M'uzuri in them, but now it seemed natural, no longer to be italicized, just as all the words come to seem the proper and natural words."

Perkins apparently accepted Hemingway's artistic reasoning, for he did not suggest bringing in an expert again. Instead, he wrote on

9 July to say that Shenton was pleased that his illustrations would be used in the book. He went on to explain how things were going with the proofs and the plans for advertisements: "Everything is all clear about the proof except with respect to the fifth installment which was sent you. . . . As for the advertising, it will be good, and will be persistent throughout the season. What you have said of it in your letter is very much what I said in a more voluble statement in the selling points I prepared for the salesmen." Despite his continuing reassurances to his author that the book was really good, Perkins added, "You must finish a novel though before very long."[119] Perkins knew that what the public—Hemingway's public—really expected was fiction, novels like *A Farewell to Arms* in particular. If Hemingway were to remain popular, he would soon need to publish a novel.

Work continued through July on the setting of the galley proofs and the incorporation of Shenton's illustrations. There is no located correspondence between Hemingway and Perkins from 9 to 30 July about the galley proofs. Perkins apparently sent Hemingway the proofs in sections. Dashiell had kept a list of mistakes in the serial text to be corrected in the book.[120] This list—undated, unsigned, and typed—specified that all the names for animals except the Grant gazelle should be in lowercase letters. It also verified the spellings of certain place-names. Most importantly, the list instructed that after chapter 3 the Swahili words should not be italicized except for emphasis.[121]

By the end of July, all the galley proofs were nearly ready for Hemingway to check, but Perkins had to verify his plans. On 30 July he wired his author, "AFRICAN SPELLINGS GALLEYS TWENTY-FIVE TO FIFTY-SEVEN SENT YOU LAST WEEK WILL BE CORRECTED HERE ACCORDING TO BLIX STOP SENDING COMPLETE PROOF THURSDAY STOP UNCERTAIN WHETHER YOU PLAN CHAPTER TITLES AND SHENTON'S SCHEME DEPENDS UPON IT STOP IF YOU DO CAN YOU HOLD THEM DOWN TO FIVE OR SIX WORDS WHICH COULD be reconciled to scheme for illustrations."[122] Although the chapters had titles in the serial, these may have been Dashiell's creation, not Hemingway's. Hemingway wrote the same day with his decision: "I don't believe we want all those subheads on the chapters in the book. Those were just for the magazine. We will make 3 or 4 main divisions. Such as Part One—Part Two—Part Three—But I have to see it all together to do this—Each one subtitled as Pursuit and Conversation—Pursuit Remembered—Pursuit as Happiness. That is the way it was originally I believe—All that breaking up in subheads I think bad for book—O.K. for magazine and done for that—Or what do you think? Makes it less like a novel too to have chapter titles."[123] The following day Hemingway wired that he would return the galleys he had the next day and reaffirmed that he did not want chapter titles.[124] Perkins responded on 5 August: "I think you are dead right about not having chapter titles, and about having the three part titles. As soon as you know exactly where they did go—I suppose they will go where they did in the original manuscript, but I haven't got it—let us know. . . . Our advertising man, Weber, who has just read the book, is most keen about it."[125]

By 19 August Perkins had all the galley proof but was still not sure about the section titles, wiring Hemingway that day, "CAN YOU WIRE PLACES FOR PART TITLES STOP CANNOT FINISH PAGING WITHOUT KNOWING."[126] Hemingway's answer has not been located. Perkins wrote on 26 August that page proofs would soon be sent and that "your wire made the titles clear."[127] There is a strong possibility that in this unlocated wire Hemingway instructed that the book be divided into four sections and added the heretofore-unmentioned third section, "Pursuit and Failure" (chapters 10 and 11).

On 30 August, writing from the Harvard Club, Perkins sent a rather unusual letter to Hemingway. Besides giving advice on revising one section of *Green Hills of Africa,* Perkins encourages Hemingway to be true to his own artistic vision:

I'm glad you're going to write some stories. All You have to do is to follow your own judgement, or instinct, + disregard what is said, + convey the absolute bottom quality of each person, situation + thing. Isn't that simple!!—But it's what you have been doing. When you're ready do a novel. That's what they all must want. That's what they all tell me they want + want me to tell you. I don't think I can tell You anything. If what I have said should worry You + I knew it I'd beg you to disregard + forget it. I can get pretty depressed but even at worst I still believe—+ its written in all the past—that the utterly real thing in writing is the only thing that counts, + the whole racket melts down before it. All you have to do is to trust Yourself. That's the truth.—I say all this mostly because I sometimes have thought that You thought I ought to advise You, or keep You advised. I do that for lots of people who write as a trade. With You it seems superfluous + absurd because those things that are important to that kind of writer + affect his fortunes, ought not to have anything to do with You,—+ so far You have not let them. I hope You never will, too.

Perkins also suggested that his author revise the section where he called Gertrude Stein a "bitch."[128] Perkins may have feared the coming critical attack on *Green Hills of Africa*. In any event, this letter was one of the clearest and best articulations of the editor's view of his role and what he saw as important in writing.

The Stein passage that Perkins objected to came at the conclusion of chapter 3; in the second installment of the serial, the passage read:

"Mr. J. P. is really awfully brave, you know he really is. He's *so* lovely."

"Yes, and he doesn't have to read books written by some bitch he's tried to help get published saying how he's yellow."

"She's just malicious. She knew that would make you angry."

"It did all right. She's skillful when she's malicious, with all that talent gone to malice and nonsense and self praise. Well, she's cashing in now. Anybody can whenever he wants. How would you like a little cash, Baby?"[129]

On 7 September, in a letter mainly dedicated to describing the effects of a hurricane that devastated the Florida Keys, Hemingway gave his thoughts on the Stein passage and his revision:

About the Stein thing—I was just trying to be completely honest. I don't mention her name and what proves it is Gertrude? what would you like me to put in place of bitch? Fat bitch? Lousy bitch? Old Bitch? Lesbian Bitch? What is the modifying adjective that would improve it? I don't know what word to replace bitch with. Certainly not whore. If anyone was ever a bitch that woman was a bitch. I'll see if I can change it. (Have just found it and read it over and don't see what the fuss is about. Unless you think it gives the critics something to burp about. For Christ sake Max don't you see that they have to attack me to believe in themselves. You can't be popular all the time unless you make a career of it like Galsworthy etc. I will survive this unpopularity and with one more good book of stories (only these are going to be with plenty of action so they can understand them) and one good novel you are in a place where they will all have to come around and eat shit again. I don't give a damn whether I am popular or not. You know I never went in for it when I was. The only thing bothers me is that your business office will not have the faith in me that I have and will not see that I am working on a long plan instead of trying to be popular every day like Mr. Roosevelt. I need a certain amount of money too

All right. Let us take up the word bitch again.

Would you prefer fat female?

That is possible. I'll change it to fat female. or just female. That's better. That will make her angrier than bitch, will please you be not calling a lady a bitch, will make it seem that I care less about her lying about me, and will please everyone but me who cares only about honesty.

Well I've fixed it up now. It's all right. Have gotten more how I really feel about her and given it the small degree of importance that it deserves. It's all right now. Don't worry. . . .

I appreciate what you wrote about writing

Enclosed is the way the Stein part goes so you can get it reset now for the page proof. This fixes it up all right and puts the emphasis where it belongs. Also betters the end of the chapter I think and avoids the word bitch as applied to a Lady writer.[130]

Hemingway revised the passage to read:

"Yes, but I'm dignified with him. Don't you think he's wonderful."

"Yes, and he doesn't have to read books written by some female he's tried to help get published saying how he's yellow."

"She's just jealous and malicious. You never should have helped her. Some people never forgive that."

"It's a damned shame, though, with all that talent gone to malice and nonsense and self-praise. It's a god-damned shame, really. It's a shame you never knew her before she went to pot. You know a funny thing; she never could write dialogue. It was terrible. She learned how to do it from my stuff and used it in that book. She had never written like that before. She never could forgive learning that and she was afraid people would notice it, where she'd learned it, so she had to attack me. It's a funny racket, really. But I swear she was damned nice before she got ambitious. You would have liked her then, really."[131]

On 10 September Perkins gave his opinion of the revision, assuring Hemingway that he had the firm's complete support:

I wish you would send back what proofs you can, without waiting until you have finished all. We can begin to cast then right away. I think it was better not to call the old girl a bitch. I wouldn't feel responsible for trying to make you compromise now on anything important, but I would not think this was like that, and for Heaven's sake, Ernest, I don't believe you have to worry about us here. I know perfectly well what you are doing, or as much so as anyone could in the circumstances, and I know it is a long course you are steering on, and that you want loyal support, and faith in you. You must know that I know you are entitled to both, and intend that you shall get both. What you say about a book of stories and a novel is completely true too.[132]

Perkins of course knew that Hemingway would be seen as petty for attacking Stein. What is strange is what Perkins did not ask him to change: the attacks on the literary critics and, most surprising, the remark about his fellow Scribners author Thomas Wolfe. In chapter 4 (l.c. 71), Hemingway had written, "I wondered if it would make a writer of him, give him the necessary shock to cut the over-flow of words and give him a sense of proportion, if they sent Tom Wolfe to Siberia or to the Dry Tortugas. Maybe it would and maybe it wouldn't. He seemed sad, really, like Carnera." Perhaps Perkins did not want to appear to Hemingway to be favoring Wolfe. In any event the passage passed without comment from Perkins.

Around 14 September Hemingway finished going over the page proof. He requested that the list of people in the book that he had used in the serial be placed on the inside flap of the jacket. He also told Perkins, who had asked on 10 September for a list of sportsmen who might speak well of the book, that he could think of none, adding, "Am afraid you will have to try to put it over as literature. You're not just trying to sell it as a sporting book are you? I think it is the best book in a lot of ways that I've written but am probably prejudiced."[133] Perkins responded on 17 September that all would be done as Hemingway had asked, noting that the publication date would be 25 October, the late date necessitated by the conclusion of the serial.[134]

Prior to publication, the firm had extensively advertised *Green Hills of Africa* to booksellers. In *Publishers Weekly,* the firm had mentioned or listed the book in four of its advertisements.[135] The most extensive mention is in the first advertisement, where the book is described as "The story of a hunting expedition in Africa told with the suspense, perception and imaginative qualities of a fine novel. For the *whole* Hemingway audience—"Death in the Afternoon" enthusiasts and "A Farewell to Arms" readers alike." The book is merely listed in the others. While this is greater exposure in *Publishers Weekly* than any other Hemingway work, it is strange that no advertisements ran closer to the date of publication. In the trade catalog for its fall list, the firm ran the following description:

> The Author: *His "Death in the Afternoon," "A Farewell to Arms," "The Sun Also Rises" are among the most popular and widely discussed books ever published in America.*
>
> Mr. Hemingway in an introductory note explains a book which records the events of an exciting hunting expedition in Africa so skillfully as to infuse into a narrative those qualities of imagination, perception and suspense which one usually finds only in a masterpiece of fiction.

After quoting in full Hemingway's preface to the book, the description continues:

> The book takes you right into a strange, wild, beautiful land so that you feel it and see it. One might have read of a shooting of a rhino a thousand times, and yet never have known about it until the two rhinos are shot in these pages. And the Kudu. One would not think that a creature by that name, even though he turns out to be a magnificent game animal, could finally become as desirable a thing to a reader as the Golden Fleece was to Jason. But it is so, and this book in which the characters are real people but become as fascinating as those in fiction, is not paper and print, but a living experience which rises at the end to a pitch of beauty

and happiness that even Hemingway's novels have not exceeded.

The Market: *The nature of the book will please the "Death in the Afternoon" enthusiasts: the manner of its treatment will excite the "Farewell to Arms" crowd. In short, the whole Hemingway audience.*[136]

The advertising department was thus marketing the work as both fiction and nonfiction, which in the long run may have hurt the book since it was not easy for salespeople to classify.

Hemingway came to New York near the end of September and stayed a month. Prior to publication, Perkins must have known that the book would not do well. On 28 September he wrote Fitzgerald, "Ernest is here, now, in fine shape. . . . He has speculated several times about seeing, you, but he is bent upon writing stories,—has done a couple. Every writer seems to have to go through a period when the tide runs against him strongly, and at worst it is better that it should have done this when Ernest was writing books that are in a general sense minor ones. That is, the kind that the trade and the run of the public are bound to regard that way. I hope we can think of something to be done about it now and October 25th."[137] *Green Hills of Africa,* Perkins seems to have thought, would not be pushed hard by either literary opinion makers or by book sellers.

Green Hills of Africa was published on 25 October 1935 at $2.75. The firm ordered a first printing of 10,550 copies on 23 September. Initial orders were good, and another printing of 5,030 copies was produced on 24 October.[138] The book received eleven reviews or mentions in major American magazines and newspapers between October and December. In addition, Hemingway's scrapbooks contain clippings of about sixty additional reviews or mentions.[139] The reviews were again mixed. Carl Van Doren, reviewing for the *New York Herald Tribune Books,* called parts of the book "tiresome" but described it as having "prose that sings like poetry."[140] Charles Poore, in the *New York Times Book Review,* called *Green Hills of Africa* "the best written story of big-game hunting anywhere I have read."[141] On the other side of the fence, Bernard DeVoto scornfully wrote in the *Saturday Review of Literature* (which featured a photograph of Hemingway on its cover) that it was a "pretty small book for a big man to write."[142] The review of the safari book by Granville Hicks in the Communist periodical *New Masses* summed up his sentiments by saying that he thought it would do Hemingway good to write about a strike instead.[143] Perkins correctly analyzed the bad reviews in a letter to Fitzgerald on 26 October: "The unfavorable reviews are mostly colored by this prevalent idea that you ought to be writing only about the troubles of the day, and are disapproving of anything so remote from present social problems as a hunting expedition."[144]

The firm ran eight advertisements that featured *Green Hills of Africa* in the *New York Times Book Review* after publication.[145] Scribners did not advertise the book extensively into 1936, nor did it take any special efforts to single out *Green Hills of Africa* in its advertisements. In all but one, the advertisement for 10 November, Hemingway's memoir is advertised with other Scribners books. At best, it is one of seven books advertised (3 November); at worst, it is one of eighteen titles featured (8 December). The advertising department's records indicate that the book was not pushed extensively in any part of the country. Scribners bought only seventy-six advertisements for *Green Hills of Africa*, all but one appearing between 8 June and 25 December 1935; the only one to appear in 1936 was in the January issue of *Scribner's Magazine*. Only eleven ads in newspapers outside New York City were bought. In total, the firm spent a scant $4,796.03 to promote the memoir.[146]

Perhaps the advertising effort was not as vigorous as those for Hemingway's previous books since the firm may have thought that the serialization would attract a great deal of attention, as had happened for *A Farewell to Arms*. This never happened. For one thing, circulation had dropped for the magazine since 1929. Within two years the firm would sell it because of its losses. Also, *Green Hills of Africa* was never subject to suppression as *A Farewell to Arms* was and thus did not attract the newspapers' attention. In any event, Hemingway and Scribners could not make the magic happen again; *Green Hills of Africa* would be the last work Hemingway published in *Scribner's Magazine*.

Green Hills of Africa had strong initial sales, but it dropped markedly after December. On 11 December, the press had 3,048 copies on hand, indicating that 12,532 of the 15,580 copies printed had been sold. However, the press had 3,988 copies on hand as of 18 October 1937: 940 copies had been returned from bookstores.[147] Therefore, the most optimistic estimate of sales from October 1935 to October 1937 is 11,592 copies. At 15 percent of $2.75, Hemingway's royalty at

Hemingway, E.

HEMINGWAY, Ernest   GREEN HILLS OF AFRICA

October 25, 1935 - 2.75

Date	Publication	Amount
June 8, 1935	Publishers Weekly	24.00
June 22	Publishers Weekly	3.50
June 15	Publishers Weekly	4.00
June 29	Publishers Weekly	3.50 - 35.00
1935-36	American News Co. Catalog	12.00
November	What to Read in Books	10.00
Sept.. 21	Publishers Weekly	5.00
1935-36	Christmas Bulletin (Baker & Taylor	55.00 - 117.00
November	Latest Books	12.00 - 129.00
Oct. 27	N. Y. Herald Tribune	300.00
Oct. 27	N. Y. Times	593.76
November	Harper's Magazine	35.00
November	Atlantic Monthly	40.00
October 26	Saturday Review of Literature	60.20
November	Scribner's Magazine	20.00 - 1127.96
Oct. 25	N. Y. Herald Tribune	93.98
Oct. 25	N. Y. Times	84.25
December	Atlantic Monthly	28.00
December	Harper's Magazine	25.00
January	Esquire	180.00
Nov. 10	N. Y. Times	518.36
December	Book Dial	6.00
Nov. 10	N. Y. Herald Tribune	60.00
Nov. 3	N. Y. Times	198.78
Nov. 3	N. Y. Herlad Tribune	152.91 - 2524.88
Nov. 16	Saturday Review of Literature	16.52
Nov. 17	N. Y. Times	120.00
Dec.	Caravan	2.50
December	Yale Review	10.00
December	Scribner's Magazine	21.00
Dec. 1	Los Angeles Times	20.00
Dec. 1	San Francisco Chronicle	13.00
Nov. 26	N. Y. Times	39.99
Nov. 26	N. Y. Herald Tribune	42.84
Nov. 30	Boston Transcript	24.80
Nov. 29	N. Y. Sun	35.98
Nov. 30	Chicago Tribune	58.90
Nov. 27	N. Y. World Telegram	41.54
Dec. 7	Philadelphia Inquirer	19.00
Dec. 7	Chicago Tribune	36.00
Dec. 4	Boston Transcript	12.00
Dec. 11	Chicago News	25.00
Dec. 14	Boston Herald	17.00
Dec. 4	N. Y. Times	39.99
Dec. 4	N. Y. World Telegram	41.54
Dec. 3	N. Y. Herald Tribune	42.84
Dec. 4	Chicago News	40.30
Dec. 2	N. Y. Times	39.99
December 1	N. Y. Times	140.00
Nov. 30	Saturday Review of Literature	17.00
Dec. 1	N. Y. Herald Tribune	85.00
1935	Bowker Book Parade	40.00 - 3567.59

(over)

First page of the advertising schedule for Hemingway's memoir of his first African safari (Scribners Archives) best would have been only $4,781.70 for these 11,592 copies—not enough to cover the $4,800 advance. In 2005 terms, he would have earned $66,011.03.

Hemingway summed up the failure on 17 December 1935 for Perkins:

> My book was ruined by three things; First that price—it was much too high for the length of the book. I protested about this in advance but it did no good.
>
> 2nd—without even thinking about it I had offended the daily critics deadlily and they ganged up on it. The sidicated critics did the same. This was my fault.
>
> 3rd—You had a big advance sale. With any book by anybody it needed advertisement to move this and get the other sale started. Nothing was done to overcome the bad daily reviews by putting ads in those paper quoting from the good weekly reviews when it would have done some good. Ads at that time would have moved our advance sale. Instead the offensive was allowed to bog down completely and never gotten moving at all.
>
> My stuff is not now judged by whether it is good or bad interesting or dull but whether it is or is not A In Our Time B The Sun Also Rises C A Farewell to Arms D Death In The Afternoon. You may have noticed how this last which was hailed as lousy when it came out is now referred to with the hushhushe. It all gives me a pain in the ass.[148]

Perkins responded on 20 December, addressing all of Hemingway's points:

> As to the points you make in your letter: I knew, and I never dreamed that you did not, that you were telling plain truths to the reviewers in "Green Hills." I could have warned you about that, but I did not think you wanted it, and I do not believe you would have heeded it for an instant. Nor do I think you should have. You have always spoken out, and insisted on your way, and I think you are right in doing it. It is all a question of how long a view you take. You told the truth about them and it won't act against you over a fairly long space of time, but only momentarily.

As for advertizing, it is a matter that nobody can ever speak of positively and it would be silly for anybody to say they might not have done wrong about it.—But this is the fact. Orders were given that irrespective of results altogether, and because we knew we were right about the real value of the book, "Green Hills" should have the same backing in advertising as Sullivan, Van Dine, and "Europa."[149] We spent more on "Europa" because of its long time of publication and its extraordinary sale, but not more within the same period. We do not believe that you can answer unfavorable reviews by following them up two or three days later. You might if you knew when they were to appear, in the same issue. We have tried every turn and twist in advertising, and we do not believe that the daily papers have any value comparable to the Times and Tribune supplements. It is stupid that this is so, but we have been convinced of it. When a book goes in great style, the daily use of advertisement does keep it in people's minds, and so we used it on "Europa." We did do a good deal of it in the dalies on "Green Hills" but not until after you spoke of it.

I am not saying all this to dispute you, but merely to tell you what our idea was.—But nobody, not one bookseller, ever doubted the price of "Green Hills." Booksellers always kick about prices, that they ought to be higher or lower, and often cause publishers to change the prices. It is the one thing they do talk about if they have any doubt. Not one unfavorable criticism was made of the price of "Green Hills." It looked its price thoroughly.[150]

Perkins's letter reveals an important aspect of Scribners' advertising strategy. Books that continued to sell well, the profits of which went back into the advertising budget, were promoted more extensively than books that did not. While this may have been good business, it could not have been much solace to Hemingway, although he was a bit more subdued when he responded around the end of the year:

About the critics, offending same, I never thought about them at all. Only put down what I told the Austrian in response to questions and what I was thinking then. You remember Winner Take Nothing came out while we were away and I got the first reviews in Arusha and read them in the plane flying to Nairobi. That was how I happened to think about critics at all when I came back hunting after that time being ill in Nairobi. I didn't set out to offend them but to tell the truth and if the truth offended them tant pis. It is all to the good in a few years. But hard on you as publishers of present book.

About the other stuff—as I say I was never around N.Y. when a book came out before and certainly never will be again. Wrote my reactions. You do right to back the book regardless of immediate sale as you have a valuable property to protect and sooner or later will have a book that will outsell any of them. There is no hurry though. With the critics hating my gut the way they do could bring out Hamlet new and they would see no good in it. But who are the most talented and best writing of the kids coming up? Cantwell, O'Hara, Malraux say.[151] They are the ones that like and respect my stuff—not the disappointed bastards who write the columns and hate your guts because they think you are in the big money, because they know you despise them, because you called them angleworms in a bottle. The novelists can see how your writing develops. The critics can't all they can do is remember how wonderful Lady Brett was in the sun also rises.[152]

Hemingway's only solace was that other writers knew what was good, even if the critics and common readers did not. He knew he would be vindicated in time.

After *Green Hills of Africa,* Hemingway never published another nonfiction book during his life. He seems to have finally been convinced that to remain popular, both with the critics and readers, he would have to produce more fiction, especially novels. The next step was to regain some of the ground he had lost since the publication of *A Farewell to Arms.* He and Scribners would do so with *To Have and Have Not.*

CHAPTER 6

"THEIR MONEY'S WORTH"

To Have and Have Not *and* The Fifth Column and the
First Forty-Nine Stories

After *Green Hills of Africa,* Hemingway turned more and more toward fiction. In the period from 1936 to 1938, he completed his third novel, *To Have and Have Not;* published seven new stories; and wrote his first (and only) play, "The Fifth Column," which was published with his collected stories in *The Fifth Column and the First Forty-Nine Stories.* During this time Hemingway also returned to newspaper work; he covered the Spanish civil war for the North American Newspaper Alliance (NANA) and contributed articles on the war to Arnold Gingrich's new magazine, *Ken.* He made four trips to Spain in 1937 and 1938. Hemingway was an ardent supporter of the Republican side during the war and lent his efforts to the cause. In 1937, he helped make *The Spanish Earth,* a propaganda film used to raise money for the Spanish Republic. The Left and Hemingway would be allied as they had never been before because of the war, and the author became for a brief time the darling of magazines like the *New Masses.* Hemingway's activism placed him more and more in the public spotlight, attracting attention to the cause, himself, and his work. The years 1936 to 1938 marked an upswing for Hemingway in terms of critical regard and sales of his books. While *To Have and Have Not* and *The Fifth Column and the First Forty-Nine Stories* did not match the success of *A Farewell to Arms,* they were good sellers for the author and the firm, helping to recoup their losses after *Winner Take Nothing* and *Green Hills of Africa.*

From the end of 1934 thorough 1935, after the completion and during the editing and publication of *Green Hills of Africa,* Hemingway had been writing stories. By April 1936, he had five long stories completed: "One Trip Across," "The Tradesman's Return," "The Capital of the World" (first published as "The Horns of the Bull"), "The Snows of Kilimanjaro," and "The Short Happy Life of Francis Macomber."[1] Hemingway and Perkins's first idea appears to have been to include these in the collected edition of stories that Hemingway had mentioned in his letter of 20 November 1934.

By April 1936, however, Hemingway and Perkins had begun making new plans. On 6 April, Perkins wrote Hemingway asking about the collected stories: "We have got soon to have a title and begin to make active plans."[2] Hemingway wired two days later, "BEEN GOING AWFULLY WELL LATELY STILL WAITING FOR ANSWER MY LETTER NEARLY TWO MONTHS AGO ASKING IF YOU WANTED TO PUBLISH NEW BOOK OF LONG SHORT STORIES BEFORE COLLECTED STORIES STOP AM CONTEMPLATING SELLING SEVERAL LONG STORIES COMPLETED TO COSMOPOLITAN."[3] Perkins, responding on 8 April to Hemingway's wire, wrote that if there were enough stories for a volume of completely new work they would do so, placing the collected stories on hold. He then asked for the title and, when Hemingway could provide it, the setting copy.[4] Perkins apparently felt that new material would sell better than a collected edition of the previously published stories.

Before he could have gotten Perkins's letter, Hemingway wrote on 9 April to lay out his ideas on the next book and to get Perkins's opinion. Hemingway wrote that he had six completed stories: "One Trip Across," "The Tradesman's Return," "The Capital of the World," "Up in Michigan," "A Budding Friendship," and "The Happy Ending." (The last two stories were retitled "The Short Happy Life of Francis Macomber" and "The Snows of Kilamanjaro," respectively.) He was unsure whether to publish these and two unfinished stories alone or to include them with the previously collected stories in an omnibus collection. He needed to make a decision about publishing a collection in the fall fairly quickly because he wanted to publish some of the new stories in *Cosmopolitan*.[5] What the "two other long stories" were is not known. It is possible it was material that was eventually incorporated into the third part of *To Have and Have Not*.

Perkins appeared optimistic about the new collection. Writing on 15 April, the editor suggested another possible approach. In addition to including the new stories, he advocated including some of Hemingway's *Esquire* essays as well as "Up in Michigan" and "Who Murdered the Vets?"[6] Perkins was resurrecting an idea Hemingway had advanced after finishing *Green Hills of Africa*.[7] Now Hemingway opposed the idea. In a letter of 19 April, after bragging about how his work was admired by the Russians, Hemingway explained why he did not want to mix fiction and nonfiction in his next book:

> Am not very hot about mixing in articles and stories, Max. That just gives them the opportunity to dismiss it all, as Wilson did, as the trash I write for that Men's Clothing Trade magazine. If I publish a book of sporting and political pieces let it be bought by those who would buy it and damned by everybody else. But don't think it would be a good idea to take a book of the best short stories I've done and get it damned as a hybred book and cursed by all that N.Y. outfit that foam at the mouthe at the mention of fishing or shooting or the idea that I ever have any fun or any right to have any fun. By being in N.Y. last fall and seeing how it worked I know that they don't read books; just look for a damning point or a praising point and that must be economic. They can't tell literature from shit and I have no more illusions on that score, nor any of fairness., nor any idea but what they want to put me out of business. Nor will I ever again notice them, mention them, pay any attention to them, nor read them. Nor will I kiss their asses, kiss their arses, make friends with them, nor truckle to them. Am going to work by myself, for myself and for the long future as I have always done.[8]

Hemingway did not want a repeat of the critical reception of *Green Hills of Africa;* he knew that a book of his *Esquire* pieces, most of which dealt with fishing and hunting, would be too tempting a target for the leftist critics like Malcolm Cowley and Edmund Wilson. Perkins accepted Hemingway's view. On 6 May he wrote his author, "Maybe some day we can make up a book of other kinds of writing,—but then it would probably have to be altogether those on sports."[9]

Through May and June, both Hemingway and Perkins held to the idea of publishing a new collection of stories. Hemingway on 2 June wired asking for an advance of $500 for the book, promising to deliver the setting copy by 15 August.[10] Perkins responded the next day that the money had been deposited in Hemingway's bank account.[11]

Hemingway soon changed his mind and shelved the idea of publishing a collection of the new stories. From Bimini, where he was vacationing with his family, he wrote Perkins on 11 July about a plan that *Esquire* editor Arnold Gingrich had advanced for a new book:

> Gingrich was down here and I showed him the 30,000 words I had done on the Key West—Havana novel of which One Trip Across and The Tradesman's Return were a part—I had taken these for the book of stories and he seemed to think that was crazy—I hadnt even looked at the 30,000 since I left off to finish the book of stories—Anyway Ive decided to go on and finish that book now when we go out West—That will only take 2 stories from a book—and will have plenty of others by the time you want the stories, and it can come out after this book—The book contrasts the two places—and shows the inter-relation—also contains what I know about the mechanics of revolution and what it does to the people engaged in it—There are two themes in it—The decline of the individual—The man Harry—who shows up first in One Trip Across—and then his re-emergence as Key West goes down around him—and the story of a shipment of dynamite and all of the consequences that happened from it—There is a hell of a lot more that I wont inflict on you—But with luck it is a good book—Gingrich was very steamed up about what he read and wanted me to promise not to bring out the stories until I'd finished this—I got the last stuff I needed for it on my last trip across—Also have the hurricane and the vets in it.

Hemingway then asked if the $1,100 advance he had taken on the story collection could be transferred to the novel. He told Perkins he had arranged with Gingrich to write only six "Letters" a year for *Esquire*—instead of one every month—so he would have time to work on the novel. He closed by noting that he would still have enough stories for a new collection: "If I can lift those 2 and finish this other then with only a couple more stories I have 2 books instead of one and one of them that thing the pricks all love—a novel."[12] After seven years, Hemingway was preparing another novel.

Contrary to Hemingway's fears, Perkins was happy, wiring on 20 July, "DELIGHTED BY YOUR CHANGE OF PLAN FOR BOOK STOP WRITING."[13] The next day he wrote his author to praise his latest story and his ideas for the novel:

> I read "The Snows of Kilimanjaro" last Thursday on a train, and with the greatest pleasure. . . . It is a very fine story,—the end magnificent. "The Short Happy Life" is not out yet,—probably in the September number. Waxman told me about that story, and I am mighty anxious to read it.
>
> About your change of plans, I wired that I was delighted, and the fact is I could not have got a letter that would have bucked me up more. It is a fine change, and the novel ought to be all by itself, and much better from our point of view, than a book of stories.—Much better to have a novel come before a book of stories. The only thing that has ever worried me is the long interval between your books of fiction—that is the way publishers look at things, being conscious of the trade—but I had actually been reflecting upon the postponement of the book of stories anyhow, this being a Presidential year, and the time of publication necessarily rather late. I hope we can bring it out very early in '37. But everything now is first-rate, and it looks to me as if things were shaping up better in many ways. . . .
>
> P.S. As for the advance, let it go against the novel, or else let it be divided between the novel and the story, either way you prefer,—or any other way you prefer. We would put it against the book of stories, for that matter, if you want it, but that would be putting it off a pretty long time.[14]

Perkins's excitement over the prospect of a new Hemingway novel and his desire not to anger him may have been the reason he did not comment in this letter about one aspect of "The Snows of Kilimanjaro." The story included a belittling comment about "poor Scott Fitzgerald" and his "romantic awe" of the rich. The comment sparked an angry exchange of letters between the two writers, with

Perkins caught in the middle.[15] Perkins, after finding out how upset Fitzgerald was, wrote him on 23 September, "As for what Ernest did, I resented it, and when it comes to book publication, I shall have it out with him."[16]

Hemingway spent the rest of the year working on the Harry Morgan novel. To "One Trip Across," he added seven new paragraphs that give the first view of Morgan at home in Key West to the end of what would be chapter 5. In "The Tradesman's Return," he changed the names of the government men who surprise Morgan and condensed the account of their confrontation with him in what would be chapter 7. By the end of September, Hemingway believed that the end was in sight. On 26 September, he wrote Perkins from Cooke City about the progress he had made and his plans for the next year:

> Have worked very hard on this novel ever since out here. . . .
>
> Have about 55,000 some words done. It has gone very well lately. . . .
>
> When finish this book hope to go over to Spain if all not over there. Will leave the completed Mss. in a vault so you will be covered on it. I can go over it again when I come back. In case anything should happen to me you would always be covered financially even without this novel by the book of stories. . . .
>
> Hope to finish my first draft this month i.e. October. If I go to Spain will see you in N.Y. on way through.[17]

With the end seemingly so near, Perkins responded on 1 October, "I hope you will let nothing prevent the publication of a novel in the Spring."[18]

Hemingway did not finish the novel in October. By November, Perkins's anxiety was great. He wired Hemingway on the fifth, "Hope you will soon send me word how things going and what you plan."[19] Writing from Piggott, Hemingway told Perkins that the publication would have to be pushed back to the fall of 1937:

> Been doing nothing but this novel. On page 354. will work probably all next month as it seems to get longer. Anyhow a long one is a better one now isnt it? Doesnt your Mr. Wolfe write very long books and Mrs. Gone With Wind too? Tell me if am misinformed.

If I dont finish until Christmas or later (and will have to leave it alone for a while before re-writing) you had better figure on it for fall instead of Spring as that would give us both plenty of time. . . . Going to have you a hell of a fine book Max full of everything poor people, rich people, reactionaries, revolutionaries, everybody. All in U.S. so far except just the opening in Cuba.[20]

Work on the novel was obviously not going as well as Hemingway would have hoped. But Perkins does not seem to have been too concerned after receiving this letter. In his answer of 13 November he wrote, "I read with greatest pleasure everything that you say about your book,—except that it won't be ready for Spring.—And the only thing against that is that I am impatient to see it, and to see it published. Otherwise it has no disadvantage, perhaps the reverse. But it sounds like a wonderful book, and that is what I feel sure it will be. . . . Don't consider the length of your book. It could not be too long. It is grand to hear that it is going so well."[21] Perkins understood that at this point what Hemingway needed was support. Five days later Perkins wrote Hemingway to clarify what money had been advanced. His records indicated that the firm had advanced Hemingway $1,250 against the royalties of the collected stories. Perkins suggested that this could easily be transferred to the collection of new stories.[22] On 24 November he wired Hemingway, "WHEN YOU DECIDE TITLE LET ME KNOW FEEL FINE ABOUT BOOK."[23]

But Hemingway apparently did not have a title yet. Writing on 2 December from Havana, where he had gone to verify information for the novel, Hemingway told Perkins that he was on page 412 of the manuscript, adding, "I wish I had this sonof a bitching novel finished. About yesterday I was ready to end it and call it vol one of a trilogy. I know now why the boys write Trilogies."[24] By the middle of the month he wired that he had gotten what he had needed and was returning to Key West to finish the novel.[25] From Key West the next day he repeated that information in a letter. He also added, "Am awfully sorry about the Tom Wolfe libel suit.[26] On this book of mine we will have to put something air tight in the front to make absolutely sure no one identifies themselves with characters."[27] Legal disclaimers had been standard for Hemingway's fiction books since the 1930 *In Our Time*. But with this novel there was a greater need.

The character of Richard Gordon was based on John Dos Passos, while the rich Helène Bradley was a thinly veiled portrait of Jane Mason, a wealthy friend of the Hemingways.[28]

On 2 January 1937, Hemingway was finally able to wire Perkins, "FINISHED BOOK TODAY." The editor sent his response by telegram: "Splendid news + best promise for Happy + Exciting New Year Many Thanks. I Know it was a great accomplishment."[29] On 7 January, Perkins wrote asking for the title and to say how pleased he was that it was set in Key West: "I was ever so glad to hear that you had finished the novel. Have you found a title? Now that it is done, it can be talked about better.—It has seemed to me that it had one great superficial advantage in being about a region that I think nobody has ever written well about, and a very rich and colorful scene. I remember the first time I was down there asking why you did not write about what you saw, and your telling me why in a way I understood. But you did get around to it when you had absorbed a sense of it and knew what part everything did play in the scheme of things. So I am not more anxious for anything than to see this novel come out."[30] Perkins would not get the title, however, until June.

The located correspondence between Hemingway and Perkins in 1937 is small compared to the surviving correspondence for the years before and after. The reason is that during that year Hemingway made seven trips to New York—en route to and from Spain, to make a speech and work on *The Spanish Earth*—and met with Perkins often during these trips.[31] This correspondence is, however, is adequate to piece together the story of the editing and publication of *To Have and Have Not*.

On 13 January, Hemingway was in New York to sign a contract to cover the Spanish civil war for the NANA. Before returning to Key West around the twentieth, he probably met with Perkins, but there is no indication that he took the manuscript with him or discussed the book with Perkins. Around this time Gingrich suggested modifying the Helène character so she would not resemble Jane Mason as much.[32] In early February, Hemingway wrote Perkins about the Spanish trip and his plans for revision:

Am working like hell on a title. Have a long list.
    Am going to go over the book entirely before and after I am in Spain. The version I complete before going to Spain. (I am

principally trying to better The Bradley part) will leave at the Guaranty Trust Co of N.Y., 4 Place de la Concorde, Paris with instructions to mail it to you in case I shouldnt be able to. But I hope to go over it again in time to get it to you to set it up in June Is that date O.K? What is the latest date you can set it up?

I found I needed more time to leave it alone to get a proper perspective on it. But you know the length, you can set up a few chapters of the first part (where I am making no changes) for the dummy as soon as we have a title and Mr Darrow can get going with it. Moe Speiser read it and liked it very much but when I told him how much I wanted to try to strengthen a part of it (which incidentally he did *not* think needed strengthening) he agreed that there was no necessity to set it up at once. We have plenty of time. I plan to leave for Spain before the end of this month. Going by way of Paris and clearing up everything so I can work on the book on the boat. I will complete a publishable draft Leave it where it can be sent to you. And then try, again, to improve it when I come out.

Will also leave one copy here with Pauline so there is no chance of losing it. When you get this will you please deposit $500.00 in my account City Bank Farmers Trust 22 Williams Street against the advance on the book. I think this brings the advance to $2000.00

Have been working on the book hard but need to be a little further away from it still to get that detached eye I need for re-writing. Am putting in more of the town too.

May be seeing you next week for a few minutes.[33]

Hemingway's statement that he wanted to improve "The Bradley part" indicates he was heeding Gingrich's advice. By 17 February, Hemingway was back in New York. The next day Perkins wrote him, "It will do very well if we get the novel in early June, but I hope it will be early. I hoped we could publish this side the middle of September, and all the proofreading might take quite a while, particularly if you were abroad. You ought to do it all the way your own instinct tells you."[34] By this point Perkins does not appear to have seen any of the completed novel.

Hemingway left for Spain on 27 February and returned to New York on 18 May, staying in the city for a week before returning to Key

West. On 4 June, he flew from Bimini to New York to deliver a speech entitled "Fascism Is a Lie" before the Second American Writers' Congress.[35] He stayed in New York for approximately four days before returning to Bimini. While in the city he must have suggested to Perkins that they publish the novel with the three new stories he had on hand. But Hemingway changed his mind after returning to Bimini, for on 10 June he wired Perkins, "HOLD EVERYTHING ON BOOK UNTIL YOU GET MY AIRMAIL LETTER NEWS GOOD STOP."[36] The letter outlined a plan to make the book into something much larger and very different from just the story of Harry Morgan. Hemingway's idea was to publish the novel with the uncollected stories and some nonfiction pieces such as "Who Murdered the Vets?" and "Facism Is a Lie":

> This would be a new sort of book—A living omnibus—and would take away the disadvantage of combining a novel with a book of stories to disadvantage of both—You could sell it as a major book by me and it would give them their moneys worth. I will be in Spain when it comes out and it will have the advantage of leaving things sort of tidied up. Also you have a good timely book in case I should run into any bad luck.
>
> It looks as though it were going to be quite a business now this summer and fall and I would like to have every thing in good order. . . .
>
> I think this is a damned good idea. An exciting novel—3 good stories—and this other stuff that brings it all up to date—But is worth preserving—For Titles I thought of
> > *The Various Arms*
> That is the novel, the story, the article, the newsdispatch and the speech.
> > or
> > Return To The Wars.
> Can maybe do better.[37]

Hemingway again thought he could win with quantity. He also seemed afraid of dying in Spain and wanted to leave the largest monument to himself that he could.

Perkins wired Hemingway on 14 June, "Think idea fine except in small details getting together material fast and will write Luck."[38] Three days later he explained what these "small details" were:

I could not get the speech until today, but now I have sent it air mail. It was this speech that made me hesitate to speak completely in favor of your plan,—though I am altogether in favor of it in every other respect. I do think that bringing in a speech, just because it is one, does tend to make the book seem too miscellaneous perhaps. I would rather favor leaving it out. I just read it, and it is as good as when delivered, but it deals with current events partly in a current way, in speaking of Bilbao, etc.—though not in what it says about writing, which is everlastingly true—and the articles, especially the New Republic one, while dealing with current events, do it in a way that raises them above that level. They make you feel the way the thing all was, and have almost the quality of fiction. I sent off the Wheeler ones right away and have only read those of them that were in the Times. But they must represent the rest.—Certainly the New Republic material is worthy of the book, and so is "Who Murdered the Vets" which I always wanted to see got into a book. I think all that will add to the value of the book.—In reading over the speech, and especially the part about writing, I thought perhaps the book might have a preface. I have got now to like the title "To Have and To Have Not" very much.—Certainly it fits the Vets in a literal fashion, and in some sense it fits everything that will be in the book. I would be for sticking to it.[39]

Hemingway made a quick trip to New York to record the voice track for *The Spanish Earth* around 20 June. It was on this trip that he delivered setting copy for the novel to Perkins, and the two must have met and decided against the omnibus plan.[40] But the reason for its rejection is not clear, since in their letters both men seem to have favored the idea. Hemingway may have concluded that since Perkins did not want to see "Fascism Is a Lie" in the book there would be little point in including the other articles. During this time Hemingway also clarified that the title, which had erroneously been printed on the salesmen's dummies as *To Have and To Have Not,* was *To Have and Have Not.*[41] There is an unsigned typed note, dated 24 June 1937, that reads: "The title of Hemingway's book is not as it appears in the Fall List, 'To Have and to Have Not' but: TO HAVE AND HAVE NOT."[42] The recipient of this note is not known, although it is logical to assume that it was sent to the sales and advertising departments.

Hemingway and director Joris Ivens flew to Hollywood on a fund-raising trip on 10 July. Galley proofs for the novel were waiting for Hemingway in New York by 16 June, as evidenced by Perkins's letter of that date: "They say at the Barclay that you are to be there tomorrow, and as we are closed tomorrow and I had to leave at five, I thought the best thing was to send all the proof around to you with your letters. . . . I have read a large part of the proof, as you will see by some of the marks at the beginnings of chapters. I shall read the rest in duplicate."[43] Hemingway stayed in New York until 21 July, during which time he and Perkins probably worked on the editing of the galley proofs. One decision that was made at this time must have dealt with obscene words. Unfortunately, no correspondence about these matters exists for the editing of *To Have and Have Not,* for in this novel Hemingway was allowed a greater latitude in regard to obscene words. For the first time, Hemingway was allowed to print in full the word *fucking.* In Harry Morgan's death speech, he tells the Coast Guard officers, "No matter how a man alone ain't got no bloody fucking chance."[44] No doubt the power and importance of the speech in the novel convinced Perkins that *fucking* should be printed.

When Hemingway finished going over the galley proofs is not known. By 5 August, he had the page proofs in hand, as indicated by a letter from Perkins on that date. In the same letter, Perkins expressed his concern over the dust jacket. Their friend Waldo Peirce had done two jackets, but neither was to their satisfaction. Perkins wanted an illustration that suggested the Gulf Stream, since "the scene of the book is in itself a great asset."[45] Peirce never got the illustration right, and in the end the novel was published with a jacket that featured only the title and author's name on the front. Hemingway wired on 9 August, "RETURNED PAGED PROOFS SATURDAY [7 August]."[46] Perkins acknowledged receipt the next day.[47] With the editing complete, the ball was wholly in Scribners' court. What remained was the launching and selling of *To Have and Have Not.*

On 10 August, Hemingway returned to New York en route to Spain for his second trip to cover the war. The next day he walked into Perkins's office to find Max Eastman there. Still angry about Eastman's "Bull in the Afternoon," Hemingway attacked the older writer, and the two ended up scuffling on the floor.[48] The fight proved to be a brief sensation in the press, resulting in three articles in the *New York Times* and one each in *Newsweek* and *Time,* as well as a satire

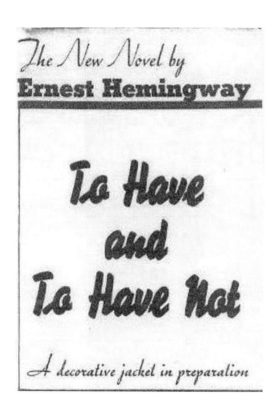

The New Novel by
Ernest Hemingway

To Have

and

To Have Not

A decorative jacket in preparation

Salesman's dummy for
To Have and Have Not
(Louis Henry Cohn
Collection, University
of Delaware Library)

in the *New Yorker*.[49] The fight and these accounts had nothing to do with *To Have and Have Not,* but they did provide a measure of free publicity to Hemingway, which may have helped the book. During 1937 Hemingway was frequently the subject of newspaper and magazine stories. From January to October 1937, there were thirty articles in important American newspapers and magazines about Hemingway and his activities. In addition, during this same period Hemingway gave four interviews and wrote sixteen dispatches for the NANA that were reprinted in newspapers around the United States. As John Raeburn has stated of Hemingway's activities at this time, "The doings of the public personality became more dramatic, more serious, more heroic, and altogether more newsworthy."[50]

Perhaps due to the amount of free publicity Hemingway generated for himself at this time, Scribners did not see the need to promote *To Have and Have Not* very extensively before publication. The book was advertised only once in *Publishers Weekly,* when the firm ran a one-page ad for the novel in the 2 October 1937 issue.[51] This was part of the firm's strategy that fall season. There was not the typical announcement of the fall list; rather, Scribners ran one-page advertisements for various books in *Publishers Weekly* throughout the season.

The Scribners advertising department decided to focus on the fact that *To Have and Have Not* was Hemingway's first novel in eight years, as was made clear by the firm's announcement of the book in its fall 1937 catalog:

To Have and Have Not
by
Ernest Hemingway
author of "The Sun Also Rises" and "A Farewell to Arms, etc.
Publication Date, October $2.50

For eight long years the public has waited impatiently for a novel from Ernest Hemingway to succeed his world famous *A Farewell to Arms.* Here it is—an exciting story of the romantic region of island and sea through which flows the blue Gulf Stream—the Keys of Florida, Cuba, and the many-colored waters between. The book teems with living characters—boatmen of Key West who must live by their wits in times of depression if not always, penniless veterans of the World War camped on the Keys, rich sportsmen and yacht owners and their restless wives, and gun-running revolutionaries from Havana.

The continuous thread of the story is the narrative of the adventures and fate of Harry Morgan, boatman, the real American individualist. He loves his wife and his child and his home, and it is up to him to take care of them.[52] He is always the independent man, but pressure of circumstances forces him into crime and involves his life with those of the wealthy and dissipated yachtsmen who throng the region. His adventures are most exciting to read of, and they affect the whole course of a series of dramatic events. Harry Morgan both has, and has not, and the wealthy characters have not, even while they have.

The Market for a Hemingway book is of course boundless.[53]

Another selling point was the American locale. However, the announcement is a bit misleading since the two threads of the story, the Morgan narrative and that of the wealthy yachtsmen, never really come together.

To Have and Have Not was published on 15 October 1937 at a price of $2.50. The contract for the novel has not been located, but Hemingway's royalty was probably his standard 15 percent of the list price for the first 25,000 copies sold, and 20 percent thereafter. Initial orders were very good. Before publication the Scribners Press produced two printings—the first of 10,130 copies on 27 July, and the second of 15,690 copies on 23 September. On the day of publication another 10,200 copies were printed, for a total of 36,020 copies.[54]

The novel received eleven reviews in major American newspapers and magazines. Hemingway's scrapbooks contain 135 clippings of reviews or mentions of the novel from American newspapers and magazines.[55] The reviews were once again mixed, but the balance was tilted toward those reviewers who did not like the book. J. Donald Adams, writing in the *New York Times Book Review,* concluded that Hemingway's reputation would have been stronger if *To Have and Have Not* had not been published.[56] *Nation* reviewer Louis Kronenberger called the novel "awkward and incompetent."[57] *Time* was by far the kindest, running a portrait of Hemingway on the cover and a feature article on him in addition to a review that declared Harry Morgan to be the best character Hemingway had ever created.[58]

Scribners spent a total of $9,325.74 on eighty-three advertisements for the novel in book trade publications and major newspapers and magazines. All but three appeared between September and December 1937. While this campaign was more extensive than the ones for Hemingway's previous three books, it was more limited than those for *The Sun Also Rises* and *A Farewell to Arms.* Only four ads appeared in Chicago and West Coast newspapers. The majority of the notices ran in New York papers.[59] After publication Scribners ran eight advertisements that featured *To Have and Have Not* in the *New York Times Book Review* in 1937.[60] Only the full-page advertisement in the 21 November issue was for Hemingway's novel alone, but the book was emphasized strongly in all the other advertisements—either by including drawings of the cover or photographs of Hemingway or by devoting more space to it than to the other books listed. For example, in the full-page advertisement for nine Scribners books that ran in the 17 October issue, four-fifths of the page was devoted to *To Have and Have Not.*

As was typical, Hemingway was not satisfied by the firm's efforts to push his book. Writing to Perkins from Key West on 1 February

1938, after his second trip to cover the war, Hemingway expressed his disappointment over the lack of advertising and the missed opportunity to make a really big sale:

> Aside from the big full page ad you sent me I didnt see much mention of the book or any sort of a campaign to push it when it had begun to sell. But as I say I was not in any position to see one if it had been made. Seems a mistake not to exploit any kind of a break-through—if there was any kind of a break-through. . . .
>
> Will you tell me, quite frankly, whether you plan to try to sell anymore copies of the book? I remember how you pushed the Sun Also after it got away to such a slow start and sold it for a long time after the first of the year. But that was a long time ago and the stock market was better and I guess it was a much more saleable book. Though the funny thing is; this is a good book. Could be sold too. But what the hell. If I sound bitter or gloomy throw it out. It's that it takes one kind of training and frame of mind to do what I've been doing and another to write prose. I'm making the shift, cutting out drinking during the day, nothing until five p.m. and nothing after dinner, and I'll write and it will be o.k. Meantime it is hell on the disposition and I also think the family and friends.[61]

In his reply of two days later, Perkins tried to show Hemingway how wrong the author was, explaining in detail the extreme measures the firm had adopted to push *To Have and Have Not*:

> I shall also send you a list of the advertising we did on "To Have."—We spent $9,500 in newspaper and magazine advertising, and we sent out hundreds of thousands of lists and circulars and Bookbuyers. We sent out through our own store, and other stores, imprinted, 87,000 postcards announcing the book to individuals, to arrive on the day of publication. We kept the book at the top of every ad. through the season. Of course it would have sold more if it had not been for what they politely call the "recession." We cannot push it in any big way, but we shall carry it along in all our regular advertising through the Spring. I know plenty of people who call this your best book, and I am sure that whether it was that or not—and comparisons always seem

pointless to me, each book being something by itself alone—it did represent a breaking through into new territory, and an enlargement of technique. It showed a lot of things.[62]

Again, the economy was blamed for the lack of a big success. Hemingway seems to have been satisfied with Perkins's explanation. His response combined a muted apology with complaints about his bad luck:

> Have never had much of a break on publishing years. Farewell to Arms came out in Oct. 1929 the day the market broke. Had to wait eight years to hit the next break right on the nose.
>
> You don't need to send the ads. I believe you, and I don't get any kick out of seeing my name in print. As you know I know very little about the business end of publishing. Certainly the Sun Also and Farewell to Arms were much easier books to sell than this. I know all the cards that were stacked against it. $9,500. sounds like a hell of a lot to have spent for advertising.
>
> I never doubted the plan nor the strength of your original attack and if you had 9500 casualties before there was any break through (and I don't even know there *was* any breakthrough; although it did look as though it had started to go once) nobody has any business to tell anybody else to gamble with their reserves.[63]

The printing records for *To Have and Have Not* bear out the fact that it was not the big success Perkins and Hemingway had expected it to be. There was only one additional printing (5,065 copies on 11 November 1937), for a total of four printings of 41,085 copies. But the card also shows that as of 9 May 1938, the firm still had 3,683 copies on hand. Therefore, only 37,402 copies had been sold in the seven months the book had been out. The last notation of the firm's inventory for *To Have and Have Not* shows 2,047 copies still on hand in 1945; the total sale was 39,038 copies.[64] Hemingway would have made $16,391 from this sale (which would equal $218,571.93 in 2005 dollars). A sale of over 37,000 copies within seven months was very good for the 1930s. *To Have and Have Not* sold better than any other Hemingway book published that decade. But the standard of success had been set for him and Perkins with *A Farewell to Arms,* with its sale in excess of 100,000 copies over two years. For the author and editor, a book would have to match or exceed those numbers to be considered a success.

Hemingway and Perkins did not dwell long on the perceived failure of *To Have and Have Not.* In addition to the idea for the collected stories, by November Hemingway had written a play about the war, "The Fifth Column." Pauline Hemingway had mentioned the play to Perkins, who then wrote Hemingway about it on 10 November.[65] No communication from Hemingway about the play was forthcoming, however.

At the end of the year Perkins started gearing up to publish the collected stories. He cabled Hemingway for his approval to set the stories in type.[66] Hemingway had another idea: to publish the play with his collected stories.[67] Perkins, however, thought this was a bad idea. On 3 January, he cabled his author, "THINK PLAY SHOULD COME OUT ALONE ON PRODUCTION AND IF THAT WILL BE BY APRIL BETTER PUBLISH IT ONLY AND STORIES IN FALL."[68] Hemingway gave his approval to proceed according to Perkins's plan on 9 January.[69] Hemingway sailed for New York on 12 January. Before returning to Key West, he may have met with Perkins. If so, it was probably during this meeting that they decided that the collected edition would include "The Capital of the World," "The Short Happy Life of Francis Macomber," "The Snows of Kilimanjaro," and "Up in Michigan."

On 1 February (in the same letter in which he complained about the *To Have and Have Not* campaign), Hemingway wrote Perkins that he would probably have to come to New York to see about getting "The Fifth Column" produced.[70] Perkins's response of two days later included his views on the play and the story volume:

I am glad you wrote. I had been expecting you would turn up almost any day because I thought you would have to come about the play.—By the way: I don't know how matters stand in that regard, but if for any reason it would help for us to publish the play before it was produced, which has sometimes been done, we could do it, of course. But the general scheme is to publish immediately on production because the production is generally what makes the play sell, and it sells most while the run is going on. We sold about 10,000 of "Idiot's Delight" by Robert Sherwood that way,—even though he did not give us the copy until the play had run for quite a while.—But this play of yours would sell without a production, and it is possible that its publication might have some value in connection with arranging for production. I am only saying this because I know almost nothing except the little Speiser told me, and it was that that made me think you would come up to New York right off. . . .

If we published a book of stories this Fall—that is, the omnibus book—we could do it quite early, even in August, and in that connection we could always carry it along as of equal importance with "To Have and Have Not." If we publish the play in the Fall too, I think it would do no harm either to the stories or to the play. A play is looked upon as a different thing altogether, generally speaking.[71]

Hemingway responded, "It may be necessary to publish play first. I'll let you know."[72]

Perkins was initially committed to waiting until the play was staged before publishing it. On 3 March, he wrote Hemingway to convey this opinion, noting that publication of "The Fifth Column" would not interfere with the story volume.[73] Hemingway was in Key West preparing for his third trip to report on the war in Spain when he wired Perkins: "NOW PLANNING PRODUCE PLAY EARLY FALL HOWS THAT EFFECT STORY BOOK PLANS MAYBE NECESSARY RETURN SPAIN WOULD LIKE ARRANGE EVERYTHING ORDERLY WILL HAVE SCRIPT PLAY FOR YOU READ THIS WEEK."[74] On receipt of this wire, Perkins telegraphed Hemingway, "NO DISADVANTAGE IN PUBLISHING PLAY AND STORIES SAME SEASON."[75]

Perkins had yet to read the play. On 15 March, four days before sailing for Spain, Hemingway sent Perkins the script, in addition to filling his editor in on details of the fall production: "Anyway the play is set for fall rehearsals guaranteed by September 15—Production by Oct. 15. May be earlier. I believe Austin Parker would like to open it in September. So that is what you need to know about publication date. I will probably change the title. Am sending the script to you, now, to read. But please return it to me as I have, as yet, no other copy and must make quite a few corrections and changes."[76] Since Hemingway mailed the play to Perkins, they probably did not see each other when Hemingway passed through New York en route to Spain. Perkins did not turn his attention immediately to the play. He finally cabled Hemingway on 6 April, "GREATLY MOVED BY PLAY

IT IS MAGNIFICENT ALL GOOD LUCK."[77] The next day he sent a fuller report of his ideas for the play and stories. Perkins thought it best to publish the play alone. As for the story collection, the editor opposed beginning with "Up in Michigan" because of its sexual content. Instead, he wanted to begin the collection with the interchapters of *In Our Time* as they had been published in *in our time.* The stories would have to go to the printer by 1 July. Perkins closed with a note on the dedication and the play's title: "I have the dedication to the play right,—'To Marty and Herbert with love.'[78] And by the way, I think that you will have a hard time beating the present title,—'The Fifth Column.'"[79] Again, Perkins was worried about the propriety of opening with "Up in Michigan." But this concern suggests that in Perkins's mind the more important of the two books was the story collection—not the play.

There is no located correspondence between Hemingway and Perkins for the rest of April. Scribners evidently began preparing for publication of the two Hemingway books—the play and the collected stories—for the fall. Hemingway, however, seems to have lacked confidence in this strategy. From Spain he wrote Perkins on 5 May to suggest a different plan:

> Anyway: here's another idea. How would it be to publish the three unpublished stories and the play in one vol? Might be fine. Remember the Gadsbys by Kipling [1889]. Was a vol of plays and stories. One of his best book of stories. Successful too. Would be a good length.
>
> Doubt now if we'll ever have time or whatall to produce it. It reads damned well. With those other three stories would make a fine book. Could lead off with the play and follow it by the three stories. Then when we publish the omnibus we would have them and the new ones I will write. Or I might even have a volume of new ones first. I would write a little introduction. Think this a good idea.[80]

Hemingway may have been feeling uneasy about the play's chances if it were published alone. He knew that the three unpublished stories were good—"The Snows of Kilimanjaro" had been included in *The Best Short Stories 1937*—and would sell the volume if the play would not. Perkins made no mention of Hemingway's idea in his answer of 13 May. Perkins had sent galley proofs for *The Fifth Column* to Paris. He had gotten Louis Henry Cohn's advice about the stories and was going to have them set in proof in chronological order based on the composition dates, which Cohn was providing.[81] Perkins could not forget the power of *in our time,* the book that had first brought Hemingway to his attention, and thought that in the omnibus collection the vignettes should be published together.

Hemingway could not have gotten Perkins's letter of 13 May when he wrote his editor on 19 May. He was still unsure about the order of the stories but was favoring putting them in the order in which they had appeared in *In Our Time, Men Without Women,* and *Winner Take Nothing.* He definitely wanted to include "Up in Michigan." He told Perkins that he had copies of the stories (probably those not previously collected) to go over and hoped to have several more stories before he had to send the setting copy to Scribners.[82]

Perkins and Scribners were preparing for the two volumes, both to be published in the fall. On the second of June, Perkins sent Hemingway a salesman's dummy for the collected story volume, now titled *The First Forty-Eight.* In the same letter he asserted that "The Fifth Column" should be published alone: "As to that, I think the play ought to stand alone, and can, and that it will do well alone even if it is published and not produced. . . . 'The Fifth Column' published by itself would make a much stronger impression than if it were in any collection. As to the stories.— I think now is the time to show what has been done and is being done by putting in the new and the old stories together."[83] Perkins's admiration for the play may not have been as great as he had told Hemingway it was. In any event, he probably was working under the impression that the story volume would not sell well without the new stories.

The play was no closer to being staged when Hemingway wrote his editor on 11 June:

> I won't know until July First whether the play is to be produced or not. The producer is supposed to have a certain sum on deposit by then otherwise they forfeit the advance and the play reverts to me. It looks as though they would have difficulty. The matter is in Speiser's hands and I am not worrying about it. It is

really a shame if it is not to be produced as that is what it was written for. Will let you know as soon as I come up, which will be June 22 for the fight I think.

About the stories haven't decided that either. That is; about the order. Have finished one new story but it needs some re-writing. It is difficult to get going and your imagination and all seems sort of cauterized. Also was drinking too much, as always at a war, and cutting it out is sort of a career in its-self for a while. Have cut it to a little under my normal limit now for ten days.[84]

The story was probably "The Denunciation," which Hemingway did not finish in time for the book's publication in the fall.[85] Hemingway's assurance that he and Perkins could decide how to publish when he got to New York did little to relieve Perkins's worries, for he had to get things moving for the fall selling season. On 15 June he wrote asking, "Have you been considering the proposal about the play in one volume, and the stories all together? We ought to get going soon."[86] Hemingway did not answer, probably preferring to do so in person.

Hemingway flew to New York on 22 June and probably stayed in the city for a week.[87] Almost certainly during this trip Hemingway and Perkins finally settled on the idea of publishing two volumes. The firm had listed both volumes in an advertisement for its fall books in the 4 June 1938 issue of *Publishers Weekly*.[88] A salesman's dummy for *The Fifth Column* was prepared.[89] The firm also prepared descriptions for the two books in its catalog. These ran on consecutive pages in *Scribners Fall Books 1938*. The description for *The First Forty-Eight* emphasized that many of the stories had been anthologized and the fact that Hemingway was known as much for his stories as for his novels. The play's description is a synopsis and promise that it would be produced in October; additionally, the play is said to "*read* as well as the best Hemingway has ever written, and the fact that it is in the form of a play makes it none the less fascinating." Publication for both was set for September, and both were priced at $2.50.[90]

On the first day of July, Perkins sent the first forty-five pages of galley proofs for *The First Forty-Eight* to Hemingway. Perkins did not think the author had to edit the proofs, but he did have other worries:

You do not have to read them, but I thought you ought to look at them so as to see the arrangement.—But the numbering is wrong, and the reason is that even before you got back, we had 30 galleys set up, but I thought it better not to say anything about that in order not to make your decision any more difficult. It would not have been very important if we had to scrap them. But I began on the strictly chronological order. The shifting around of the numbers won't amount to anything at all, and will have to be done in the galleys when they are complete. And the new stories will all be at the end and will not be in the right order when they come. It is better not to give a printer directions after he has got started.—It gives him an alibi for not getting on fast. The only point is "Up In Michigan." I enclose a clipping from Publisher's Weekly about the situation in Detroit which shows that so far everything is right enough.[91] But in reading over "Up In Michigan" I did begin to feel nervous about it. When I remembered it, it did not seem to me that there was any serious question. I did not remember the two phrases in it which would arouse the vindictiveness of a certain very numerous kind of person. I remembered it as in a sense a sad story. And it is. Except for those two phrases it is all right from any point of view. I think maybe you ought to read that story through. I certainly do not like to furnish those people with amunition with which to misrepresent your work. The story ought to be in because of its quality, and because it was your first story. We would not really be carrying out the idea of the book without it. Anyhow, we'll read a duplicate proof here so that you need do no more reading than you want to.[92]

Perkins did not want to see the new book banned because of a fifteen-year-old story.

When Hemingway responded on 12 July, he argued that there was nothing wrong with "Up in Michigan" and that, even though a bit of the dialogue was "wooden," it should stay in the collection. He also introduced an idea that changed the whole direction of the publisher's plans. Hemingway was finding it difficult to get the play produced. He suggested that it should be published in one volume with the stories because he thought this would be stronger and more impressive than publishing two books. He also sent a new story, "The Old Man at the Bridge."[93] Now instead of two books, Hemingway wanted to publish just one big book; now instead of forty-eight stories there would be forty-nine. The new story, like "Chi Ti Dice la

Partia?" before it, had first been published as a nonfiction article.[94] The only revision made when it was published in *The Fifth Column and the First Forty-Nine Stories* was the deletion of the first "the" in the title.[95]

Later that same day Hemingway was still undecided as to how to publish the stories. After going through the galleys, he wrote another letter to Perkins. He pointed out that the *in our time* section contained two vignettes that had eventually been published as stories in *In Our Time* and that the supposed chronological order was wrong. It was in the latter part of this letter that the final form of *The Fifth Column and the First Forty-Nine Stories* was finally established. Hemingway's suggestion was to place the uncollected stories first, followed by the stories as they had appeared in *In Our Time, Men Without Women,* and *Winner Take Nothing.* He asked that the piece titled "An Introduction by the Author" in the 1930 *In Our Time* be retitled "On the Quai at Smyrna." He also promised to write an introduction for the book.[96] Although he would still consider other options, the book was finally published with "The Fifth Column" first, followed by the four new stories, "Up in Michigan," and the previously collected stories.

Perkins's response of 18 July was restrained, but he was ready to acquiesce to Hemingway's demands: "If the odds are what you say against production this Fall, we might well reserve *separate* publication of the play until production occurred, when it would be required. We can therefore keep standing the type of the present setting for a later separate publication, and rest to line up with 'The First Forty-Nine' and do as you say.—That is, publish a book to be called 'The Fifth Column and the First Forty-Nine Stories, etc.'"[97] Again Perkins probably thought it best to do what Hemingway wanted rather than argue with him. However, with the plans to publish the play and the stories in two books already in motion, Perkins could not have been pleased with the change.

Hemingway finished correcting proofs for the play on 3 August. In his letter that accompanied the proof, Hemingway expressed his continuing uncertainty over how to proceed. The play, he wrote, could be produced if he would let it be "play doctored" (i.e., allow sections to be rewritten by a playwright). He was still uncertain about publishing the play and the stories together and requested that Perkins advise him on the matter.[98] Perkins, perhaps preoccupied by Thomas Wolfe's illness,[99] did not argue, writing Hemingway on 9 August that he favored joint publication.[100] Perhaps the editor thought it best to come to a definite decision, however bad it might prove to be.

From Cooke City, Hemingway sent the proofs for the stories on 17 August. They were still in reverse chronological order—the new stories first, then the stories as they had appeared in *Winner Take Nothing, Men Without Women,* "Up in Michigan," and *In Our Time.* But Hemingway strongly suggested that this arrangement be changed in his accompanying letter:

> Although it does seem sort of goofy to work backwards all the way like that and it would probably be sounder since we are not following chronology completely either backwards or forward to simply state in the preface that the play and the first four stories were the last things written and so are put first and then follow with the other stories in the order of Up In Michigan In Our Time, Men Without Women, and Winner Take Nothing. I think that give the book a more logical reading arrangement.
>
> But if you want it the other way go ahead.
>
> I put the Old Man at the Bridge between the Francis Macomber and The Snows of Kilimanjaro quite arbitrarily because it is better for the readability. Will mention in the preface that it is the last story written and Up In Michigan the first.
>
> The only proof that needs to be read now is the Old Man at the Bridge and the In Our Time italics.
>
> I really think it is best to put the order In Our Time, Men Without Women and, Winner Take Nothing with the play first followed by the new stories.

Before closing, Hemingway asked, "Did what I changed make it all right about Scott?"[101] He had changed the name "Scott Fitzgerald" to "Scott" in "The Snows of Kilimanjaro." But Perkins was not happy. In his reply of 23 August, the editor requested further changes:

> As to the Scott passage, you amended it very neatly.—But I greatly wish his name could come out altogether. If people reading the story do not identify "Scott" as F.S.F., it might as well be some other name (one realizes he is a writer in the very next sentence)

and if they do identify him, it seems to me it takes them out of the story for a moment. It takes their attention to the question of what this means about Scott. You did take out the things that could hurt and I showed the amended passage to two people who had never read the story and they thought Scott might still feel badly, being very sensitive, but that they hardly thought there was much reason for it now. If his name could come out without hurting, it would be good.—But I'll bring up the matter when you are here.[102]

Hemingway flew to New York on 29 August for a two-day visit before sailing for France on 31 August. Perkins must have convinced him to emend "Scott" to "Julian" in the story at this time.[103]

Despite his assurances to Hemingway that publishing the play and the stories in one volume was a good one, Perkins never really seemed to like the plan. More than likely he saw that he could not convince Hemingway that this large book with its cumbersome title would not impress readers and critics. An indication of this feeling on Perkins's part is given in his letter of 1 September to Fitzgerald:

Hem went through here like a bullet day before yesterday, to sail for France. He is going to take at least another look at Spain, but his real purpose was to work. I wish I could talk to you about him: he asked me about a plan he has, and I advised him quite vigorously, and yet had some doubts of the wisdom of it afterward. But I think it is right enough. I only would like to talk to someone who really would understand the thing. We are publishing, after a great deal of argument and frequent changes of plan which were made to meet Hemingway's wishes mostly, a book which is to be called "The Fifth Column and the First Forty-Nine Stories." It is the play, "The Fifth Column," the four new stories, and then all the old ones, in an omnibus volume. The play appears simply as if it were a story, and it can be read that way mighty well.—If later it is produced, we shall publish separately the version used, for there will be a demand for it in that form.—But here it appears as if it were one of his stories, you might say. There is a good introduction. One of the new stories is "The Snows of Kilimanjaro" and you are not in it.[104]

It seems, then, that Perkins merely gave up trying to convince Hemingway of the folly of publishing everything in one book.

The firm listed *The Fifth Column and the First Forty-Nine Stories* in the announcement of its fall list in the 17 September 1938 issue of *Publishers Weekly.* The book was one of nine listed, and the description emphasized that it contains a full-length play about the Spanish civil war and all of Hemingway's short stories.[105] The firm also issued a revised catalog for its fall list with a lengthy description of Hemingway's new book:

The Fifth Column
and The First Forty-Nine
by ERNEST HEMINGWAY
Publication Date: October $2.75

The Author and the Book: Here are combined all the short stories by the American writer who is recognized as the leading contemporary practitioner of this type of fiction, and Ernest Hemingway's first full length play—The Fifth Column—which will be produced in New York in October.

About the short stories it is necessary to say but little. Such masterpieces as "The Undefeated," "The Snows of Kilimanjaro" and "Big Two-Hearted River" are internationally famous, and there are many others that thousands of readers will want to have in one book. The volume includes, moreover, several stories never before published. For sheer reading enjoyment this collection offers an unmatched value.

"The Fifth Column" deals with the intrigues of the Fascist organization that works inside the Loyalist lines in Spain. The scene of the play is besieged Madrid, the leading characters—an American agent on the Loyalist Intelligence Staff, an American girl, a German who is also doing intelligence work for the Loyalists, and a Moorish girl who is intensely pro-Loyalist, but otherwise no better than she should be. It reads as well as the best Hemingway has ever written. Here is the Hemingway who wrote the tremendous Caporetto scenes of "A Farewell to Arms" working his own particular magic on the bloody conflict in Spain.

The Market: The play alone is a "must" for the Hemingway audience, and so are the short stories.[106]

Again, the emphasis is placed on how well the play reads and how similar it is to Hemingway's novels and stories.

The Fifth Column and the First Forty-Nine Stories was published on 14 October 1938 and sold for $2.75. Hemingway's contract for the collection has not been located, but he no doubt received his standard royalty (15 percent of the list price for the first 25,000 copies sold and 20 percent thereafter). The firm ordered an initial printing of 5,350 copies on 6 September, and a second of 3,525 on 14 October, for a total of 8,875 copies printed before publication.

The book did not impress reviewers as Hemingway had hoped. The collection received only eight reviews in major American newspapers and magazines. Hemingway had clippings of about eighty notices and reviews of the book from American periodicals.[107] The reviews were for the most part good, and the stories were praised by most critics. The play, however, fared worse. The *Time* reviewer called it "ragged and confused."[108] The *New Masses* reviewer, Edwin Berry Burgum, gave a glowing notice to the whole book, no doubt more in recognition of Hemingway's support of the Loyalist cause than for the qualities of the drama.[109] Peter Monro Jack, writing in the *New York Times Book Review,* praised the play, but only because it read like a story: "It is doubtful this is to be his gift to the stage."[110] In short, the book, especially the play, did not make the splash with reviewers that Hemingway had expected.

The firm's promotion of the volume was extremely limited, perhaps due to the changes in the publication plans. Between June 1938 and July 1939, fifty-four advertisements were purchased. All but five ran in 1938 (most in November and December). Aside from three ads in West Coast papers and one each in the *Chicago News* and the *Philadelphia Inquirer,* all ran in book trade journals, national magazines and New York newspapers. The publisher spent only $3630.79 on promotion.[111] From October to December 1938, Scribners ran nine advertisements in the *New York Times Book Review* that featured *The Fifth Column and the First Forty-Nine Stories.*[112] Only two of these notices, the ones of 27 November and 11 December, were for Hemingway's book alone. In addition to using quotes from reviewers, some of these advertisements emphasized the new material. *The Fifth Column and the First Forty-Nine Stories* was not advertised in 1939 in the *New York Times Book Review.*

The firm ordered two more printings after 14 October 1938: one of 3,290 copies on 23 November 1938, and one of 2,935 copies on 10 April 1940. The total for this edition was 15,100 copies.[113] The best Hemingway could have realized if all of these copies were sold would have been $6,228.75, which would equal $80,173.36 in 2005.

From Paris, writing on 28 October 1938, Hemingway expressed his anger at the lackluster reception:

> Well we thought we had something pretty unbeatable in that book didn't we? But you can't beat those guys. They can gang up to play it down. You know Max I think I'll still be around and going pretty good when there is a whole new generation of critics. You see those guys all buried me and it is awkward and difficult for them to see you rising like Lazarus. . . .
>
> I don't give a shit about any of it except the aspect of interfering with my livelihood. When I got the book and saw all those stories I knew I was all right as a sort of lasting business if I kicked off tomorrow. Which, by the way,—oh well let us neither talk nor write balls.[114]

Despite the disappointment that he felt, the facts bear out that both *To Have and Have Not* and *The Fifth Column and the First Forty-Nine Stories* were good sellers—marked improvements over *Winner Take Nothing* and *Green Hills of Africa*. But these two books could not match the success that Hemingway's publications of the 1920s had enjoyed. Perhaps the many changes Hemingway had made had not allowed Scribners adequate time to successfully market the books, or Hemingway's attention to the events in Spain had led him to cut corners with his work that he would not have otherwise. Readers of the time just might not have wanted to read what Hemingway was writing. In the end, though, the time Hemingway had spent in Spain during the latter part of the 1930s would pay off when, in 1940, he published *For Whom the Bell Tolls*.

CHAPTER 7

THE BLOCKBUSTER

For Whom the Bell Tolls

After 1938, Hemingway gave up reporting (at least until 1944) and political activism and, for the first time since 1929, concentrated almost wholly on fiction writing. Beginning in March of 1939, after producing six stories about the Spanish civil war, Hemingway began writing a novel about the conflict.[1] Unlike *To Have and Have Not,* this novel was not constructed by the fusing together of new material with previously published stories. It would be Hemingway's first true novel since *A Farewell to Arms.* When this new novel, titled *For Whom the Bell Tolls,* was issued in the fall of 1940, it would prove to be Hemingway's most successful publication. Part of its success must be attributed to Hemingway's willingness to seek and follow the advice of Perkins and Charles Scribner III; the novel was the first Hemingway book that Scribner took an active role in editing and publishing. *For Whom the Bell Tolls* marked the pinnacle of Hemingway's association with Charles Scribner's Sons.

Around the time of the publication of *The Fifth Column and the First Forty-Nine Stories,* Hemingway seems to have started working on what would become *For Whom the Bell Tolls*.[2] In a letter to *Esquire* editor Arnold Gingrich (dated 22 October 1938), Hemingway wrote that he had "two chapters done on a novel," a claim he also made to Perkins on 28 October.[3] On 7 February 1939 he wrote to Perkins to suggest publishing a collection of short stories "to support the family for the rest of the year and can then start on the novel again. I have to know how the war comes out to get that right anyway."[4] Perkins responded on 9 March, tactfully trying to dissuade Hemingway from publishing the story volume first: "If you had to do a book of stories first it would have been all right with us, and it would have been a book of distinction, but it is much better strategy if it turns out that way, to have a novel first. One reason I did not say this was because I knew you knew it, and the other was that you could not do a novel for any such reason as strategy. But nothing could be more satisfactory than to hear what this letter says."[5] Perkins seems to have understood that what Hemingway had to publish to save his reputation was a real novel, not a short-story collection or a novel that he made by fusing together a group of short stories. Hemingway and Perkins may have discussed the publishing strategy Perkins mentions here when the author was in New York in November 1938.[6]

The first clear indication that Hemingway was writing what would become *For Whom the Bell Tolls* is in a 25 March 1939 letter to Perkins: "And then started on another [story] I'd had no intention of writing for a long time and working steadily every day found I had fifteen thousand words done; that it was very exciting; and that it was a novel. So I am going to write on on that until it is finished. I wish I could show it to you so far because I am very proud of it but that is bad luck too. So is talking about it." Hemingway went on to tell his editor that he was going to stay in Cuba until the novel was done, that he was rereading what he had written every day, and that he felt as good as when he was working on *A Farewell to Arms*.[7]

Throughout the year Hemingway continued to send Perkins and Scribner progress reports. Both responded to their author by giving him praise and money but made no attempt to learn anything about the nature of the novel. Perkins wrote Hemingway on 18 April, "I am mighty glad the book is going so well, and fast."[8] Hemingway informed Perkins on 10 May that he was "averaging between 700 and 1000 words a day and have to hold down not to do more."[9] Perkins responded on 19 May, "It was fine to read about the book, how well it was going. I won't ask any questions at all. I'll just wait to for you to tell me."[10]

Hemingway also gave his publisher, Charles Scribner III reports on his progress. On 23 May, he wrote: "Work goes good. Am on page 199 of the Mss. now. That should be over half through. . . . After I started this book the first of March and saw how it was going I wrote Tommy [Shevlin] in early April that I couldn't interrupt the book and to get some one else."[11] This letter also provides the first evidence of Hemingway's ideas on publication: "Cosmopolitan are after me about the serializing but am not thinking about that while writing it. After I finish will see if it is serializable and if so we can then figure on what time that will take to know when to publish. If we don't want to serialize can figure then, without worrying about that. So far I should think it would be quite serializable (pretty word) but do not want to think about that; only to write a good novel."[12] Scribner responded on 1 June as Perkins had earlier: "I was delighted to receive your letter and hear that you are making such fine progress. I won't write anything more as I do not wish to interrupt you even for a minute."[13] Hemingway wrote Perkins on 30 May that he was on page 213 of the manuscript.[14] In a letter of 16 June, Perkins wrote, "Hope all goes well with the novel but will ask no questions," maintaining his hands-off attitude.[15]

After a nearly month and a half silence, Hemingway on 10 July updated his editor on the status of the work: "Have 56,000 words done now. Fourteen chapter 342 pages of Mss. . . . Guess it is about 2/3 through. Wish you could read it. Went well yesterday and today." He also intimated that he might go west to escape the Cuban heat and that he was sure that it would take all summer to finish the novel.[16] At this point, the novel was in reality only a little over one-third of the way to being finished. Chapter 14 (which is chapter 15 in the published text) is the account of Anselmo watching the bridge during the snowstorm. Hemingway had greatly underestimated both the novel's eventual length and the time it would take for him to finish it.

Around the middle of July, Hemingway wrote Perkins that he had 64,000 words done and requested $500 to be drawn against the advance on the book, adding, "This is the 1st money drawn. Will be drawing plenty more."[17] Perkins's response on 19 July contains the assurance, "I knew you would have to draw against the book,—at least you intimated as much when you were last here. So we are prepared for it, and only have to be told when and how."[18] On 28 July he sent Hemingway a check for $500, his only comment being "I am mighty glad to hear of the 64,000 words. That is fine."[19] A month later, from St. Louis en route to Wyoming, Hemingway reported to Perkins, "Am on 74,000 words. Getting it copied. Will be about 115,000 words." He also requested $840 against the advance.[20]

Not until 27 October did Hemingway send Perkins a fuller report of his progress, providing for the first time an indication of the subject of the novel and the type of characters in it: "Have something over 90,000 words done on the novel and it gets longer and longer. You don't have to worry about competition with Bessies or other Spanish books.[21] This is a novel and it is also from the inside. How it really was. All the things that people with party obligations could never write and what most of them could never know or, if they knew, allow themselves to think. Have two wonderful women (Spanish) in it so far. Maybe more later. It will either be about fifteen or twenty thousands words longer or else fifty thousand words longer. There is a part about Madrid I don't know whether to write or not. I think I will."[22] Perkins was his usual reassuring self when he replied on 1 November: "I was mighty glad to get your letter. It sounded fine, about the book especially."[23]

By mid-November, Hemingway reported that he was "on page 474 of the typewritten mss." But he also raised again the possibility of bringing out a collection of short stories: "Did you ever read that story of mine, Under The Ridge that Cosmo published in September? If finish this novel in January or Feb the novel will come out in the fall I suppose. Was just thinking that I have six stories already on a book of stories. . . . Christ I will be glad to get this book done and write some stories. Do you know that I have been working hard on it ever since March 1?"[24] Hemingway may have begun to feel that the novel would not be finished by the time he predicted and was preparing to offer a story volume as a substitute. Perkins's response of 21 November contained praise for the Spanish civil war stories, but he was clearly against publishing them in a book before the novel came out. He also made his first request for information about the novel:

> But it would be unwise in the circumstances, to publish a collection of stories until after this novel.—And if the novel is finished

in January, it could comfortably come out in the Spring. It would be all right if it were a late Spring book because it could carry over safely into the Fall. It would not be hurt by the fact that the Spanish war seems to have been pushed far back into the past in the sense of a historical event. It will sell as a novel about the people and the way things were, and such things as other people writing about the war wouldn't have any effect upon it. But I would give anything if I knew just a few of the elements in it to make a note from, and the title. Even if the title were changed later it would be O.K. And I would not need to know much to build up a note for the time being.[25]

Perkins clearly was preparing for late spring publication and wanted to get the machinery of promotion running.

By 8 December, Hemingway was optimistically stating from Sun Valley, Idaho, "It goes well and can see the finish." He also told Perkins that he would go to Cuba and not leave there until the book was finished if it were impossible to work in Key West, a situation created by the disintegration of his marriage to Pauline Pfeiffer Hemingway.[26] Perkins may or may not have known of the Hemingways' marital problems, but his 19 December reply to Hemingway was full of praise and encouragement: "I know perfectly well what feats of concentration you must have performed to work as you have in all the circumstances, and I am delighted the book is going on as it must be. I am sure it will be a great book."[27]

In early January, Hemingway sent Perkins eight pages of the first chapter and Pilar's story about the opening days of the war (chapter 10 in the published text). He also informed Perkins that he had "let various people that I trust read this one and they think it's the best I ever wrote. Hope to God so. People like Esther Chambers, Joris Ivens, Chris LaFarge, Otto Bruce." He also told Perkins not to show the samples to the "ideology boys," that is, reviewers on the Left such as Alvah Bessie. He added that there would be no problem with obscenities in the book: "And in writing this I have learned how to give the effect of all the bad words without using them. I had to because Spanish is so truly obscene that you can't translate most of the stuff and have people believe it even. So have learne how to do that and there is not one obscene word in the book. If I have it right that is something to have learned."[28] The practices described in this letter were atypical for Hemingway. He had never sent Perkins samples of his work in progress or let other people read his manuscripts, and he usually fought for the inclusion of obscene words in his works. Perhaps he thought Perkins needed proof of the novel's existence and worth or wanted Perkins to have an idea of what the book was about in order to prepare promotional material. There is little doubt that fear of suppression was a factor in Hemingway's editing, but it is also likely that Hemingway knew the novel would be more marketable if it were "clean." Hemingway was writing and editing the novel with a view toward serialization and perhaps even book club selection, since postal regulations would prohibit a book club from shipping a book judged to be obscene.[29]

Perkins cabled on 18 January that he was "extremely impressed."[30] Hemingway responded the same day that he was "awfully happy you liked the sample. . . . Finished chapter 23 today. . . . Am going to go straight on working now until the novel is finished. Plenty cavalry in this last chapter."[31] The novel was about two-thirds complete; he had eighteen chapters left to write.

The next day Perkins wrote to Hemingway in greater detail of his reactions to the samples:

> The impressions made by it are even stronger after the lapse of time. The scenes are more vivid and real than in the reading. That has always happened to me after reading your novels, and it is true of mighty few writers. That chapter eight is terrific, and as one gets further away from it the characters of those different men when they came out to be killed, and the ways they took it, seem as if one had seen it all, and had known them. It is truly wonderful,—the way the temper of the people changed as things went on, and they got drunk with killing, and with liquor too. The first chapter, or the first eight pages, had the old magic. . . . Well, of course I am mighty impatient to see more.[32]

Perkins may have included these comments because he believed that Hemingway was becoming discouraged over the length of time the composition was taking him. His letters display a mixture of bragging about the quality of the work and dismay at the amount of time it had taken. Around 23 January, he reported that he had finished chapter 24, the account of Jordan and Augustín on guard (chapter

25 in the published text).[33] By February, the search for a title had begun: "Want a big one. I don't have to worry about over-titling this one. She'll carry quite a lot. I think it is good that it is a long book. You know there are pricks who are impressed by length."[34] Hemingway wrote Perkins on 18 February to tell him that he had rewritten two chapters and now had "old Sordo fighting on a lousy hill in this chapter now where they get wiped out."[35]

On 21 February, Perkins sent the samples back and told Hemingway that Scribner might be going over to Cuba from Palm Beach.[36] Two days later, Hemingway complained to Perkins that he wished the book were finished but assured his editor that "it reads like a short book."[37] Perkins responded on 26 February that Scribner was "definitely going down there" then went on to assure Hemingway that he was not taking too much time: "As to the length of time you have been doing the novel, I do not think it is *long*. I am glad you have done it that way. It is a long novel anyhow, and material of great implications in depth and breadth. It couldn't but be a struggle, and if you had asked anybody how long it ought to take to do such a novel, they certainly would not have put it at less than a year."[38] Perkins again met his author's worries with assurances.

On 3 March, Hemingway wrote Perkins that "Harry Burton of Cosmo came down to see me about serialization." He also asked for another $500.[39] At about the same time Scribner and his wife Vera visited Havana. Scribner's report to Perkins on Hemingway's progress is partially repeated by Perkins in a 12 March letter to Maurice Speiser:

> Here is a report, *confidential*, about Ernest's progress, from Charles Scribner: "I read about 350 typed pages of Ernest's ms and he read me part of the rest—not yet fully typed. It is really a swell novel: all takes place in four days and three nights—the underlying theme being that a man may complete himself and live a complete life in that space of time. It has great unity—no digressions and as a *story* every page has movement, action and suspense that holds the reader. You don't want to put it down anywhere, and it speeds up as it goes along. It is to a great extent a love story and there is no propaganda about Spain. Ernest has lost none of his fire or his close knit style, but he has gained warmth and understanding. His characters ring true but even the worst have a side which makes

them likable. He is now working hard on the last morning but doesn't quite see his ending yet."[40]

Why Perkins thought he had to inform Hemingway's lawyer of the author's progress is not known—although the most probable explanation is that Speiser was already working on selling the film rights—but the report suggests that Perkins, Scribner, and Speiser were more concerned with Hemingway's progress than their letters to him indicate. On the same day, Perkins informed Hemingway of Scribner's report: "In the first place, I was most delighted with the letter I got from Charlie about the book, extremely enthusiastic, and giving me quite an idea of it as a whole. I suppose the situation about the ending is that you don't know exactly how to do it yet, but you know what it is to be. Well, endings are mighty difficult anyhow."[41] Perkins understood that at this point he could only encourage his author and hope for the best.

On 4 April, Perkins sent the following request to Hemingway: "If we could get the title by 22 April it would be a mighty good thing, but I know you don't want to think about that yet."[42] Perkins probably knew that the book would never make the spring publication goal but wanted the title anyway for a press release on the novel as a way to build interest for a fall publication.

Hemingway had probably not received Perkins's 4 April letter when he sent another progress report on 6 April. He had finished chapter 32 and was well into 33; he also updated Perkins on serialization plans and the search for a title:

> Harry Burton is after me for serialization in Cosmo. I let him read 16 Chapters when he was down here. He was very enthusiastic. Now he says that if I will send him 28 chapters he will make a definite decision and offer. I might as well have that decision and offer so am sending him the 28 chapters. But am sending them just typed and uncorrected as I do not want to interrupt now for anything. So if you want I will have him deliver them to you and you can read them before you send them back to me. Only remember they are uncorrected and probably full of every sort of mistake and probably won't even make sense. So when it is that way don't think it will really be that way. I have

26 titles but none of them are right and am still working. Sixteen chapters are o.k. to go ahead on serializing with right now if they should buy it.[43]

Perkins's response of 9 April indicates that from the firm's point of view serialization in *Cosmopolitan* was a bad idea: "I tried to get hold of Burton on the telephone. I do want to read those twenty-eight chapters, whatever shape they are in, as soon as I can, and I was going to tell Burton you would probably ask him to turn them over to me when he was through with them.—The devil of the serial question though, is that they have already made up their July number and if they take five months, the book would almost have to go over into 1941."[44] Perkins probably thought that having the serial still running during the fall when the book was published would water down the book's impact. The book, if it came out toward the end of the serial's run, would be published between the fall and spring selling seasons; Christmas sales would be lost.

In a mid-April letter, Hemingway briefed Perkins on the serial situation. Burton, he reported, was less than enthusiastic now that a decision had to be made. Hemingway went on to tell Perkins that he had nearly finished chapter 35 (chapter 36 in the published text, the account of Andrés and the anarchists) and had let Ben Finney read the manuscript. Finney reportedly had two erections after reading the descriptions of Jordan and Maria making love, a good sign, Hemingway thought, since "Finney pretty well fucked out."[45] He was still working on a title, the best so far being "The Undiscovered Country," but had still not found exactly what he wanted.[46] However, by 19 April Perkins had yet to hear from Burton and was anxious to read the manuscript.[47] He had it in hand by the next day.[48] Perkins's anxiety no doubt was heightened by the fast approach of the 22 April deadline; he had needed a clear idea of the nature of the work and the title in order to write a press release about it.

On 21 April, Hemingway finally wrote Perkins,

> How about this for a title
> For Whom The Bell Tolls
> A Novel
> By Ernest Hemingway

He also included in the letter the source of the title, "Meditation XVII" by John Donne, which Hemingway had found in *The Oxford Book of English Prose*. Aside from his concern that the title might invoke images of the Bell Telephone Company, he was pleased.[49] The next day he wired the title to Perkins, along with a report on his dealings with *Cosmopolitan:* "SENT BURTON FOLLOWING WIRE WHAT PERKINS EYE HAVE TO KNOW TO DECIDE WHETHER SERIALIZATION MONTHLY MAGAZINE JUSTIFIES DELAYING PUBLICATION IS WHAT WILL YOU PAY HOW MANY INSTALLMENTS WHEN WOULD START AND FINISH STOP SRIBNERS= MAKEING UP CATALOGUE MONDAY STOP BETWEEN FIFTEEN AND TWENTY THOUSAND MORE WORDS COMEING COMPLETING END MAY."[50] Perkins responded via wire the same day, telling Hemingway, "ALL KNOCKED OUT BY FIRST FIVE HUNDRED TWELVE PAGES. . . . TITLE BEAUTIFUL CONGRATULATIONS."[51] Two days later, he wrote about his reactions more fully:

> I am just sending you a line to say that I have read all of the manuscript there is here, and am still in a kind of a daze, half in that land, and half in this,—which has happened to me twice before in reading your manuscripts. I think this book has greater power, and larger dimensions, greater emotional force, than anything you have done, and I would not have supposed you could exceed what you had done before. . . . Well, by God, that fight piece, where El Sordo dies, is a wonder. That surprises you, and you know for dead sure that that is the way it would be. The nearest thing I ever saw to that fight was perhaps one or two pieces in Tolstoi. . . . If the function of a writer is to reveal reality no one ever so completely performed it. . . .
>
> As to the title, I don't believe you can possibly improve it, and I almost hope you won't try to,—and especially when you read that passage.[52]

This letter could not have failed to please Hemingway.

A notice of the book's impending publication, with the title given as *For Whom Tolls the Bell,* appeared in the 26 April 1940 *New York Times.*[53] Hemingway wired Perkins on 5 May to point out the mistake. Perkins responded that the mistake was the paper's and the title was correct everywhere else.[54] In Hemingway's scrapbooks, there are twenty clippings from various newspapers that were reprints of this release.[55]

Sometime before 13 May, Burton declined the book for serialization. The problem seems to have been Hemingway's asking price, as indicated in his May 13 letter to Perkins: "Harry makes me sick. I interrupted my work, paid $150 to a mother and daughter to type the Mss. day and night on his promise to give me an instant and absolute decision on 28 chapters and then he tries to jew me down to a 30,000 serial price and no decision until he has it all so as to know about cutting." But in the conclusion to this letter, Hemingway raised a new possibility for an extra source of income and exposure: "Have you gone into Book of Month business and thought how that would affect us both and whether would be better to or not to (always provided they wanted it). I hate to put that many copies out for such a chickenshit sum."[56] This is the first mention of placing *For Whom the Bell Tolls* with the Book-of-the-Month Club in the Hemingway/Perkins correspondence. One or the other may have brought the matter up earlier in a letter now lost, or Hemingway may have discussed the matter with Charles Scribner in Cuba. In any event, the possibility of submitting the book to a book club was unprecedented for Hemingway. In previous situations, both he and Perkins had thought doing so would take sales away from the trade edition. For example, when the idea of placing *Death in the Afternoon* (1932) with a book club was brought up, Hemingway said he would allow it only under certain conditions; he was worried that Scribners would not push the book as hard if they had a guaranteed $7,000 from the club, but his main concern was that there would be pressure to "emasculate" the book (i.e., remove the obscene words).[57] In his response, Perkins stated, "As for the Book Club, we don't like it any more than you do."[58] Perkins had even more reasons to dislike the Book-of-the-Month Club when its selection of Marjorie Kinnan Rawlings's *South Moon Under* (1933) forced a delay in its appearance, which hurt sales.[59]

But Perkins and the firm's fear of book clubs softened over time. In 1938, Rawlings's *The Yearling* had been the April main selection of the Book-of-the-Month Club and had enjoyed remarkable sales.[60] Perkins was open to trying to get *For Whom the Bell Tolls* chosen by the club. In his 15 May letter, he informed Hemingway that he had sent the manuscript back and outlined what must be done to secure Book-of-the-Month Club approval, as well as the possible benefits:

We can't do anything about the Book of the Month Club until we can show them proofs. I wish to God we could do it, for I think it would be well if they took it,—for many reasons, not only financial ones. It is a great book and people will say so when they get it, and the talk will go from the Book of the Month Club people too. . . . Now Charlie or I could approach Schurman of the Book of the Month Club himself, and tell him about the book. But no decision would be possible until their judges—for the thing is absolutely on the level—had read it, and that would mean that there would have to be either four copies, or four sets of proofs. Whenever we can do it, we shall set it up with extreme rapidity though.[61]

For the firm, the main benefit of Book-of-the-Month Club selection would be the word-of-mouth advertising campaign it would create, but they and Hemingway would have to move quickly in order to secure it.

Hemingway's pace seems to have picked up after this letter from Perkins. On 21 May, he wired his editor that he had finished chapter 40.[62] Two days later, he wrote Perkins that he thought there would be two more chapters.[63] On the last day of the month, Hemingway informed his editor that he was "writing Chapter 42. It's either the last or the next to last."[64] Finally, after a month of silence, Hemingway wired Perkins on 1 July, "BRIDGE ALL BLOWN AM ENDING LAST CHAPTER."[65] But Hemingway did not appear to be finished. In a 13 July letter to Perkins, he wrote, "Hope to get to N.Y. by the end of next week with the Mss. They are copying it all now except the last chapter where I am still working on the end. The last chapter is the most exciting in the book. Is almost unbearably exciting during and after the bridge is blown. . . . I knew I had to write a hell of a last chapter—But have it all now except the very end—the action and the emotion are all done."[66] He was going to New York to work on the manuscript there so as to have the book in proof as soon as possible for submission to the Book-of-the-Month Club. But the last chapter was not finished.

The contract between Hemingway and Charles Scribner's Sons for *For Whom the Bell Tolls* is dated 15 July 1940, but evidence suggests that Hemingway signed it during his New York trip. Evan Shipman was Hemingway's witness, but he was not in Cuba or Key West in 1940. He probably did see Hemingway in New York. The contract stipulates a royalty of 15 percent of the retail price for the first 25,000 copies, with an increase to 20 percent on all copies sold thereafter. An advance of $6,040, which Hemingway had already drawn while working on the book, was to be paid to the author. Mention of sub rights is limited to one sentence: "It is further agreed that the profits arising from any publication of said work, during the period covered by this agreement, in other than book form shall be divided equally between said PUBLISHERS and said AUTHOR."[67]

Hemingway arrived in New York around 25 July and left in early August.[68] Two notes from Perkins to Hemingway at this time indicate that Hemingway was progressing rapidly with his revisions and that the typescript was being sent to the printer as soon as he finished. On 31 July, Perkins wrote that he did not know how much copy Hemingway had given the printer, "but the press say they have enough to last until tomorrow afternoon."[69] The next day he requested another two hundred pages, "if humanly possible."[70] During this same trip, Hemingway was interviewed by Robert Van Gelder for the *New York Times Book Review*. Van Gelder intimated in his article that the new novel was better than *A Farewell to Arms*. Hemingway was quoted as saying, "This one had to be all right or I had to get out of line, because my last job, 'To Have and Have Not,' was not so good."[71] Whether Hemingway or Scribners had anything to do with setting up the interview is not known, but it serves as an example of the type of publicity and attention the book and its author were receiving more than two months before publication.

On 12 August, Scribner sent Hemingway a sketch for the wrapper and said he would be forwarding some minor suggestions in a few days.[72] The next day Perkins forwarded to his author a memo prepared by Wallace Meyer on "points of style, uniformity, spelling." He also indicated that his suggestions would be very minor and that the salesmen who had read the book were "enthusiastic."[73] Finally, the next day Perkins sent Hemingway a four-page letter containing his suggestions. Most of the suggestions have to do with matters of style, such as Hemingway's use of "thee" and "thou" and the defining of certain Spanish words. He questioned the relating of Pilar's thoughts in the last paragraph of chapter 4, since it might "break the reader out of the story by the change from one person to another." Another passage Perkins wanted modified was in chapter 13, where

Jordan thinks about bigotry. Hemingway had included a passage about marriage: "But what was the other thing that made as much for bigotry as continence? Sure. Being married to an unattractive wife and being faithful to her. Being married to such a woman and working at it was twice as strong a force for bigotry as continence. Twice as strong. Sure. But look at that old one from home with a beautiful wife who seemed, when you talked to her, twice as bigoted and witch-hunting as he was. Sure, he told himself. You'll have quite a time writing a true book. You better confine yourself to what happens. Now, back to Maria."[74] Perkins thought that this passage led to confusion about Jordan: "when I read this and came to that about being married, etc., I thought that Robert was married. But he was not." He also wanted Jordan's reminiscences of Madrid and the smell-of-death episode (chapters 18 and 19) shortened, because they "delay the story possibly longer than is advantageous." He questioned the naming of "'a certain American journalist' who happens to be named Mitchell" (chapter 18) because of the possibility for a libel suit. Concerning El Sordo's fight, Perkins thought that Hemingway's identification of a dead Fascist officer as "the same one who had ridden up the pass to Pablo's camp" would distract the reader from the episode (chapter 27). Perkins also wrote that he would reread the last chapters when the final 1,500 words came.[75]

Around this same time, proof copies were submitted to the Book-of-the-Month Club. Believing that the proof was missing the last two chapters, Perkins prepared a typed statement that was inserted on the last page of the proof copies:

Two short chapters, amounting 1,500 in all, will bring the book to a conclusion. In the first of these Karkov and Goltz meet after the failure of the attack, and in driving back from the front they talk together about it, and about Robert's message and his success in blowing the bridge. In the second, Andrés and Gomez motorcycle back to the outpost and then Andrés makes his way over ground he covered before, and eventually reaches the abandoned camp, sees the ruined bridge, and knows all that has happened there.

These chapters are written, but not yet to the complete satisfaction of the author. He wished to wait until after reading the proof up to this point before perfecting the end.[76]

While Hemingway seems to have started these chapters, there is no evidence that he got beyond the first page.[77] In any event, no one at Scribners saw any of these two chapters.

On 15 August, Hemingway wrote to Scribner about suggestions the publisher had made. He thanked him for the advice about the horse's injury. The jacket seemed to Hemingway all right, except for the bridge, which should have been "a thin, high-arching, metal, cantilever bridge instead of a stone bridge," and he included his own drawing of a bridge for the artist to follow. Hemingway suggested changing the journalist's nationality from American to British. He also wrote that he would cut part of Jordan's "soliloquay" but would not change the smell-of-death section. He also indicated that he would see about "Onan."[78] Hemingway asked Scribner to check into the possibility of whether Andre Marty could sue and directed him to show the letter to Perkins, to whom Hemingway would write "on his points" as he took them up.[79]

After receiving Hemingway's letter of 15 August, Scribner wrote to Harry Scherman of the Book-of-the-Month Club about the revisions: "Just a line to say that I have just received the first revisions of Ernest Hemingway's book. He is apparently in a most docile mood and has accepted therefore all of our suggestions—such as modifying the rather forced repetition of the words 'obscenity' and 'unprintable' in the places where they were bunched without resorting to any four-letter words, and in having Jordan say he was 'antifascist' rather than 'communist.'[80] I believe that such passages that might be irritating to some readers will be ironed out. I don't suppose this has any great bearing on your decision but I am so damned interested in the book that I felt I had to pass this on to you."[81] This letter indicates that Scribner took the lead in all of the firm's dealings with the Book-of-the-Month Club and that the revisions he had asked Hemingway to make were requested in order to facilitate acceptance by the club.

On 26 August, Scribner wrote to Hemingway that *For Whom the Bell Tolls* had been accepted by the book club.[82] The next day he repeated the news and informed Hemingway that one of the judges, Christopher Morley, had suggested including a map of the novel's setting as the end papers. Scribner stressed, however, that Hemingway did not have to seriously consider this idea. He also told Hemingway that he could not decide whether to publish the book at $2.50 or $2.75; he favored the former, since his ambition was to "plaster the country with the novel." Prospects looked good. The book club would pay within the week between $10,000 and $14,000, which would be divided equally between the publisher and the author. Advance sales of the trade edition had jumped from $30,000 to $60,000 to $100,000. As Scribner pointed out, "Complete success is a great stimulant."[83] No written agreement between Scribners and the Book-of-the-Month Club has been found. However, figures calculated on 22 January 1941 for a royalty statement for Hemingway indicate that he received fifteen cents from each Book-of-the-Month Club copy.[84] Scribners no doubt also got fifteen cents per copy, as an even split of book club moneys between author and publisher was standard. In addition, Scribners Press was also paid for printing the Book-of-the-Month Club copies, although how much the firm received for this is not known.

There is at least a hint that Perkins did not think much of the selection of *For Whom the Bell Tolls* by the Book-of-the-Month Club. In a letter to F. Scott Fitzgerald, dated 19 September 1940, Perkins wrote, "I suppose you have heard of the good fortune that has befallen Ernest. "For Whom the Bell Tolls" has been taken by the Book of the Month Club.—The stamp of bourgeois approval. He would hate to think of it that way, and yet it is a good thing, practically speaking."[85] From the contents of this letter, it would appear that Charles Scribner, not Perkins, had taken the lead in placing the book with the Book-of-the-Month Club, which is indicative of Hemingway's relationship with various members of the firm during the editing of the book. Typically, matters concerning money and publishing were handled by Scribner, while Perkins acted almost solely as editor, giving advice and responding to Hemingway's questions.

On 27 August, Hemingway returned to Perkins 123 galleys. He cut the Mitchell section to remove all libel, repeated that the "thees" and "thous" were correct as written, replaced "unprintable" with "un-nameable or some other word," kept the smell-of-death episode as written, and revised the Sordo fight as Perkins had suggested. He modified Jordan's thoughts on masturbating in chapter 31 because Scribner had been bothered by it. He also deleted Jordan's reflections on marriage. Hemingway also included a style sheet on the Spanish names and phrases and asked Perkins's advice on the revision of the meeting between Karkov and Marty in chapter 42.

Much of the letter, however, is dominated by Hemingway's questions about the conclusion:

> What would you think of ending the book as it ends now without the epilogue?
>
> I have written it and re-written it and it is o.k. but it seems sort of like going back into the dressing room after the fight or following Catherine Barclay to the cemetery (as I originally did in Farewell to Arms) and explaining what happened to Rinaldi and all.
>
> I have a strong tendency to do that always on account of wanting everything completely knit up and stowed away ship-shape. . . .
>
> Please write me air-mail on this the day you get this. Ask everybody if they think it ends all right as it is. . . .
>
> You see the epilogue only shows that good generals suffer after an unsuccessful attack (which isn't new); that they get over it (that's a little newer) Golz haveing killed so much that day is forgiveing of Martybecause he has that kindliness you get sometimes. I can and do make Karkov see how it will all go. But that seems to me to date it. The part about Andres at the end is very good and very pitiful and very fine.
>
> But it really stops where Jordan is feeling his heart beating against the pine needle floor of the forest. . . .
>
> Should I put on the epilogue? Is it needed? Or would it just be grand manner writing and take you away from the emotion that the book ends on?
>
> Please write me when you get this.[86]

He also wired Perkins the same day asking for an immediate response to the question of the ending.[87] He seems not to have been able to finish these chapters to his satisfaction. But Hemingway was clearly worried over the novel's need of them and Perkins's reaction. Now he needed Perkins to agree with him.

Hemingway must have sent the galleys and his letter via airmail, because the next day Perkins sent two wires answering Hemingway's questions and commenting on the revisions: "GALLEYS AND DIRECTIONS RECEIVED IN FINE SHAPE STOP CAN WAIT TILL SEPTEMBER TWELFTH FOR LAST CHAPTER BUT WOULD PREFER TENTH STOP DE-

CISION ON ENDING IS HARD BUT WE KNOW PRESENT ENDING IS IM-
MENSELY EFFECTIVE AND COMPLETELY SATISFYING STOP ALL HERE
FELT NOTHING MORE COULD BE SAID ON READING GALLEYS BEFORE
QUESTION WAS RAISED STOP I THINK WE SHOULD DECIDE AGAINST
THE EPILOGUE."[88] After examining the corrections, Perkins wired,
"THINK DEATH PASSAGE RIGHT AS WRITTEN AND ONAN AS CORRECT-
ED AND MARTY PARAGRAPH MUCH BETTER WITHOUT FIRST PART
FIRST SENTENCE AND LAST SENTENCE WRITING SUN VALLEY."[89]

Hemingway must have been extremely anxious, because he telephoned Perkins about the ending. Perkins mentioned this in his 30
August letter to Hemingway, which accompanied 171 pages of page
proof to Sun Valley, Idaho:

> Of course the hardest question of all was that about the ending. I
> didn't get your letter of the 26th in which you talked about it un-
> til the day after you telephoned.—I thought it over all the time
> that afternoon and night, and I had arrived at the conclusion
> myself that the only thing there was doubt about was Andres. It
> really was only a question of that. The ending is tremendously
> effective. . . . I do see the value of Andres coming back because
> then the reader would feel it as Andres felt it.—But it was only
> about that question that I was still hesitating. On the other hand
> we know that the ending really is an ending, a wonderful ending.
> Then you have amended it, or are doing so. I therefore thought
> that if we must decide, we ought to decide to have no epilogue.

Perkins also informed Hemingway that all corrections had to be in
by 12 September.[90]

Scribner informed Scherman on 29 August of the decision not to
add the proposed chapters to the end:

> In the last day or two we have had a number of telegrams, letters,
> and telephone conversations with Ernest Hemingway regarding
> the ending of his novel. As we had told you, he intended to add
> two short chapters at the end of the proof that we sent to you.
> He does not seem, however, to be able to work them out so that
> they do not form an anti-climax, and we have practically arrived
> at the conclusion that it would be best and most dramatic to stop
> the book at the death of Jordan where your proof ends. He tells

me that he has refined the last galleys considerably and that he thinks they are very much better. I don't suppose that this makes any difference to you and your jury. It is something of a relief to me as he got badly stuck at the end of "Farewell to Arms" and wrote forty seven different endings, which took three months' time, before he hit on the right one. He has now returned all but eighteen galleys of the proof, so we can start printing in another week, which greatly simplifys the situation. He has made quite a number of minor changes and cuts, all of which are to the good, and the word "unprintable" is now completely out of the book and only a very few obscenities left. I never felt more certain that we have a really good book.[91]

If Hemingway was tentative about how to end his novel in his letters to Perkins, in his letters to Scribner about money matters he was very sure of himself and his position. On 29 August, he wrote the publisher to outline his plans. He could not decide about the map idea but was going to work on it. The biggest problem was the division of the Book-of-the-Month Club money:

You say there could be no question between us regarding the division as it has become a fixed precedent etc. and that this fee includes the use of the publishers plates of the book.

It would seem to me that in this particular book, not a first novel, not etc. you enjoyed from the Book of the Month selection considerably greater benefits than you would have if it had been a first book say. Not to mention recovering your costs before you start.

Something else that slipped both our minds perhaps; would it be perfectly o.k. for me to make a comeing out present of one half of the $35,000 cash I turned down for serialization to you and to Charles Scribner's Sons? . . .

I would suggest a 50-50 split on the first money; i.e. $14,000 received from the book of the Month Club to maintain your precedent in dealing with future authors etc. And recover costs.

I would suggest, and accept, a split of 60-40 ie 60 to me and 40 to you on all subsequent money received from the book of the month. At this rate if the book sold an extra 300,000 I would recover *a part of one half* of the cash I put into the pot to bring this miracle about. . . .

Tell them that when they [other authors] have written Farewell To Arms, had a first printing of 200,000 on the novel in question and turned down $35,000 for serial rights in order to piblish in the fall rather than the spring you will discuss the split I suggest with them. You won't have to make it many times and if you ever do make it you will be makeing plenty of money.[92]

Scribner's response, if there was one, has not been located. There is no located evidence to suggest that the fifty-fifty division of the Book-of-the-Month Club money between the author and the publisher was emended in Hemingway's favor.

On 9 and 10 September Hemingway wired corrections to Perkins and Scribner. All the corrections were matters of spelling and punctuation. The wire of the tenth also included his rejection of the map idea.[93] The 12 September deadline was set back; no reason is indicated in the correspondence. On 16 September, Hemingway wired the last corrections to Charles Scribner, concluding, "THAT'S ALL MAY COMMENCE FIRING."[94] On 20 September, Perkins wrote Hemingway to congratulate him on a job well done.[95]

While Hemingway worked with Perkins and Scribner to get the book into shape for publication, the firm's advertising and sales departments set about promoting the novel. The book occupied the second page of *Scribner's Fall 1940 Trade Catalog.* The description stressed that the novel was the true follow-up to *A Farewell to Arms:* "The books between that great novel and 'For Whom the Bell Tolls' have been successful and highly praised by critics . . . but none approaches in stature, or in tremendous impact, this new novel." Under "The Market," the copywriter optimistically predicted a bigger sale than that of *A Farewell to Arms,* with every novel reader knowing about and wanting to read it.[96] Salesmen's dummies with temporary dust jackets, the title, copyright statement, epigraph, and six pages of text had been prepared sometime in the summer.[97] The first mention of the novel in *Publishers Weekly* was in the 15 June 1940 issue, where it was listed with fourteen other titles.[98] Scribners' advertisement in the 7 September issue was led by a single page devoted to what the ad calls "Ernest Hemingway's first full-length novel since 'A Farewell to Arms.' The 'big' Hemingway novel that booksellers and the reading public have been waiting for."[99] Two weeks later, in the issue announcing the fall publications, the listing of the book and Hemingway's picture occupied a quarter of the second page of a two-page Scribners spread.[100] In the same issue's "A Few High Spots Among Fall Ad Campaigns," which outlined what books various houses were pushing, the section on Charles Scribner's Sons began, "With a strong list headed by the new Ernest Hemingway novel, 'For Whom the Bell Tolls,' which is the November selection of the Book-of-the-Month Club, and Allan Nevins' 'John D. Rockefeller: The Heroic Age of American Enterprise,' the Scribner promotion campaign will be unusually extensive."[101]

The prepublication ads in the *New York Times Book Review* had a similar tone to those in *Publishers Weekly*. The first ad for the novel appeared on 22 September with twenty other works, but it and *John D. Rockefeller* were set apart in white type on a black background. Again, the ad predicted that the novel would be a greater success than *A Farewell to Arms*.[102] In the same issue, Hemingway's novel, flanked by his picture, was listed on the first page of "Books to Be Published During the Fall Months."[103] In the 13 October issue, the novel was again in the same white-on-black format at the bottom of a Scribners ad listing nine other titles.[104] In addition, more publicity was provided by the October *Book-of-the-Month Club News,* which included a glowing review of the novel by Henry Seidel Canby on pages 2 and 3 (in which the novel was called "one of the most touching and perfect love stories in modern literature") and an article on the author by Perkins on page 4. In it, Perkins concentrated on Hemingway's biography, never mentioning the new novel. The editor repeated certain apocryphal stories about Hemingway's life, stating as fact that Hemingway had run away from home at age sixteen and had led troops in combat during World War I.[105] The book's selection by the Book-of-the-Month Club was reported in several newspapers, as evidenced by the clippings Hemingway kept.[106] The attention devoted to the novel was extensive, but nothing compared to what it would be after publication.

In early October, Hemingway, still smarting over the fact that no one had informed him in September of the publication delay, joked with his editor about the Book-of-the-Month Club article: "Somebody out here had the book of month bulletin so I saw it. Why the hell did they make you write about me? I didn't know you were a writer. You guys certainly were willing to do anything to put that over. Charlie reading the man's book on Gold. You writing about a son of a bitch like me and makeing him out to be a fine fellow. Now all we've got to do is try to keep some of the books in the bookstore. I think Darrow ought to lecture on me as a Clubman. Couldn't we arrange that? On A Fellow Player by Whitney Darrow.[107] We could send him across the country with it."[108] Perkins responded that "it just had to be done, and for a deadline," claiming the article would have been better if two anecdotes had not been cut from it.[109]

While the book world awaited publication of the new novel, Speiser was busy trying to sell the novel to Hollywood. On 7 October, a request for twenty-five copies to be sent to Donald Friede, a former publisher turned agent in Hollywood, was made to Perkins.[110] Around 12 October, Hemingway informed Perkins, "There are some very big money negotiations going on for picture rights and I believe we have turned down 100,000 for the book and may get 150,000. Wouldn't that be bloody wonderful?"[111] On all fronts, success seemed within Hemingway's grasp. The book had yet to be published but was already famous.

The book was published on 21 October 1940, selling for $2.75. In the market, the work had to compete with, among other books, Thomas Wolfe's *You Can't Go Home Again,* Jan Struther's *Mrs. Miniver,* James Hilton's *Random Harvest,* Van Wyck Brooks's *New England: Indian Summer,* and John O'Hara's *Pal Joey.* The initial printing was for 210,192 copies, with 135,000 going to the Book-of-the-Month Club.[112] The black dust jacket, printed in red, white, blue, and grey, had an illustration of mountains with a steel bridge and house, which appeared between the title and the author's name. A photo of Hemingway appeared on the back cover. The inside flaps included a quote from Canby's *Book-of-the-Month Club News* review and a description of the novel emphasizing the action and love elements of the story and that it is "twice as long as 'A Farewell to Arms.'"[113] To mark the event, the Scribner Book Store devoted its three windows to displays featuring the novel and the author.[114]

The novel was widely and, for the most part, very favorably reviewed. Hemingway's scrapbook contains clippings of over a hundred reviews.[115] On 20 October, a day before publication, both the *New York Times Book Review* and the *New York Herald Tribune Books* featured reviews of *For Whom the Bell Tolls* on their front pages. The *Times* review, by editor J. Donald Adams, called the novel "the best book Ernest Hemingway has written, the fullest, the deepest, the truest."[116] For John Chamberlain, writing in the *Herald Tribune,* the novel "redeems a decade of futility" on Hemingway's part.[117] By far the most enthusiastic review of the day was Dorothy Parker's for *PM.* In her conclusion, Parker stated, "I think that what you do about this book of Ernest Hemingway's is to point to it and say, 'Here is a book.' As you would stand below Everest and say, 'Here is a mountain.'"[118] Ralph Thompson in the *New York Times* and the unsigned reviewers for *Time* and *Newsweek* all unreservedly praised the novel on the day of publication.[119] Margaret Marshall, reviewing the novel for the *Nation,* saw it as "superior" to *A Farewell to Arms,* and the book that set "a new standard for Hemingway."[120] Writing in the *New Yorker,* Clifton Fadiman called the book "not merely an advance on 'A Farewell to Arms.' It touches a deeper level than any sounded in the author's other books."[121] The reviewer for the *Saturday Review of Literature* (which featured a photo of Hemingway on its front cover), Howard Mumford Jones, declared that *For Whom the Bell Tolls* was "probably one of the finest and richest novels of the last decade."[122] Edmund Wilson, writing in the *New Republic,* echoed the sentiments of the other reviewers of the week, stating, "Hemingway the artist is with us again, and it is like having an old friend back."[123]

Most of the reviews that appeared in the following months were positive, but Hemingway did not enjoy the unanimous support of the critics. Perhaps the most negative review was by novelist Alvah Bessie in the *New Masses,* but he faults Hemingway mainly for his criticisms of the Communist Party.[124] Burton Rascoe was also critical of the novel. In his review for the *American Mercury,* he saw the novel as proof that Hemingway was "the most infantile-minded writer of great talent in our time."[125] The reviewer for the *Commonweal,* J. N. Vaughan, took the opposite view of most of the critics, calling the novel "infinitely inferior to Hemingway's prior work."[126] The January–February 1941 *Partisan Review* contained both a negative and a positive review. Dwight Macdonald condemned the novel because of Hemingway's "lack of political consciousness."[127] Lionel Trilling, in the same issue, stated that "here, we feel at once, is a restored Hemingway writing to the top of his bent."[128] Playwright and fellow Scribners author Robert Sherwood called the novel "a rare and beautiful work" in the *Atlantic Monthly.*[129] Malcolm Cowley provided the *New Republic* with another review of the novel on 20 January 1941, in which he called the work "an ambitious undertaking" with "everything in it."[130] For most of the critics, *For Whom the Bell Tolls* was the novel they had been waiting for since *A Farewell to Arms*. It was almost as if they were taking their cues from the Scribners advertising department.

As he got reviews, Perkins sent them along to Hemingway with his comments. On 11 October, a week before publication, he wrote Hemingway, "We have just heard from Time that they have in type a very fine review,—may get proof of it this afternoon to send to you."[131] Four days later, Perkins reported on Adams's and Chamberlain's reviews: "Here is a magnificent review from Adams who never previously was very friendly.—And as you know, the Times is far more important and effective than any other reviewing medium.— And here also is a review which except for the silliness of its beginning, is quite good—anyhow it is very good from a sales standpoint even in the silliness—by John Chamberlain, for the front page of the Herald Tribune. I am getting both of these supplements tomorrow for Speiser who will have them photostated in furtherance of the movie sale."[132] On the date of publication, Perkins forwarded more reviews and comments: "Here are two more, and both of them very fine, but Dorothy Parker's is unbeatable.—And I understand that there is to be a magnificent one in the next issue of The Saturday Review which, while it has a very small circulation, has a great deal of prestige."[133]

About a week after the book was published, Hemingway wrote Perkins about the closing of the movie deal. He was to get $100,000, plus ten cents a copy from a special movie tie-in edition of the novel.[134] Hemingway thought it best to make the deal "before the counterattack started." He also included his own reactions to the reviewers: "I thought Bunny Wilson's review very dull. He is interested only In the political and sectarian political aspect and writing means nothing to him anymore. Same for the Nation one. He, Chamberlain etc. all the non-fuck-men unite against the girl. Calling that unreal is the only thing they have left to attack. Well it isn't nreal and the thee and the thou way of speaking is the one thing they would know about if they were ever in a revolution."[135] Critics, it would seem, would always be distrusted and disliked by Hemingway, even when the majority of what they said was favorable.

In addition to being widely reviewed, the book was advertised by the firm more extensively than any other Hemingway title. Between 15 June 1940 and 3 December 1941, the firm bought 504 advertisements for the novel, spending $43,567.09 on the effort. Space was purchased in newspapers and magazines across the country, not merely in publications on the East Coast. In addition, Scribners bought in January 1941 "4000 Hemingway Window Displays," presumably for bookstores, at a cost of $1,672.80.[136] From 20 October 1940 to 15 June 1941, twenty-nine ads for the novel appeared in the *New York Times Book Review.*[137] Nine of these are for the novel alone; in thirteen, the novel was the most prominent in the ads because more space was devoted to it, its copy was in a different typeface, or it had a different border. After the full-page advertisement of 10 November, Scribners used quotes from the reviewers in these advertisements. In most of them, the fact that the novel was a Book-of-the-Month Club selection was mentioned. Such extensive advertisement was not confined to the *New York Times Book Review,* as evidence from the *New York Herald Tribune Books* and the *Chicago Tribune* shows. From October 20 to the end of the year, fourteen ads for the novel appeared in the *New York Herald Tribune Books.* The *Chicago Tribune* had seven ads for the novel in the same period.[138]

Scribners also ran two post-publication ads in *Publishers Weekly.* The first appeared in the 30 November 1940 issue. This two-page spread featured seventeen quotes from bookstores around the country.[139] A one-page ad ran in the 1 February 1941 issue and included the statement, "A National Advertising campaign reaching more than 10,000,000 readers is now under way."[140] In the 25 January issue's "The Publishers Plan Promotion for High Spots of Spring Lists," the Scribners section began with the firm's plans for the novel: "A new and impressive advertising campaign has been scheduled to keep up the big sales of Ernest Hemingway's 'For Whom the Bell Tolls.' Copy will be run in all the national media and a special series of ads is planned for more than 30 newspapers throughout the country. A new poster, a handsome 3-panel affair, will soon be sent to bookstores."[141] The firm also devoted one-page sections to the novel on the second page of both its spring 1941 and fall 1941 trade catalogs.[142] Clearly, Scribners was doing everything it could to maintain the demand for the novel.

The firm was aided in this endeavor by publicity it did not have to buy. As the novel became more successful and well known, so did Hemingway; as Hemingway's fame grew, so did the novel's. Between the date of publication and June 1941, Hemingway was the subject of six interviews.[143] From the time of publication to the end of 1941, there were fourteen magazine and newspaper articles on Hemingway or the novel. Many related information about his divorce from Pauline Hemingway and marriage to Martha Gelhorn.[144] In addition to this coverage, John Raeburn points out that in regard to Hemingway's divorce and remarriage, "syndicated columnist Walter Winchell reported the details of the alimony settlement, *Harper's Bazaar* ran a full-page photograph taken of the 'co-adventurers' after their wedding, and the tabloid New York *Mirror* featured a human interest story on Hemingway's love life."[145] Hemingway attracted attention that had nothing to do with his literary creations but that could also sell books.

Beyond the money the club paid to Hemingway, *For Whom the Bell Tolls* benefited greatly from its selection by the Book-of-the-Month Club. No doubt the novel did help create and maintain a word-of-mouth campaign among readers, the scope of which is impossible to assess. One aspect of the Book-of-the-Month Club's impact is easy to judge. From 20 October 1940 to 28 December 1941, the Book-of-the-Month Club ran twenty-three ads in the *New York Times Book Review* that featured the book.[146] While the main purpose was to advertise the club, they also served to keep the book in the public eye. By seeking to share the fame of the novel, these ads helped make the book better known.

The novel was widely regarded as one of the best novels of 1940. In the *New York Herald Tribune Books*'s survey of seventy critics and authors, which ran in the 1 December 1940 issue under the title "Books I Have Liked," twenty-four listed Hemingway's novel.[147] Fanny Butcher, in the *Chicago Tribune,* placed it second, behind *You Can't Go Home Again,* on her list of the ten best novels of the year.[148] The *Saturday Review of Literature* included the novel with thirteen other titles on its recommended Christmas list.[149]

In addition to these honors, the novel was the odds-on favorite to win the Pulitzer Prize for Fiction. In a poll of thirty-nine reviewers by the *Saturday Review of Literature,* twenty-one picked *For Whom the Bell Tolls* as the winner for fiction.[150] However, no award for fiction was given that year. Nicholas Murray Butler, president of Columbia University (which administered the Pulitzer Prize selections), vetoed the choice of *For Whom the Bell Tolls* as winner for fiction. John Hohenberg, in his book on the prize, writes that Butler told the advisory board for the prize at its meeting on 2 May 1941, "I hope you will reconsider before you ask the university to be associated with an award for a work of this nature." Butler's prestige and power were so great that "no member of the Board at that time dared to stand against him."[151] As Albert Marrin states, "Evidently Robert Jordan's politics and love affair with Maria offended the educator's sense of propriety."[152] Hemingway at least appeared unaffected by the slight, telling a *St. Louis Star-Times*'s interviewer, "If I'd won that prize, I'd think I was slipping. I've been writing for twenty years and never have won a prize. I've gotten along all right."[153] There is no mention of the Pulitzer Prize in Hemingway's letters to Perkins.

Scribners pushed the book until it was not economically sound to push it anymore. Responding to one of Hemingway's perpetual complaints that the book was not being advertised enough, Perkins wrote on 3 September 1941 to correct Hemingway:

> On straight newspaper and magazine advertising we spent a few cents short of $43,000.00. On special trade advertising, which includes circulars, posters (partly explained by the enclosed circular), and such things as that box enlargement of the book, we spent approximately five thousand dollars, not less.
>
> The preliminary trade advertising began in June 1940, but the actual amount spent in advertising did not begin to amount to very much until October 20th. We then advertised steadily to August, 1941.
>
> We did not stop except in the face of returns diminishing to a point where spending close to 50¢ a copy sold, in advertising on the average in the 1941 months. That is, in 1940 we sold 189,529 copies and in that year we spent (excluding the special trade advertising) $26,397.92. From December 31st through August 28, 1941, we had sold about 35,000 copies, and we had spent in advertising $16,598.97. Fifty cents a copy is very much too much in the face of long discounts that have to be given with a book selling in great quantity, and the royalty we pay. . . . We actually advertised "The Bell" steadily for nine months. A publisher very seldom gets a chance to do that.[154]

Based on these figures, Hemingway's income from the Scribners edition of *For Whom the Bell Tolls* would have been $120,053.45 by this time. If a 40-percent discount to bookstores is assumed, the firm

TITLE Hemingway For Whom Bell Tolls   EDITION_____   CODE_____ 2.

PUBLISHED October 21, 1940   PRINTED_____

	SHEET STOCK					BOUND STOCK			
DATE	ON HAND	JOB NO.	ORDER	BALANCE	DATE	DELIVERIES	RECEIPTS	NET SALES	BALANCE
1940					1940				
Nov. 1	117627	20000	64000	53627	1940	26074	1355		
14		18211	1000	52627	Nov. 28	24124	1950		
1		20000	51127	1500	28	23305	819		
22		18277	500	1000	29	22330	975		
26		18284	500	500	Dec. 2	20038	2292		
Dec. 2		18319	500	0	3	17113	2925		
Nov. 27	25000	21000	24500	500	3	11759	5354		
Dec. 10		18350	500	0	4	5855	5904		
Nov. 27	50000	21000	26650	23350	5	5327	528		
Dec. 16		18389	350	23000	6	528	4799		
1940		22000	2750	250	Nov. 9	0	528		
1941 Jan. 6		18469	250	0		500	12		
					Dec. 10	0	500		
		See New Card				24500	1355		
					6	20652	3848		
					9	19833	819		
	BOUND STOCK				9	18195	1638		
DATE	DELIVERIES	RECEIPTS	NET SALES	BALANCE	11	8836	9359		
1940	500	12			12	7198	1638		
Nov. 22	0	500			10	5530	1668		
	500	12			11	3892	1638		
26	0	500			12	3812	80		
	500	12			13	402	3410		
Dec. 3	0	500			16	0	1053		
	51127	1355				22750	1374		
Nov. 15	48565	2562			13	20956	1794		
18	47242	1323			16	19319	1638		
19	46714	528			17	15223	4095		
20	40981	5733			18	13345	1878		
25	36589	4392			20	10230	3115		
26	30856	5733			24	8592	1638		
27	26074	4782			26	4497	4095		
					27	3678	819		
					30	2040	1638		
					30	402	1638		

Bindery card for Hemingway's *For Whom the Bell Tolls*, reflecting the first two printings of the novel (Scribners Archives)

would have grossed $370,472.85 by September 1941. This would have left Charles Scribner's Sons with $202,422.51 (excluding the amount paid to the firm from the Book-of-the-Month Club) to cover other expenses after paying Hemingway's royalty and the cost of advertising.

The demand for the work was good, but not as great as the ads would lead one to believe. On 22 October, a day after publication, 50,417 copies were printed—20,000 going to the Book-of-the-Month

Club, 30,417 to Scribners. During the last two months of the year, 192,627 copies were printed, of which the Book-of-the-Month Club got 92,000. From January to April of 1941, Scribners printed 115,000 copies—60,000 for itself and 55,000 for the Book-of-the-Month Club. The printing records indicate that after a print run of 25,000 copies for themselves on 19 February 1941, Scribners did not need to print any more copies for themselves until September 1942. From that date until 23 July 1945, the firm printed only 28,650 copies of its own edition. The press also continued to print for the Book-of-the-Month Club; that firm took an additional 96,600 copies between 22 December 1941 and 23 July 1945. In all, the Scribners Press printed a total of 693,486 copies of the novel—398,600 for the Book-of-the-Month Club, 294,886 for Scribners.[155] Assuming every copy sold, Hemingway would have made $158,749.80 from the Scribners edition by 1945; at fifteen cents a copy, he would have made only $59,790 from the Book-of-the-Month Club. This equals $218,539.80 in royalties by 1945, which would equal $2,295,721.38 in 2005 terms.

Earning the author well over $300,000—from the Scribners and Book-of-the-Month Club editions and the movie rights—*For Whom the Bell Tolls* was Hemingway's high-water mark. Responding to his need to publish a novel, he produced the longest and perhaps finest of his career, or, as he might have called it, a long book that reads like a short one. However, much of the success of the work was the result of what Perkins, Scribner, and the other associates of Charles Scribner's Sons did to promote and sell both the work and the author. In short, the miracle of *For Whom the Bell Tolls* might be the fact that everyone did the right thing while writing, editing, packaging, and selling this novel.

CHAPTER 8

AFTER PERKINS

Across the River and Into the Trees *and*
The Old Man and the Sea

For Whom the Bell Tolls was the last Hemingway work that Perkins edited. Although Perkins gave his author advice when he was editing *Men At War,* an anthology of war stories in 1942, Hemingway never sent his editor another manuscript.[1] After 1941, Hemingway's attention was focused almost exclusively on World War II. From 1942 to 1943, he searched for German submarines in the *Pilar,* which had been modified as a Q-boat; from 1944 to 1945 he covered the war in Europe as a correspondent for *Collier's.*[2] After the war Hemingway worked on two novels, both of which he never finished: *The Garden of Eden* and a novel he described as being about the war from the perspectives of "the land, sea and air"—the "sea section" was eventually published as *Islands in the Stream.*[3] Hemingway would not submit a new book to Scribners until 1950, three years after Perkins's death. In 1950, Scribners published *Across the River and Into the Trees,* Hemingway's fifth novel. Two years later, Hemingway followed with the novella *The Old Man and the Sea.* These would be the last new books that Hemingway published. Both could be considered to be successful books, which in part was a result of the work of Charles Scribner III and Wallace Meyer. Both stepped in to fill the role that Perkins had played in Hemingway's career. Although they would never edit Hemingway the way Perkins had, they were adept at handling the other aspects of book publication and helped maintain Hemingway's prominence as the most famous American writer of his day.

Maxwell Perkins died on 17 June 1947. From Cuba, Hemingway wired Charles Scribner, "WHAT AWFUL LUCK DEEPEST SYMPATHY YOU AND ALL AT SCRIBNERS HAVE CABLED LOUISE."[4] Scribner on 25 June wrote Hemingway to express his sense of loss and to assure Hemingway that the firm would protect his interests and not put undue pressure on him. After giving an account of Perkins's last days and death, Scribner described how the firm was reacting. He then wrote:

> Naturally, I am most concerned that the fact that Max is no longer here may affect your relationship with Charles Scribner's Sons. I have not seen you or written to you as much as I would like to have because I knew how close you were to Max and that you would rather hear from and see him which I could very well understand. Your are not an author who needs inspiration from an editor or editorial work done on your books and if you entrust us with your novel, I believe that your friend, Wallace Meyer, can see it through the press as well as any man I know of. It would seem best, however, if you carried on any correspondence in the meantime directly with me. When we meet there are many things I would like to talk over with you. One matter that is very much on my mind is making a new edition of A FAREWELL TO ARMS about which Max and I were talking the last day he was here.[5] I feel sure you will like Norman Snow who has taken Whitney Darrow's place and he is entirely in accord with me in believing that we should put far more pressure on the promotion of the older books that we publish. I think that Whitney Darrow was oversold on the importance of reprint houses. They can do a good job, but it is all-important for our authors, as well as the House, to maintain a strong backlog of seasoned books.[6]

In addition to feeling grief over Perkins's death, Scribner feared the loss of many of the firm's authors, especially Hemingway.

Hemingway was naturally upset over the loss of Perkins, who had been his editor for over twenty-one years. But in his response of 28 June he seemed more concerned for Scribner and the firm than for himself. After recounting the last time he saw Perkins, giving his approval to the changes Scribner had made, and assuring his publisher that he had enough money, Hemingway attempted to lay the groundwork for his future editorial relationship with the firm: "If it would do any good you might let it be known that while Max was my best and oldest friend at Scribners and a great, great editor he never cut a paragraph of my stuff nor asked me to change one. One of my best and most loyal friends and wisest counsellors in life as well as in writing is dead. But Charles Scribner's Sons are my publishers and I intend to publish with them for the rest of my life."[7] Hemingway's statement that Perkins never asked him to change any paragraph was untrue. The author was trying to control the editorial input of Scribner and other members of the firm. The first test of this would come with the publication of *Across the River and Into the Trees.*

The story of the publication of Hemingway's fifth novel really begins in the spring of 1948. *Cosmopolitan* had sent a young editor, A. E. Hotchner, to Cuba to convince Hemingway to write an article on "The Future of Literature" for a proposed series. After meeting with Hotchner, Hemingway agreed not only to write the article but also to submit two stories and serialize a novel (most likely *Islands in the Stream*) in the magazine. The contract, dated 11 June 1948, stated that an acceptable manuscript of the novel had to be delivered by 1 January 1950. Hemingway received $15,000 for the proposed series and articles. The amount would equal $124,093.35 in 2005 terms. The series was cancelled, and Hemingway never wrote the article, nor did he submit any stories.[8]

The novel was another matter. In March of 1949 Hemingway began writing a novel about a U.S. Army colonel's last visit to Venice.[9] The first information he gave Scribner about the novel was on 24 August 1949:

Anyway here is the gen: TOP SECRET EQUALS BRITISH MOST SECRET. I dislike very much much oweing money; even to you and with adequate security. Therefore when some seven doctors, all of whom were wrong up until this date and hour, were convinced that I would die shortly, I started a short novel to show

how well I could write (which is all I give a shit about) except loving Miss Mary and to pay my debts to you since I owe no money to anyone else.

It is a very fine novel, written to beat all comers, and written as well or better than I can write. I guaranty you that is sound in wind and limb. Now we have to gen out when to publish it. This is the point where *you* pay attention. Thank you. . . . Now, you knowing you will have it by the end of October, and that there will be the big one comeing later, we have to start figureing how to launch it. It is better novel than any other son of a bitch, alive or dead, can write and I will not consent to haveing it launched as a secondary, or substitute, effort. It is a beauty novel; short and clear and even those saw-dust headed goons and ghouls that work for you in that defected edifice could probably understand it.[10]

Two days before, Hemingway had written Hotchner that he had "a pretty nice surprise" for him, an intimation that he had a novel for the magazine. After visiting the Hemingways in Cuba in early September, Hotchner returned to New York and ironed out an agreement for *Cosmopolitan* to serialize it in two installments beginning in the February 1950 issue. The magazine would pay $85,000 for the serial, equivalent to $658,904.10 in 2005. Hotchner also met with Charles Scribner, who asked him about the portion of the novel the magazine editor had read.[11] At this point, Hemingway had not sent any of the novel to his publisher.

Hemingway's decision to publish this novel at this time—and thus to abandon work on both *Islands in the Stream* and *The Garden of Eden*—may have had another spur besides his poor health. First, he may have felt the pressure to produce a novel about World War II that could compete with those being published at the time (such as Irwin Shaw's *The Young Lions*, Norman Mailer's *The Naked and the Dead*, and James Gould Cozzens's *Guard of Honor*). He had not published a novel since 1940 and may have seen the new work as a way to regain his prominence as America's best-known writer, especially after William Faulkner ranked him fourth among his contemporaries, telling students at the University of Mississippi that "he has no courage, has never climbed out on a limb."[12] And he had taken an advance for two stories from *Cosmopolitan*. Perhaps this perceived pressure is what led Hemingway to compose and publish the novel as he did.

The novel was not yet complete, but Hemingway was already discussing serialization and publishing strategies. On 31 August, Hemingway wrote Scribner that he could figure on having the setting copy on his desk by 1 December.[13] The next day he wrote his publisher that he did not want to submit the book to any book club, no doubt not wanting to split the money with Scribners as he had had to do with *For Whom the Bell Tolls*.[14] By the twenty-first of the month, he optimistically wrote Scribner, "Have the book under control and needs less than 3 weeks to finish. Am stacking up a list of titles and the latest is ACROSS THE RIVER AND INTO THE TREES. It is an abbreviation of the last words, supposedly, uttered by the late Stonewall Jackson."[15] But the writing was not going as well as Hemingway had hoped or reported. Mary Hemingway, the author's fourth wife, reported her impressions of the novel at this time in her memoir: "I was unhappy about the middle and later parts of the manuscript I had read since my return from Chicago. But I had not figured out why and mentioned it to no one, not even my notebook. It made me feel disloyal, but I was finding Colonel Cantwell's and his girl's conversations banal beyond reason and their obsession with food and the ploy of the emeralds a mysterious lapse of judgement. I kept my mouth shut. Nobody had appointed me my husband's editor or the bombardier of his self-confidence. Someone at Scribner's would help him improve those passages, I hoped."[16] Mary Hemingway was saying, in short, that Hemingway lacked critical judgment when it came to this book.[17] At this date, neither Hotchner nor anyone at Scribners had seen any of the manuscript.

While Hemingway continued work in Cuba, the firm and *Cosmopolitan* issued a press release on 12 October 1949 to promote the novel. The release stated that *Cosmopolitan* would serialize the novel in two installments beginning with the February 1950 issue and that Scribners would publish in March 1950. Emphasis was placed on the fact that it was Hemingway's first novel since *For Whom the Bell Tolls* but was not the big novel he had been working on for some time. Rather, the statement said that Hemingway had started this short book after he had been told that he was going to die from blood poisoning in February of 1949. The statement closed with the following: "Expecting the present novel to be his final work, Mr. Hemingway determined to make it the finest of his writing career. Those who have read the manuscript feel that this novel will rank above anything he has ever written."[18] The notice ran in various newspapers, including the *New York Times*.[19]

From Cuba, where he was preparing to leave for Europe, Hemingway gave Scribner the first intimation that the novel was not progressing as well as he had originally stated: "Have postponed sailing until Nov. 19 because it is not humanly possible to complete novel by Nov. 1. Did 3,243 in four days last week, fished yesterday morning. Actual word count, just words, is 51,700."[20] The slowed progress may have led Hemingway to cannibalize the manuscript of his big novel. On 31 October, he wrote his publisher that he had "decided to save nothing from the ground fighting in this war and all the best goes in."[21] The section on the Hürtgen Forest had originally been part of the "land" section of the big novel. Now it became part of *Across the River and Into the Trees*. During the first part of November, Hemingway reported to Scribner that he had sent about 65 pages of typescript to Hotchner. He had an additional 126 pages on hand.[22] On 16 November, he and Mary flew to New York en route to Paris. It was during this visit that Lillian Ross gathered material for her profile of Hemingway.[23] On 19 November, the Hemingways sailed for France.

From Paris—where Hotchner had joined him—Hemingway wrote Scribner thanking him for advice he had given and for "the news." Apparently, Scribner had at this time moved the publication date from March to June 1950, no doubt because *Cosmopolitan* was going to have to run the novel in more than two installments. He then went on to give Scribner a report on his progress: "But Jesus Christ I am certainly glad to have time to do it right. I believe I would have done it right anyway; but there might have been holes like (such as) you pointed out. . . . Then there is 87,000 (it was 187,000) of another book. I boiled down, and distilled 100,000 out of it to make 17,000 for the book."[24] This was the account of the Hürtgen Forest fight.

On 10 December, Hemingway was finally able to write Scribner, "Finished first draft of book and am naturally beat to the wide."[25] Three days later he wrote Scribner and outlined his revision process:

> The way I am working with Hotch is to have several copies (five) made of all the MSS. I went over on the boat and the MSS. I wrote here. He gets one of these and corrects, cuts etc. for Cosmo. Anything he wants to know he asks me. He also corrects from original mss. with stenographer.

I will then have an original, un-cut, but corrected Mss. to work on for you.

I worked out the problem of the High Brass by name yesterday. Hotch is a lawyer and I read law one winter and so far in 30 years of newspaper and book and magazine work nobody has ever been sued for libel on acct. me.[26]

As it would turn out, the revisions Scribner did ask for were those made to avoid libel suits.

Hotchner was editing for the *Cosmopolitan* serialization—not for Scribners. Nevertheless, some of Hotchner's corrections were retained by Hemingway for the book publication. Albert DeFazio, in his study of the Hemingway/Hotchner relationship, has documented Hotchner's revisions for *Across the River and Into the Trees*. Hemingway had instructed Hotchner to "use your good taste" in the editing. Hotchner modified Cantwell's interior monologue in chapter 18 to eliminate all anti-Semitic references. He also eliminated or modified other passages "that were potentially libelous or sexually explicit as well as language that was profane."[27] Hotchner returned to New York to deliver the setting copy for the serial in January. The serial ran in five installments, beginning in the February 1950 issue.[28] Obscene words were deleted, but some were restored for the book publication. In addition, Hemingway added passages about "the Honorable Pacciardi," and d'Annunzio, as well as all of chapter 37 before the book was published.[29]

From New York, Scribner wrote Hemingway on 12 January 1950 that "We all agree that the ideal time to publish it would be in the first week of August."[30] By 2 February, the publisher had a copy of the version being serialized, for he cabled his author on that date "TRULY DELIGHTED WITH WHAT I HAVE READ OF REVISED VERSION OF NOVEL STOP IT IS NOW BECOMING YOU AT YOUR BEST."[31] Hemingway wrote on 18 February to tell Scribner, "Don't worry about un-necessary fucks and shits. I put them in when it is how a man thinks and later take them out."[32] Before leaving for Paris, Hemingway wrote that he had finished the first revision and removed all but the "absolutely necessary" obscene words but still wanted to strengthen the Hürtgen section.[33]

By this point Wallace Meyer had read all of the *Cosmopolitan* version. On 13 March, he wrote Scribner (who with his wife, Vera, was in London en route to Paris), giving the publisher his impressions of the novel:

> Betty Youngstrom tells me that you're expecting to see Ernest in Paris on the 17th, and I'm hoping this letter will find you before you leave London. We sent the final part of the Cosmo manuscript off by airmail on Monday the 27th, and it must have reached London almost as soon as you did. I can't honestly say that I found it greatly reassuring. The basic trouble is that this book hasn't the idea of a novel. There isn't the essential core there. It should have been a short story, only a moderately long one at that. If Ernest had handled it in its proper medium, the things that so greatly trouble us would have dropped away as excess, and it would have been, I think, a genuinely moving thing. My hope is still what yours has been—that Ernest, when the manuscript had grown cold for him, as it must have done by now, would see the passages and aspects as padding, and would manage somehow to rework and rewrite to give the whole real depth and validity.[34]

Meyer apparently hoped Scribner could convince Hemingway to make the needed revisions to fix the novel. Hemingway, however, did not seem to be willing to take much advice. He wrote Scribner on 14 March, "Don't worry about book. Tell me anything you think and I will fix it if agree, chances are have fixed it already. I don't agree with you worth a damn about the Col. and the headwaiter being cut or that I wrote it because it was fun."[35] The Scribners arrived around the fifteenth. Any editorial exchanges between the two men at this time were not recorded.

The Hemingways landed in New York on 27 March and stayed until 6 April. On 5 April, Hemingway worked with Meyer on the novel. On the day after Hemingway left the city, Meyer sent Scribner a report of his session with Hemingway:

> You have probably wondered why you haven't heard from me about Ernest. But until now I have had nothing substantial to report, and I know that in the meantime he has written to you.
> Ernest and I had half a dozen phone conversations, and it was agreed that as soon as he was ready to see me I'd hold myself at

his disposition. A week went by during which I was kept busy fending off people who were trying to find out where he was. The summons finally came on Wednesday. Ernest wanted me to bring Irma Wyckoff with me if possible, to do some work on the manuscript. I was with him from 11 to 4, and Irma stayed for half an hour after I left. She brought back the manuscript with her, and your son now has it in hand for composition. Ernest and Mary left the next day (Thursday).

The manuscript is not changed in any fundamental respect. Ernest had cleaned it up quite a bit in the matter of language and personal allusions. There are new touches which will strengthen some of the passages a little, but essentially it is the book that we first saw. The galleys will be in his hands before you get back, and I am frankly hoping that he does quite a bit of work on them. He has several possibilities in mind, I know. Any revision he may make now will be in the right direction.

Ernest was friendliness itself. Mary went out for lunch some-where else after a brief hello, and along toward two o'clock Ernest gave us lunch. We'd had the inevitable champagne before that, and there was wine with the lunch, though not, I suspect, Valpolicella. We went over photographs for possible use, and I brought back the jacket design, which Miss DeVoy now has in hand. She feels that it will work out effectively in three colors. Everyone here agrees with you that we must do some work on the lettering. Ernest seemed to consider it fine as it was. But I don't think he will ever be captious about it. He wants the original design back eventually, and it follows that he will be able to compare our product with the original.

I read some of Ernest's shorter things, and he gave me one of his long poems, which I found strange and individual and really moving. He fairly trembled looking over my shoulder as I read—it evidently means a tremendous lot to him—and I was very much aware of the same effect that you had spoken of. In the course of the day I discovered the reason: Ernest eats a raw onion sandwich for breakfast every morning. . . . Ernest did not seem to me to be very well. There's no question but what he's in a transition phase, physically speaking. I think too that he's in a transition phase as a creative artist, and that we can only let him develop freely, as freely as his health will permit. It seemed to me, though, that as I read the poem I began to understand a little better.[36]

For Meyer, the book was still not improved, and it seems that he and Scribner did not know how to approach Hemingway to get him to make the necessary revisions to the structure and concept of the novel. He hoped instead that Hemingway would see the defects for himself.

On 14 April, Meyer wrote Hemingway a letter with queries about some of the place-names.[37] Scribner wrote his author on 21 April that he would read the novel when he got back to New York. He added that Hemingway could revise as much as he wanted on the galley proofs and would not be charged for any alterations.[38] By 1 May, Hemingway had the galley proofs.[39] Three days later, Scribner wrote about possible libelous references. One was the reference to the "pitted" writer (i.e., Sinclair Lewis). Scribner also objected to the reference to Dwight David Eisenhower as a "mediocre general." Of utmost concern was Cantwell calling his ex-wife—a very thinly veiled portrait of Martha Gelhorn—a "bitch."[40] Hemingway, writing on 7 May, thought that neither Lewis nor Gelhorn could sue, but he did change "bitch" to "woman." He promised to send the galleys the next day.[41] On 8 May, Scribner sent another letter about possible libelous references. He reiterated that the worst were those about Lewis, Eisenhower, and Gelhorn.[42] The next day, after reading Hemingway's revised galleys, Scribner still wanted the Lewis and Gelhorn references changed and told his author, "I don't care who that old bastard of a colonel was, but Martha is still very easily recognized."[43] In none of their letters to their author did Meyer or Scribner indicate that they had more serious concerns about the novel.

Hemingway was convinced about the Lewis reference, for on 15 May he sent Scribner a revision to be inserted in galley 26. He also changed "mediocre general" to "Political General." He told Scribner that an Italian friend, Gianfranco Ivancich (brother of Adriana Ivancich), had checked the novel twice for errors in geography and Italian. But Hemingway made it clear to the publisher that his patience was running thin: "I am getting sick of all this and of the necessary, I suppose, emasculation and of Wallace telling me there is no such place as Fornace and that Fossalta is on the Po. I'm not even permitted to know where I lost my right knee cap. Next they will tell me there is no such place as Pertica, nor Asalone—I'll leave it alone."[44] Hemingway no doubt thought that Scribner was overstepping his bounds. Scribner wrote on 16 May that the publication date had been moved from August to 7 September so that the novel would be considered a fall book rather than be "handicapped as being on the list of books classed as Summer books."[45] Hemingway replied on 20 May: "About the rest of it: It's your business. I met all my datelines and usually was ahead. If you want to start on Sept. 7 that's o.k. . . . But do not let any one be given the impression that you are publishing a month later than I have told people, because there is something wrong with the book. We have been trying to make a good book better. Not make a bad book good."[46] Hemingway may have feared that news of such a delay would lead to a "gang-up" by the critics.

The next day Hemingway sent Scribner another letter, this one containing information about a new work: "Started to re-read a short story I was interrupted on and found it ran over 30,000 words. I'll finish it with 10, to 15,000 more and then we can call it The Longest Short Story In The World and use it as an anchor story in the book of Short Stories. It's a hell of a story. Think you will like it."[47] The book of stories was never published. The story was probably *The Old Man and the Sea.*

Scribner mailed a set of revised galley proofs of *Across the River and Into the Trees* to the author on 23 May; he noted that there were a few queries but told Hemingway, "Whether you make any changes or not is entirely up to you. I shall be completely happy with the book whatever you decide to do."[48] Hemingway returned this set on 2 June.[49] Scribner wired on 5 June to see if Hemingway wanted to see page proofs.[50] These were mailed on 14 June, Scribner noting in his cover letter, "I am entirely happy with what you have done."[51] Hemingway finished going over these and mailed them to the publisher on 30 June.[52] The editing of *Across the River and Into the Trees* was complete.

Scribner did bring up one mistake Hemingway had made. On 18 July, he wrote Hemingway about Cantwell's address to his driver: "I know very little about the infantry, thank heaven, but I do know just enough to have discovered that you pulled a boner in your book. Your Colonel addresses his driver as sergeant, but Jackson is also referred to in other places as T-5 which, if you will go back to your manuals of marching, you will find is a corporal's rank. The references are on page 160 and 273. Maybe the Colonel is dumb, but in any event, I am delighted with my technical knowledge of such matters."[53] Scribner's tone indicates that he was joking. But Hemingway was not amused. He wrote Scribner a letter on 21 July (annotating the date "my goddamned birthday") in which he stated: "I got sort of angry at your letter about T/5 etc. and wrote a sort of bad one back. But didn't send it. . . . Also please do not apologize for the book or pick flaws in it *once it is being printed.* Any criticisms or suggestions you have to make should have been made while it was still fluid. Now I would wish to see you fight and to *ride* the horse for better or for any amount of worse."[54] No one at Scribners pointed out another error in the book to Hemingway.

Scribners had two months from receipt of the page proofs to publication—ample time to prepare a big campaign. On 28 July Scribner wrote his author that review copies would be sent the next week. He added, "We are definitely committed to the largest advertising appropriation than we have invested on any book since your last was published ten years ago, and the copy for the advertising looks very good to me."[55] Scribners had begun promoting the book in the fall of 1949. In the firm's spring catalog a notice for the novel appeared on page 1; the copy stated, "Probable Publication Date: July / Watch *Publishers Weekly* for further details."[56] In the catalog for the fall, the firm included a three-page spread announcing *Across the River and Into the Trees,* which featured a photograph of Hemingway and a reproduction of the dust jacket. The copy stressed the similarities of the new novel to *For Whom the Bell Tolls* and *A Farewell to Arms.* After giving a plot summary, the description promised the bookseller: "The Hemingway market extends into the hundreds of thousands. *Across the River and Into the Trees* will be given the strongest possible promotion, with heavy announcement advertising at publication and a continuing campaign through the whole fall season. Please note that although an early version of *Across the River and Into the Trees* was serialized in the spring, this book presents the novel in its completed and final form, with passages which are wholly new and without deletion or expurgation. Initial advertising appropriation: $20,000. Return post card. Poster available."[57] The notice for the novel in the "Buyers' Forecast" in the 29 July issue of *Publishers Weekly* made it clear how important the publisher and the trade believed the novel to be:

New passages and passages deleted from the serialized *Cosmopolitan* version are included in this 300-page novel, Hemingway's first in ten years, his first since "For Whom the Bell Tolls." However, not of the stature of that novel. Scribner has an initial ad appropriation of $25,000 for heavy announcement ads and a campaign through the whole fall. A postwar story of an American Colonel, whose fifty years and heart condition weigh heavily upon him, as he spends a weekend in Venice, the city he loves, and sees the 18-year-old Italian contessa who is his "only, last and true love." Scribner's most important fall book, it will have advance postcards and window posters available.[58]

Clearly Scribners was positioning *Across the River and Into the Trees* to be the book of the season.

The post-publication advertisement schedule was, as promised, extensive. On 23 August, Julien Dedman of the firm's advertising department sent Scribner, Meyer, and Snow a two-page schedule for the firm's print advertisements across the country. Between 7 September and 15 October, the firm had scheduled advertisements to run in fourteen newspapers, Sunday book supplements, and magazines. Most of the advertisements were to be placed in New York City newspapers. In all, the firm was going to spend $14,325.30 on these post-publication notices.[59] The balance of the $20,000 was probably for posters and other promotional materials for bookstores.

Across the River and Into the Trees was published on 7 September 1950 and sold for $3.00.[60] Hemingway's contract, dated 18 November 1949, includes a clause for his standard royalty rate: 15 percent of the trade list price for the first 25,000 copies sold, 20 percent thereafter. Hemingway received an advance of $25,000.[61] Initial orders were very good. On 7 June, the Scribners Press ordered a printing of 76,000 copies. On 14 August, an additional 25,500 copies were ordered, for a total of 101,500 copies.

As expected, since this was Hemingway's first novel in ten years, *Across the River and Into the Trees* was widely reviewed and created something of a sensation. In major American newspapers and magazines, the novel received twenty-two reviews. Raeburn states that "About 150 newspaper and magazine critics reviewed *Across the River and Into the Trees*."[62] Most were unimpressed. Lewis Gannett, writing in the *New York Herald Tribune,* stated, "Some of the book is

Hemingway at his worst, and the whole does not add up to Hemingway at his best."[63] In *Harper's Magazine,* Richard H. Rovere called the book "a disappointing novel."[64] Malcolm Cowley, reviewing for the *New York Herald Tribune Book Review,* wrote that the book "was below the level of his earlier novels."[65] Most of the positive reviews came from other novelists. John O'Hara, in his front-page review for the *New York Times Book Review,* wrote: "The most important author living today, the outstanding author since the death of Shakespeare, has brought out a new novel. The title of the novel is *Across the River and Into the Trees.* The author, of course, is Ernest Hemingway, the most important, the outstanding author out of the millions of writers who have lived since 1616."[66] Sections from Evelyn Waugh's review for the British magazine *Tablet* (in which he wrote, "What, in fact [Hemingway] has done is to write a story entirely characteristic of himself, not his best book, perhaps his worst, but still something very much better than most of the work to which the same critics give their tepid applause") were printed in *Time* in the 30 October issue.[67] William Faulkner sent a letter to *Time,* which was printed in the 13 November issue, in support of Waugh's opinion.[68] The disagreement among the two camps was news in itself, resulting in at least five additional articles or columns just on the reception alone.[69]

Despite the hype generated by the publication, a truly large sale did not result. In a memo dated 19 April 1951, Whitney Darrow reported to Scribner that the firm had 25,701 copies of the novel still on hand. The memo goes on to report that since the first of that year, about 1,500 copies had been sold. What was even worse was the fact that there had been "somewhere around 10,000" returns during the same period.[70] A chart of Hemingway's royalty income for 1 August 1951 to 1 February 1954 shows that as of 1 August 1951, eleven months after publication, the firm had sold 93,738 copies, paying Hemingway a royalty of $50,960.70. (In 2005 terms, this amount would equal $395,037.82.) The chart also records that there were no sales after this date.[71] The discount Scribners gave bookstores and jobbers at this time was 44 percent of the list price (i.e., they sold copies of *Across the River and Into the Trees* for $1.68). The firm would have grossed $157,479.84 on these 93,738 copies. After paying Hemingway's royalty and the $20,000 advertising cost, the firm would have had $86,519.14 left to cover its other expenses. Including the $85,000 paid by *Cosmopolitan* for serial rights, Hemingway received $135,960.70 for *Across the River and Into the Trees.*

The novel can therefore be seen as a success. But the success was short-lived, and the bad reviews were sure to have left a bad taste in Hemingway's mouth. It was not the work that would cement his reputation. His next project, *The Old Man and the Sea,* would.

Hemingway first presented the idea for *The Old Man and the Sea* in "On the Blue Water: A Gulf Stream Letter," which appeared in the April 1936 issue of *Esquire.* In it, he tells of an old commercial fisherman who caught a large marlin after a fight of two days and nights, only to lose over half the fish to sharks after it was caught.[72] In a letter dated 7 February 1939 to Maxwell Perkins, Hemingway raised the possibility of publishing a new book of stories that would contain the old man's story but added that he had not written it yet.[73] The idea lay dormant until 1950, when he began writing or rewriting the story. Mary Hemingway reported that Hemingway began working on the story after the Christmas holidays:

> As the holidays ended Ernest set out by himself on a new adventure, a story about an old Cuban fisherman he had put on the tape recorder inside his head years before and had sketched in a piece *Esquire* published in April 1936. This was happy work. Every morning he unwound a bit of the tape, the words falling smoothly onto the paper in his battered Royal portable, with none of the problems of disciplining turbulent emotions, rephrasing meannesses, smoothing roughnesses that had so troubled him in the writing of *Across the River.* Every evening after supper when our guests had retired and the house was quiet I read the manuscript, beginning each time at the first page.[74]

By 17 February 1951 the story was finished.[75] At his home in Cuba Hemingway showed it to visitors, including Charles Scribner, but did not send it to Scribners to be published, since he wanted it to serve as an epilogue to the three books, which were posthumously published as *Islands in the Stream.*[76]

On 11 February 1952 Charles Scribner III died. Hemingway had lost another editor. On 21 February, Hemingway wrote Wallace Meyer, giving his reaction to the news:

When Max died I did not think I could stand it. We understood each other so well that it was like haveing a part of yourself die. But it happened so there was nothing to do until I saw that there was something to do about Charlie. He was takeing an awful beating filling in for Max and I thought the only thing I could do to give him confidence was to give him absolute loyalty. We had been friends for a long time (although we made friends fairly reluctantly) but finally we got to be very close friends. I used to get angry sometimes and so did he. But when he came down here and I saw how ill he had been dureing a time when I had thought he had been inefficient I knew I must never hurt nor worry him if I could help it. I wish to Christ I could have done something for him. But what can you do, Wallace? I loved Charlie very much and I understood him and appreciated him I hope and feel like hell that he is dead.[77]

Hemingway would eventually honor both Perkins and Scribner when *The Old Man and the Sea* was published by dedicating the book to them.

Hemingway's plans for the story changed drastically when Leland Hayward read it in early March 1952. Hayward, the Broadway producer of *South Pacific* and other shows, suggested to Hemingway that it should be published as soon as possible. Mary Hemingway recorded the encounter. According to her, Hayward wanted the work published in "a big magazine, *Life* or *Look*." Hemingway replied that Scribners "wouldn't like that." Hayward claimed that magazine publication would mean "millions of dollars of free advertising" for Scribners and that the magazine piece should appear "just ahead of the book" or at the same time. Hemingway countered that Scribners would not sell a copy with such an arrangement, but Hayward claimed, "People will read the magazine and rush out to buy the book." When Hayward left a day or two later, he had a copy of the manuscript in hand to peddle in New York.[78]

While Hayward worked on *Life*, Hemingway sent a typescript copy of the work to Scribners. He included a letter, dated 4 March, to Meyer. Hemingway mentioned Hayward's idea of magazine publication but did not say whether he thought that it was a good idea or not. He did not mail the letter until 7 March, a day after Hayward's departure. On the page he added to the letter, Hemingway told more of Hayward's plan and subtly tried to get Meyer to agree with it:

> Hayward suggested that the Book of the Month club might take it as a selection along with another full sized book. He said that he wanted to have lunch with the editor of LIFE and talk the Mss. over with him. I asked him to wait until after Scribners had read it. In times like these I do not want you or young Charlie to have any impression that I am going over anybody's heads in anything. You will naturally hear the usual false rumours that I am negotiating with other publishers etc. There is no way from stopping those lies. But never believe any movement of mine that you do not hear from me.
>
> Charlie wrote me a couple of times asking me if I did not want to serialize this and to be sure to do so if I wanted to.[79]

Without coming out and saying it directly, Hemingway implied in the letter that he wanted to publish the work in a magazine. He also tried to sell Meyer on the idea by claiming that Charles Scribner had essentially given him permission to do so—although there is no evidence to indicate that the author and the publisher had ever discussed the matter—and by giving assurances to Meyer that he would do nothing to hurt the company.

After reading the work, Meyer telegraphed Hemingway on 12 March that it was "magnificent" and that they should plan for publication in the fall.[80] In a follow-up letter the next day, Meyer told Hemingway, "By all means it should go into one of the weeklies—Life or The New Yorker—where it will not be divided, and for a very good price. There is also the advantage of flexibility in having four issues a month and the ability to synchronize magazine publishing and book publishing dates. The Book-of-the-Month Club idea in your letter should be a certainty for a dual selection, and perhaps even for a single selection. I should think that the quality of it would completely over-ride any considerations of length."[81] Undoubtedly, Meyer, like Hayward, saw the magazine publication as free advertising for the book.

In a letter dated 21 March, Meyer informed Hemingway that he had met with Hayward on the day before and was ready to proceed. As soon as Hemingway had sent the final typescript, copies would be made so that Hayward could present it to *Life* and Scribners could do the same with the Book-of-the-Month Club. Again, Meyer emphasized that the scheduling of the book publication should wait until the "other two considerations" were set.[82] In his next letter to Hemingway, dated 28 March, Meyer stated that he had arranged a meeting with the Book-of-the-Month Club officials and that they could expect a decision on the day the club's judges met (4 April). Meyer also said that Norman Snow thought that September would be the ideal time to publish. The only thing was to "get the synchronization worked out, keeping very quiet on the outside until things are all set."[83]

On 4 April, Meyer wired Hemingway that the Book-of-the-Month Club had accepted the book and could publish in September with Scribners. However, until *Life* made its decision the date was still tentative.[84] In a follow-up letter dated 7 April, Meyer explained that the Book-of-the-Month Club wanted *The Old Man and the Sea* as part of its October dual selection but would use it in September if Scribners wanted. Meyer suggested two possible publication dates based on the club's decision: 8 September if it was a September selection or 29 September if it was an October selection. The only remaining problem was if and when *Life* would publish, a cause for concern for both Scribners and the Book-of-the-Month Club: "The ideal timing would be for *Life* to bring out their number just about a month before book publication, ideal both for us and for The BOMC. To have it practically simultaneous with the book would undercut the importance of book publication considerably. The BOMC are a little nervous about that. A month ahead ought to be just right to build interest toward the appearance of the book. The atmosphere created is bound to be good."[85] Meyer saw the advantage of the *Life* publication in creating interest in the book but knew that it could just as easily overshadow the book if the two came out at the same time.

When *Life* finally did agree to publish the novella, a new problem arose. Hayward wrote to Hemingway on 11 April 1952 that *Life* definitely wanted the piece and would pay between $40,000 and $50,000, but that their publication plans differed radically from those of Scribners:

There was a school of thought at LIFE that the way to do the book was to run it at Christmas, and instead of running the usual kind of insert they do of sixteen pages of beautiful reproductions of some kind or other, they would like to run your story as a Christmas feature. I told them that I thought this would conflict with the Book-of-the-Month Club and with Scribner's plan of publishing either September 1st or October 1st, but that I would check it. I checked with Meyer who said it would completely screw up everything. So, I told Sidney James [managing editor of *Life*] that it would have to be September 1st or October 1st. They are still arguing about it as of tonight at seven o'clock. Sidney James and Dan Longwell [chairman of the board of editors at *Life*] want to publish it Labor Day Weekend because they feel they would get a big kick-off on it because of the holiday weekend.[86]

Hayward's letter caused Hemingway considerable worry. On 15 April, he wrote Meyer to give his views and to distance himself from the *Life* business:

> I think Life should publish around Labour Day so you can publish the end of Sept. even if I have to take less money from them. Christmas publication would seem to me to be very destructive for the book from our point of view.
>
> Wallace please understand that the LIFE business was Leland's suggestion and that I routed everything through you and no one saw it or had any offer of it until you had seen Leland. I did not know, nor do I know, how publishing conditions are changed and I would certainly not want to imperil book sale by publication in a magazine. But Leland assured me that such a wide diffusion helped rather than hurt now.[87]

Meyer tried, in a letter dated 25 April, to assure his author that he was well within his rights to get "the maximum reward" for the book, but he also explained the way things had to be. Since the Book-of-the-Month Club had given a guarantee of $40,000 for the book, they were nervous about the *Life* publication undercutting them. Since the club would send questionnaires to their members around the first of August for their September selections, they wanted *Life* to publish around the first of September. October publication was still a possibility but seemed unlikely, since *Life* would want to devote more space then to the presidential campaign. So it was publication for all three parties around the first of September or nothing.[88]

By 2 May, the arrangements with *Life* were settled.[89] Hemingway would receive $40,000 from *Life* for the serial rights (equivalent to $284,525.02 in 2005).[90] Hemingway wrote Meyer on 7 May to say he did not see how the Book-of-the-Month Club could offer the book without telling its members that it would appear in *Life;* this did not seem ethical to him.[91] It would appear that since all three parties had come to an agreement on publication dates, Hemingway was trying to see where the deal would go wrong. Meyer wrote to Hemingway on 9 May to assure him that no secret would be made of the *Life* publication by the Book-of-the-Month Club or by Scribners: "We will be open about it in our presentation to the book trade." Meyer also admitted that magazine publication could hurt book sales but emphasized its possible advantages:

> The Book-of-the-Month Club is prepared to accept the possible handicap of a one-shot in *Life*, and so are we. We frankly don't know whether it will turn out to be a handicap and neither do they. It may very well work out the other way. Coming practically all at once the way it will—*Life*, the book in the stores and in the reviews, The Book-of-the-Month selection and publicity—the effect may be a boost that would over-ride any possible handicap. . . . As for the timing, I think they figure it this way. If the BOM circular reached members just at the time the *Life* issue came on the stands, subscribers would say, "All right, I'll read that in *Life* and spend my money on some other book." But with *Life* publication coming later, just ten days or a week before the BOM edition goes out, THE OLD MAN AND THE SEA will be enhanced in the eyes of BOM people who will have ordered it—that the book which is on the way will be something to prize. The *Life* one-shot will be something of sensation; *Life* has never done anything like that before. An issue of *Life* gets kicked around and covered with beer stains, but a book is a book, and with you forever if you want it.[92]

Thus Meyer saw *Life* publication as a mere curiosity, the only value of which would probably be the positive publicity it would generate for the book.

By 13 May every detail concerning publication dates had been set. *Life* would publish *The Old Man and the Sea* in its 1 September

1952 issue (which would be on newsstands on 28 August), Scribners would publish on 8 September, and the Book-of-the-Month Club would begin its distribution on 9 September. Scribners was contractually obligated to mention that the book was a Book-of-the-Month Club main selection on the book's jacket and in advertising that included sales figures but did not have to mention the *Life* publication in its advertisements or sales material.[93]

With all the publication dates worked out, Meyer began working on getting the work in shape to be published. On 21 May, he sent Hemingway marked galley proofs. The only questions he had dealt with were matters of style: uniform capitalization of the points of the compass and The Terrace (a restaurant in the novella), the spelling of the White Sox by the old man, and punctuation.[94] Meyer informed Hemingway that as soon as page proofs were made from the marked set of galleys a set would be given to Sidney James of *Life*.[95]

Page proofs were ready by the first week of June.[96] Along with a letter dated 19 June, Meyer sent Hemingway the dummy of the book's front matter. He also responded to Hemingway's concerns about Alfred Eisenstaedt, a photographer *Life* had sent to Cuba. The magazine wanted photos from which drawings could be made to illustrate the story. Hemingway had telephoned to give his approval for the photographer to go ahead, and he and Mary had helped Eisenstaedt with his task.[97] But both Hemingway and Meyer were worried that *Life* would overwhelm the work with illustrations or photographs. Again, Meyer emphasized the good that could result: "We had been told they planned to use small sketchy illustrations, something the would run in the margins, but I suppose the photographer was there to get background photographs. Even if *Life* goes further and works up the illustrations more than had been our understanding, I do not see what harm it could do. The more effective their presentation, the better. We hope that it will have an effect that will work to the eventual benefit of our trade edition and of the Book-of-the-Month Club's edition. I really believe that it will."[98] But Hemingway does not seem to have been convinced, because in a letter dated 25 June, Meyer informed Hemingway that he had "passed on to Dan Longwell of *Life* what you told me about the illustrations."[99] He wrote to Hemingway on 2 July to calm his fears, sending him a set of proofs for the *Life* version and informing him that *Life* wanted to present *The Old Man and the Sea* "as nearly like a book as possible. Hence, the illustrations, as I say are to be used as symbols."[100] Longwell also sent a copy of the letter to Meyer, who responded the next day that "It is exactly the reassurance Ernest needed, and I think your handling of the story will please him in every detail."[101] Hemingway wrote to Longwell on 6 July to thank him for writing. Throughout the letter Hemingway discussed the work and how he "had gotten finally what I had been working for all my life." He also told Longwell that publication by *Life* made him "much happier than to have a Nobel prize."[102] The letter is vintage Hemingway, containing nothing but praise for the magazine.

Longwell saw Hemingway's letter as perfect advertising copy and wrote asking for permission to quote from it. In a letter dated 27 July, Hemingway gave permission for *Life* to use some excerpts from his letter of 6 July in a teaser for the 1 September 1952 issue but questioned some of Longwell's choices, because they might make him seem "conceited or self satisfied."[103] Longwell eventually used paragraphs two, three, and five of Hemingway's 6 July 1952 letter in a full-page advertisement entitled "From Ernest Hemingway to the Editors of *Life*" on the last page of the 23 August 1952 issue of *Life*.[104] A similar advertisement appeared in the 30 August issue of the *Saturday Review of Literature*.[105]

Meanwhile, Scribners began launching the book in trade circles. The front cover of the 19 July 1952 issue of *Publishers Weekly* featured the book alongside the quote "On September 8 . . . this book will burst upon the literary world." On the next two pages were a brief description of the book and a mention that it was a Book-of-the-Month Club selection and that Scribners had allocated $15,000 for the initial advertising. There was no mention of the *Life* publication.[106] *Scribner's Fall List: July—December 1952* also presented the work prominently on pages 2 and 3 and repeated the essential information of the *Publishers Weekly* ad. A "nation-wide promotional campaign" and the $15,000 for initial advertising were promised. Again, there was no mention of the *Life* publication.[107] In addition, none of the ads for the book in the *New York Times Book Review* in 1952 mentioned the *Life* publication.

Scribners, despite Meyer's earlier assurances, may have been trying to distance itself from *Life* in this matter for fear of upsetting booksellers. The initial advertising appropriation, however, indicates that the firm was banking on the publicity *Life* would provide to push the book. More money had been spent on the advertising budget for *Across the River and Into the Trees,* perhaps because it was Hemingway's first novel in ten years. *The Old Man and the Sea* would come out just two years after that novel and would have what the previous novel had not: promotion by the Book-of-the-Month Club and by one of the most popular magazines in America.

Initially, Scribners' plan appeared to be working. The 1 September 1952 issue of *Life* began appearing on newsstands the last week of August. The cover featured a picture of Hemingway and the words "AN EXTRA DIVIDEND IN THIS ISSUE | "THE OLD MAN AND THE SEA" BY HEMINGWAY | A COMPLETE NEW BOOK | FIRST PUBLICA-TION."[108] Matthew J. Bruccoli, in his introduction to *Conversations with Ernest Hemingway,* describes the stir created by the magazine's appearance: "Late one August night in 1952 I noticed a small crowd around a Times Square newsstand where the next day's new magazines were being put out. The people were waiting to buy the *Life* issue with *The Old Man and the Sea*—which sold 5,300,000 copies in two days."[109] *Life* eventually sold 5,449,833 copies of this issue.[110]

The novelty of *Life* devoting so much space to a work of original fiction gave the piece attention it may not have received otherwise. Meyer wrote Hemingway on 11 September 1952 to describe the effect:

> One thing I didn't foresee—perhaps it was impossible to fore-see—was the effect the *Life* one-shot would have as news. It was a first time, of course, for *Life,* and it was a Hemingway, and natu-rally it was news. The result was an AP [Associated Press] release by Rogers, their book man. He was under orders from above, probably. That release, when it went out, brought orders from managing editors to their daily book reviewers to review—the New York Times and Herald Tribune, for example. A good many other book reviewers throughout the country beat the gun, for the same reason, and booksellers began selling the book. The reg-ular book supplements and book pages were timed for the official publication date. But the handling of the book as news on August 28th was something that couldn't have been forestalled.[111]

Scribners was not ready to take advantage of the publicity the *Life* publication created. Copies had not been shipped to some stores, and the major reviews, like the one in the *New York Times Book*

Review, were keyed to the official publication date. By then, the momentum could have been lost for good.

The Old Man and the Sea was published on 8 September 1952 and sold for $3.00. Hemingway's contract for the novella, dated 19 May 1952, includes the author's standard royalty rate. It also includes a clause stating that Scribners and Hemingway would split equally whatever the Book-of-the-Month Club paid.[112] The reviews were overwhelmingly good. In all, the book received twenty-one reviews in major American newspapers and magazines. Raeburn describes the reception this way: "By any standard the novel was a triumph. Nearly all reviewers praised it, and many called it a masterpiece, the crowning achievement of his career. After reaching a low point in 1950, his literary reputation turned so sharply upward two years later that at least one reviewer could again refer to him, without irony, as 'the champ.'"[113] The advertising was also extensive. Between the date of publication and 9 November, the firm ran advertisements in twelve different newspapers and magazines across the country, including the *New York Times,* the *Chicago Tribune,* the *Boston Post,* and the *San Francisco Chronicle.*[114]

Hemingway was naturally fearful that Scribners' sales would be hurt by the magazine publication. In a letter to Longwell dated 1 September, he revealed his concerns about what the booksellers would do: "But to read some people you would have thought I'd entered into a conspiracy to destroy publishing. Wallace Meyer and Charles Scribner Jr. had written me all along that they thought the Life publication was a good thing for the book. Certainly hope it works out that way."[115] Hemingway's fears were still not quelled by the end of the month, as a 28 September letter to Longwell shows: "I hope it will work all right with the Book Sellers. Scribners always thought it would or they wouldn't have agreed to the timeing and neither would I. . . . Now if the book sellers just decided that no one wished them harm and go ahead and take advantage of everything Life has done to sell the book it will be wonderful."[116]

Hemingway had cause to be concerned, according to reports from observers of the book business. In his 7 September 1952 "In and Out of Books" column for the *New York Times Book Review,* David Dempsey wrote that how the *Life* publication would affect trade sales "was the $3 question disturbing publisher and booksellers alike."[117] In his 19 October 1952 column, Dempsey reported that trade sales had been hurt by the magazine: "Four out of seven buyers for local bookstores thought that they were in the same boat with the 'old man'—the customers just weren't biting like they ought to. Since one of these buyers represents the 31-store Doubleday chain, the evidence seemed pretty conclusive. Sales were running disappointingly behind the author's last book, despite superlative reviews."[118] A similar conclusion was drawn in a *Publishers Weekly* report. In its 13 September 1952 "News and Trends of the Week" column, the magazine reported on a test conducted by Sylvan Baruch, owner of The Book Bar in the Port of New York Authority Bus Terminal. Baruch put one hundred copies of the magazine—which sold for twenty cents—beside twenty-five copies of the trade edition, which retailed for $3.00 a piece. At the end of the week, eighty-eight copies of the magazine had sold, an unimpressive number to Baruch, since he typically had "a traffic numbering 1600 to 1700 people a day." But since the shop sold mainly cheap paperback and remaindered books, he thought the twelve copies of the book that he sold was very impressive. However, Baruch added that his shops at LaGuardia and Idlewild airports did not receive the book until 8 September and had between them only one inquiry for it. He thought that "display and promotion of the book was required to sell it in the face of the *Life* publication."[119]

The same issue of *Publishers Weekly* included an editorial by one of its editors, Peter S. Jennison. While admitting that some problems had been caused by the *Life* publication, he concluded that both the book and the industry would be helped in the long run:

> Certainly this advance publication has caused some confusion and not a little grief in the trade. But it is unfair to criticize the publishers, who did not engineer the arrangement, or those reviewers who timed their columns to coincide with *Life's* [*sic*] appearance on the newstands; and one can hardly blame those booksellers who broke the publication date set for them and put the book on sale when it was news.
>
> What does matter very much is that here we have a Book that has been brought dramatically into focus for millions of readers, the mass-market that ordinarily only a segment of the industry taps. . . . One thing is clear: for once, the public has been introduced to a book, rather than a book to the public. Reading and

books, particularly fiction, have been given a badly-needed shot-in-the-arm; "The Old Man and the Sea's" [sic] wide penetration into the public's awareness may well be felt to the trade's advantage for some time to come.[120]

This view was echoed by Bennett Cerf, owner of Random House, in his 18 October "Trade Winds" column for the *Saturday Review of Literature*:

> FOR THE RECORD, *Life*'s use of Ernest Hemingway's "The Old Man and the Sea" complete in one issue has not hurt the sale of the book in the slightest degree. It is not only a thumping best seller throughout the country, but Book-of-the-Month Club executives indicate that it has had wider acceptance with members than any other selection in many months. And, indeed, why not? Publishers are always seeking publicity for their new offerings. What greater publicity could any author hope for than to see his book picked up and heavily featured by one of the most popular magazines in the country? The issue of *Life* that contained the Hemingway story was sold out clean in most localities within eight hours of publication. Disappointed customers had only one recourse: to buy the book. I'll bet thousands of them hadn't been in a bookstore in years.[121]

Officials at Scribners seemed to agree with Jennison and Cerf's view and had the sales figures to support it. In a letter, dated 23 September, Meyer stated that "As of a week ago (the 17th) our sales of THE OLD MAN AND THE SEA were over 50,000 with reorders coming in most encouragingly." He also gave Hemingway a list of bookstores and jobbers and the amount of their original orders and reorders. Reorders ranged from 50 percent of the original order to increases of 333 percent over the original. Meyer also reported that for 22 September alone, reorders totaled 2,400 copies. It was clear to Meyer that despite what appeared at first to be a negative effect, *Life*'s publication of the novella had given a big boost to the book: "The *Life* one-shot which we told the booksellers about in advance, did have the effect of holding down the advance sale, but I think it will stimulate continuing sales, in the long run. We now have a mounting sales psychology with booksellers selling out their original orders and reordering. It seems to us better, in this very special situation, than huge original orders that take a long time to move out."[122] Charles Scribner Jr. (who had become president of the firm after his father's death), repeated Meyer's idea in a letter of 30 September to Hemingway. Scribner stated that the book "has gained momentum markedly, and the actual results contradict the few outsiders who theorized that the *Life* publication would scotch book sales."[123]

The firm's printing records confirm Meyer's and Scribner's statements. In addition to the first two printings—which totaled 61,950 copies—ordered before publication, the firm ordered another nine printings for a total of 133,650 copies.[124] If all these copies were eventually sold, Hemingway would have received $76,440 ($543,727.31 in 2005 terms). No exact figures for the Book-of-the-Month Club sales are known. Scribners did not print copies for the club, though they did provide plates for them; their initial run, printed by the Kingsport Press, consisted of 153,000 copies.[125] No documents have been located to verify Hemingway's royalty from the Book-of-the-Month Club. However, in 1 February 1954 Scribners credited Hemingway $148.12 from the sale of 1,500 copies of the Book-of-the-Month Club edition.[126] This indicates that Hemingway received only ten cents for each copy sold. Adding the $20,148.12 that the Book-of-the-Month Club paid and the $40,000 *Life* paid for serial rights to what Scribners potentially had to pay for the novella, Hemingway might have grossed $136,588.12, which would have been equivalent to $950,654.04 in 2005.

Scribners also turned a profit. On 27 January 1953, the firm estimated that it had spent $97,810.17 on the book. This figure included $21,551.88 spent on advertising and $44,850 for Hemingway's royalty. The publisher had made $136,080 from the sale of 81,000 copies (at a 44-percent discount of the list price, or $1.68). Its gross profit was therefore $38,269.83. In a memo from Snow to Scribner that accompanied this report, Snow pointed out that the firm had spent nearly 16 percent of the gross sales on advertising and promoting the book. He concluded, "Although . . . we will want to continue including it in our general ads, it does not seem feasible to make any large reappropriation at this time."[127]

There is no question that *Life* and the Book-of-the-Month Club publications took sales away from Scribners' publication. *Life* printed 5,449,833 copies of its 1 September 1952 issue. When added to the 153,000 copies known to have been printed by the Book-of-the-Month Club, this adds up to at least 5,602,833 potential readers, who had no reason to buy the book from Scribners. There is no way of knowing how sales would have been affected if *Life* or the Book-of-the-Month Club had not taken *The Old Man and the Sea* or if *Life* had published it a month before Scribners, as originally planned. What is clear is that the magazine publication created a great deal of interest in the book, which officials at Scribners thought boosted sales. The novella was a success. Hemingway reached more readers with this book than he had ever before. The book sold very well and, unlike *Across the River and Into the Trees,* had helped his critical reputation. In 1953 it also garnered him the Pulitzer Prize for Fiction, an award he had been denied in 1941. *The Old Man and the Sea* solidified Hemingway's position as America's foremost writer.

EPILOGUE

HEMINGWAY AFTER *THE OLD MAN AND THE SEA*

The *Old Man and the Sea* capped Hemingway's career as a professional writer and marked the end of his active collaboration with Charles Scribner's Sons. The novella was awarded the Pulitzer Prize for Fiction in 1953 and was a major factor in the decision to give him the Nobel Prize for Literature in 1954. Both prizes increased Hemingway's critical stature and brought more readers to his works, as Wallace Meyer told his author in a letter of 17 February 1955:

> Here's the royalty report for the six-months period ending February 1, 1955, and payment of the total of $15,898.01 will be due you on June 1.
>
> In a letter dated November 29, I gave you a sort of estimate of what this would be. It didn't undertake to be accurate, but it was way too low. One factor that was underestimated was the stimulus to sales in the Nobel award. THE OLD MAN AND THE SEA, for example, accounts for over $9,000 in this total,[1] but the effect of the award shows all along the line.[2]

In 1954, Scribners began issuing new printings of Hemingway's works, first in a uniform hardback format and then (after the reprint licenses from firms such as Bantam and Dell had expired) as trade paperbacks. These reprints sold well, especially since Hemingway's novels and short stories were becoming part of the standard curriculum in high school and college English classes. With healthy sales from his backlist, Hemingway would never have to worry about money again.

Regardless, he did not stop writing. He had on hand the two incomplete novels he had started in the 1940s (*Islands in the Stream* and *The Garden of Eden*) and continued work on both during the 1950s. His 1953 safari, like his first in 1934, also prompted him to write about his experiences. In 1957, he focused his efforts on his memoirs of the early years in Paris.[3] Finally, in the summer of 1959, with an entourage that included his wife Mary and A. E. Hotchner, Hemingway traveled through Spain, following the mano a mano competition between matadors Antonio Ordóñez and Luis Miguel Domínguín in order to write an article about the fights for *Life*. But his account ran nearly 120,000 words long by 28 May 1960. Eventually, an abridged version was published in three installments in *Life*.[4]

Either Hemingway was unable to complete any of these works during his lifetime or he could not bear to let these works in progress go. Suffering from depression and paranoia that worsened as the decade progressed, he seems to have been unable, or unwilling, to edit his works himself, and he did not trust anyone at Scribners to do so. He killed himself in Ketchum, Idaho, on 2 July 1961.

In the decades since then, Scribners has brought out twelve "new" Hemingway books. Working in conjunction with Mary Hemingway, the Hemingway sons, and the Hemingway Foundation, the firm has published versions of his unfinished works, starting with his Paris memoirs (*A Moveable Feast*) in 1964, and followed by *Islands in the Stream* (1970), *The Dangerous Summer* (1986), *The Garden of Eden* (1986) and *True at First Light* (the second African book, 1999).[5] In addition, Scribners issued three story collections containing hitherto uncollected and unpublished stories: *The Fifth Column and Four Stories of the Spanish Civil War* (1969), *The Nick Adams Stories* (1972), and *The Complete Short Stories of Ernest Hemingway: The Finca Vigía Edition* (1987). Two collections of Hemingway's nonfiction articles, both edited by William White, have also been brought out by the firm: *By-Line: Ernest Hemingway* (1967) and *Dateline: Toronto* (1985). Scribners is the publisher of two collections of Hemingway's letters: *Ernest Hemingway: Selected Letters, 1917–1961,* edited by Carlos Baker (1981), and *The Only Thing That Counts: The Ernest Hemingway/Maxwell Perkins Correspondence,* edited by Matthew J. Bruccoli (1996).

All the major works of the Hemingway canon—the twelve listed above and the thirteen published by Scribners during Hemingway's lifetime (including the 1930 edition of *In Our Time*)—are thus published under the Scribners imprint or that of its parent company, Simon and Schuster. The Hemingway family's control—and thus Scribners' control—of Ernest Hemingway's works is secure until at least the year 2020, when *In Our Time* is scheduled to enter public domain.[6]

For eighty years, Hemingway's works have been published by one firm in the United States. Part of the reason for such a long relationship was the trust the members of the firm engendered in the often-suspicious Hemingway; he stayed with the firm because he had faith in Maxwell Perkins, Charles Scribner III, and Wallace Meyer. They let him work the way he wanted, although they made sure that he published nothing that lead to libel suits or suppressions. In return for being given a relatively free hand, Hemingway produced books that continue to make money for the firm decades after the principals involved in their creations have passed.

Samuel Johnson, in a plea for more biographies of writers, observed that for these men, "Every publication is a new period of time from which some increase or declension of fame is to be reckoned. The gradations of a hero's life are from battle to battle, and of an author's from book to book."[7] This study has been an attempt to illustrate how the gradations of Ernest Hemingway's life were affected by his work with Charles Scribner's Sons. There is little doubt that he would have continued to write and publish and would probably have been as famous as he was if he had worked with another firm, but the writer Ernest Hemingway became, and the way he was and is perceived by readers, was shaped in large part by the efforts of Maxwell Perkins and the other employees of Charles Scribner's Sons. Hemingway's fiction and nonfiction, in the forms in which they were published and in which they still appear, were the result of the editing of Perkins, Meyer, and Scribner, mostly in order to make them conform to a now-outdated concept of decency. The linking of Hemingway's image and lifestyle with his writings—which persists to this day, as the trademarked signature and photograph are used to sell cars and furniture—began early in his association with Scribners, when Perkins placed Blomshield's drawing of Hemingway on the back cover of *The Sun Also Rises* because it could be more widely reproduced in newspapers than a photograph could be. While he early on resisted the efforts the firm made to use his biography to market his works, by 1940 and the publication of *For Whom the Bell Tolls,* Hemingway willingly allowed newspapers and magazine interviewers access as a way to promote his new novel, a strategy that reached its zenith with the appearance of Hemingway on the cover of the 7 September 1952 issue of *Life* containing *The Old Man and the Sea.* And the primary focus on Hemingway's fiction—particularly his novels—rather than on his nonfiction ultimately can be traced back to the fact that Scribners' advertising department spent less to advertise *Death in the Afternoon* and *Green Hills of Africa* and spent more on his novels.

To equate the development of an author's career and his reputation wholly to the influence of his publisher is misguided. There are too many influences and pressures on a writer to say that he was formed by only one relationship. But to ignore the relationship between Hemingway and the employees of Charles Scribner's Sons is to ignore an important force in his development as an artist and as a professional writer and to ignore how our perception of the writer and his work was shaped. For thirty-five years, the most stable relationship Hemingway had was with his publisher, and this relationship still colors the reception of his works. By understanding the facts of this relationship, our understanding of the works—the most important legacy Hemingway left—is hopefully richer.

APPENDIXES

1. Hemingway's Potential Earnings from Charles Scribner's Sons

Book	Advance	Royalty Rate	Potential Earnings
TS	$500	15%	$626.63
SAR	$1,000	15%	$10,842
MWW	$750	15%	$7,144.50
FTA	$5,000[a]	15/20%[b]	$47,712.50
IOT	0	15/20%	$1,603.13
DIA	0	15/20%	$10,909.50
WTN	$6,000	15/20%	$6,090.00[c]
GHA	$4,800	15/20%	$5,169.45[d]
THHN	$2,000	15/20%	$17,415 [e]
First 49	0	15/20%	$6,228.75
FWTBT	$6,040	15/20%	$218,539.80[f]
ARIT	$25,000	15/20%	$57,000[g]
OMATS	0	15/20%	$76,440

[a]On the serial, not the book.

[b]Fifteen percent of the list price on the first 25,000 copies sold, and 20 percent thereafter.

[c]The firm sold only 18,300 copies, making Hemingway's earnings $5,490.

[d]The firm sold only 11,592 copies, making Hemingway's earnings $4,781.70.

[e]The firm sold only 39,038 copies, making Hemingway's earnings $16,391.

[f]Scribners' share would have been $158,749.80; the Book-of-the-Month Club's share would have been $59,790.

[g]The firm sold only 93,738 copies, making Hemingway's earnings $50,960.70.

2. Advertising for Hemingway's Books

Book	Budget	Ads Purchased	First Ad	Last Ad
TS	$796.54	35	13 March 1926	Oct 1926
SAR	$6,557.93	179	Sept. 1926	1 Dec. 1927
MWW	$4,599.70	153	Oct. 1927	Dec. 1928
FTA	$20,578.17	325	Sept 1929	Dec. 1930
IOT	$1,564.71	48	20 Sept. 1930	17 Jan. 1931
DIA	$8,581.14	178	11 June 1932	Feb. 1933
WTN	$2,442.16	90	20 May 1933	March 1934
GHA	$4,796.03	76	8 June 1935	Jan. 1936
THHN	$9,325.74	83	Sept. 1937	12 June 1938
First 49	$3,630.79	54	4 June 1938	July 1939
FWTBT	$43,567.09	504	15 June 1940	3 Dec. 1941
ARIT	$20,000	unknown	unknown	unknown
OMATS	$21,551.88	unknown	19 July 1952	27 Jan. 1953

3. Scribners' Printings of Hemingway's Books

Book	Date Published	No. of Printings	First Printing	Total Printed
TS	28 May 1926	4	1,250	2,785
SAR	22 Oct. 1926	14	5,090	36,140
MWW	14 Oct. 1927	7	7,650	23,815
FTA	27 Sept. 1929	7	31,050	101,675
IOT	24 Oct. 1930	2	3,240	4,275
DIA	23 Sept. 1932	5	10,300	20,780
WTN	27 Oct. 1933	1	20,300	20,300
GHA	25 Oct. 1935	2	10,550	12,532
THHN	15 Oct. 1937	4	10,130	41,085
First 49	14 Oct. 1938	4	5,350	15,110
FWTBT	21 Oct. 1940	7	210,192[a]	693,486[b]
ARIT	7 Sept. 1950	2	76,000	101,500
OMATS	8 Sept. 1952	11	51,700	133,650

[a]Scribners printed 75,192 copies for itself and 135,000 copies for the Book-of-the-Month Club.

[b]Scribners printed 294,886 copies for itself and 398,600 copies for the Book-of-the-Month Club.

ABBREVIATIONS

AL	Autograph Letter
ALS	Autograph Letter Signed
CC	Carbon Copy
TCD	Typed Cable Draft
TCDS	Typed Cable Draft Signed
TL	Typed Letter
TLS	Typed Letter Signed

Abbreviations for Works by Hemingway

ARIT	*Across the River and into the Trees*
DIA	*Death in the Afternoon*
First 49	*The Fifth Column and the First Forty-Nine Stories*
FTA	*A Farewell to Arms*
FWBT	*For Whom the Bell Tolls*
GHA	*Green Hills of Africa*
IOT	*In Our Time*
MWW	*Men Without Women*
OMATS	*The Old Man and the Sea*
SAR	*The Sun Also Rises*
TS	*The Torrents of Spring*
WTN	*Winner Take Nothing*

Abbreviations for Publishers

Scribners	Charles Scribner's Sons
B&L	Boni and Liveright
BOMC	Book-of-the-Month Club

Abbreviations for Library Collections

JFK	Ernest Hemingway Collection at the John F. Kennedy Library
PUL	Princeton University Library

NOTES

Introduction: Hemingway as Professional Author and the House of Scribner

1. Carlos Baker, ed., *Ernest Hemingway: Selected Letters, 1917–1961* (New York: Scribners, 1981), 155.

2. William Charvet, *The Profession of Authorship in America, 1800–1870,* ed. Matthew J. Bruccoli (Columbus: Ohio State Univ. Press, 1968), 3.

3. Bernice Kert, *The Hemingway Women* (New York: Norton, 1983), 200.

4. Carlos Baker, *Ernest Hemingway: A Life Story* (New York: Scribners, 1969), 178, 183, 191, 210, 221, 226.

5. Kert 344.

6. Baker, *A Life Story* 175, 177, 182. Adjustments for inflation were made using "The Inflation Calculator" at www.westegg.com/inflation and are based on information (for years prior to 1975) from the Consumer Price Index statistics from *Historical Statistics of the United States* (Washington, D.C.: USGPO, 1975) and (for years after 1975) from the annual Statistical Abstracts of the United States. This site will be used for inflation calculations throughout this study.

7. F. Scott Fitzgerald, *F. Scott Fitzgerald's Ledger: A Facsimile,* introduction by Matthew J. Bruccoli (Washington, DC: Bruccoli Clark/Microcard Editions, 1973), 63.

8. Fitzgerald 65.

9. Ernest Hemingway, *Green Hills of Africa* (New York: Scribners, 1935), 109.

10. Ernest Hemingway, *Death in the Afternoon* (New York: Scribners, 1932), 2.

11. Hemingway, *Death in the Afternoon* 192.

12. Ernest Hemingway, "The Doctor and the Doctor's Wife," in *The Complete Short Stories of Ernest Hemingway: The Finca Vigía Edition* (New York: Scribners, 1987), 73–76.

13. Ernest Hemingway, *The Only Thing That Counts: The Ernest Hemingway/Maxwell Perkins Correspondence,* ed. Matthew J. Bruccoli, with the assistance of Robert W. Trogdon (New York: Scribners, 1996), 105.

14. Hemingway, *Only Thing* 208.

15. Hemingway, *Only Thing* 188.

16. Carlos Baker, *Hemingway: The Writer as Artist* (Princeton, NJ: Princeton Univ. Press, 1952); Philip Young, *Ernest Hemingway* (New York: Rinehart, 1952); John Atkins, *The Art of Ernest Hemingway* (London: Peter Nevill, 1952); Charles Fenton, *The Apprenticeship of Ernest Hemingway: The Early Years* (New York: Farrar, Straus and Young, 1954).

17. John Raeburn, *Fame Became of Him: Hemingway as Public Writer* (Bloomington: Indiana Univ. Press, 1984), 144.

18. A. Scott Berg, *Maxwell Perkins: Editor of Genius* (New York: Dutton, 1978), 11.

19. Berg 41.

20. Malcolm Cowley, *Unshaken Friend: A Profile of Maxwell Perkins* (New York: Roberts Rinehart, 1985), 6. This profile originally appeared in the *New Yorker,* 1 Apr. 1944: 32–36, 39–42; and 8 Apr. 1944: 30–34, 36–43.

21. As reported by McCormack in Berg 6.

22. John Kuehl and Jackson R. Bryer, eds., *Dear Scott/Dear Max: The F. Scott Fitzgerald and Maxwell Perkins Correspondence* (New York: Scribners, 1971), 47.

23. Hemingway, *Only Thing* 98.

24. John Hall Wheelock, ed., *Editor to Author: The Letters of Maxwell Perkins* (New York: Scribners, 1950), 121–22.

25. Roger Burlingame, *Of Making Many Books: A Hundred Years of Reading, Writing, and Publishing* (New York: Scribners, 1946), 112.

26. Berg 62.

27. Hemingway, *Only Thing* 224.

28. Scribner also was the only member of the firm, other than Perkins, to visit Hemingway. In 1940 and 1951, he went to Cuba to visit Hemingway. In addition, the two men met in Paris in March of 1950 to discuss the editing and publishing of *Across the River and into the Trees.*

29. Hemingway may have had a valid complaint in this area. Evidence shows that more money was spent to advertise his novels than was allocated to promote his short-story collections or his nonfiction books.

1. Learning the Trade

1. Kuehl and Bryer 78.

2. Audre Hanneman, *Ernest Hemingway: A Comprehensive Bibliography* (Princeton, NJ: Princeton Univ. Press, 1967), 5–6.

3. Matthew J. Bruccoli, *Some Sort of Epic Grandeur: The Life of F. Scott Fitzgerald,* rev. ed. (New York: Carroll and Graf, 1991), 158, 193.

4. Berg 11.

5. Kuehl and Bryer 79.

6. Kuehl and Bryer 87.

7. Hemingway, *Only Thing* 33.

8. Kuehl and Bryer 97.

9. Maxwell Perkins to Ernest Hemingway, 26 Feb. 1925, CC, 1 p., PUL.

10. Baker, *A Life Story* 144.

11. Baker, *A Life Story* 133.

12. Baker, *A Life Story* 138–39.

13. Michael Reynolds, *Hemingway: The Paris Years* (Oxford: Basil Blackwell, 1989), 271–72.

14. *In Our Time* contract, 17 Mar. 1925, Cohn Collection, Univ. of Delaware. *In Their Time/1920–1940: Fiestas, Moveable Feasts, and "Many Fêtes": An Exhibition at the University of Virginia Library, December 1977–March 1978* (Bloomfield Hills, MI: Bruccoli-Clark, 1977), item 41.

15. Baker, *Selected Letters* 154–55.

16. Hemingway, *Only Thing* 33–34.

17. Maxwell Perkins to Ernest Hemingway, 28 Apr. 1925, CC, 1 p., PUL.

18. Baker, *Selected Letters* 162–63.

19. Baker, *Selected Letters* 160–61.

20. William Gilmore, *Horace Liveright: Publisher of the Twenties* (New York: David Lewis, 1970), 90–91.

21. Kuehl and Bryer 119.

22. Matthew J. Bruccoli, *Fitzgerald and Hemingway: A Dangerous Friendship* (New York: Carroll and Graf, 1994), 46.

23. "Good Books: Fall 1925," Boni and Liveright Sales Pamphlet, 8 pp., Cohn Collection, Univ. of Delaware.

24. Later in his career, Hemingway, in his preface to Jerome Bahr's *All Good Americans* (New York: Scribners, 1937), commented on the problem of an author whose first book was a short-story collection:

> But, when you are a young writer, the only way you can get a book of stories published now is to have some one with what is called, in the trade, a name write a preface to it. Otherwise you must write a novel first. A novel, even if it fails, is supposed to sell enough copies to pay for putting it out. If it succeeds, the publisher has a property, and when a writer becomes a property he will be humored considerably by those who own the property. He will be, that is, as long as he continues to make them money, and sometimes for a long time afterwards on the chance that he will produce another winner. But when he is starting out he is not humored at all and many natural, good story writers lose their true direction by having to write novels before they want to earn enough at their trade to eat; let alone to marry and have children. (Robert W. Trogdon, ed., *Ernest Hemingway: A Literary Reference* [New York: Carroll and Graf, 2002], 188)

25. Hanneman 7. Later printings were ordered in March 1927, October 1928, and December 1929.

26. Jennifer McCabe Atkinson, *Eugene O'Neill: A Descriptive Bibliography* (Pittsburgh: Univ. of Pittsburgh Press, 1974), 163; Robert Woodham Daniel, *A Catalogue of the Writings of William Faulkner* (New Haven, CT: Yale Univ. Library, 1942), 8.

27. Boni and Liveright advertisement, *Publishers Weekly,* 26 Sept. 1925: 912.

28. *In Our Time* entry, Boni and Liveright ledger, 1925–1950, Annenberg Rare Book and Manuscript Library, Univ. of Pennsylvania, Philadelphia.

29. *Boni and Liveright Fall 1925: An Announcement of New Publications* 25, Cohn Collection, Univ. of Delaware.

30. Boni and Liveright ledger.

31. *Catalog of the Ernest Hemingway Collection at the John F. Kennedy Library* (Boston: G. K. Hall, 1982), 2:342–47.

32. Boni and Liveright ledger.

33. F. Scott Fitzgerald to Maxwell Perkins, c. 6 Oct. 1925, ALS, 1 p., PUL.

34. Maxwell Perkins to F. Scott Fitzgerald, 27 Oct. 1925, CC, 2 pp., PUL.

35. Matthew J. Bruccoli and Margaret Duggan, eds., *Correspondence of F. Scott Fitzgerald* (New York: Random House, 1980), 182.

36. Maxwell Perkins to F. Scott Fitzgerald, 15 Dec. 1925, CC, 3 pp., PUL.

37. Kuehl and Bryer 106.

38. See Frederic Joseph Svoboda, *Hemingway and "The Sun Also Rises": The Crafting of a Style* (Lawrence: Univ. Press of Kansas, 1983); William Balassi, "The Writing of the Manuscript of *The Sun Also Rises,* with a Chart of Its Session-by-Session Development," *Hemingway Review* 6.1 (1986): 65–78; and Michael Reynolds, *Hemingway: The Paris Years* (Oxford: Basil Blackwell, 1989), 306–24, for fuller accounts of the composition of *The Sun Also Rises.*

39. Ernest Hemingway to Harold Loeb, c. Nov. 1925, TL, 2 pp., JFK.

40. Gilmore 115.

41. Baker, *Selected Letters* 172–74.

42. Bruccoli and Duggan 183.

43. Bruccoli, *Fitzgerald and Hemingway* 34.

44. Gilmore 123.

45. Gilmore 123–25.

46. Liveright was mistakenly including *In Our Time* in his calculations.

47. Bruccoli and Duggan 184.

48. Bruccoli, *Fitzgerald and Hemingway* 43–46.

49. Kuehl and Bryer 127–28.

50. Bruccoli, *Fitzgerald and Hemingway* 47.

51. F. Scott Fitzgerald to Maxwell Perkins, cable with Perkins's holograph response, 11 Jan. 1926, 1 p., PUL. See also Bruccoli, *Fitzgerald and Hemingway* 47.

52. Kuehl and Bryer 21.

53. Kuehl and Bryer 129.

54. Kuehl and Bryer 130–31.

55. Kuehl and Bryer 135.

56. F. Scott Fitzgerald to Maxwell Perkins, c. 8 Feb. 1926, ALS, 2 pp., PUL. This section of the letter was cut in the published version in Kuehl and Bryer 133.

57. Baker, *Selected Letters* 190–91.

58. Reynolds, *Hemingway: The Paris Years* 350–52.

59. Horace Liveright, typed note, 10 Feb. 1925, 1 p., Cohn Collection, Univ. of Delaware.

60. Scott Donaldson, "The Wooing of Ernest Hemingway," *American Literature* 53.4 (1982): 697.

61. Contract for *The Torrents of Spring* and *The Sun Also Rises,* 15 Feb. 1926, 2 pp., PUL.

62. Baker, *Hemingway* 164.

63. Kuehl and Bryer 136.

64. Kuehl and Bryer 137.

2. Strengthening the Bond

1. Maxwell Perkins to Ernest Hemingway, 15 Feb. 1926, CC, 1 p., PUL.

2. Maxwell Perkins to Ernest Hemingway, 17 Feb. 1926, CC, 1 p., PUL.

3. Maxwell Perkins to Ernest Hemingway, 19 Feb. 1926, CC, 2 pp., PUL.

4. Maxwell Perkins to Ernest Hemingway, 15 Mar. 1926, CC, 4 pp., PUL.

5. Ernest Hemingway to Maxwell Perkins, 10 Mar. 1926, TLS, 1 p., PUL.

6. Maxwell Perkins to Ernest Hemingway, 24 Mar. 1926, CC, 2 pp., PUL.

7. Maxwell Perkins to Ernest Hemingway, 15 Mar. 1926, CC, 4 pp., PUL.

8. The actress named in the satire is Lenore Ulric, who, like Adams, appeared in *Peter Pan* in the 1924 production.

9. Ernest Hemingway to Maxwell Perkins, 1 Apr. 1926, ALS, Venetia-Hotel stationery, 6 pp., PUL.

10. Surprisingly, Fitzgerald was not on this list. Hemingway did give him the typescript, which he inscribed, "To Scott and Zelda with love from Ernest."

11. Ernest Hemingway to Maxwell Perkins, 8 Apr. 1926, ALS, 6 pp., PUL.

12. Maxwell Perkins to Ernest Hemingway, 19 Apr. 1926, CC, 2 pp., PUL.

13. *Charles Scribner's Sons Supplement to List of Spring Publications—1926:* 1. All citations of Scribners trade catalogs are to the microfilm copies in the South Caroliniana Library, Univ. of South Carolina, Columbia.

14. Advertising schedule for *The Torrents of Spring,* Advertising Department, Charles Scribner's Sons, n.d., 1 p., PUL.

15. Scribners advertisement, *New York Times Book Review,* 30 May 1926: 19.

16. Scribners advertisement, *New York Times Book Review,* 13 June 1926: 26.

17. Scribners advertisement, *New York Times Book Review,* 27 June 1926:

22. Hemingway kept scrapbooks for each of his books. Many of the clippings are reprints (various copies of syndicated columns and reviews, etc.). It is

also sometimes difficult to tell which clippings deal only with *The Torrents of Spring* and which are about it and his other books.

18. *Catalog of the Ernest Hemingway Collection,* 2:347–88.

19. Review of *TOS, New York Times Book Review,* 13 June 1926: 8.

20. Printing card for *The Torrents of Spring,* Scribners Press, 1 p., PUL.

21. Kuehl and Bryer 142.

22. Maxwell Perkins to Ernest Hemingway, 12 Apr. 1926, CC, 2 pp., PUL.

23. Kuehl and Bryer 139.

24. Hemingway typically used the word "manuscript" or the abbreviation "Mss." to refer to both holograph and typescript.

25. Hemingway, *Only Thing* 36–37.

26. Hemingway, *Only Thing* 36.

27. Berg 95–96.

28. "Report by Brownell on Hemingway's 1st Book," n.d., TL, 1 p., PUL.

29. Berg 96.

30. Hemingway, *Only Thing* 38–39.

31. Ernest Hemingway to Maxwell Perkins, 5 May 1926, ALS, 1 p., PUL.

32. Bruccoli, *Fitzgerald and Hemingway* 63–69.

33. Baker, *Selected Letters* 208–9. See also Hemingway, *Only Thing* 40–41.

34. Maxwell Perkins to Ernest Hemingway, 16 June 1926, CC, 2 pp., PUL.

35. Maxwell Perkins to Ernest Hemingway, 29 June 1926, 2 pp., PUL.

36. Hemingway, *Only Thing* 43.

37. "Tell him the bulls have no balls" was restored in Scribners' 1953 uniform edition of *The Sun Also Rises.*

38. Hemingway, *Only Thing* 41–43.

39. Hemingway recycled the story in "Ford Maddox Ford and the Devil's Disciple," in *A Moveable Feast* (New York: Scribners, 1964), 79–96.

40. Maxwell Perkins to Ernest Hemingway, 27 July 1926, CC, 1 p., PUL.

41. Hemingway, *Only Thing* 44–45.

42. Maxwell Perkins to Ernest Hemingway, 31 Aug. 1926, TCD, 1 p., PUL.

43. Maxwell Perkins to Ernest Hemingway, 8 Sept. 1926, TCD, 1 p., PUL.

44. After the third printing, the second verse of the Ecclesiastes quote was dropped per Hemingway's instructions in a letter to Perkins dated 19 November 1926: "That makes it much clearer. The point of the book to me was that the earth abideth forever—having a great deal of fondness and admiration for the earth and not a hell of a lot for my generation and caring little about Vanities. I only hesitated at the start to cut the writing of a better writer—but it seems necessary" (Hemingway, *Only Thing* 51).

45. Maxwell Perkins to Ernest Hemingway, 8 Sept. 1926, CC, 4 pp., PUL.

46. Maxwell Perkins to Ernest Hemingway, 9 Sept. 1926, CC, 1 p., PUL.

47. Baker, *Selected Letters* 215–16.

48. Robert Bridges to Ernest Hemingway, 15 Sept. 1926, CC, 1 p., PUL.

49. Baker, *Selected Letters* 219.

50. *Charles Scribner's Sons List for Fall 1926:* 32.

51. Dust jacket of *The Sun Also Rises* (New York: Scribners, 1926).

52. Maxwell Perkins to Ernest Hemingway, 26 Nov. 1926, CC, 4 pp., PUL.

53. Hemingway, *Only Thing* 121,176, 253.

54. *Publishers Weekly*, 25 Sept. 1926: 1153.

55. *Publishers Weekly*, 30 Oct. 1926: 1745.

56. *Publishers Weekly*, 25 Dec. 1926: 2307.

57. Advertising sheet for *The Sun Also Rises,* advertising department, Charles Scribner's Sons, n.d., 4 pp., PUL.

58. The advertisements for *The Sun Also Rises* appeared in the following issues of the *New York Times Book Review:* 24 Oct. 1926: 37; 31 Oct. 1926, 21; 7 Nov. 1926: 10; 14 Nov. 1926: 12; 21 Nov. 1926: 17; 28 Nov. 1926: 17; 5 Dec. 1926: 16 and 40; and 12 Dec. 1926: 15.

59. *Catalog of the Ernest Hemingway Collection,* 2:347–92.

60. Conrad Aiken, review of *SAR, New York Herald Tribune Books,* 31 Oct. 1926: 4.

61. Review of *SAR, New York Times Book Review,* 31 Oct. 1926: 7.

62. Ernest Boyd, review of *SAR, Independent,* 20 Nov. 1926: 594.

63. Allen Tate, review of *SAR, Nation,* 15 Dec. 1926: 644.

64. Review of *SAR, Time,* 1 Nov. 1926: 48.

65. Review of *SAR, Dial,* Jan. 1927: 73.

66. Hemingway, *Only Thing* 47.

67. Hemingway, *Only Thing* 48.

68. Maxwell Perkins to Ernest Hemingway, 26 Nov. 1926, CC, 4 pp., PUL.

69. Baker, *Selected Letters* 230; Ernest Hemingway to Maxwell Perkins, 22 Nov. 1926, TLS, 1 p., PUL.

70. Baker, *Selected Letters* 230; Manuel Komroff to Ernest Hemingway, 29 Dec. 1926, TLS, 1 p., PUL.

71. Maxwell Perkins to Ernest Hemingway, 22 Nov. 1926, CC, 4 pp., PUL.

72. Maxwell Perkins to Ernest Hemingway, 3 Dec. 1926, CC, 4 pp., PUL.

73. Hemingway, *Only Thing* 52–53.

74. Printing card for *The Sun Also Rises,* Scribners Press, 4 pp., PUL.

75. Maxwell Perkins to Ernest Hemingway, 10 Dec. 1926, CC, 4 pp., PUL.

76. Advertising sheet for *The Sun Also Rises,* advertising department, Charles Scribner's Sons, n.d., 4 pp., PUL.

77. Printing card for *The Sun Also Rises,* Scribners Press, 4 pp., PUL.

78. This total does not include income derived from reprints of *The Sun Also Rises* by the Modern Library (25 Feb. 1930), Grosset and Dunlap (Sept. 1930), Colliers (1942), or Bantam (Sept. 1949), nor does it include Scribners' own reprints of the novel in the Sun Rise edition (May 1938) or in the uniform edition of Hemingway's works (Apr. 1953).

79. RKO voucher, 5 July 1932, 1 p., PUL.

80. Baker, *Selected Letters* 239–40.

81. Maxwell Perkins to Ernest Hemingway, 14 Jan. 1927, CC, 3 pp., PUL.

82. "A Lack of Passion" was never published in Hemingway's lifetime;

see Susan Beegel, ed., "The 'Lack of Passion' Papers," and Beegel, "'A Lack of Passion': Its Background, Sources," *Hemingway Review* 9:2 (1990): 69–93 and 50–68.

83. Baker, *Selected Letters* 241.

84. Maxwell Perkins to Ernest Hemingway, 4 Feb. 1927, CC, 3 pp., PUL.

85. Baker, *Selected Letters* 245–46.

86. Maxwell Perkins to Ernest Hemingway, 28 Feb. 1927, CC, 2 pp., PUL.

87. Baker, *Selected Letters* 246–47.

88. His lawyers, Maurice Speiser and, later, Alfred Rice, served as ad hoc agents, but they mainly handled movie deals and foreign publication rights; in the 1950s A. E. Hotchner arranged the sales of several of Hemingway's works for television and stage adaptations. But for the most part Hemingway dealt directly with his American and British publishers and with magazine editors when selling his stories and articles.

89. Baker, *Selected Letters* 247.

90. Hemingway, *Only Thing* 61.

91. Maxwell Perkins to Ernest Hemingway, c. 1 May 1927, TLS with holograph inserts, 2 pp., PUL.

92. Maxwell Perkins to Ernest Hemingway, 9 May 1927, CC, 3 pp., PUL.

93. Kuehl and Bryer 147.

94. Kuehl and Bryer 148.

95. Baker, *Selected Letters* 250–51.

96. Maxwell Perkins to Ernest Hemingway, 16 May 1927, CC, 2 pp., PUL.

97. Baker, *Selected Letters* 251–53.

98. Maxwell Perkins to Ernest Hemingway, 8 June 1927, CC, 4 pp., PUL.

99. Maxwell Perkins to Ernest Hemingway, 27 May 1927, CC, 2 pp., PUL.

100. Contract for *Men Without Women,* 27 May 1927, 2 pp., PUL.

101. The story appeared in the August 1927 issue of *transition;* Hemingway probably sent it to this little magazine because he knew that its at-the-time frank focus on abortion would make the story unacceptable for an American periodical.

102. In two instances in "A Pursuit Race" the word *shit* was replaced by *s——*. A rough translation of "Che Ti Dice La Patria?" is "What do you hear from home?" For "Ten Indians," see Ernest Hemingway to Maxwell Perkins, 10 June 1927, TLS with holograph inserts, 2 pp., PUL.

103. Ernest Hemingway to Maxwell Perkins, 17 Aug. 1927, TLS, 3 pp., PUL.

104. Ernest Hemingway to Maxwell Perkins, 6 Sept. 1927, Cable, 1 p., PUL.

105. Maxwell Perkins to Ernest Hemingway, 14 July 1927, CC, 3 pp., PUL.

106. Maxwell Perkins to Ernest Hemingway, 25 July 1927, CC, 3 pp., PUL.

107. Maxwell Perkins to Ernest Hemingway, 9 Sept. 1927, CC, 2 pp., PUL.

108. *Charles Scribner's Sons Books for Fall 1927,* 34.

109. *Publishers Weekly,* 24 Sept. 1927: 1027.

110. "Books to Come Before Christmas," *New York Times Book Review,* 25 Sept. 1927: 7.

111. Printing card for *Men Without Women,* Scribners Press, 5 pp., PUL.

112. *Catalog of the Ernest Hemingway Collection* 2:393–99.

113. Advertising sheet for *Men Without Women,* advertising department, Charles Scribner's Sons, n.d., 3 pp., PUL.

114. Advertisements for *Men Without Women* appeared in the following issues: 16 Oct. 1927: 29; 23 Oct. 1927: 27; 30 Oct. 1927: 17; 6 Nov. 1927: 19; 13 Nov. 1927: 19; 20 Nov. 1927: 23; 27 Nov. 1927: 26; 4 Dec. 1927: 37; 11 Dec. 1927: 17; 18 Dec. 1927: 14; 4 Mar. 1928: 31; and 20 May 1928: 26.

115. *Men Without Women* dust jackets, first and third printings (New York: Scribners, 1927). Cohn Collection, Univ. of Delaware.

116. There is compelling evidence that the plates for this edition were used in the printing of three other editions. In 1938, 510 copies were ordered; this coincides with the publication of the Sun Rise edition by Scribners. Another 510 copies were produced in 1942, followed by a printing of 505 copies in 1943. In 1955, a last printing of 2,000 copies was ordered; this coincides with the publication of the uniform edition of the works of Hemingway. In addition, there were two editions issued by the World Publishing Company in 1944 and in 1946 (the latter an illustrated edition). In all except the 1946 World edition, the pagination is the same as the 1927 Scribners edition, suggesting that Scribners used the same plates for all its editions and that World bought its sheets in 1944 from Scribners. See Hanneman 20–23

117. Printing records for *Men Without Women,* Scribners Press, 5 pp., PUL.

118. Baker, *Selected Letters* 276–77.

119. Bruccoli, *Fitzgerald and Hemingway* 241–42.

3. "It's No Fun for Me on Acct. of the Blanks"

1. Baker, *Selected Letters* 272–74; Hemingway, *Only Thing* 65.

2. The unfinished novel, the working titles of which were "A New Slain Knight" and "Jimmy Breen," was never published in Hemingway's lifetime; portions of it were published as "A Train Trip" and "The Porter," in *The Complete Short Stories of Ernest Hemingway: The Finca Vigía Edition* (557–78) in 1987.

3. Hemingway, *Only Thing* 69.

4. Hemingway, *Only Thing* 62–63.

5. Alfred Dashiell to Robert Bridges, c. mid-1927, AL, 15 pp., PUL.

6. Hemingway, *Only Thing* 66.

7. Hemingway, *Only Thing* 71–72.

8. Hemingway, *Only Thing* 72.

9. Baker, *Selected Letters* 280.

10. Hemingway, *Only Thing* 74–75.

11. Hemingway, *Only Thing* 76.

12. Hemingway, *Only Thing* 77.

13. Hemingway, *Only Thing* 78.

14. Hemingway, *Only Thing* 79.

15. Hemingway, *Only Thing* 80–81.

16. Hemingway, *Only Thing* 81.

17. Baker, *Hemingway* 197–98.

18. Baker, *Hemingway* 198.

19. Baker, *Hemingway* 198–99.

20. Hemingway, *Only Thing* 85.

21. Hemingway, *Only Thing* 86.

22. Hemingway, *Only Thing* 86.

23. Hemingway, *Only Thing* 88–90.

24. Hemingway, *Only Thing* 88.

25. Hemingway, *Only Thing* 91–92.

26. Robert Bridges to Ernest Hemingway, 19 Feb. 1929, TLS, *Scribner's Magazine* stationery, 2 pp., JFK.

27. See Huddleston, *Paris Salons, Cafés, Studios: Being Social, Artistic and Literary Memories* (Philadelphia: Lippincott, 1928), 121–23.

28. Hemingway's 16 Feb. 1929 letter to Perkins.

29. Hemingway, *Only Thing* 92–93.

30. Hemingway, *Only Thing* 93.

31. Hemingway, *Only Thing* 94.

32. *A Farewell to Arms,* serial galley proofs, second installment, 5 Mar. 1929, JFK, box 73.

33. Ernest Hemingway to Robert Bridges, 11 Mar. 1929, ALS, 3 pp., UVA.

34. Hemingway, *Only Thing* 95–96.

35. Hemingway, *Only Thing* 96.

36. Ernest Hemingway to Robert Bridges, 18 May 1929, ALS, 1 p., PUL.

37. See Michael Reynolds, *Hemingway's First War: The Making of "A Farewell to Arms"* (Princeton, NJ: Princeton Univ. Press, 1976), 45–51, for a full discussion of Hemingway's drafts of the ending.

38. Hemingway, *Only Thing* 96–97.

39. Letter to Lord Chesterfield, 7 Feb. 1755. Samuel Johnson, *Selected Poetry and Prose,* ed. Frank Brady and W. K. Wimsatt (Berkeley: Univ. of California Press, 1977), 33.

40. Alan Price, "'I'm Not an Old Fogey and You're Not a Young Ass': Owen Wister and Ernest Hemingway," *Hemingway Review* 9.1 (1989): 83.

41. Price 85.

42. Price 87.

43. Hemingway, *Only Thing* 97.

44. Price 88.

45. Price 88. Hemingway's letter has not been located. He later, in a 24 June 1929 letter, instructed Perkins to destroy his mid-May 1929 letter (*Only Thing* 105). Perkins reported that he had done so in a 14 Aug. 1929 letter to Hemingway (*Only Thing* 115).

46. Hemingway, *Only Thing* 100.

47. Hemingway, *Only Thing* 104–5.

48. Bruccoli, *Fitzgerald and Hemingway* 111–20.

49. Maxwell Perkins to Ernest Hemingway, 16 Apr. 1929, CC, 2 pp., PUL.

50. Maxwell Perkins to Ernest Hemingway, 12 June 1929, CC, 3 pp., PUL.

51. Baker, *Selected Letters* 298–99.

52. Hemingway, *Only Thing* 98–99.

53. *A Farewell to Arms,* galley proof 23, JFK.

54. The galley proofs, which are at the Kennedy Library, are incomplete. Galleys 13, 38, 39, 50, 51, 52, 54, 55, 57, and 60 are missing. These correspond to galleys that Hemingway mentions as having obscene material and that Perkins had marked.

55. Hemingway, *Only Thing* 101–4.

56. Scott Donaldson, "Censorship and *A Farewell to Arms,*" *Studies in American Fiction* 19.1 (1991): 85.

57. "Boston Police Bar Scribner's Magazine," *New York Times,* 21 June 1929: 2.

58. Donaldson 89.

59. Hemingway, *Only Thing* 106–7.

60. Gilmore 153–57.

61. Hemingway, *Only Thing* 108.

62. Bruccoli, *Fitzgerald and Hemingway* 128–29.

63. Since the Book-of-the-Month Club and the Literary Guild shipped books through the mail, they were subject to the same oversight by the U.S. Post Office as magazines were and were thus careful to publish books with no obscene content or words.

64. Harry Hansen wrote the "First Reader" column for the *New York World Telegram.*

65. Hemingway, *Only Thing* 111, 109.

66. Hemingway, *Only Thing* 115.

67. Hemingway, *Only Thing* 114–15.

68. The advertisements ran in the following issues of *Publishers Weekly,* 20 Apr. 1929: 1883; 11 May 1929: 2216; 8 June 1929: 2655; 22 June 1929: 2833; and 10 Aug. 1929: 526.

69. *Catalog of the Ernest Hemingway Collection* 2:402–4.

70. *Charles Scribner's Sons Books for Fall 1929,* 21.

71. *Publishers Weekly,* 21 Sept. 1929: 1292–93.

72. *New York Times Book Review,* 23 June 1929: 12; and 22 Sept. 1929: 10 and 22.

73. *Catalog of the Ernest Hemingway Collection,* 2:405–29.

74. Fanny Butcher, review of *FTA, Chicago Daily Tribune,* 28 Sept. 1929: 11.

75. Clifton Fadiman, review of *FTA, Nation,* 30 Oct. 1929: 498.

76. Robert Herrick, "What Is Dirt?" *Bookman,* Nov. 1929: 258–62.

77. Henry Seidel Canby, "Chronicle and Comment," *Bookman,* Feb. 1930: 641–47; Scribners advertisement, *Bookman,* Mar. 1930: xiv–xv.

78. Advertisements that mention or feature *A Farewell to Arms* ran in the following issues of the *New York Times Book Review:* 29 Sept. 1929: 21; 6 Oct. 1929: 38; 13 Oct. 1929: 17; 20 Oct. 1929: 16; 27 Oct. 1929: 19; 3 Nov. 1929: 19; 10 Nov. 1929: 19; 17 Nov. 1929: 36; 24 Nov. 1929: 21; 24 Nov. 1929: 21; 1 Dec. 1929: 27; 8 Dec. 1929: 16–17; 22 Dec. 1929: 23; 29 Dec. 1929: 19; 19 Jan. 1930: 18; 26 Jan. 1930: 21; 2 Feb. 1930: 18; 9 Feb. 1930: 14; and 16 Feb. 1930: 23.

79. Cape published the novel in England on 11 November 1929.

80. Advertising records for *A Farewell to Arms,* advertising department, Charles Scribner's Sons, 6 pp., PUL.

81. Printing cards for *A Farewell to Arms,* Scribners Press, 4 pp., PUL.

82. Hemingway, *Only Thing* 117–19.

83. Ernest Hemingway to Maxwell Perkins, 22 Oct. 1929, TL and ALS, 2 pp., PUL.

84. Maxwell Perkins to Ernest Hemingway, 14 Mar. 1929, CC, 2 pp., PUL.

85. Hemingway, *Only Thing* 122.

86. Hemingway, *Only Thing* 122–23.

87. William Curtis, review of *FTA, Town and Country,* 1 Nov. 1929: 86.

88. Hemingway, *Only Thing* 128.

89. Hemingway, *Only Thing* 134.

90. This rate was not applied to reprints by the firm. For example, for the separate publication of *The Fifth Column* (contract dated 15 July 1940), the royalty was a straight 15 percent of the list price.

91. Contract for *A Farewell to Arms,* 25 Sept. 1929, 3 pp., PUL.

92. Margo Horn, "Lifestyles and Social Trends," in *American Decades: 1920–1929,* ed. Judith Baughman (Detroit, MI: Gale, 1996), 268.

93. Hemingway, *Only Thing* 154.

94. Maxwell Perkins to Ernest Hemingway, 11 June 1931, CC, 3 pp., PUL.

4. "A Writer Should Never Repeat"

A portion of this chapter appeared in "The Composition, Revision, Publication, and Reception of *Death in the Afternoon,*" in *A Companion to Hemingway's "Death in the Afternoon,"* ed. Miriam B. Mandel (New York: Camden House, 2004), 21–41.

1. Hemingway, *Only Thing* 34.

2. Baker, *Hemingway* 205–6.

3. Ernest Hemingway, "Bullfighting, Sport and Industry," *Fortune* 1.2 (1930): 83–88, 139–46, 150.

4. Baker, *Selected Letters* 799.

5. Maxwell Perkins to Ernest Hemingway, 25 Nov. 1929, CC, 3 pp., PUL.

6. Horace Liveright to Charles Scribner's Sons, 31 Dec. 1929, TLS, Horace Liveright and Publisher stationery, 1 p., PUL.

7. Baker, *Selected Letters* 320–21.

8. Maxwell Perkins to Ernest Hemingway, 30 Apr. 1930, CC, 4 pp., PUL.

9. Baker, *Hemingway* 210–11.

10. Horace Liveright to Charles Scribner's Sons, 16 June 1930, CC, 1 p., Horace Liveright Papers, Annenberg Rare Book and Manuscript Library, Univ. of Pennsylvania.

11. Hanneman 10.

12. Horace Liveright, Inc., to Charles Scribner's Sons, 21 Nov. 1930, CC, 1 p., Liveright Publishing Corporation Archives, Annenberg Rare Book and Manuscript Library, Univ. of Pennsylvania.

13. Maxwell Perkins to Ernest Hemingway, 1 July 1930, CC, 3 pp., PUL.

14. Paul Smith, *A Reader's Guide to the Short Stories of Ernest Hemingway* (Boston: G. K. Hall, 1989) 189–90.

15. Ernest Hemingway to Maxwell Perkins, 24 July 1930, ALS, 3 pp., PUL.

16. Maxwell Perkins to Ernest Hemingway, 1 Aug. 1930, CC, 4 pp., PUL.

17. Hemingway, *Three Stories and Ten Poems* (Paris: Contact Press, 1923), with Hemingway's holograph revisions. Cohn Collection, Univ. of Delaware.

18. Hemingway, *Only Thing* 144–46.

19. Maxwell Perkins to Ernest Hemingway, 18 Aug. 1930, CC, 1 p., PUL.

20. "A girl in Chicago—*Tell us about the French women, Hank. What are they like?*" "Bill Smith—*How old are the French women, Hank?*"

21. See Henry S. Villard and James Nagel, *Hemingway in Love and War: The Lost Diary of Agnes von Kurowsky, Her Letters, and Correspondence of Ernest Hemingway* (Boston: Northeastern Univ. Press, 1989).

22. Hemingway, *Only Thing* 146–49.

23. Maxwell Perkins to Ernest Hemingway, 9 Sept. 1930, CC, 1 p., PUL.

24. Maxwell Perkins to Ernest Hemingway, 24 Sept. 1930, TCD, 1 p., PUL.

25. Maxwell Perkins to Ernest Hemingway, 27 Sept. 1930, CC, 4 pp., PUL.

26. Ernest Hemingway to Maxwell Perkins, 28 Sept. 1930, ALS, 2 pp., PUL.

27. Ernest Hemingway to Maxwell Perkins, 3 Oct. 1930, wire, 1 p., PUL.

28. Maxwell Perkins to Ernest Hemingway, 3 Oct. 1930, TCD, 1 p., PUL.

29. Maxwell Perkins to Ernest Hemingway, 14 Oct. 1930, CC, 4 pp., PUL.

30. *Scribners Fall Books 1930, Revised to August 1:* 19.

31. *Publishers Weekly,* 20 Sept. 1930: 1232–33.

32. These advertisements ran in the following issues of the *New York Times Book Review:* 26 Oct. 1930: 13; 2 Nov. 1930: 17; 16 Nov. 1930: 27; 23 Nov. 1930: 17; 30 Nov. 1930: 24–25; and 7 Dec. 1930: 34.

33. Advertising records of *In Our Time,* Scribners Advertising Department, 1 p., PUL.

34. *Catalog of the Ernest Hemingway Collection* 2:437–40.

35. Hanneman 9–10.

36. This conclusion was reached by the author after a comparison of the Scribners edition with the Boni and Liveright edition using a Hinman Collator at the Harry Ransom Humanities Research Center, Univ. of Texas, Feb. 2002.

37. Contract for *In Our Time,* 10 Nov. 1930, 2 pp., PUL.

38. Ernest Hemingway to Maxwell Perkins, 28 Oct. 1930, ALS, 3 pp., PUL.

39. Baker *Hemingway* 216–21.

40. *Death in the Afternoon,* manuscript, 303 pp., Ernest Hemingway Collection, box 2, folders 4–6, Harry Ransom Humanities Research Center, Univ. of Texas, Austin. See also Robert W. Lewis, "The Making of *Death in the Afternoon,*" in *Ernest Hemingway: The Writer in Context,* ed. James Nagel (Madison: Univ. of Wisconsin Press, 1984), 34–37.

41. Ernest Hemingway to Maxwell Perkins, 28 Dec. 1930, TL, 2 pp., PUL.

42. Hemingway, *Only Thing* 156.

43. Ernest Hemingway to Maxwell Perkins, c. 2 May 1932, ALS, 2 pp., PUL.

44. Ernest Hemingway to Maxwell Perkins, 1 Aug. 1931, ALS, 2 pp., PUL.

45. Ernest Hemingway to Maxwell Perkins, 14 Sept. 1931, wire, 1 p., PUL.

46. Ernest Hemingway to Maxwell Perkins, c. 20 Oct. 1931, ALS, 1 p., PUL.

47. Spanish government rules that regulate bullfights. A translation of this document did not appear in *Death in the Afternoon.*

48. Ernest Hemingway to Maxwell Perkins, c. 20 Nov. 1931, ALS, 4 pp., PUL.

49. Maxwell Perkins to Ernest Hemingway, 25 Nov. 1931, CC, 3 pp., PUL.

50. Hemingway, *Only Thing* 157–58.

51. Ernest Hemingway to Maxwell Perkins, 14 Jan. 1932, wire, 1 p., PUL.

52. Wheelock 77–78.

53. Ernest Hemingway to Maxwell Perkins, 21 Jan. 1932, ALS, 4 pp., PUL.

54. Maxwell Perkins to Ernest Hemingway, 20 Jan. 1932, TCD, 1 p., PUL.

55. Hemingway, *Only Thing* 158.

56. See Susan F. Beegel, "'The Excellence of the Stuff Cut Out': A Discarded Passage from *Death in the Afternoon,*" in *Hemingway's Craft of Omission: Four Manuscript Examples* (Ann Arbor, MI: UMI Research Press, 1988), 51–67; and Donald Junkins, "The Poetry of the Twentieth Chapter of *Death in the Afternoon,*" in *Hemingway in Italy and Other Essays,* ed. Robert W. Lewis (New York: Praeger, 1990), 113–21.

57. "Fall Book Prices Are Lower," *Publishers Weekly,* 12 Nov. 1932, 1866.

58. Maxwell Perkins to Ernest Hemingway, 5 Feb. 1932, CC, 3 pp., PUL.

59. Alfred Dashiell to Ernest Hemingway, 5 Feb. 1932, CC, 2 pp., PUL.

60. Ernest Hemingway to Alfred Dashiell, 7 Feb. 1932, ALS, 12 pp., PUL.

61. Hemingway, *Only Thing* 180.

62. Alfred Dashiell to Ernest Hemingway, 15 Feb. 1932, CC, 4 pp., PUL.

63. Maxwell Perkins to Ernest Hemingway, 2 Feb. 1932, CC, 3 pp., PUL.

64. Maxwell Perkins to Ernest Hemingway, 2 Apr. 1932, CC, 3 pp., PUL.

65. Hemingway, *Only Thing* 163–64.

66. Hemingway, *Only Thing* 165.

67. Maxwell Perkins to Ernest Hemingway, 2 Apr. 1932, CC, 3 pp., PUL.

68. Ernest Hemingway to Maxwell Perkins, 4 Apr. 1932, TLS with holograph inserts and postscript, 5 pp., PUL.

69. Hemingway, *Only Thing* 164–65.

70. Hemingway, *Only Thing* 165.

71. Maxwell Perkins to Ernest Hemingway, 13 Apr. 1932, CC, 2 pp., PUL.

72. Ernest Hemingway to Maxwell Perkins, 15 Apr. 1932, wire, 1 p., PUL.

73. See also Anthony Brand's essays "'Far from Simple': The Published Photographs in *Death in the Afternoon*" and "Deleted 'Flashes': The Unpublished Photographs of *Death in the Afternoon*," in *A Companion to Hemingway's "Death in the Afternoon*," ed. Miriam Mandel (New York: Camden House, 2004): 165–87, 189–204.

74. Michael Reynolds, *Ernest Hemingway: An Annotated Chronology* (Detroit, MI: Manly/Omnigraphics, 1991), 67.

75. c. mid-Feb. 1932. Townsend Ludington, ed., *The Fourteenth Chronicle: Letters and Diaries of John Dos Passos* (Boston: Gambit, 1973), 402–3.

76. Baker, *Selected Letters* 355.

77. Baker, *Selected Letters* 356.

78. Ludington 410.

79. Baker, *Selected Letters* 360.

80. *Death in the Afternoon,* galley proofs (2–117), Hemingway Collection, JFK; the first galley is missing from the JFK set. A completed set of marked galleys, in addition to the salesmen's dummy, is held in the Cohn Collection at the Univ. of Delaware. The Cohn set seems to be the one onto which a copy editor at Scribners transferred Hemingway's revisions.

81. Hemingway, *Only Thing* 185. Hemingway's contract for *Death in the Afternoon,* dated 20 Sept. 1932, included the following clause: "Expenses incurred for alterations in type or plates, exceeding twenty per cent. of the cost composition and electrotyping said work, are to be charged to the AUTHOR'S account" (PUL). This clause was standard for all contracts the firm issued at this time.

82. Hemingway, *Only Thing* 161, 167.

83. Michael S. Reynolds, *Hemingway: The 1930s* (New York: Norton, 1997), 73.

84. Hemingway, *Only Thing* 91.

85. Ludington 409–10. Dos Passos, in his introduction to the Modern Library edition of *Three Soldiers* (New York: Random House, 1932), addresses the same concerns that Hemingway had in the deleted sections of *Death in the Afternoon*'s twentieth chapter:

> Making a living by selling daydreams, sensations, packages of mental itch-ingpowders [*sic*], is all right, but I think few men feel it's much of a life for a healthy adult. You can make money by it, sure, but even without the collapse of capitalism, profit tends to be a wornout [*sic*] motive, tending more and more to strangle on its own power and complexity. No producer

of the shoddiest five and ten cent store goods, can do much about money any more; the man who wants to play with the power of money has to go out after it straight, without any other interest. Writing for money is as silly as writing for self-expression. The nineteenth century brought us up to believe in the dollar as an absolute like the law of gravitation. History has riddled money value with a relativity more scary than Einstein's. The pulpwriter [sic] of today writes for a meal ticket, not for money. . . .

Well you're a novelist. What of it? What are you doing it for? What excuse have you got for not being ashamed of yourself?

Not that there's any reason, I suppose, for being ashamed of the trade of novelist. A novel is a commodity that fulfills a certain need; people need to buy daydreams like they need to buy icecream [sic] or aspirin or gin. They even need to buy a pinch of intellectual catnip now and then to liven up their thoughts, a few drops of poetry to stimulate their feelings. All you need to feel good about your work is to turn out the best commodity you can, play the luxury market and to hell with doubt. (vi, vii)

Whether Hemingway read this preface is not known.

86. Hemingway, *Only Thing* 167–69.

87. John S. Sumner was secretary of the New York State Society for the Suppression of Vice.

88. Hemingway, *Only Thing* 169–70.

89. Hemingway, *Only Thing* 172.

90. *Death in the Afternoon,* galley proofs, Cohn Collection, Univ. of Delaware.

91. Hemingway, *Only Thing* 171.

92. Hemingway, *Only Thing* 172–73.

93. Ernest Hemingway to Maxwell Perkins, 15 July 1932, ALS, 2 pp., PUL.

94. Maxwell Perkins to Ernest Hemingway, 28 June 1932, TCD, 1 p., PUL.

95. *Death in the Afternoon,* salesman's dummy (New York: Scribners, 1932), Cohn Collection, Univ. of Delaware.

96. *Scribner's Fall Books 1932:* 6.

97. Publicist Benjamin Gayelord Hauser.

98. Hemingway, *Only Thing* 171–72.

99. Ernest Hemingway to Maxwell Perkins, 15 July 1932, ALS, 2 pp., PUL.

100. Hemingway, *Only Thing* 176.

101. *Publishers Weekly,* 10 Sept. 1932: 826.

102. *Publishers Weekly,* 17 Sept. 1932: 1007.

103. *Catalog of the Ernest Hemingway Collection* 2:444–54.

104. Review of *DIA, Time,* 26 Sept. 1932: 47.

105. Laurence Stallings, review of *DIA, New York Sun,* 23 Sept. 1932: 34.

106. Ben Ray Redman, review of *DIA, Saturday Review of Literature,* 24 Sept. 1932: 121.

107. R. L. Duffus, review of *DIA, New York Times Book Review,* 25 Sept. 1932: 5, 17; Curtis Patterson, review of *DIA, Town and Country,* 15 Oct. 1932: 50.

108. Robert M. Coates, review of *DIA, New Yorker,* 1 Oct. 1932: 61–63; H. L. Mencken, review of *DIA, American Mercury,* Oct. 1932: 506–7.

109. Advertising records for *DIA,* advertising department, Charles Scribner's Sons, 4 pp., PUL.

110. Advertisements for *Death in the Afternoon* appeared in the following issues of the *New York Times Book Review:* 25 Sept. 1932: 13; 2 Oct. 1932: 16; 9 Oct. 1932: 15; 16 Oct. 1932: 20; 23 Oct. 1932: 19; 30 Oct. 1932: 21; 6 Nov. 1932: 22; 13 Nov. 1932: 24; 20 Nov. 1932: 11; 27 Nov. 1932: 15; 4 Dec. 1932: 13; 11 Dec. 1932: 15; and 18 Dec. 1932: 13.

111. Printing card for *Death in the Afternoon,* Scribners Press, 1 p., PUL. The Scribners Press also printed copies for the Halcyon House edition (Oct. 1937) using the same plates.

112. Maxwell Perkins to Ernest Hemingway, 8 Oct. 1932, CC, 3 pp., PUL.

113. Maxwell Perkins to Ernest Hemingway, 3 Nov. 1932, CC, 2 pp., PUL.

114. Maxwell Perkins to Ernest Hemingway, 12 Nov. 1932, CC, 4 pp., PUL.

115. Maxwell Perkins to Ernest Hemingway, 21 Nov. 1932, CC, 1 p., PUL. These circulars have not been located.

116. In 1906, Harry Thaw shot architect Stanford White, whom Thaw believed had had an affair with his wife, former chorus girl Evelyn Nesbit. The scandal was covered extensively by the press. After two lengthy trials, Thaw was declared sane and set free.

117. A. E. Howard, "Ernest Hemingway," *New York Times Book Review,* 9 Oct. 1932: 25.

118. This figure is based on Hemingway's royalty rate, as stipulated in the *Death in the Afternoon* contract: 15 percent of list price for the first 25,000 copies, and 20 percent for every copy thereafter.

119. Hemingway, *Only Thing* 185–86.

120. Maxwell Perkins to Ernest Hemingway, 3 Apr. 1933, CC 4 pp., PUL.

5. "You Can't Be Popular All the Time"

1. Maxwell Perkins to Ernest Hemingway, 19 Sept. 1932, CC, 3 pp., PUL.

2. Ernest Hemingway to Maxwell Perkins, 14 Oct. 1932, ALS, 4 pp., PUL.

3. Ernest Hemingway to Maxwell Perkins, 26 Oct. 1932, ALS, 2 pp., PUL.

4. Baker, *Selected Letters* 376–77.

5. Maxwell Perkins to Ernest Hemingway, 18 Nov. 1932, CC, 3 pp., PUL.

6. Hemingway, *Only Thing* 178.

7. Hemingway, *Only Thing* 181.

8. Hemingway, *Only Thing* 182.

9. Probably the start of *To Have and Have Not* (New York: Scribners, 1937).

10. Hemingway, *Only Thing* 183–84.

11. Maxwell Perkins to Ernest Hemingway, 3 Mar. 1933, CC, 2 pp., PUL.

12. Ernest Hemingway to Maxwell Perkins, 3 Mar. 1933, ALS, 1 p., PUL.

13. Maxwell Perkins to Ernest Hemingway, 29 Mar. 1933, CC, 3 pp., PUL.

14. Hemingway, *Only Thing* 186.

15. Maxwell Perkins to Ernest Hemingway, 3 Apr. 1933, CC, 4 pp., PUL. See chapter 4 for a fuller discussion of this incident.

16. F. Scott Fitzgerald, *All the Sad Young Men* (New York: Scribners, 1926); and Ring Lardner, *Round Up* (New York: Scribners, 1929).

17. Ernest Hemingway to Maxwell Perkins, 8 Apr. 1933, TLS with holograph postscripts, 3 pp., PUL.

18. Maxwell Perkins to Ernest Hemingway, 10 Apr. 1933, TCD, 1 p., PUL.

19. Maxwell Perkins to Ernest Hemingway, 12 Apr. 1933, CC, 4 pp., PUL.

20. Ernest Hemingway to Maxwell Perkins, 24 Apr. 1933, wire, 1 p., PUL.

21. Ernest Hemingway to Maxwell Perkins, 20 May 1933, ALS, Hotel Ambos Mundos stationery, 3 pp., PUL.

22. Hemingway, *Only Thing* 190.

23. Maxwell Perkins to Ernest Hemingway, 12 June 1933, TCD, 1 p., PUL.

24. Baker, *Hemingway* 241.

25. Baker, *Selected Letters* 393–94.

26. Hanneman 36–37. The Cohn Collection at the Univ. of Delaware and the Speiser and Easterling-Hallman Collection of Ernest Hemingway at the Univ. of South Carolina have copies of this dummy.

27. Contract for *Winner Take Nothing,* 15 June 1933, 2 pp., PUL.

28. Maxwell Perkins to Ernest Hemingway, 16 June 1933, CC, 2 pp., PUL.

29. Hemingway, *Only Thing* 191–92.

30. Maxwell Perkins to Ernest Hemingway, 18 July 1933, wire, 1 p., PUL.

31. Hemingway, *Only Thing* 193–94.

32. Ernest Hemingway to Maxwell Perkins, 29 July 1933, TLS, 1 p., PUL. Hemingway misdated this letter "Sat July 28?"

33. Maxwell Perkins to Ernest Hemingway, 31 July 1933, TCD, 1 p., PUL.

34. Ernest Hemingway to Maxwell Perkins, 31 July 1933, wire, 1 p., PUL.

35. "Oh go and jack off." The phrase did not appear in the *Winner Take Nothing* version of the story.

36. Hemingway, *Only Thing* 195.

37. Hemingway, *Only Thing* 195–97.

38. Maxwell Perkins to Ernest Hemingway, 14 Aug. 1933, CC, 2 pp., PUL.

39. Maxwell Perkins to Ernest Hemingway, 15 Aug. 1933, TCD, 1 p., PUL.

40. Hemingway, *Only Thing* 197.

41. Hemingway, *Only Thing* 198–200.

42. Ernest Hemingway to Maxwell Perkins, 2 Sept. 1933, ALS, Hotel Ambos Mundos stationery, 1 p., PUL.

43. Maxwell Perkins to Ernest Hemingway, 14 Sept. 1933, TCD, 1 p., PUL; Maxwell Perkins to Ernest Hemingway, 21 Sept. 1933, TCD, 1 p., PUL.

44. Hemingway, *Only Thing* 200–201.

45. Maxwell Perkins to Ernest Hemingway, 25 Sept. 1933, CC, 1 p., PUL.

46. Maxwell Perkins to Ernest Hemingway, 5 Oct. 1933, CC, 3 pp., PUL.

47. Ernest Hemingway to Maxwell Perkins, 20 Oct. 1933, Cable, 1 p., PUL.

48. Maxwell Perkins to Ernest Hemingway, 25 Oct. 1933, TCD, 1 p., PUL.

49. Printing card for *Winner Take Nothing,* Scribners Press, 1 p., PUL.

50. "Fall Book Index, 1933," *Publishers Weekly,* 16 Sept. 1933: 958.

51. *Publishers Weekly,* 20 May 1933: 1587.

52. *Charles Scribner's Sons Books for Fall 1933:* 6.

53. *Publishers Weekly,* 16 Sept. 1933: 864.

54. *Catalog of the Ernest Hemingway Collection* 2:455–58.

55. Horace Gregory, review of *WTN, New York Herald Times Books* 29 Oct. 1933: 5; Clifton Fadiman, "A Letter to Mr. Hemingway," review of *WTN, New Yorker,* 28 Oct. 1933: 74–75.

56. Advertisements for *Winner Take Nothing* appeared in the following issues of the *New York Times Book Review:* 29 Oct. 1933: 15; 12 Nov. 1933: 25; 19 Nov. 1933: 17; 26 Nov. 1933: 17; 3 Dec. 1933: 13; and 10 Dec. 1933: 15.

57. *Publishers Weekly,* 11 Nov. 1933: 1661–64; 18 Nov. 1933: 1722.

58. Hemingway, *Only Thing* 202.

59. Maxwell Perkins to Ernest Hemingway, 3 Nov. 1933, TCD, 1 p., PUL.

60. Maxwell Perkins to Ernest Hemingway, 10 Nov. 1933, CC, 3 pp., PUL.

61. Maxwell Perkins to Ernest Hemingway, 12 Dec. 1933, CC, 3 pp., PUL.

62. Hemingway, *Only Thing* 204.

63. Printing card for *Winner Take Nothing,* Scribners Press, 1 p., PUL.

64. Reynolds, *Hemingway: The 1930s* 155–67.

65. Hemingway, *Only Thing* 207.

66. Reynolds, *Hemingway: The 1930s* 169.

67. See Bruccoli, *Fitzgerald and Hemingway* 166–68.

68. Hemingway, *Only Thing* 207–10.

69. Hemingway had contributed articles on any subject he wished since the magazine's first issue (fall 1933), receiving $250 for his efforts; his fee was subsequently raised to $500 per article or story.

70. Ernest Hemingway to Maxwell Perkins, 20 June 1934, TLS with holograph postscript, 2 pp., PUL.

71. *Green Hills of Africa,* holograph manuscript, 492 pp., Alderman Library, Univ. of Virginia.

72. See Berg 236–48.

73. Hemingway, *Only Thing* 212n2.

74. Hemingway, *Only Thing* 212.

75. Hemingway, *Only Thing* 213.

76. Hemingway, *Only Thing* 214–16.

77. "Spring Freshets" is the novella by Ivan Turgenev, better known as *The Torrents of Spring* (1871).

78. Hemingway, *Only Thing* 217–18.

79. Ernest Hemingway to Maxwell Perkins, 14 Dec. 1934, TLS, 2 pp., PUL.

80. Hemingway, *Only Thing* 218–19.

81. Berg 250–51.

82. Maxwell Perkins to Ernest Hemingway, 4 Feb. 1935, TCD, 1 p., PUL.

83. Maxwell Perkins to Ernest Hemingway, 5 Feb. 1935, CC, 4 pp., PUL.

84. Baker, *Hemingway* 270.

85. Ernest Hemingway to Maxwell Perkins, c. 7 Feb. 1935, TLS with holograph postscript, 1 p., PUL.

86. Maxwell Perkins to Ernest Hemingway, 8 Feb. 1935, CC, 2 pp., PUL.

87. Maxwell Perkins to Ernest Hemingway, 11 Feb. 1935, TCD, 1 p., PUL.

88. Hemingway, *Only Thing* 220.

89. Maxwell Perkins to Ernest Hemingway, 15 Feb. 1935, TCD, 1 p., PUL.

90. Maxwell Perkins to Ernest Hemingway, 15 Feb. 1935, CC, 2 pp., PUL.

91. Hemingway, *Only Thing* 220.

92. Hemingway, *Only Thing* 221.

93. Hemingway, *Only Thing* 221.

94. Maxwell Perkins to Ernest Hemingway, 19 Feb. 1935, TCD, 1 p., PUL.

95. Ernest Hemingway to Maxwell Perkins, 22 Feb. 1935, TLS, 2 pp., PUL. The portion of this letter published in *Only Thing* (p. 222) does not include the material quoted.

96. Maxwell Perkins to Ernest Hemingway, 27 Feb. 1935, CC, 2 pp., PUL.

97. Maxwell Perkins to Ernest Hemingway, 20 Feb. 1935, TCD, 1 p., PUL.

98. Maxwell Perkins to Ernest Hemingway, 5 Mar. 1935, CC, 4 pp., PUL.

99. Ernest Hemingway to Maxwell Perkins, c. 8 Mar. 1935, TLS, 1 p., PUL.

100. Maxwell Perkins to Ernest Hemingway, 2 Apr. 1935, CC, 4 pp., PUL.

101. Hemingway, *Only Thing*. 222–23.

102. Peter Fleming, *Brazilian Adventure* (New York: Scribners, 1933). This account of the author's trip up the Amazon River was a nonfiction best seller for the firm in that year.

103. Ernest Hemingway to Maxwell Perkins, c. 13 Apr. 1935, TL with holograph additions, 1 p., PUL.

104. Ernest Hemingway, *Green Hills of Africa* (New York: Scribners, 1935), 27, 108–9.

105. *Green Hills of Africa* appeared in the following issues of *Scribner's Magazine:* May 1935: 257–68; June 1935: 334–44; July 1935: 14–21; Aug. 1935: 74–83; Sept. 1935: 157–65; Oct. 1935: 200–6; Nov. 1935: 262–73.

106. Ernest Hemingway to Maxwell Perkins, 1 May 1935, ALS, 2 pp., PUL.

107. Alfred Dashiell to Ernest Hemingway, 6 May 1935, TLS, Charles Scribner's Sons stationery, 1 p., JFK.

108. Ernest Hemingway to Maxwell Perkins, 3 June 1935, TLS, 2 pp., PUL.

109. Maxwell Perkins to Ernest Hemingway, 5 June 1935, CC, 4 pp., PUL.

110. Alfred Dashiell to Ernest Hemingway, 10 June 1935, TLS, Charles Scribner's Sons stationery, 1 p., JFK.

111. Ernest Hemingway to Maxwell Perkins, 19 June 1935, ALS, 4 pp., PUL.

112. Maxwell Perkins to Ernest Hemingway, 28 June 1935, CC, 4 pp., PUL.

113. Ernest Hemingway, "*Green Hills of Africa,* Part IV," *Scribner's Magazine,* Aug. 1935: 79; *Green Hills of Africa 149–50.*

114. Ernest Hemingway, "*Green Hills of Africa,* Part V," *Scribner's Magazine,* Sept. 1935: 157; *Green Hills of Africa* 172.

115. Ernest Hemingway to Maxwell Perkins, 2 July 1935, ALS, 4 pp., PUL.

116. Contract for *Green Hills of Africa,* 15 Oct. 1935, 2 pp., PUL.

117. Maxwell Perkins to Ernest Hemingway, 2 July 1935, TCD, 1 p., PUL.

118. Ernest Hemingway to Maxwell Perkins, 4 July 1935, ALS, 3 pp., PUL.

119. Maxwell Perkins to Ernest Hemingway, 9 July 1935, CC, 4 pp., PUL.

120. Alfred Dashiell to Ernest Hemingway, 17 July 1935, TLS, Charles Scribner's Sons stationery, 1 p., JFK.

121. *Green Hills of Africa* style sheet, n.d., TS, 1 p., PUL.

122. Maxwell Perkins to Ernest Hemingway, 30 July 1935, TCD, 1 p., PUL.

123. Ernest Hemingway to Maxwell Perkins, 30 July 1935, ALS, 4 pp., PUL.

124. Ernest Hemingway to Maxwell Perkins, 31 July 1935, wire, 1 p., PUL.

125. Maxwell Perkins to Ernest Hemingway, 5 Aug. 1935, CC, 2 pp., PUL.

126. Maxwell Perkins to Ernest Hemingway, 19 Aug. 1935, TCD, 1 p., PUL.

127. Maxwell Perkins to Ernest Hemingway, 26 Aug. 1935, CC, 4 pp., PUL.

128. Hemingway, *Only Thing* 224–25.

129. Ernest Hemingway, "*Green Hills of Africa,* Part II," *Scribner's Magazine,* June 1935: 339.

130. Hemingway, *Only Thing* 227–28.

131. Hemingway, *Green Hills of Africa* 65–66.

132. Maxwell Perkins to Ernest Hemingway, 10 Sept. 1935, CC, 3 pp., PUL.

133. Ernest Hemingway to Maxwell Perkins, c. 14 Sept. 1935, TLS, 2 pp., PUL.

134. Maxwell Perkins to Ernest Hemingway, 17 Sept. 1935, CC, 1 p., PUL.

135. Advertisements in *Publishers Weekly* mentioning *Green Hills of Africa* appeared in the following issues: 8 June 1935: 2200; 15 June 1935: 2226; 22 June 1935: 2398; 21 Sept. 1935: 964.

136. *Charles Scribner's Sons Books for Fall 1935,* 4.

137. Kuehl and Bryer 224–25.

138. Printing card for *Green Hills of Africa,* Scribners Press, 1 p., PUL.

139. *Catalog of the Ernest Hemingway Collection* 2:467–75.

140. Carl Van Doren, review of *GHA, New York Herald Tribune Books,* 27 Oct. 1935, 3.

141. Charles Poore, review of *GHA, New York Times Book Review,* 27 Oct. 1935: 3.

142. Bernard DeVoto, review of *GHA, Publishers Weekly,* 26 Oct. 1935: 5.

143. Granville Hicks, review of *GHA, New Masses,* 19 Nov. 1935: 23.

144. Kuehl and Bryer 226.

145. Advertisements featuring *Green Hills of Africa* appeared in the following issues of the *New York Times Book Review:* 27 Oct. 1935: 13; 3 Nov. 1935: 15; 10 Nov. 1935: 18; 17 Nov. 1935: 13; 1 Dec. 1935: 15; 8 Dec. 1935: 13; 15 Dec. 1935: 13; 22 Dec. 1935: 15.

146. Advertising records for *Green Hills of Africa,* Advertising Department, Charles Scribner's Sons, 2 pp., PUL.

147. Printing card for *Green Hills of Africa,* Scribners Press, 1 p., PUL.

148. Hemingway, *Only Thing* 229.

149. Mark Sullivan's *Our Times: The Twenties,* S. S. Van Dine's *The Garden Murder Case,* and Robert Briffault's *Europa* were Scribners' best sellers for the fall of 1935.

150. Hemingway, *Only Thing* 230–31.

151. Robert Cantwell (*The Land of Plenty*), John O'Hara (*Appointment in Samarra*), and André Malraux (*Man's Fate*).

152. Hemingway, *Only Thing* 232.

6. "Their Money's Worth"

A portion of this chapter was previously published as "'Their Money's Worth': The Composition, Editing, and Publication," in *One Man Alone: Hemingway and "To Have and Have Not,"* ed. Toni Knott (Lanham, MD: Univ. Press of America, 1999), 47–63.

1. *Cosmopolitan,* Apr. 1934: 20–23, 108–22; *Esquire,* Feb. 1936: 27, 193–96; *Esquire,* June 1936: 31, 190–93; *Esquire,* Aug. 1936: 27, 194–201; *Cosmopolitan,* Sept. 1936: 30–33, 166–72.

2. Maxwell Perkins to Ernest Hemingway, 6 Apr. 1936, CC, 3 pp., PUL. The letter to which Hemingway refers has not been located.

3. Ernest Hemingway to Maxwell Perkins, 8 Apr. 1936, wire, 1 p., PUL.

4. Maxwell Perkins to Ernest Hemingway, 8 Apr. 1936, CC, 3 pp., PUL.

5. Hemingway, *Only Thing* 238–39.

6. Hemingway, *Only Thing* 241.

7. Ernest Hemingway to Maxwell Perkins, 20 Nov. 1935, ALS, 4 pp., PUL.

8. Hemingway, *Only Thing* 242–43.

9. Maxwell Perkins to Ernest Hemingway, 9 May 1936, CC, 4 pp., PUL.

10. Ernest Hemingway to Maxwell Perkins, 2 June 1936, wire, 1 p., PUL.

11. Maxwell Perkins to Ernest Hemingway, 3 June 1936, TCD, 1 p., PUL.

12. Hemingway, *Only Thing* 243–44.

13. Maxwell Perkins to Ernest Hemingway, 20 July 1936, TCD, 1 p., PUL.

14. Maxwell Perkins to Ernest Hemingway, 21 July 1936, CC, 4 pp., PUL. A portion of this letter appears in Hemingway, *Only Thing* 245.

15. See Bruccoli, *Fitzgerald and Hemingway* 190–94.

16. Kuehl and Bryer 232.

17. Ernest Hemingway to Maxwell Perkins, 26 Sept. 1936, TLS with holograph inserts, 1 p., PUL.

18. Maxwell Perkins to Ernest Hemingway, 1 Oct. 1936, CC, 4 pp., PUL.

19. Maxwell Perkins to Ernest Hemingway, 5 Nov. 1936, TCD, 1 p., PUL.

20. Ernest Hemingway to Maxwell Perkins, c. 8 Nov. 1936, ALS, 2 pp., PUL.

21. Maxwell Perkins to Ernest Hemingway, 13 Nov. 1936, CC, 2 pp., PUL.

22. Maxwell Perkins to Ernest Hemingway, 17 Nov. 1936, CC, 2 pp., PUL.

23. Maxwell Perkins to Ernest Hemingway, 24 Nov. 1936, TCD, 1 p., PUL.

24. Ernest Hemingway to Maxwell Perkins, 2 Dec. 1936, TLS with holograph inserts and postscripts, 2 pp., PUL.

25. Ernest Hemingway to Maxwell Perkins, 14 Dec. 1936, wire, 1 p., PUL.

26. Wolfe's former landlady, Marjorie Dorman, had been the basis for "Mad Maude" Whittaker in the story "No Door." The firm reached an out-of-court settlement with Dorman in December. The suit precipitated Wolfe's break with Scribners. See Berg 311–312.

27. Baker, *Selected Letters* 455–56.

28. Reynolds, *Hemingway: The 1930s* 236–38.

29. Hemingway, *Only Thing* 247.

30. Hemingway, *Only Thing* 248.

31. Reynolds, *Chronology,* 86–90.

32. Baker, *Hemingway* 299–300.

33. Hemingway, *Only Thing* 248–49.

34. Maxwell Perkins to Ernest Hemingway, 18 Feb. 1937, CC, 2 pp., PUL.

35. This speech was published in *New Masses,* 22 June 1937: 4.

36. Ernest Hemingway to Maxwell Perkins, 10 June 1937, wire, 1 p., PUL.

37. Hemingway, *Only Thing* 249–50.

38. Maxwell Perkins to Ernest Hemingway, 14 June 1937, TCD, 1 p., PUL.

39. Hemingway, *Only Thing* 251.

40. Baker, *Hemingway* 315.

41. See Hanneman 41.

42. Typed note, 24 June 1937, 1 p., PUL.

43. Maxwell Perkins to Ernest Hemingway, 16 July 1937, CC, 2 pp., PUL.

44. *To Have and Have Not* (New York: Scribners, 1937), 225.

45. Hemingway, *Only Thing* 252.

46. Ernest Hemingway to Maxwell Perkins, 9 Aug. 1937, wire, 1 p., PUL.

47. Maxwell Perkins to Ernest Hemingway, 10 Aug. 1937, TCD, 1 p., PUL.

48. For accounts of the fight, see Baker, *Hemingway* 317–18, and Kuehl and Bryer 238–240.

49. See "Hemingway Slaps Eastman in Face; Clash in Publisher's Office Has To Do with 'Bull' and 'Death' Both 'in Afternoon,'" *New York Times,* 14 Aug. 1937: 15; "Eastman Claims Title," *New York Times,* 16 Aug. 1937: 21; "Literary Slug Fests," *New York Times,* 17 Aug. 1937: 18; *Newsweek,* 21 Aug. 1937: 4; *Time,* 23 Aug. 1937: 66; and *New Yorker,* 28 Aug. 1937: 17.

50. Raeburn 81.

51. *Publishers Weekly,* 2 Oct. 1937: 1403.

52. This statement was inaccurate, since the Morgans have three daughters.

53. *Scribner Fall Books 1937:* 2.

54. Printing card for *To Have and Have Not,* Scribners Press, 1 p., PUL.

55. *Catalog of the Ernest Hemingway Collection* 2:477–92.

56. J. Donald Adams, review of *THHN, New York Times Book Review,* 17 Oct. 1937: 2.

57. Louis Kronenberger, review of *THHN, Nation,* 23 Oct. 1937: 440.

58. Review of *THHN, Time,* 18 Oct. 1937: 79–85.

59. *To Have and Have Not* advertising records, Advertising Department, Charles Scribner's Sons, 2 pp., PUL.

60. Advertisements for *To Have and Have Not* ran in the following issues of the *New York Times Book Review:* 17 Oct. 1937: 13; 24 Oct. 1937: 23; 31 Oct. 1937: 13; 7 Nov. 1937: 24; 14 Nov. 1937:13; 21 Nov. 1937: 19; 5 Dec. 1937: 13; and 12 Dec. 1937: 11.

61. Hemingway, *Only Thing* 253–54.

62. Hemingway, *Only Thing* 254.

63. Hemingway, *Only Thing* 256.

64. Printing card for *To Have and Have Not,* Scribners Press, 1 p., PUL.

65. Maxwell Perkins to Ernest Hemingway, 10 Nov. 1937, CC, 4 pp., PUL.

66. Maxwell Perkins to Ernest Hemingway, 29 Dec. 1937, TCD, 1 p., PUL.

67. Ernest Hemingway to Maxwell Perkins, c. 1 Jan. 1938, Cable, 1 p., PUL.

68. Maxwell Perkins to Ernest Hemingway, 3 Jan. 1938, TCD, 1 p., PUL.

69. Ernest Hemingway to Maxwell Perkins, 9 Jan. 1938, Cable, 1 p., PUL.

70. Hemingway, *Only Thing* 253.

71. Hemingway, *Only Thing* 254–56.

72. Ernest Hemingway to Maxwell Perkins, mid-Feb. 1938, TLS, 1 p., PUL.

73. Maxwell Perkins to Ernest Hemingway, 3 Mar. 1938, CC, 3 pp., PUL.

74. Ernest Hemingway to Maxwell Perkins, 9 Mar. 1938, wire, 1 p., PUL.

75. Maxwell Perkins to Ernest Hemingway, 10 Mar. 1938, TCD, 1 p., PUL.

76. Ernest Hemingway to Maxwell Perkins, 15 Mar. 1938, TLS with holograph postscript, 1 p., PUL.

77. Hemingway, *Only Thing* 257.

78. This dedication was not used. "Marty" was Martha Gelhorn, a correspondent with whom Hemingway was having an affair; the two married in 1940. "Herbert" was *New York Times* reporter Herbert Matthews. They and Hemingway had covered the Spanish civil war together.

79. Maxwell Perkins to Ernest Hemingway, 7 Apr. 1938, CC, 3 pp., PUL.

80. Baker, *Selected Letters* 466–67.

81. Hemingway, *Only Thing* 258–59.

82. Ernest Hemingway to Maxwell Perkins, 19 May 1938, TLS with holograph postscript, *S.S. Ile de France* stationery, 1 p., PUL.

83. Maxwell Perkins to Ernest Hemingway, 2 June 1938, CC, 4 pp., PUL.

84. Ernest Hemingway to Maxwell Perkins, 11 June 1938, TLS, 2 pp., PUL.

85. The story was first published in *Esquire,* Nov. 1938: 39, 111–14.

86. Maxwell Perkins to Ernest Hemingway, 15 June 1938, CC, 1 p., PUL.

87. Reynolds, *Chronology* 91.

88. *Publishers Weekly,* 4 June 1938: 2202.

89. Hanneman 50–51.

90. *Scribners Fall Books 1938:* 5–6.

91. *To Have and Have Not* had been suppressed in Detroit. The action was being fought by a bookseller named Alvin Hamer. Scribners took no part in the fight, and Hemingway did not seem to have been too concerned about the action.

92. Hemingway, *Only Thing* 260.

93. Hemingway, *Only Thing* 260–62.

94. "The Old Man at the Bridge" appeared in *Ken,* 19 May 1938: 36.

95. Smith 362–63.

96. Hemingway, *Only Thing* 262–63.

97. Maxwell Perkins to Ernest Hemingway, 18 July 1938, CC, 5 pp., PUL.

98. Hemingway, *Only Thing* 264–66.

99. See Berg 349–51.

100. Maxwell Perkins to Ernest Hemingway, 9 Aug. 1938, CC, 3 pp., PUL.

101. Hemingway, *Only Thing* 267–68.

102. Hemingway, *Only Thing* 268–69.

103. Hemingway, *Only Thing* 351.

104. Kuehl and Bryer 248.

105. *Publishers Weekly,* 17 Sept. 1938: 975.

106. *Scribners Fall List Books, 1938, Revised to Aug. 1:* 4.

107. *Catalog of the Ernest Hemingway Collection* 2:496–505.

108. Review of *First 49, Time,* 17 Oct. 1938: 75.

109. Edwin Berry Burgum, review of *First 49, New Masses,* 22 Nov. 1938: 21–24.

110. Peter Monro Jack, review of *First 49, New York Times Book Review,* 23 Oct. 1938: 4.

111. Advertising records for *First 49,* advertising department, Charles Scribner's Sons, 2 pp., PUL.

112. These advertisements appeared in the following issues of the *New York Times Book Review:* 16 Oct. 1938: 19; 23 Oct. 1938: 17; 30 Oct. 1938: 13; 6 Nov. 1938: 17; 13 Nov. 1938: 13; 20 Nov. 1938: 15; 27 Nov. 1938: 14; 4 Dec. 1938: 13; 11 Dec. 1938: 28.

113. Printing card for *First 49,* Scribners Press, 1 p., PUL.

114. Hemingway, *Only Thing* 270.

7. The Blockbuster

1. The stories were "The Denunciation," *Esquire,* Nov. 1938: 39, 111–14; "The Butterfly and the Tank," *Esquire,* Dec. 1938: 51, 186, 188, 190; "Night Before Battle," *Esquire,* 11 Feb. 1939: 27–29, 91–92, 95, 97; "Nobody Ever

Dies!" *Cosmopolitan,* Mar. 1939: 28–31, 74–76; and "Under the Ridge," *Cosmopolitan,* Oct. 1939: 34–35, 102–6. "Landscape with Figures" was not published during Hemingway's life. None of these stories was collected in book form until after Hemingway's death.

2. Hemingway would later state that he started work on the novel on 1 Mar. 1939, five months later than the date suggested by Hemingway's letters to Gingrich and Perkins.

3. Baker, *Selected Letters* 472; Hemingway, *Only Thing* 271.

4. Hemingway, *Only Thing* 273.

5. Maxwell Perkins to Ernest Hemingway, 9 Mar. 1939, CC, 4 pp., PUL.

6. Baker, *Hemingway* 338.

7. Hemingway, *Only Thing* 274–75.

8. Maxwell Perkins to Ernest Hemingway, 18 Apr. 1939, CC, 3 pp., PUL.

9. Ernest Hemingway to Maxwell Perkins, 10 May 1939, TLS, 1 p., PUL.

10. Maxwell Perkins to Ernest Hemingway, 19 May 1939, CC, 4 pp., PUL.

11. Shelvin, a wealthy sportsman, had invited Hemingway to fish in a tuna tournament.

12. Baker, *Selected Letters* 485–86.

13. Charles Scribner III to Ernest Hemingway, 1 June 1939, CC, 2 pp., PUL.

14. Ernest Hemingway to Maxwell Perkins, 30 May 1939, TLS, 1 p., PUL.

15. Maxwell Perkins to Ernest Hemingway, 16 June 1939, CC, 3 pp., PUL.

16. Ernest Hemingway to Maxwell Perkins, 10 July 1939, TLS, 2 pp., PUL.

17. Ernest Hemingway to Maxwell Perkins, mid-July 1939, ALS, 1 p., PUL.

18. Maxwell Perkins to Ernest Hemingway, 19 July 1939, CC, 3 pp., PUL.

19. Maxwell Perkins to Ernest Hemingway, 28 July 1939, CC, 2 pp., PUL.

20. Ernest Hemingway to Maxwell Perkins, 27 Aug. 1939, TLS, 2 pp., PUL.

21. Alvah Bessie had been a member of the Abraham Lincoln Brigade. In 1939, he published *Men in Battle: A Story of Americans in Spain* (New York: Scribners).

22. Ernest Hemingway to Maxwell Perkins, 27 Oct. 1929, TLS, 2 pp., PUL.

23. Maxwell Perkins to Ernest Hemingway, 1 Nov. 1939, CC, 3 pp., PUL.

24. Ernest Hemingway to Maxwell Perkins, c. mid-Nov. 1939, TLS with holograph inserts and postscript, 1 p., PUL.

25. Maxwell Perkins to Ernest Hemingway, 24 Nov. 1939, CC, 3 pp., PUL.

26. Hemingway, *Only Thing* 275.

27. Maxwell Perkins to Ernest Hemingway, 19 Dec. 1939, CC, 3 pp., PUL.

28. Hemingway, *Only Thing* 277–78.

29. See Robert W. Trogdon, "Money and Marriage: Hemingway's Self-Censorship in *For Whom the Bell Tolls,*" *Hemingway Review* 22.2 (2003): 6–18, for a fuller discussion of how Hemingway rendered obscene language in the novel and his possible motivations for doing so.

30. Hemingway, *Only Thing* 279.

31. Ernest Hemingway to Maxwell Perkins, 18 Jan. 1940, TLS, 1 p., PUL.

32. Hemingway, *Only Thing* 279.

33. Ernest Hemingway to Maxwell Perkins, c. 23 Jan. 1940, TLS, 1 p., PUL.

34. Baker *Selected Letters* 500–2.

35. Ernest Hemingway to Maxwell Perkins, 18 Feb. 1940, TLS, 1 p., PUL.

36. Maxwell Perkins to Ernest Hemingway, 21 Feb. 1940, CC, 2 pp., PUL.

37. Ernest Hemingway to Maxwell Perkins, 23 Feb. 1940, TLS, 1 p., PUL.

38. Maxwell Perkins to Ernest Hemingway, 26 Feb. 1940, CC, 3 pp., PUL.

39. Ernest Hemingway to Maxwell Perkins, 3 Mar. 1940, TLS, 1 p., PUL.

40. Maxwell Perkins to Maurice Speiser, 12 Mar. 1940, CC, 1 p., PUL.

41. Maxwell Perkins to Ernest Hemingway, 12 Mar. 1940, CC, 3 pp., PUL.

42. Maxwell Perkins to Ernest Hemingway, 4 Apr. 1940, CC, 3 pp., PUL.

43. Ernest Hemingway to Maxwell Perkins, 6 Apr. 1940, TLS with holograph postscript, 1 p., PUL.

44. Maxwell Perkins to Ernest Hemingway, 9 Apr. 1940, CC, 4 pp., PUL.

45. Finney was an adventurer and soldier of fortune. His account of reading the manuscript of *For Whom the Bell Tolls* in his autobiography *Feet First* (New York: Crown, 1971) confirms Hemingway's report to Perkins.

46. Hemingway, *Only Thing* 280–82.

47. Maxwell Perkins to Ernest Hemingway, 19 Apr. 1940, CC, 3 pp., PUL.

48. Maxwell Perkins to Ernest Hemingway, 20 Apr. 1940, CC, 1 p., PUL.

49 Hemingway, *Only Thing* 282.

50. Hemingway, *Only Thing* 283.

51. Hemingway, *Only Thing* 283.

52. Hemingway, *Only Thing* 283–84.

53. "Books and Authors," *New York Times Book Review,* 12 May 1940: 14.

54. Ernest Hemingway to Maxwell Perkins, 5 May 1940, wire with Perkins's holograph response, 1 p., PUL.

55. *Catalog of the Ernest Hemingway Collection* 2:506–8.

56. Ernest Hemingway to Maxwell Perkins, 13 May 1940, TLS, 1 p., PUL.

57. Hemingway, *Only Thing* 161–64. Cf. chapter 4 for a fuller discussion of the publication of *Death in the Afternoon.*

58. Hemingway, *Only Thing* 165.

59. Berg 211–12.

60. Berg 300.

61. Maxwell Perkins to Ernest Hemingway, 15 May 1940, CC, 3 pp., PUL.

62. Ernest Hemingway to Maxwell Perkins, 21 May 1940, wire, 1 p., PUL.

63. Ernest Hemingway to Maxwell Perkins, 23 May 1940, TLS, 1 p., PUL.

64. Ernest Hemingway to Maxwell Perkins, 31 May 1940, TLS, 1 p., PUL.

65. Hemingway, *Only Thing* 284.

66. Hemingway, *Only Thing* 285.

67. Contract for *For Whom the Bell Tolls,* 15 July 1940, 3 pp., PUL.

68. Reynolds, *Chronology* 96.

69. Maxwell Perkins to Ernest Hemingway, 31 July 1940, CC, 1 p., PUL.

70. Maxwell Perkins to Ernest Hemingway, 1 Aug. 1940, CC, 1 p., PUL.

71. Robert Van Gelder, "Ernest Hemingway Talks of Work and War," *New York Times Book Review*, 11 Aug. 1940: 2; reprinted in Matthew J. Bruccoli, ed., *Conversations with Ernest Hemingway* (Jackson: Univ. Press of Mississippi, 1986), 17–20.

72. Charles Scribner III to Ernest Hemingway, 12 Aug. 1940, CC, 2 pp., PUL.

73. Maxwell Perkins to Ernest Hemingway, 13 Aug. 1940, CC, 3 pp., PUL.

74. *For Whom the Bell Tolls* galley proofs, galley 50, JFK.

75. Hemingway, *Only Thing* 286–89.

76. Hemingway, *Only Thing* 285.

77. In 2002, a single typescript page titled "Epilogue," dealing with Golz, was found in Hemingway's papers at the Finca Vigía in Cuba. See Jenny Phillips, "The Finca Vigía Archives: A Joint Cuban-American Project to Preserve Hemingway's Papers," *Hemingway Review* 22.1 (2002): 12.

78. In Genesis 38:8–10, Onan spilled his seed on the ground rather than impregnate his brother's wife; God was displeased and slew him. The story of Onan has served as a warning against masturbation. In chapter 31, Jordan, unable to have sexual intercourse with Maria, thinks, "I'll keep any oversupply of that for tomorrow. I'll need all of that there is tomorrow. Who was it cast his seed upon the ground in the Bible? Onan. How did Onan turn out? he thought. I don't remember ever hearing any more about Onan. He smiled in the dark."

79. Ernest Hemingway to Charles Scribner III, 15 Aug. 1940, TLS with holograph postscript, 3 pp., PUL.

80. Originally in chapter 6, Jordan had told Pilar and Maria that he was a Communist (galley 21). Following Scribner's advice, Hemingway changed Jordan to an "anti-fascist."

81. Charles Scribner III to Harry Scherman, 23 Aug. 1940, CC, 2 pp., PUL.

82. Charles Scribner III to Ernest Hemingway, 26 Aug. 1940, CC, 2 pp., PUL.

83. Charles Scribner III to Ernest Hemingway, 27 Aug. 1940, CC, 2 pp., PUL.

84. *For Whom the Bell Tolls* royalty report, 22 Jan. 1941, holograph note, 1 p., PUL.

85. Kuehl and Bryer 266.

86. Hemingway, *Only Thing* 289–93.

87. Hemingway, *Only Thing* 293–94.

88. Hemingway, *Only Thing* 294.

89. Maxwell Perkins to Ernest Hemingway, 28 Aug. 1940, TCDS, 1 p., PUL.

90. Maxwell Perkins to Ernest Hemingway, 30 Aug. 1940, CC, 4 pp., PUL; partially reprinted in Hemingway, *Only Thing* 294–95.

91. Charles Scribner III to Harry Scherman, 29 Aug. 1940, CC, 2 pp., PUL.

92. Ernest Hemingway to Charles Scribner, 29 Aug. 1940, TLS, 2 pp., PUL.

93. Ernest Hemingway to Maxwell Perkins, 9 Sept. 1940 (1:05 P.M.), wire, 1 p.; 9 Sept. 1940 (1:19 P.M.), wire, 1 p.; 9 Sept. 1940 (8:30 P.M.), wire, 1 p.; 10 Sept. 1940 (4:05 P.M.), wire, 1 p., PUL. The last wire is included in Hemingway, *Only Thing* 298.

94. Ernest Hemingway to Charles Scribner III 16 Sept. 1940, wire, 1 p., PUL.

95. Hemingway, *Only Thing* 298.

96. *Charles Scribner's Sons Fall 1940 Trade Catalog* 2.

97. *In Their Time,* Item 151.

98. "Scribner Leaders for the Fall of 1940," *Publishers Weekly,* 15 June 1940: 2052–53.

99. "Scribner: Leaders from a Strong List," *Publishers Weekly,* 7 Sept. 1940: 785.

100. "A Handy Guide to Notable Books of 1940," *Publishers Weekly,* 21 Sept. 1940: 1073.

101. "A Few High Spots Among Fall Ad Campaigns," *Publishers Weekly,* 21 Sept. 1940: 1125.

102. "Scribner Books for Every Taste," *New York Times Book Review,* 22 Sept. 1940: 17.

103. "Scribner Books for Every Taste," 9.

104. *New York Times Book Review,* 13 Oct. 1940: 11.

105. *Book-of-the-Month Club News,* Oct. 1940: 2–4. Perkins's article is reprinted in its entirety in Hemingway, *Only Thing* 295–97.

106. *Catalog of the Ernest Hemingway Collection* 2:510–11.

107. Both Hemingway and Darrow were members of the Players Club of New York.

108. Ernest Hemingway to Maxwell Perkins, c. 2 Oct. 1940, TLS, 3 pp., PUL.

109. Maxwell Perkins to Ernest Hemingway, 5 Oct. 1940, CC, 2 pp., PUL.

110. Donald Friede to Maxwell Perkins, 7 Oct. 1940, wire, 1 p., PUL.

111. Baker, *Selected Letters* 517–18.

112. Scribners printing card for *For Whom the Bell Tolls,* Scribners Press, 1 p., PUL. See also R. H. Miller, "For Whom The Bell Tolls: Book-of-the-Month Club Copies," *Fitzgerald/Hemingway Annual* (1979): 407–9.

113. *For Whom the Bell Tolls,* Cohn Collection, Univ. of Delaware. See also Hanneman 51–52.

114. "Hemingway Novel a Smash," *Publishers Weekly,* 2 Nov. 1940, 1751.

115. *Catalog of the Ernest Hemingway Collection* 2:514–28.

116. J. Donald Adams, review of *FWTBT,* "The New Novel By Hemingway," *New York Times Book Review,* 20 Oct. 1940: 1.

117. John Chamberlain, review of *FWTBT,* "Hemingway Tells How Men Meet Death," *New York Herald Tribune Books,* 20 Oct. 1940: 1.

118. Dorothy Parker, review of *FWTBT,* "Mr. Hemingway's Finest Story Yet," *PM,* 20 Oct. 1940: 42.

119. Ralph Thompson, "Books Of the *Times,*" *New York Times,* 21 Oct. 1940: 15; "Death in Spain," *Time,* 21 Oct. 1940: 94–95; "Hemingway's Spanish War," *Newsweek,* 21 Oct. 1940: 50.

120. Margaret Marshall, "Books and the Arts," *Nation,* 26 Oct. 1940: 395.

121. Clifton Fadiman, review of *FWTBT,* "Hemingway Crosses the Bridge," *New Yorker,* 16, 26 Oct. 1940: 82.

122. Howard Mumford Jones, "The Soul of Spain," *Saturday Review of Literature,* 26 Oct. 1940: 5.

123. Edmund Wilson, "Return of Ernest Hemingway," *New Republic,* 28 Oct. 1940: 591.

124. Alvah Bessie, "Hemingway's 'For Whom the Bell Tolls,'" *New Masses,* 5 Nov. 1940: 25–29.

125. Burton Rascoe, "The Library," *American Mercury,* Dec. 1940: 495.

126. J. N. Vaughan, "Books of the Week," *Commonweal,* 13 Dec. 1940: 210.

127. Dwight Macdonald, "Reading from Left to Right," *Partisan Review,* Jan.–Feb. 1941: 27.

128. Lionel Trilling, "An American in Spain," *Partisan Review,* Jan.–Feb. 1941: 63.

129. Robert E. Sherwood, "The Atlantic Bookshelf," *Atlantic Monthly,* Nov. 1940: front section.

130. Malcolm Cowley, "Death of a Hero," *New Republic,* 20 Jan. 1941: 89.

131. Maxwell Perkins to Ernest Hemingway, 11 Oct. 1940, CC, 3 pp., PUL.

132. Maxwell Perkins to Ernest Hemingway, 15 Oct. 1940, CC, 3 pp., PUL.

133. Maxwell Perkins to Ernest Hemingway, 21 Oct. 1940, CC, 1 p., PUL.

134. This edition was never published.

135. Hemingway, *Only Thing* 298.

136. Advertising records for *For Whom the Bell Tolls,* advertising department, Charles Scribner's Sons, 9 pp., PUL.

137. Advertisements for the novel appeared in the following issues of the *New York Times Book Review:* 20 Oct. 1940: 17; 27 Oct. 1940: 11; 3 Nov. 1940: 25; 10 Nov. 1940: 11; 17 Nov. 1940: 15; 24 Nov. 1940: 12; 1 Dec. 1940: 11, 43; 8 Dec. 1940: 11; 15 Dec. 1940: 13; 22 Dec. 1940: 13; 12 Jan. 1941: 20; 19 Jan. 1941: 15; 26 Jan. 1941, 13; 2 Feb. 1941: 11; 9 Feb. 1941: 22; 16 Feb. 1941: 14; 23 Feb. 1941: 14; 2 Mar. 1941: 12; 16 Mar. 1941: 25; 23 Mar. 1941: 16; 4 May 1941: 18; 11 May 1941: 23; 1 June 1941: 14, 18; 8 June 1941: 12; and 15 June 1941: 16, 17, 19.

138. Ads for the novel ran in the *New York Herald Tribune Books* on 20 Oct. (11); 10 Nov. (26); 17 Nov. (12); 24 Nov. (21); 1 Dec. (19, 30, 34, 38, 44); 8 Dec. (9); 15 Dec. (7); 22 Dec. (9, 11); and 29 Dec. (9). Ads for the novel appeared in the *Chicago Tribune* on 30 Oct. (19); 6 Nov. (24); 13 Nov. (19); 27 Nov. (17); 4 Dec. (sec. 2, p. 6); 11 Dec. (21); and 18 Dec. (20).

139. "The Fastest Selling Book in the United States," *Publishers Weekly,* 30 Nov. 1940: 2010–11.

140. *Publishers Weekly,* 1 Feb. 1941: 614.

141. *Publishers Weekly,* 25 Jan. 1941: 419–20.

142. *Charles Scribner's Sons Spring 1941 Trade Catalog* 2; *Charles Scribner's Sons Fall 1941 Trade Catalog* 2.

143. "Back to His First Field," *Kansas City Times,* 26 Nov. 1940: 1; "Author in the Forenoon," *New Yorker,* 28 Dec. 1940: 10; Ralph Ingersoll, "Hemingway Is on the Way to Far East for *PM,*" *PM,* 31 Jan. 1941: 12; Stanton Dalplane, "For the Hemingways, There'll Be No Farewell to Arms," *San Francisco Chronicle,* 31 Jan. 1941: 13; "Hemingway, Here for a Visit, Says He'd Think He Was Slipping If He Had Won Pulitzer Prize," *St. Louis Star-Times,* 23 May 1941: 3; "Ernest Hemingway Interviewed by Ralph Ingersoll," *PM,* 9 June 1941: 6–10.

144. Stephen Vincent Benét and Rosemary Benét, "Ernest Hemingway: Byron of Our Day," *New York Herald Tribune Books,* 3 Nov. 1940: 7; "Ernest Hemingway Is Divorced," *New York Times,* 5 Nov. 1940: 13; "Hemingway Weds Magazine Writer," *New York Times,* 22 Nov. 1940: 25; "Hemingways on Way Here," *New York Times,* 23 Nov. 1940: 15; "The Hemingways in Sun Valley: The Novelist Takes a Wife," *Life,* 6 Jan. 1941: 49–51; "Ernest Hemingway Meets Ingrid Bergman," *Life,* 23 Feb. 1941: 48, 51; David Daiches, "Ernest Hemingway," *English Journal* 30 (1941): 175–86; "Hemingway Novel Wins Critics' Vote," *New York Times,* 26 Apr. 1941: 13; "The Nation's Book Reviewers Nominate Their Pulitzer Prize Favorites," *Saturday Review of Literature,* 26 Apr. 1941: 7; "Eire Bans Hemingway Book," *New York Times,* 12 June 1941: 3; Maxwell Geismar, "No Man Alone Now," *Virginia Quarterly Review* 17 (1941): 517–34; Eleanor Sickels, "Farewell to Cynicism," *College English* 3 (1941): 31–38; "Hunting at Sun Valley," *Life,* 24 Nov. 1941: 116–19; "Hemingway Gets Medal for Book," *New York Times,* 27 Nov. 1941: 21.

145. Raeburn 107. Raeburn cites the following: Walter Winchell in the *Philadelphia Record,* 16 Dec. 1940; Photograph in *Harper's Bazaar,* Jan. 1941: 50–51; and Ruth Reynolds, "Love Collaborates with Hemingway," *New York Mirror,* 1 Dec. 1940.

146. BOMC ads appeared in the *New York Times Book Review* in the following issues: 20 Oct. 1940: 40; 10 Nov. 1940: 48; 17 Nov. 1940: 40; 1 Dec. 1940: 56; 29 Dec. 1940: 16; 12 Jan. 1941: 28; 2 Feb. 1941: 26; 16 Feb. 1941: 32; 9 Mar. 1941: 38; 30 Mar. 1941: 32; 20 Apr. 1941: 32; 17 Aug. 1941: 24; 24 Aug. 1941: 30; 7 Sept. 1941: 32; 14 Sept. 1941: 26; 21 Sept. 1941: 38; 28 Sept. 1941: 38; 5 Oct. 1941: 38; 12 Oct. 1941: 30; 19 Oct. 1941: 40; 9 Nov. 1941: 48; 7 Dec. 1941: 62; and 28 Dec. 1941: 16.

147. "Books I Have Liked," *New York Herald Tribune Books,* 1 Dec. 1940: 2, 3, 4, 6, 8, 9, 14.

148. Fanny Butcher, "Fanny Butcher Selects 10 Best Novels of 1940," *Chicago Tribune,* 4 Dec. 1940: sec. 2, 1–2.

149. "The *SRL* Christmas List," *Saturday Review of Literature,* 7 Dec. 1940: 10.

150. "The Nation's Book Reviewers Nominate Their Pulitzer Prize Favorites," *Saturday Review of Literature,* 26 Aug. 1941: 7–8.

151. John Hohenberg, *The Pulitzer Prizes: A History of the Awards in Books, Drama, Music, and Journalism, Based on the Private Files over Six Decades* (New York: Columbia Univ. Press, 1974), 144–45.

152. Albert Marrin, *Nicholas Murray Butler* (Boston: Twayne, 1976), 85.

153. "Hemingway, Here for a Visit," 1; Bruccoli, *Conversations with Ernest Hemingway,* 29–30.

154. Maxwell Perkins to Ernest Hemingway, 3 Sept. 1941, CC, 4 pp., PUL.

155. Printing cards for *For Whom the Bell Tolls,* Scribners Press, 4 pp., PUL.

8. After Perkins

1. Ernest Hemingway, *Men At War* (New York: Crown, 1942). See Hemingway, *Only Thing* 317–22, for Hemingway and Perkins's correspondence about this volume.

2. Michael Reynolds, *Hemingway: The Final Years* (New York: Norton, 1999), 56–89, 92–123.

3. *The Garden of* Eden was published in a truncated and heavily edited version by Scribners in 1986. *Islands in the Stream,* edited by Carlos Baker, was published by Scribners in 1970.

4. Hemingway, *Only Thing* 342.

5. Ernest Hemingway, *A Farewell to Arms,* illustrated by Daniel Rasmusson (New York: Scribners, 1948).

6. Hemingway, *Only Thing* 343–44.

7. Hemingway, *Only Thing* 344–45.

8. Albert J. DeFazio III, ed., *Dear Papa, Dear Hotch: The Correspondence of Ernest Hemingway and A. E. Hotchner* (Columbia: Univ. of Missouri Press, 2005), 15–16.

9. Reynolds, *Hemmingway: The Final Years* 190.

10. Ernest Hemingway to Charles Scribner III, 24 Aug. 1949, TLS with holograph inserts and postscript, Finca Vigía stationery, 2 pp., PUL.

11. DeFazio, *Dear Papa, Dear Hotch* 37–41.

12. Faulkner, "Classroom Statements at the Univ. of Mississippi," *Lion in the Garden: Interviews with William Faulkner,* ed. James B. Meriwether and Michael Millgate (Lincoln: Univ. of Nebraska Press, 1968), 58. See also Reynolds, *Hemingway: The Final Years* 157–58.

13. Ernest Hemingway to Charles Scribner III, 31 Aug. 1949, TLS, 2 pp., PUL.

14. Ernest Hemingway to Charles Scribner III, 1 Sept. 1949, TLS with holograph postscript, Finca Vigía stationery, 1 p., PUL.

15. Ernest Hemingway to Charles Scribner III, 21 Sept. 1949, TLS, Finca Vigía stationery, 1 p., PUL.

16. Mary Hemingway, *How It Was* (New York: Knopf, 1976), 246.

17. One must take Mary Hemingway's account with grain of salt, however. Her memoir was not published until 1976, and her opinion of *Across the River* may have been colored by jealousy over her husband's infatuation with Adriana Ivancich, upon whom the character of Reneta in the novel was based.

18. "News of Scribner Books and Authors," 12 Oct. 1949, TL, 2 pp., PUL.

19. "Hemingway Novel Slated for March," *New York Times,* 13 Oct. 1949: 25.

20. Ernest Hemingway to Charles Scribner III, 17 Oct. 1949, TLS, Finca Vigía stationery, 2 pp., PUL.

21. Ernest Hemingway to Charles Scribner III, 28 and 31 Oct. 1949, TLS with holograph inserts, Finca Vigía stationery, 2 pp., PUL.

22. Ernest Hemingway to Charles Scribner III, 8 Nov. 1949, TLS, Finca Vigía stationery, 1 p., PUL.

23. "How Do You Like It Now, Gentlemen?" *New Yorker,* 13 May 1950: 36–62.

24. Ernest Hemingway to Charles Scribner III, 28 Nov. 1949, ALS, *S.S. Ile de France* stationery, 5 pp., PUL.

25. Ernest Hemingway to Charles Scribner III, 10 Dec. 1949, TLS with holograph inserts, 3 pp., PUL.

26. Ernest Hemingway to Charles Scribner III, 13 Dec. 1949, TLS with holograph inserts, 1 p., PUL. There is no evidence to support Hemingway's claim that he studied law.

27. DeFazio, *Dear Papa, Dear Hotch* 7. See also 63–64, and Albert J. DeFazio, III, "The Hemhotch Letters: The Correspondence and Relationship of Ernest Hemingway and A. E. Hotchner" (PhD diss., Univ. of Virginia, 1992), 593–1243, for a full explanation of Hotchner's editorial contribution.

28. *Across the River and Into the Trees, Cosmopolitan,* Feb. 1950: 31–33, 156–67; Mar. 1950: 34–35, 79–91; Apr. 1950: 58–59, 119–29; May 1950: 50–51, 130–39; June 1950: 56–57, 79–83.

29. Hanneman 62.

30. Charles Scribner III, to Ernest Hemingway, 12 Jan. 1950, CC, 4 pp., PUL.

31. Charles Scribner III, to Ernest Hemingway, 2 Feb. 1950, cable, 1 p., PUL.

32. Ernest Hemingway to Charles Scribner III, 18 Feb. 1950, TLS with holograph inserts, 2 pp., PUL.

33. Ernest Hemingway to Charles Scribner III, 3 Mar. 1950, TLS, 2 pp., PUL.

34. Wallace Meyer to Charles Scribner III, 13 Mar. 1950, ALS, Charles Scribner's Sons stationery, 6 pp., PUL.

35. Ernest Hemingway to Charles Scribner III, 14 Mar. 1950, TLS, Hotel Ritz stationery, 2 pp., PUL.

36. Wallace Meyer to Charles Scribner III, 7 Apr. 1950, TLS with holograph postscript, Charles Scribner's Sons stationery, 3 pp., PUL.

37. Wallace Meyer to Ernest Hemingway, 14 Apr. 1950, CC, 2 pp., PUL.

38. Charles Scribner III to Ernest Hemingway, 21 Apr. 1950, ALS, 6 pp., JFK.

39. Ernest Hemingway to Charles Scribner III, 1 May 1950, TLS, 2 pp., PUL.

40. Charles Scribner III to Ernest Hemingway, 4 May 1950, CC, 3 pp., PUL.

41. Ernest Hemingway to Charles Scribner III, 7 May 1951 [1950], TLS, 2 pp., PUL.

42. Charles Scribner III to Ernest Hemingway, 8 May 1950, CC, 4 pp., PUL.

43. Charles Scribner III to Ernest Hemingway, 9 May 1950, CC, 2 pp., PUL.

44. Ernest Hemingway to Charles Scribner III, 15 May 1950, TLS with holograph inserts, 6 pp., PUL.

45. Charles Scribner III to Ernest Hemingway, 16 May 1950, CC, 2 pp., PUL.

46. Ernest Hemingway to Charles Scribner III, 20 May 1950, TLS with holograph postscript, Finca Vigía stationery, 2 pp., PUL.

47. Ernest Hemingway to Charles Scribner III, 21 May 1950, ALS, Finca Vigía stationery, 6 pp., PUL.

48. Charles Scribner III to Ernest Hemingway, 23 May 1950, CC, 2 pp., PUL.

49. Ernest Hemingway to Charles Scribner III, 1 and 2 June 1950, TLS with holograph postscript, 1 p., PUL.

50. Charles Scribner III to Ernest Hemingway, 5 June 1950, TCD, 1 p., PUL.

51. Charles Scribner III to Ernest Hemingway, 14 June 1950, CC, 3 pp., PUL.

52. Ernest Hemingway to Charles Scribner III, 30 June 1950, TLS, Finca Vigía stationery, 1 p., PUL.

53. Charles Scribner III to Ernest Hemingway, 18 July 1950, CC, 2 pp., PUL.

54. Ernest Hemingway to Charles Scribner III, 21 July 1950, TL and ALS, Finca Vigía stationery, 3 pp., PUL.

55. Ernest Hemingway to Charles Scribner III, 28 July 1950, CC, 2 pp., PUL.

56. *Scribners Spring List: January to June 1950*: 1.

57. *Scribners Fall List: July to December 1950*: 1–3.

58. Alice Hackett, "*PW* Buyers' Forecast for Sept. 6–12," *Publishers Weekly*, 29 July 1950: 487.

59. Julien Dedman, memo to Charles Scribner Sr., Wallace Meyer, and Norman Snow, "The Advertising Schedule for Ernest Hemingway's ACROSS THE RIVER AND INTO THE TREES," 23 Aug. 1950, TL, 2 pp., PUL.

60. Due to miscommunication, the English edition (published by Jonathan Cape) was published three days earlier. *Across the River and Into the Trees* is the only Hemingway book that appeared in Britain before its release in the United States.

61. Contract for *Across the River and Into the Trees,* 18 Nov. 1949, 2 pp., PUL.

62. Raeburn 125.

63. Lewis Gannett, review of *ARIT,* *New York Herald Tribune,* 7 Sept. 1950: 23.

64. Richard H. Rovere, review of *ARIT, Harper's,* Sept. 1950: 104.

65. Malcolm Cowley, review of *ARIT, New York Herald Tribune Book Review,* 10 Sept. 1950: 1.

66. John O'Hara, "The Author's Name Is Hemingway," *New York Times Book Review,* 10 Sept. 1950: 1.

67. Evelyn Waugh, review of *ARIT, Tablet,* 30 Sept. 1950: 290; *Time,* 30 Oct. 1950: 44.

68. William Faulkner, Letter, *Time,* 13 Nov. 1950: 6.

69. "Item," *Commonweal,* 22 Sept. 1950: 572–73; John K. Hutchens, "Nobody on the Fence," *New York Herald Tribune Book Review,* 24 Sept. 1950: 3; J. Donald Adams, "Speaking of Books," *New York Times Book Review,* 24 Sept. 1950: 2; Ben Ray Redman, "The Champ and the Referees," *Saturday Review of Literature,* 28 Oct. 1950: 15–16, 38; Elise Morrow, "The Hemingway View of His Critics," *St. Louis Post-Dispatch,* 15 Jan. 1951: 1C.

70. Whitney Darrow, memo to Charles Scribner III, 19 Apr. 1951, TL, 2 pp., PUL.

71. "Itemized Record of Credits to Ernest Hemingway Royalty Account: February 1951 to February 1954," 1 p., PUL.

72. "On the Blue Water: A Gulf Stream Letter," *Esquire,* Apr. 1936: 31, 184.

73. Baker, *Selected Letters* 478–79.

74. Mary Hemingway, *How It Was* 283.

75. Baker, *Hemingway* 490.

76. Baker, *Hemingway* 492.

77. Baker, *Selected Letters* 750–52.

78. Mary Hemingway, *How It Was* 295.

79. Baker, *Selected Letters* 757–60.

80. Wallace Meyer to Ernest Hemingway, 12 Mar. 1952, TCD, 1 p., PUL.

81. Wallace Meyer to Ernest Hemingway, 13 Mar. 1952, CC, 3 pp., PUL.

82. Wallace Meyer to Ernest Hemingway, 21 Mar. 1952, CC, 1 p., PUL.

83. Wallace Meyer to Ernest Hemingway, 28 Mar. 1952, CC, 3 pp., PUL.

84. Wallace Meyer to Ernest Hemingway, 4 Apr. 1952, TCD, 1 p., PUL.

85. Wallace Meyer to Ernest Hemingway, 7 Apr. 1952, CC, 2 pp., PUL.

86. Leland Hayward to Ernest Hemingway, 11 Apr. 1952, CC, 3 pp., PUL.

87. Ernest Hemingway to Wallace Meyer, 15 and 21 Apr. 1952, TL and ALS, Finca Vigía stationery, 2 pp., PUL.

88. Wallace Meyer to Ernest Hemingway, 25 Apr. 1952, CC, 4 pp., PUL.

89. Ernest Hemingway to Wallace Meyer, 6 May 1952, TLS, Finca Vigía stationery, 1 p., PUL.

90. Agreement between Ernest Hemingway and Time, Inc., c. 6 May 1952, CC, 1 p., PUL.

91. Ernest Hemingway to Wallace Meyer, 7 May 1952, TLS, Finca Vigía stationery, 1 p., PUL.

92. Wallace Meyer to Ernest Hemingway, 9 May 1952, CC, 3 pp., PUL.

93. Whitney Darrow, memorandum to Messrs. Scribner, Meyer, Snow, Schieffelin, and Poli, 13 May 1952, CC, 2 pp., PUL.

94. *The Old Man and the Sea,* galley proofs, Rare Book and Manuscript Division, New York Public Library.

95. Wallace Meyer to Ernest Hemingway, 21 May 1952, CC, 2 pp., PUL.

96. Wallace Meyer to Ernest Hemingway, 3 June 1952, CC, 3 pp., PUL.

97. Ernest Hemingway to Daniel Longwell, 6 July 1952, 2 pp., Daniel Longwell Papers, Butler Library, Columbia Univ.

98. Wallace Meyer to Ernest Hemingway, 19 June 1952, CC, 2 pp., PUL.

99. Wallace Meyer to Ernest Hemingway, 25 June 1952, CC, 1 p., PUL.

100. Daniel Longwell to Ernest Hemingway, 2 July 1952, CC, 2 pp., PUL.

101. Wallace Meyer to Daniel Longwell, 3 July 1952, CC, 3 pp., PUL.

102. Ernest Hemingway to Daniel Longwell, 6 July 1952, ALS, Finca Vigía stationery, 3 pp., Daniel Longwell Papers, Columbia Univ.

103. Ernest Hemingway to Daniel Longwell, 27 July 1952, TLS, Finca Vigía stationery, 2 pp., Daniel Longwell Papers, Columbia Univ.

104. "From Ernest Hemingway to the Editors of *Life,*" *Life,* 25 Aug. 1952: 124.

105. *Saturday Review of Literature,* 30 Aug. 1952: 2.

106. *Publishers Weekly,* 19 July 1952: 161–63.

107. *Scribners Fall List: July-December 1952:* 1–3.

108. *Life,* 1 Sept. 1952.

109. Matthew J. Bruccoli, introduction to *Conversations with Ernest Hemingway* (Jackson: Univ. Press of Mississippi, 1986), ix.

110. Hanneman 166.

111. Wallace Meyer to Ernest Hemingway, 11 Sept. 1952, CC, 3 pp., PUL.

112. Contract for *The Old Man and the Sea,* 19 May 1950, 2 pp., PUL.

113. Raeburn 141.

114. Julien Dedman, memo to Wallace Meyer, 15 Sept. 1952, TL, 1 p., PUL.

115. Ernest Hemingway to Daniel Longwell, 1 Sept. 1952, ALS, Finca Vigía stationery, 2 pp., Daniel Longwell Papers, Columbia Univ.

116. Ernest Hemingway to Daniel Longwell, 28 Sept. 1952, ALS, Finca Vigía stationery, 3 pp., Daniel Longwell Papers, Columbia Univ.

117. David Dempsey, "In and Out of Books," *New York Times Book Review,* 7 Sept. 1952: 8.

118. David Dempsey, "In and Out of Books," *New York Times Book Review,* 19 Oct. 1952: 8.

119. "News and Trends of the Week," *Publishers Weekly,* 13 Sept. 1952: 991.

120. P. S. J. [Peter S. Jennison], "'The Old Man' and the Book," *Publishers Weekly,* 13 Sept. 1952: 1011.

121. Bennett Cerf, "Trade Winds," *Publishers Weekly,* 18 Oct. 1952: 6.

122. Wallace Meyer to Ernest Hemingway, 23 Sept. 1952, CC, 2 pp., PUL.

123. Charles Scribner Jr., to Ernest Hemingway, 30 Sept. 1952, CC, 2 pp., PUL.

124. Printing cards for *The Old Man and the Sea,* Scribners Press, 4 pp., PUL. Printings for *The Old Man and the Sea* were ordered on 28 May 1952 (51,700), 28 Aug. 1952 (10,250), 18 Sept. 1952 (15,400), 24 Nov. 1952 (10,200), 5 May 1953 (5,175), 24 June 1953 (4,400), 14 Oct. 1953 (5,025), 2 Mar. 1954 (6,500), 1 Nov. 1954 (10,000), 7 Dec. 1954 (5,000), and 11 Jan. 1955 (10,000). The plates for this edition were destroyed on 23 Aug. 1955.

125. Hanneman 64.

126. "Itemized Record of Credits to Ernest Hemingway Royalty Account: February 1951 to February 1954," 1 p., PUL.

127. Norman Snow, memo to Charles Scribner Jr., 27 Jan. 1953, TL, 2 pp., PUL.

Epilogue

1. More than 15,000 copies sold at a 20-percent royalty for Hemingway.

2. Wallace Meyer to Ernest Hemingway, 17 Feb. 1955, TLS, 1 p., JFK.

3. Reynolds, *Hemingway: The Final Years* 285.

4. *Life,* 5 Sept. 1960: 78–109; 12 Sept. 1960: 60–82; 19 Sept. 1960: 74–96.

5. The "African Journal" was published, in an extremely abridged form, in three issues of *Sports Illustrated:* 20 Dec. 1971: 5, 40–52, 57–66; 3 Jan. 1972: 26–46; and 10 Jan. 1972: 22–30, 43–30, 43–50. In 1999, Scribners issued *True at First Light,* a fuller yet still incomplete version edited by Patrick Hemingway. In 2005, Kent State University Press published *Under Kilimanjaro* (edited by Robert Lewis and Robert Fleming), a fuller version of the work as Hemingway left it.

6. Under the provisions of the Copyright Act of 1976, works published during Hemingway's lifetime were protected for seventy-five years from the date of publication. With the passage of the Sonny Bono Copyright Term Extension Act in 1998, the term was extended another twenty years.

7. Samuel Johnson, "The Idler, No. 102," *Selected Poetry and Prose,* 273.

BIBLIOGRAPHICAL NOTE

As this is the first book-length examination of Ernest Hemingway's relationship with Charles Scribner's Sons, the author has relied most heavily on unpublished archival material, mainly from the Archives of Charles Scribner's Sons at the Princeton University Library and from the Hemingway Collection at the John F. Kennedy Library. However, many published works have examined aspects of Hemingway's career as a professional author and should be mentioned.

First and foremost are Audre Hanneman's *Ernest Hemingway: A Comprehensive Bibliography* (Princeton, NJ: Princeton University Press, 1967) and *A Supplement to Ernest Hemingway: A Comprehensive Bibliography* (Princeton, NJ: Princeton University Press, 1975). Among the many biographical studies that have appeared since 1961, Carlos Baker's *Ernest Hemingway: A Life Story* (New York: Scribners, 1969) remains the best single-volume biography. A more detailed account of his life can be found in Michael Reynolds's five-volume account: *The Young Hemingway* (New York: Blackwell, 1986), *Hemingway: The Paris Years* (Cambridge, MA: Blackwell, 1989), *Hemingway: The American Homecoming* (Cambridge, MA: Blackwell, 1992), *Hemingway: The 1930s* (New York: Norton, 1997), and *Hemingway: The Final Years* (New York: Norton, 1999). While not a biography per se, John Raeburn's *Fame Became of Him: Hemingway as Public Writer* (Bloomington: Indiana University Press, 1984) is an indispensable study of Hemingway's public persona. The only biography of any member of the Scribners firm is A. Scott Berg's *Maxwell Perkins: Editor of Genius* (New York: Dutton, 1978).

The most valuable letter collection for those interested in Hemingway and Scribners is *The Only Thing That Counts: The Ernest Hemingway/Maxwell Perkins Correspondence*, ed. Matthew J. Bruccoli (New York: Scribners, 1996). Carlos Baker's *Ernest Hemingway: Selected Letters, 1917–1961* (New York: Scribners, 1981) reprints a few letters to Perkins not found in the previously mentioned collection as well as correspondence with other members of the firm. Albert. J. DeFazio's *Dear Papa, Dear Hotch: The Correspondence of Ernest Hemingway and A. E. Hotchner* (Columbia: University of Missouri Press, 2005) provides tremendous insight into Hemingway's creative and publishing activities in the 1950s. Most of the important reviews of Hemingway's works have been excerpted in Robert O. Stephens's *Ernest Hemingway: The Critical Reception* (N.p.: Franklin, 1977) and Jeffrey Meyers's *Hemingway: The Critical Heritage* (London: Routledge and Keegan Paul, 1982).

Three specific instances of Hemingway's career have been the subject of a great deal of scholarly attention: his break with Boni & Liveright and the writing and publishing of *The Sun Also Rises* and *A Farewell to Arms*. Two biographies of Horace Liveright—William Gilmore's *Horace Liveright: Publisher of the Twenties* (New York: David Lewis, 1970) and Tom Dardis's *Firebrand: The Life of Horace Liveright* (New York: Random House, 1995)—deal with this incident from the publisher's point of view. The chapter on Hemingway in *The House of Boni and Liveright, 1917–1933*, ed. Charles Eggleston, *Dictionary of Literary Biography* volume 288 (Detroit: Gale, 2004) reproduces the important documents of Hemingway's brief tenure as a Liveright author. F. Scott Fitzgerald's role in Hemingway's move to Scribners is detailed in Bruccoli's *Fitzgerald and Hemingway: A Dangerous Friendship,* paperback edition (New York: Carroll and Graf, 1996) and in Scott Donaldson's "The Wooing of Ernest Hemingway," *American Literature* 53.4 (1982): 691–710. The composition and editing of Hemingway's first novel is fully covered by Frederic J. Svoboda's *Hemingway and "The Sun Also Rises": The Crafting of a Style* (Lawrence: University Press of Kansas, 1983) and William Balassi's "The Writing of the Manuscript of *The Sun Also Rises,* with a Chart of Its Session-by-Session Development," *Hemingway Review* 6.1 (1986): 65–78. The best works on the writing of *A Farewell to Arms* are Reynolds's *Hemingway's First War: The Making of "A Farewell to Arms"* (Princeton: Princeton University Press, 1976) and Bernard Oldsey's *Hemingway's Hidden Craft: The Writing of "A Farewell to Arms"* (University Park: Pennsylvania State University Press, 1979). Owen Wister's role in the publishing of the novel is explicated in Alan Price's "'I'm Not an Old Fogey and You're Not a Young Ass': Owen Wister and Ernest Hemingway," *Hemingway Review* 9.1 (1989): 82–90. Perkins's editing and the Boston ban of the novel are fulsomely covered by Scott Donaldson's "Censorship and *A Farewell to Arms, Studies in American Fiction* 19.1 (1991): 85–93.

Any work of scholarship worth anything is built on the works of the scholars of the past. *The Lousy Racket* is no exception. The author gratefully acknowledges the contributions that his elders and betters made to this work. Their work made my work easier.

INDEX

Cowley, Malcolm, 171, 220, 239
Crowley, Aleistair, 42
Crowley, Malcolm H., 78

Darrow, Whitney, 11, 128, 156, 177, 219,
   228, 240, 290n107
Dashiell, Alfred, 10, 41, 61, 62, 68, 79,
   108, 147, 151, 153, 154, 157
Dedman, Julien, 239
Dempsey, David, 250–51
DeVoto, Bernard, 163
Dial, 47
Dineson, Frank, 154
Dixon, Thomas, 18
Doran, George, 15
Dos Passos, John, 34, 104; and DIA, 106,
   110–13, 115–16, 120, 276–77n85; and
   THHN, 176
Dreiser, Theodore, 18
Duffus, R. L., 122

Eastman, Max, 131, 132, 134; fight with
   Hemingway, 180, 284n49
Esquire, 142, 143, 145–46, 171–72, 199, 241

Fadiman, Clifton, 86, 140, 220
Faulkner, William, 4, 19, 230, 240
Finney, Ben, 206, 288n45
Fisherman, 7
Fitzgerald, F. Scott, 18, 25, 52, 74, 76,
   143; books by: The Beautiful and
   Damned, 8, 14; Tender Is the Night,
   143, 148; This Side of Paradise, 7,
   14, 25; career helped by Perkins, 7;
   correspondence with Hemingway,
   59, 81, 163; earnings and printings,
   2–3, 14; editorial advice to Hemingway, 43; and FTA, 75–76, 88; and
   Hemingway's move to Scribners,
   23–27; literary scout for Scribners,
   13, 24, 29–30; relationship with
   Perkins, 8, 9, 15, 17, 21, 35, 147, 164,
   194, 213; and SAR, 36, 39–41; and
   "The Snows of Kilimanjaro," 173–74,
   193–94; and TS, 23–24; and "Up
   in Michigan," 53–54; writing style
   compared to Hemingway's, 5
Fleischman, Leon, 15, 18
Ford, Ford Maddox, 14, 20, 42, 267n39
Forum, 34, 122

Frank, Waldo, 20; and DIA, 111, 112, 113,
   118
Franklin, Sidney, 116, 144
Freide, Donald, 18, 219

Gannett, Lewis, 239
Gingrich, Arnold, 142, 199; and THHN,
   172–73, 176
Gregory, Horace, 140
Grosset & Dunlap, 94

Hansen, Harry, 82, 85, 272n64
Harper's Bazaar, 52, 223
Harper's Magazine, 240
Harper's Monthly, 104, 122
Hearst's International, 51
Hemingway, Ernest: anger over revisions and assistance, 73–76; as businessman, 3, 22, 23–35, 27–29, 87–94,
   128–29, 148–51, 204, 205, 208–9,
   216–17, 229; choice of topics, 3; concept of readership, 6, 130–31, 151–52;
   death of Perkins, 228–29; death
   of Scribner, 241–42; fame, 6–7, 59,
   222–23; hunting and fishing, 67, 142,
   143, 171; newspaper reporting, 14,
   176, 180, 183–84, 198, 227; obscene
   language, 5–6, 10, 40–42, 62, 64, 68,
   77–78, 82–83, 99, 107, 109, 116, 122,
   133, 154–55, 180, 202–3, 233; opinion
   of short-story collections, 52, 130–31,
   137, 142–42, 145, 264n24; problems
   with book promotion, 18–20, 45,
   58, 87–88, 120–21, 141, 166, 183–84,
   224; relationship with Perkins, 67,
   69, 229; use of image and biography
   in promotions, 20, 45–46, 52, 210,
   218–19, 248; writing style, 4–5
   Books by:
   Across the River and Into the Trees
      (1950), 10, 227, 229; advertising,
      260; composition, 229–30, 232;
      contract, 239; earnings, 3, 229,
      240–41, 260; libel, 233, 236; print-
      ings, 239, 259; promotion, 231–32,
      238–39, 260; publication, 239;
      reviews, 239–40; revision, 232–33,
      236–38; Scribner and Meyer's
      concerns about quality, 233–36;
      serialization, 229–31

19–20; contract, 16; Perkins' opinion, 21; printings, 19; purchase by Scribners, 97–98; reviews, 20–21, 32; revisions, 17, 19

In Our Time (1930), 126–27, 140, 144, 166, 175, 188, 189, 192, 193, 257; advertising, 101, 102–4, 260; dust jacket, 103; earnings, 104, 259; printings, 104, 260, 275n37; reviews, 104; revisions and additions, 98–102; Wilson's introduction, 100–102

Islands in the Stream (1970), 227, 229, 230, 241, 256

Men Without Women (1927), 31, 51, 60, 61, 85, 102, 126, 139, 140, 189, 192, 193; advertising, 57, 58, 260, 270n114; connection to *SAR*, 48, 49–50; contents, 50–51, 54–56; contract, 56; dust jacket, 57; earnings, 53, 58, 259; printings, 58–59, 260, 270n116; proposed inclusion of "Up in Michigan," 50, 53–54; publication, 57; reviews, 57–58; salesman's dummy, 52

A Moveable Feast (1964), 2, 256

The Nick Adams Stories (1972), 256

The Old Man and the Sea (1952), 6, 227, 241, 254, 255, 258; advertising, 248–50, 260; composition, 237, 241; contract, 250; dedication, 242; earnings, 3, 244, 245, 253, 255, 260; printings, 253, 259, 298n124; publication, 250; reaction to *Life* publication, 249–52; sales, 252–53; selection by BOMC, 242–47, 253; serialization in *Life,* 242–48, 253–54

The Only Thing That Counts, The Ernest Hemingway-Maxwell Perkins Correspondence (1996), 257

The Sun Also Rises (1926), 10, 20, 25, 26, 32, 34, 57, 75, 85, 166, 258, 300; acceptance by Scribners, 37–39; advertising, 9, 11, 44–47, 49, 141, 183, 260, 268n58; composition, 19, 264n38; contract, 22, 27, 29; dust jacket, 45; earnings, 29, 49, 259; film rights, 49; obscene words in, 78; Perkins' opinion, 36–37; printings, 49, 87, 90, 260, 268n78; publication, 24, 29, 31, 51,

60; and *Publisher's Weekly,* 139, 162, 182; reviews, 47, 58; revision, 33, 36, 39–43, 267n37; salesman's dummy, 36

Three Stories and Ten Poems (1923), 13, 13, 51; Hemingway's marked copy, 98–99; printings, 14

To Have and Have Not (1937), 45, 168, 169, 170, 171, 186, 187, 197, 198, 210; advertising, 181–82, 259, 285n60; composition, 172–73, 174–76; contract, 183; dust jacket, 180; earnings, 185, 260; Hemingway-Eastman fight, 180–81; Hemingway's reaction to promotion, 183–84, 185; obscene words, 180–81; omnibus plan, 178; Perkins' defense of promotion, 184–85; Perkins' reaction, 173; printings, 183, 185–86, 260; publication, 183, 286n91; reviews, 183; revision, 176–77, 180; salesman's dummy, 181; title mistake, 179, 181

The Torrents of Spring (1927), 31, 126; advertising, 33–35, 260; book design, 32; composition, 31, 126; contract, 29; earnings, 29, 35, 43, 259; Fitzgerald's opinion, 26–27; Perkins' opinion, 35; printings, 35, 260; rejection by Boni & Liveright, 23, 27–29; reviews, 35; revision, 32–33

True at First Light (1999), 256, 298n5

Under Kilimanjaro (2005), 298n5

Winner Take Nothing (1933), 126, 155, 167, 169, 189, 192, 193, 197; advertising, 139–41, 260; contents, 6, 126–28, 131, 132–33, 142–43; contract, 132; dust jacket, 138–39; earnings, 12, 128–29, 142, 259; printings, 139, 260; publication, 139; reviews, 140; revision, 133–38, 139; sales, 141–42; salesman's dummy, 129, 132; title problems, 130–31

Stories and articles by:
"After the Storm," 96, 127, 132, 134
"An Alpine Idyll," 31, 39, 50, 51, 54, 57
"Banal Story," 50, 51, 54, 56
"The Battler," 16
"Big Two-Hearted River," 21, 145, 195
"The Butterfly and the Tank," 286n1